Congressmen's Voting Decisions

SECOND EDITION

JOHN W. KINGDON
The University of Michigan

HARPER & ROW, PUBLISHERS, New York
Cambridge, Hagerstown, Philadelphia, San Francisco,
London, Mexico City, São Paulo, Sydney

1817

To Kirsten, James, and Tor

Sponsoring Editor: John L. Michel
Project Editor: Pamela Landau
Senior Production Manager: Kewal K. Sharma
Compositor: American–Stratford Graphic Services, Inc.
Printer and Binder: The Murray Printing Company
Art Studio: Vantage Art Inc.

Congressmen's Voting Decisions, Second Edition
Copyright © 1981 by Harper & Row, Publishers, Inc.

Library of Congress Cataloging in Publication Data
Kingdon, John W
   Congressmen's voting decisions.

   Includes bibliographical references and index.
      1.   United States. Congress. House—Voting.
2.   Legislators—United States.   3.   Decision-making.
I.   Title.
JK1319.K53   1981   328.73'0775   80-15782
ISBN 0-06-043657-3

Contents

Preface to the Second Edition

I have decided to revise *Congressmen's Voting Decisions* for essentially two reasons. First, since the data for this study were originally gathered in 1969, several dramatic changes have occurred in Congress. There has been a wholesale turnover in the House of Representatives, both through defeat of incumbents and through voluntary retirements. Partly because of that turnover, several practices of the House have undergone rather substantial revision. The seniority system for selecting committee chairs, for instance, has been seriously eroded. Rules changes have provided for the ratification of committee and Appropriations subcommittee chair nominations by the majority party caucus and for the election of subcommittee chairs by the majority party members of the parent committee. Using those rules changes, three committee chairs were dumped in 1975, and relatively junior members have been elected subcommittee chair.

Other changes have occurred. The sheer number of floor voting decisions has increased dramatically. The numbers of staff on the Hill have also increased, in personal and committee staffs and in staff agencies responsible to the Congress. Subcommittees have been strengthened and made more autonomous. The Nixon administration came to its ignominious end with the Watergate scandal and with the Ford and then the Carter administrations succeeding Nixon's. There appeared to be a substantial rise in the numbers and intensity of single-issue interest groups, combined with a decline in party. And incumbents were winning by even larger margins than they had previously.

All of these changes and others raise the possibility that in some respects, the conclusions of a book written on the basis of information gathered in 1969 might be out of date. I have therefore taken the occasion of the second edition to update the original conclusions of the book at several points. As the reader will see, most of the conclusions emerge from this second look rather encouragingly intact. If anything, their persuasiveness has been enhanced by the passage of these dramatic events, rather than diminished. In the few cases in which generalizations have been found in need of modification in light of subsequent events, I have discussed those modifications.

The second major purpose for revising the book is that I have done some further thinking about the processes of decision described in the first edition, which would have occurred as an analytical matter independent of changes in Congress. An earlier version of that further work was found in the *Journal of Politics*

(August 1977), and I wish to thank the *Journal* for their permission to include material from that article. Thus, Chapter 10 and Appendix F have been rather thoroughly revised in light of that new analysis.

Other changes appear throughout the book. I think that the fundamental character of the book has not been altered. I hope that readers who liked the first edition will find that a good book has been made better. At least, that was my purpose.

John W. Kingdon

Preface to the First Edition

This book reports the results of a research project which was designed to explore how congressmen make their decisions when voting on the floor of the United States House of Representatives. The study is based primarily on interviews which concentrated on given decisions which congressmen had recently been called upon to make. Rather than asking a congressman to discuss decision-making in general, I asked him to give a kind of life history of one specific decision, the political actors to whom he paid attention, and the considerations he weighed in making his decision. I could then generalize from these instances about the importance of various actors and about the decision rules which were being employed.

During the process of designing and carrying out this research and writing this book, I have greatly benefited from the help so generously offered by a number of individuals and institutions. I owe a special debt of gratitude to the many congressmen, staff members, journalists, lobbyists, and other observers who gave so freely of their time to talk to me during the field stages of this research in 1969. Since I promised them their anonymity, I cannot acknowledge their contributions by name, but my gratitude is great nonetheless.

I want most particularly to express my deep appreciation to Ralph Huitt, both for his helpful suggestions about this research and for his encouragement and stimulation through the years. I am much indebted to Richard Fenno, Robert Peabody, and Herbert Weisberg, who provided many useful suggestions from the very beginning of this research and who made many extremely helpful comments on an earlier draft of this book. I am grateful to Herbert Asher and Robert Jervis for offering their own perceptive criticisms of that earlier version and to Ronald Brunner for his very useful commentary on portions of the manuscript. At various times during this research, I have also profited from the counsel of various colleagues at the University of Michigan and elsewhere, among them Donald Stokes, Warren Miller, Leslie Kish, and Lewis Froman. Students at the University of Michigan have been a continuing source of ideas and stimulation. I also share with other observers of politics a great intellectual debt to Lewis Dexter.

I am happy to acknowledge generous grants from the Social Science Research Council for field work and initial analysis and from the Ford Foundation for the final stages of this study. I am grateful to the Brookings Institution in Washington for an appointment as Guest Scholar and for the gracious hospitality tendered me while I was there. I have been very pleased with help given by Suzanne Hart, an able and conscientious research assistant. Mary Lou Gaul typed two versions of the manuscript with her usual high level of competence.

This book is dedicated to my wife, Kirsten, and to my sons, James and Tor. My life is much the richer for their companionship.

John W. Kingdon

PART I

Introduction

1

Introduction

Congressman: I actually taught political science years ago, and I didn't know a thing about Congress until I came here. It seemed like the whole idea in political science was to take the politics out of it. You sure got an inaccurate picture.

Kingdon: That's why some of us recently have been coming here to find out how congressmen behave.

Congressman: If we do.

How do legislators make decisions? That question is of considerable interest to wide varieties of people. The casual but interested political spectator, to whom politics is a fairly murky realm filled with intrigue and backroom dealings, notices any tidbits of scandal that reveal the "real" process, sizes up his representatives' positions in terms of his own, and follows the progress of close and highly visible legislative battles. The mass media fill their pages and the public airwaves with provisions of the latest major bill to pass the Congress, progress of the current legislative battles, statements of leading congressmen on the issues of the day, and feature stories which attempt to "get behind" the public facade and report what is "really" happening. Bureaucrats, who have spent weeks, months, and years devising legislative proposals, scratch their heads in amazement as legislators twist, contort, mangle, and even entirely reverse the product of their hard labors. Lobbyists and interest groups of every description calculate what legislators are likely to accept, consider how they can achieve their goals through the legislative process, decide which strategies work and which do not, and assess the reasons for their successes and failures in shaping legislative decisions in accordance with their wishes. Scholars are interested in legislative decisions, partly because elected legislators stand at the center of the relationship between the people and their government. And congressmen themselves occasionally pause in the bustle of daily events to ask, "Now, why did I do that?"

One interesting kind of legislative decision is that which a legislator makes as he casts his votes on the floor of the body to which he has been elected. The final points of decision in an American legislature are the votes which take place during consideration by the whole chamber. What transpires on the floor of a legislature defines the end product of the law-making apparatus. The whole chamber is also the ultimate arbiter of conflicts which take place within the body. Thus, floor voting is important in its own right.

Beyond that, however, floor voting decisions also influence the behavior of committees and other actors in the political system. Fenno maintains, for example, that as powerful a committee as the House Appropriations Committee acts as a subsystem of the whole House, within the boundaries set for it by the parent body.[1] To the extent that standing committees attempt to anticipate what will happen to their proposals on the floor, it can be said that the whole House has influenced the committees' actions. Similarly, administrators anticipate "what will go" in Congress when formulating their proposals, by judging both the likely response of the committees and the more general mood on the Hill.[2]

Voting on the floor not only is central to an understanding of policy-making, but also is of importance in the larger polity. When a congressman casts his vote, he is highly visible. Various interest groups use his votes to determine whether he is a "good" congressman deserving of their support. The reaction of his constituents, at least of the more attentive ones, is based to a degree upon his voting record. The congressman himself pays some attention to the political consequences which follow from having a voting record of one general description or another. Beyond the individual congressman, furthermore, the general voting records of the parties in Congress are ready cannon fodder in a nationwide election year.

A study of legislative voting on the floor should also have some relevance for the understanding of many other sorts of political decisions. It would seem unlikely that a legislator would make his voting decisions in a fashion totally unlike his many other decisions. Becoming better acquainted with congressmen's floor decisions, then, may help us to understand committee behavior, decisions to take certain kinds of public stands apart from the voting context, and other kinds of important political behavior.

Legislative voting, finally, is not devoid of more general human interest. The basic problem which a congressman faces in his voting is quite general to the human condition. As a nonexpert who is obliged to make unavoidable decisions about matters in which he is little schooled and to which he is able or willing to devote only limited time and attention, how does he go about making up his mind? How are the alternatives presented to him and how does he choose among these alternatives? How does he handle political and psychological conflict? The answers to such questions would speak not only to the political topics just discussed, but also to more general notions of decision-making and information-processing.

This book reports on empirical research designed to discover how congressmen make their decisions when voting on the floor of the U.S. House of Representatives. It investigates such matters as their sources of information and vote cues, their decision rules, and the importance of various actors (e.g., constituents, interest groups, administration) in floor votes. The study is based primarily on extensive interviews conducted throughout the first session of the Ninety-first Congress (1969) with congressmen and with others who are close to the process. The conclusions have been updated where appropriate.

SOME GENERAL CONSIDERATIONS

There are a number of political actors—constituents, party leaders, administration, fellow congressmen, and the like—who may have some influence on legislative voting decisions. It would be interesting to know how important these actors are, both taken singly and in relation to one another, a task to which Part II of this book is directed. More general propositions about decision-making are not tied so specifically to these actors. These interests include the congressman's general modes of decision, his search for information, the place of ideology and past voting history, various constraints on decision-making, and the flow of information within the system. A discussion of these points is found in Part III. Finally, one would also want to know not only what the general patterns appeared to be, but also what degrees and kinds of variation there were.

The actors
The legislative process has been interpreted in a number of ways throughout the years. Congressional decision-making has

been conceived alternatively as following the leads of political parties, the executive branch, the constituencies of the members, colleagues within the legislature, interest groups that present their demands, and perhaps other actors in the system. Legislative studies have tended to concentrate separately on the place of each of these actors in the legislative system. We therefore have a rich literature on representation of constituents, another literature on parties, another on interest groups. The research reported in this book attempts to pull together these various political actors into one design and, thus, to treat somewhat more comprehensively their importance in the context of voting decisions, providing some information on the extent to which and the ways in which each of these actors influences voting decisions.

One logical beginning is the constituency. Congressmen are first nominated and elected in local districts, and serve at the pleasure of their constituents. Many of their contacts with the political system at large are with constituents. There is already an extensive literature on the place of constituencies in the legislative process.[3] An interesting question, therefore, is the extent to which and the conditions under which the constituency plays a part in congressmen's voting decisions on the floor of the House. What do they think their constituents want them to do, and do they heed these wishes? How do they reach their conclusions about what their constituents want? Are the attentive, active constituents different from others, and what impact does this have? What are possible mechanisms of constituency influence?

Once they are elected with a given constituency base, congressmen interact with their colleagues in the House. It has long been held that congressmen specialize, and then turn to each other for guidance in areas outside their own specialty.[4] Scholars have also recently studied the patterns of informal communications within legislative bodies.[5] Fellow congressmen could be expected to have some influence on voting because they are readily accessible to the deciding congressman, and because he can learn through experience who can be trusted to give him reliable substantive and political information about the pending legislation. Consequently, it is important to know how often, and under what conditions, a congressman pays attention to the advice of his colleagues. How does he choose his informants in the House—does he pick those who agree with him substantively, who are on the committee that considered the bill, who are from his state delegation? What kinds of interactions are involved—face-to-face conversations, listening to the debate, reading the committee report? How do the patterns vary from one subgroup of congressmen to another?

One particular set of colleagues has had a special place in political science literature: the House leadership, both party and committee leadership. We know a good deal about the operations of the party leadership,[6] and about the place of standing committees in the legislative process.[7] It is important, then, to understand the place of the party and committee leadership in voting decisions. How often and when does the leadership become involved? How much influence do congressmen in leadership positions have over their fellow members? What are the patterns in the relationships between committees and the whole House?

Since interest groups have long been considered important in the thinking of both academic and nonacademic observers of the legislative process,[8] it is natural to consider them as possible influences on congressmen's votes. When and how are they important? What strategies do they employ and with what effectiveness? How much do they work indirectly through other actors in the legislative system such as friends in Congress and constituents, and if they do so, why?

Somewhat akin to interest groups, in the sense that they also want to influence legislative outcomes, are the administration and executive branch. The administration differs from lobbyists, however, in the greater degree of public exposure which the president and cabinet officers are capable of attracting, in their ability to call upon the expertise of the federal bureaucracy, and in the unique place which the president has in the thinking of his own party's congressmen. The relationship between the executive and legislative branches has long captured the attention of students of American government.[9] It may be relevant, therefore, to discover how often the administration takes a position, what attempts are made to see that position enacted, and with what success. When does the administration become involved in congressmen's thinking? How much do administration officials contact congressmen personally, and on whom do they concentrate? How much do they work indirectly through other actors in the system such as the party leadership, committee members, and mass media?

Another possible influence on votes is the congressional staff, including staffs of individual congressmen, the committees, and the leadership. How extensively are they consulted, when, and to what effect? Do they have some kinds of indirect influence, and if so, of what types?

Finally, congressmen's reading and listening may affect their votes. They may pay attention to the printed and broadcast mass media, and they do have available other kinds of reading, such as committee reports and more detailed information. What kinds of media and publications do they follow? How important are their reading and listening? What kinds are influential, how often, and under what conditions?

General Decision-making

Beyond an actor-by-actor mode of analysis, a study of congressional decision-making would seek to understand and develop propositions about some more general aspects of decision-making. One of these general aspects is information flow and search. The decision rules of congressmen probably have some consequences for the patterns through which information flows in the legislative system. Do the legislator's way of deciding and the actors which he does or does not seriously consider play a part in structuring communications nets in the larger system, and if so, how? What are the congressman's major sources of information, and through what paths does it reach him? Apart from information which comes to him, what sources and kinds of information does the member seek out, through what means, and with what results?

A theory of congressional decision-making should also be addressed in part to what may be a dominant mode of decision. Several such decision models have been developed.[10] It may be true that the average congressman makes up his mind according to a certain mode of decision, or in an identifiable sequence of steps. We would want to discover if there is such a dominant mode, and what the alternative modes might be. Not only would these models of decision be interesting for their own sake, but they might help us understand the way politics is conducted in the larger political system. If most congressmen decide in a given manner, for instance, do those who wish to influence legislative outcomes adapt their behavior to the congressmen's decision rules; if so, how, and with what implications for our understanding of politics generally?

The place of the legislator's own policy attitudes or ideology is another general theme with considerable potential interest. Patterned dimensions of legislative voting have been discovered,[11] leading to the logical inference that congressmen can at least be conceived as voting ideologically. Others have argued, however, that ideology is an inadequate guide to decision, since it is difficult to connect one's general policy attitudes with specific bills or amendments, since congressmen often do not have well-formed or intense opinions on many subjects before them, and, even if their opinions are well defined, they still need the advice of specialists in areas not immediately within their own competence.[12] Thus, an interesting question is the extent to which legislators' own attitudes on questions of public policy are important influences on their votes. If so, how do they translate attitudes into votes? If not, why not, and what might take the place of ideology?

Congressmen and other governmental decision-makers have also often been portrayed as deciding according to an incremental method.[13] They presumably take their past behavior as given, and their basic exercise is to preserve continuity or to consider only modest changes from their past behavior. If this is an accurate picture, then the congressman's voting history could be quite important in the consideration of present votes.

Constraints on decision are also among the general aspects of decision-making. It is possible to see the larger political system, or given sets of actors within it, as setting constraints on congressmen. Rather than conceiving the legislator as being influenced in some positive way, or as having his vote caused by a set of actors or forces, we might rather view the process as one in which these actors or forces set limits or boundaries within which congressmen are obliged to operate. Under what conditions does the congressman's constituency, for instance, influence him *to* vote in a certain way? If the constituency does not do so, can it at least be said that it obliges him *not* to vote in certain ways?

Finally, stepping back from the actual process of choice, the prior steps of agenda-setting and alternative-specifying are also of vital importance. Why are certain subjects added to the decisional agenda in the first place and why are others omitted, and with what consequences? Once a subject is on the agenda, how is it determined which alternatives will be seriously considered and which will be discarded? Which actors in the political system appear to be most important in these stages of decision-making?

Variations

Clearly, we want to know not only what the general patterns of actor importance and decision rules are, but also what variations exist within these patterns and what appears to account for such variations. One congressman, in fact, told me early in my research that I would find as many ways of making decisions as there are congressmen. While I have not found the process to be quite so complex as that, analysis of the variations is still a question of considerable interest. At least as interesting as the extent of each actor's influence, for instance, are the conditions under which each is influential. The structure of variations in the general aspects of decision-making is also important. Are high-salience issues, for example, different from those of lower salience? Do congressmen from one type of district decide differently from congressmen from other types? Does a freshman congressman decide according to criteria and cue sources which differ from those utilized by his more senior colleague? What differences exist among congressmen because of party affiliation or size of the state party delegation? (The standard independent variables used in this study are discussed in more detail in Appendix D.)

At any rate, in this introductory discussion of the actors, the general decision-making process, and variations, I have reviewed the kinds of questions to which a study of legislative decision-making might be directed. These questions were among those with which my own study began, and thus constitute a preview of the subjects which are considered in the pages of this book.

WAYS OF STUDYING LEGISLATIVE VOTING

If one is interested in studying legislative voting, there are a number of approaches which have been or could be taken. Two of the most prominent are roll call analysis and standard survey techniques.

Social scientists have traditionally studied legislative voting by analyzing roll call data. This rich body of material, perhaps unique in the field of political science, combines the singular virtues of being "hard" quantified data, while at the same time being readily accessible in published documents. We have learned a good deal about congressional voting from roll call data. The bloc structure in voting has been explored.[14] The major dimensions along which congressmen cast their votes have been investigated.[15] We have learned something about the major systemic variables such as party, constituency, and region, which help to account for voting on the floor.[16] Other studies have not only cut into the process at one point in time, but have also considered a longitudinal element.[17] For all that we have learned, however, the deficiencies of roll call and aggregate data have also been evident. Even if we find persistent blocs in a legislature, for instance, it is still a matter of inference to suggest that legislators vote together because of some communication process among those in the same bloc. If Congressman A votes with Congressman B, we do not know why. Similarly, discovery of dimensions in congressional voting leaves unanswered the question of why the dimensions arise as they do.

In more general terms, few would expect roll call data to answer a number of crucial questions of political and human behavior. What are the actual grounds on which a legislator bases his decisions? What are the influences brought to bear on the congressman, the strategies employed to gain his vote? Which of these strategies are ultimately successful and which fail? What are the patterns of interaction in the legislative process, including the cues on which congressmen do or do not rely? To which actors in the system do they pay attention and which do they ignore? In the words of Jewell and Patterson, "Roll call statistics can tell us *how* legislators vote. . . . The roll calls cannot tell us *why* legislators vote that way."[18] To cite one prominent example of the problem, nearly all roll call studies have discovered the central importance of political party in the explanation of legislative cleavage. Yet we know little about the process by which the party influences its congressmen. Party voting may be a function of some constituency factor, coalition support of different kinds, sanctions employed by legislative leaders, administration pressure, cue-giving within the Congress, ideological similarity among fellow party members, and other possible factors, or various combinations of them.

Another technique to which social scientists are accustomed, the standard survey instrument, has been used to good effect for many purposes and could be employed here to ask congressmen in general how they make their decisions. Such a method has successfully been used in the study of respondents' political attitudes and orientations, which they have no difficulty in articulating. But in the study of legislative voting or other decision-making, the basic exercise which would usually be demanded of a respondent by using this procedure is that he removes himself from the concrete context within which he makes his decisions, and that he endeavors to abstract or generalize about the process. This exercise encounters a number of difficulties, whether the interview is structured or unstructured.

First, a respondent under such circumstances may speak in generalizations which may or may not have a relationship to his actual votes. He may see himself as deciding in the national interest, or as doing his best to represent his constituents, or as following the lead of the experts on the committees. The general notions that legislators have about their work may be quite crucial in explaining their behavior, but there is little that interviews about the general decision-making process can do to discover whether, and under what conditions, they are important. To cite one example of this problem among several such cases in my own interviewing, a congressman painted a coherent, rational picture of his decision process when considering it in the abstract: "You find out that you can't possibly know about everything. Your constituents expect you to, but you just can't. So you start to seek out fellow members who are of the same philosophical bent as you and who are on the committee that heard the experts and considered the legislation. You rely on them." Appealing as this cue-passing theory might be in the explanation of his legislative voting, the fact is that on four of the five specific votes which I explored with him, this congressman did not rely on fellow members.

The second problem with using a standard survey instrument is the reputational problem. It is tempting for a respondent to judge others' reputations in the legislative system rather than their actual influence. For instance, the general question, "How important is organized labor in your decisions?" is very different from the question, "How much did you take labor's view into account on X vote?" These two questions might yield drastically different findings, and the results obtained by the second approach would probably be a better indication of the forces at work in decision-making.

Finally, participants in a process often find it difficult to step back from their activities and abstract about the process. They know only their own reactions and not the reactions of others. It is also possible, even in their own cases, that some may not be able to verbalize what moves them to act, when asked about it in the abstract. The closer the interview is to the actual context within which the decision-maker is operating, the more valid the results will be. One congressman told me, "I don't know how I vote. It's like driving a car. How do you decide to drive the car? Really, I don't know." But he had no trouble in speaking of specific decisions which he had recently made.

FEATURES OF THE STUDY DESIGN

This book reports the results of a study which utilizes another design—one which is aimed at developing information on congressmen's decision-making without encountering some of the problems of alternative approaches. The core of my study is a set of interviews with a cross-sectional sample of members of the U.S. House of Representatives. Each of these interviews concentrated on some specific vote or votes that were currently or very recently under consideration. It sought to develop a kind of life history of that decision, including the steps through which the congressman went, the considerations which he weighed, and the political actors who influenced him. By cumulating a number of these decisions over the entire session, it was possible to discern generalizations and patterns. These interview data were supplemented by a good deal of immersion in the process: repeated conversations with staffs, lobbyists, and journalists, the reading of documents, and my observations of committee meetings and floor debates.

This unusual issue-by-issue approach yields a number of important advantages. When asked how congressmen decide, one staffer made a much more sophisticated methodological point than he probably realized: "You almost have to take it by the issue." Indeed you do. As I have stated above, it is only an unusually reflective decision-maker who is able to take himself away from his concrete decisions and abstract about the process, and even if he appears to do so, his generalizations may not reflect his own behavior. For the purposes of understanding his decision-making, I have reasoned that asking a congressman to describe instead a concrete decision which he has recently made yields not only a more valid result, but one which is much more complete, more frank, and less productive of the clichés which alternative techniques often encourage.

The core of my interviewing was done during the first session of the Ninety-first Congress, the calendar year of 1969 and the first year of the Nixon administration. We were presented with an instance of government divided in partisan terms between the presidency and the Congress, and with the new administration not really mobilized to push a legislative program on the Hill until several months had elapsed. Even though unusual, divided government provided a research opportunity. A timeworn proposition, in both academic and lay literature, is that Congress is increasingly a rubber stamp for the executive branch, responding to executive initiatives and yielding to executive influence. But a session in which the same party controls both branches does not lend itself to a complete test of this proposition, since the apparent congressional ineffectiveness may simply be cooperation among partisans. Only when government is divided in partisan terms would one be able to observe institutional rivalries independent of this partisan cooperation.

The session under study proved to be interesting in several other respects. Despite the slow start, there were a number of issues on which the administration was extremely active in promoting its point of view, such as the surtax extension, antiballistic missile (ABM) deployment, opposition to increased education funding, and protection of the poverty program from further state control. This was also the start of a time of budgetary constraint which lasted at least through the 1970s. Given a limit on the size of the federal budgetary pie, the resultant competition for the scarce resources produced several disputes over the issue of national priorities, with its attendant tests of what the prevailing ideology was and "who gets what"[19] from the government. During the session under study, furthermore, there were several instances which illuminated the relationships between committees and the whole House, occasions on which committee majorities and committee chairmen found their views out of keeping with those of the whole House, and for which they were faced with an adaptation problem, which had to be resolved in some way—by capitulation, compromise, or resistance. Finally, with the society in grave upheaval over the Vietnam war, issues of race, the changing values in the younger generation, the state of the economy, and other prominent issues, this period of time provided some insight into governmental response to societal conditions which might not have been provided in a more placid time.

The entire issue of the typicality of a given congressional session, of course, may prove illusory. In order to embark upon a study such as this one, some session of Congress must be chosen. It is something of an open question whether *any* session of Congress would prove to be typical. All would have some entirely usual aspects and some very unusual ones. As one congressman remarked, "There hasn't been a year since I've been here that has been a usual year." It is also true that if there are regularities in legislative decision-making behavior, they ought to manifest themselves in a number of different contexts, including some fairly unusual ones. In fact, coping with unfamiliar situations with standard decision rules is a fascinating phenomenon in its own right, one which also puts the standard rules into sharper focus. Finally, the ultimate test of the generalizations in this book is whether they still apply in times different from the late 1960s. I examine throughout this book many instances in which the findings of the study might have been expected to change with the passage of time, and with few exceptions, the generalizations prove to be quite durable.

This study concentrated on the House of Representatives rather than on the Senate, in the belief that access to the former would be somewhat easier to obtain. Some patterns may, of course, be different in the Senate, and such possibilities are discussed throughout the book when appropriate. The central sample of congressmen is a cross-sectional sample of the House, selected so that each congressman has an equal statistical chance of falling into the sample; it also has been stratified by party, seniority, and one regional category (Southern Democrats) to ensure that the sample will be representative of the whole House. Congressmen were interviewed several times during the course of the session on different votes, with such resultant benefits as increased rapport and frankness in the interviews as the session progressed through its more hurried phases.

I should emphasize that the usual unit of analysis in this book, therefore, is the *decision,* not the congressman, or in other words, the number of congressmen multiplied by the number of decisions on which each was interviewed. A decision is also not necessarily the one-to-one equivalent of a vote. One decision may, in effect, determine several of the congressman's votes. For instance, if a congressman were to decide early in the session under study that he would vote to seat Adam Clayton Powell only on the condition that the House exact some penalty before the seating, this one decision determined his votes on five different roll calls. On occasion, the "cluster" of votes that is determined by one decision may be separated by the space of weeks, as in some logrolling exchanges. So when I say that decisions are the unit of analysis, I do so by way of contrasting decisions to both congressmen and votes as possible units. (More of the sampling details can be found in Appendix A.)

I intentionally designed the project to keep the interviews short in order to conserve the congressman's valuable time. To minimize recall deficiencies, I saw him at the time of the vote or within the following few days. I made every effort to conduct the interviews in an entirely conversational manner, using no notes or tapes, and writing up the interview immediately afterward. I had a set interview schedule committed to memory which does yield comparable responses capable of quantification. But I also inserted other questions liberally, tailored to the respondent, to the issue, or to something just said. The result was the necessary precision in the data, combined with good rapport and issue- or respondent-specific information. (Details on interviewing procedures can be found in Appendix B.)

The selection of the votes to study is a particularly vexing and important question. Given the issue-by-issue approach of this study, votes had to be selected within each week, as they came up for floor consideration. Therefore, I could not rely on conventional sampling procedures, which require a final population list of votes as a base. But beyond that, many votes cast in Congress are politically uninteresting from nearly every point of view. Political scientists cannot avoid choices about what is interesting to study, inexact as these choices may be. I chose for the core sample which forms the quantitative base of this study, votes which attracted the attention of the public, press, congressmen, and other participants, in which there were many political actors (e.g., interest groups, administration, constituents) involved, and which created controversy of some intensity. These were not necessarily votes which turned out to be won or lost by close margins, nor were they all of uniformly high importance or salience. But they were among the "big" votes of the session. This core sample of votes was supplemented by interviewing on more minor matters and on "nondecisions," that is, questions which could have come to a vote but did not, and by quite a volume of informal conversations and observations of committee and floor proceedings. (Appendix A contains a list of the votes in the core sample, in addition to a more extended discussion of the selection.)

A STATISTICAL PREVIEW

Before turning to a consideration of various influences on voting decisions, it is appropriate to place the findings about each political actor in a general framework. This final section, then, presents a simplified statistical preview of the importance of the several actors. Once this general skeleton is presented, the real flesh and blood of the decisional processes involving each of these actors is filled out in the chapters to follow.

One way to judge whether a given actor is important in a congressman's decision is to notice whether the congressman mentions that actor spontaneously, without any prompting from an interviewer's questions. Presumably, if the congressman did mention the actor spontaneously, then the actor was enough on his mind to be weighed into the decision. The interview was designed to allow for the possibility of these spontaneous references, since the first question always was very general: "How did you go about making up your mind?" Each actor could then be coded as having been mentioned spontaneously, as having been mentioned in response to a question (i.e., having some importance in the decision but not having been spontaneously mentioned), or as having no apparent impact on the decision. The results of this coding appear in Table 1–1.

It appears that none of these actors is of such overwhelming importance when compared with the others as to be spontaneously mentioned in the interviews over half the time. Three of the possible influences—the party leadership, the staff, and reading—receive far fewer spontaneous mentions than the others. Apparently, the two actors most in the minds of congressmen as they decide are fellow congressmen and constituencies, with interest groups and administration coming next.

Another way to assess the importance of each actor is simply to code its apparent overall importance in the congressman's decision, regardless of the time it is mentioned in the interview. In this case, the congressman's comments relative to each actor were coded into four categories: (1) the actor was of no importance in the decision; (2) the actor was of minor importance, that is, the congressman noticed the actor's position, checked it, or the like, but the actor was of no greater importance; (3) the actor was of major importance, that is, whether or not the congressman ended up voting with the actor, he weighed the actor's

Table 1-1 Spontaneous Mentions of Actors

mention	constituency	fellow congressmen	party leadership	interest groups	adminis- tration	staff	reading
Spontaneously mentioned	37%	40%	10%	31%	25%	5%	9%
Mentioned in response to question	50	35	28	35	14	29	40
Not involved	13	25	62	35	60	66	52
Total %	100%	100%	100%	101%ᵃ	99%	100%	101%
Total n	222	221	222	222	222	221	221

ᵃ In this and in subsequent tables, some column totals will not be exactly 100%, due to rounding error.

Table 1-2 Actor Importance

importance	constituency	fellow congressmen	party leadership	interest groups	adminis- tration	staff	reading
Determinative	7%	5%	0%	1%	4%	1%	0%
Major importance	31	42	5	25	14	8	17
Minor importance	51	28	32	40	21	26	32
Not important	12	25	63	35	61	66	52
Total %	101%	100%	100%	101%	100%	101%	101%
Total n	222	221	222	222	222	221	221

position carefully and the actor had a major impact on his thinking; (4) the actor determined the decision, to the exclusion of other influences. (A discussion of coding procedures appears in Appendix C.)

The results appear in Table 1–2.[20] The pattern is roughly the same as is seen in Table 1–1. Party leadership and staffs turn out to be the least important of the potential influences on the decision, and reading is not much more important than they. Fellow congressmen and constituency are the most important actors, followed again by interest groups and administration, in that order. Single actors very rarely determine the congressman's vote to the exclusion of other influences, and the only actor which approaches being of major importance half the time is fellow congressmen, followed by constituency.

Up to this point, the measurements of actor influence have been subjective. In other words, the congressman's own words are used as a basis for indicating the importance of the actor in his decision. Another approach is to arrive at a best estimate of the actor's position and then compare it to the congressman's eventual vote. While it is not possible definitively to state by this method that a political actor influenced the decision, we can at least see whether the congressman's vote agreed with the actor's position.[21]

The resulting agreement scores can be stated in a variety of ways. (Appendix E presents the calculations involved.) The conditional probability (listed in Table 1–3) is the probability that the congressman will vote with the actor, given the actor's position. For example, once a constituency position on the issue is ascertained, be it in the liberal or conservative direction, congressmen in this sample voted with the constituency position 76 percent

Table 1–3   Agreements Between Actor Position and Congressman's Vote

actor	conditional probability	correlation coefficient	partial correlation (6-variable)	partial correlation (4-variable)
Constituency	.76	.49	.35	.47
Fellow congressmen	.96	.78	.71	—
Party leadership	.57	.15	−.08	.04
Interest groups	.62	.21	−.05	.05
Administration	.56	.12	.12	.19
Staff	.89	.44	.19	—

of the time. The congressman could be expected to vote with any of these actors about half the time by chance alone.

Three of the actors—constituency, fellow congressmen, and staff—represent a considerable improvement on chance occurrence. If we know the position of fellow congressmen to whom the congressman pays attention, indeed, it is 96 percent certain that he will vote in the same direction. For constituency, the comparable figure is 76 percent; for staff, 89 percent. By contrast, party leadership and administration positions do not improve a great deal upon chance prediction. The position of interest groups, while a slightly better predictor, is not as good as the top three.

In the correlation model, the positions of the six actors can be viewed as six independent variables, predicting the congressman's vote. The product-moment correlation coefficients for each actor, that is, a measure of the strength of the relationship between the actor's position and the congressman's vote, are presented in the second column of Table 1–3. The multiple correlation for all six variables together as a predictor of the vote is .83. Once again, the order of importance of the actors remains roughly the same as in the case of conditional probability: The position of fellow congressmen to whom the congressman pays attention is the best predictor, followed at some distance by constituency and staff, with the other three actors far below.

What happens when one controls for the effects of the other variables? Do the relationships persist, or are they reduced? To obtain an answer, the third column of Table 1–3 presents the partial correlation for each actor, that is, the correlation between the position of the actor and the congressman's vote, controlling for all the other five actors simultaneously. It appears that whatever the relationship was that party leadership and interest groups had with the vote, it is eliminated by controlling for the others. But the relationship of the third weak actor, the administration, persists. As for the three variables which were most important in the uncontrolled relationships, the importance of fellow congressmen is reduced slightly, the figure for constituency is reduced somewhat more, but still remains above the other four; however, the relationship between staff position and the vote is very decidedly reduced, from .44 to .19. It can thus be said that fellow congressmen retain their importance independent of the other actors; that constituency still has a significant importance independent of the others; but that administration and staff exhibit rather low relationships with the vote, once the effects of other actors are taken into account; and that party leadership and interest group influence is eliminated altogether.

One major reason why fellow congressmen turn out to be so preeminently important in the six-variable model is that, unlike most of the other actors, a congressman has a free choice among fellow congressmen. If he doesn't like the advice he gets from one colleague, he is perfectly free to turn to another, in contrast to the cases in which, say, the administration or his constituents take a position. This possibility for freely shopping among fellow congressmen for cues quite naturally results in a high agreement between the cue and the vote. For the purposes of control, therefore, it might be interesting to develop another partial correlation model which excludes the variables in which this free-selection feature is evident. Those two excluded variables are: fellow congressmen, for reasons just cited; and staff, since the congressman hires his own staff and would find it surprising if they disagreed with him at least vocally for any significant part of the time.

The multiple correlation of the remaining four predictor variables with the congressman's vote is .53, indicating that while one has lost a good deal of predictive power by excluding fellow congressmen, one still has noticeable power left. When one controls the effects of each variable for the other three, the results are presented in the last column of Table 1–3. It appears that the reduction of the power of constituency in the six-variable model was due to the effects of fellow congressmen, since this four-variable partial correlation hardly disturbs the original relationship. But the influence of interest groups and party leadership is eliminated in this four-variable model, as well as in the more expanded model. The administration retains its original limited importance, and in fact is slightly enhanced by this partialling.

In conclusion, at least according to the highly simplified picture presented in this preview, fellow congressmen appear to be the most important influence on voting decisions, followed by constituency. With some measures, constituency is nearly as important as fellow congressmen; with others, it is somewhat lower. But these two actors appear to stand out in all tables as the most important ones in the legislative system. Two other actors, by contrast, appear to be relatively weak influences on a congressman's voting decisions, the administration and the party leadership of his own party. Because the leadership position in the core sample was always the same as the position of that party's ranking members, the poor showing of the party leadership in the correlation models also represents a poor showing by committee leadership. Between these extremes of consistent importance and unimportance lie interest groups and staff. Interest groups are fairly important in the subjective view of the congressman making the decisions, but turn out to be unimportant when one considers the agreement scores. The staff shows another pattern: It is very unimportant in the congressman's view, but demonstrates high agreement with the congressman's vote, yet loses that importance when the other actors in the system are controlled.

Finally, the findings presented here barely scratch the surface. The anomalies in these findings, the subtleties, and complexity, the examination of different patterns within subgroups of the House—all this and more are left for later chapters. Why is it, for example, that interest groups seem to be more important subjectively than objectively? Is the Nixon administration more important to Republicans than has been shown here? What effects can we describe that do not show up in the quantitative analysis? In short, much remains for consideration, but given this context, we are now in a position to discuss each of the actors in the system.

NOTES

1. Richard F. Fenno, Jr., *The Power of the Purse* (Boston: Little, Brown, 1966), chaps. 1–2.
2. Wildavsky provides an example of this anticipation in the budgetary process. See Aaron Wildavsky, *The Politics of the Budgetary Process* (Boston: Little, Brown, 1964), pp. 21–31.
3. Among recent writings on constituency-legislator relationships are the following: Morris P. Fiorina, *Representatives, Roll Calls, and Constituencies* (Lexington, Mass.: D. C. Heath, 1974); David Mayhew, *Congress: The Electoral Connection* (New Haven: Yale University Press, 1974); Richard Fenno, *Home Style* (Boston: Little, Brown, 1978); Lewis A. Dexter, "The Representative and his District," *Human Organization* 16(1957):2–13, reprinted in *New Perspectives on the House of Representatives*, ed. Robert L. Peabody and Nelson W. Polsby (Chicago: Rand McNally, 1969); Warren E. Miller and Donald E. Stokes, "Constituency Influence in Congress," *American Political Science Review* 57(1963):45–56; Julius Turner, *Party and Constituency: Pressures on Congress* (Baltimore: Johns Hopkins Press, 1951); John C. Wahlke, Heinz Eulau, William Buchanan, and Leroy C. Ferguson, *The Legislative System* (New York: Wiley, 1962), chaps. 12–13; James David Barber, *The Lawmakers* (New Haven: Yale University Press, 1965); Lewis A. Froman, Jr., *Congressmen and their Constituencies* (Chicago: Rand McNally, 1963); and

John W. Kingdon, *Candidates for Office: Beliefs and Strategies* (New York: Random House, 1968).

4. See Woodrow Wilson, *Congressional Government* (New York: Meridian, 1956; originally published in 1885), chap. 2; and Donald R. Matthews, *U.S. Senators and Their World* (Chapel Hill: University of North Carolina Press, 1960).

5. David Kovenock, "Influence in the U.S. House of Representatives," *American Politics Quarterly* 1(1973):407–464. Robert Huckshorn, "Decision-making Stimuli in the State Legislative Process," *Western Political Quarterly* 18(1964):164 ff.; Wayne L. Francis, "Influence and Interaction in a State Legislative Body," *American Political Science Review* 56(1962):953–960. Simulation models have also dealt with communications. See Cleo H. Cherryholmes and Michael J. Shapiro, *Representatives and Roll Calls* (Indianapolis: Bobbs-Merrill, 1969); and Donald Matthews and James A. Stimson, "Decision-making by U.S. Representatives," in *Political Decision-Making*, ed. S. Sidney Ulmer (New York: Van Nostrand, 1970); and Matthews and Stimson, *Yeas and Nays* (New York: Wiley, 1975).

6. See Ralph K. Huitt, "Democratic Party Leadership in the Senate," *American Political Science Review* 55(1961):331–344; David Truman, *The Congressional Party* (New York: Wiley, 1959); Randall B. Ripley, *Party Leaders in the House of Representatives* (Washington, D.C.: Brookings, 1967); Ripley, *Majority Party Leadership in Congress* (Boston: Little, Brown, 1969); Charles O. Jones, *The Minority Party in Congress* (Boston: Little, Brown, 1970); Robert L. Peabody, "Party Leadership Change in the House of Representatives," *American Political Science Review* 61(1967):675–693; and Peabody, *Leadership in Congress* (Boston: Little, Brown, 1976).

7. Recent committee studies include Richard F. Fenno, Jr., *The Power of the Purse* (Boston: Little, Brown, 1966); John F. Manley, *The Politics of Finance* (Boston: Little, Brown, 1970); James A. Robinson, *The House Rules Committee*, (Indianapolis: Bobbs-Merrill, 1963); Ralph K. Huitt, "The Congressional Committee: A Case Study," *American Political Science Review*, 48(1954):340–365; and the following three articles in *New Perspectives on the House of Representatives*, ed. Robert L. Peabody and Nelson W. Polsby (Chicago: Rand McNally, 1969); Charles O. Jones, "The Agriculture Committee and the Problem of Representation"; Lewis Dexter, "Congressmen and the Making of Military Policy"; and Richard Fenno, "The House of Representatives and Federal Aid to Education."

8. Group theories of politics are propounded in Arthur F. Bentley, *The Process of Government* (Chicago: University of Chicago Press, 1908); and David B. Truman, *The Governmental Process* (New York: Knopf, 1951). A fascinating study of interest groups in trade policy is that of Raymond A. Bauer, Ithiel de Sola Pool, and Lewis Anthony Dexter, *American Business and Public Policy* (New York: Atherton, 1964). See also Lester W. Milbrath, *The Washington Lobbyists* (Chicago: Rand McNally, 1963); and Mancur Olson, Jr., *The Logic of Collective Action* (Cambridge, Mass.: Harvard University Press, 1965).

9. See Wilfred E. Binkley, *President and Congress* (New York: Vintage, 1962); Joseph P. Harris, *Congressional Control of Administration* (Washington, D.C.: Brookings, 1964); and R. Douglas Arnold, *Congress and the Bureaucracy* (New Haven: Yale University Press, 1979). A key study in executive-legislative relationships in the budgetary process is that of Aaron Wildavsky, *The Poli-*

tics of the Budgetary Process (Boston: Little, Brown, 1964). See also two articles by Richard E. Neustadt, "Presidency and Legislation: The Growth of Central Clearance," *American Political Science Review* 48(1954):641–671; and "Presidency and Legislation: Planning the President's Program," *American Political Science Review* 49(1955):980–1021.

10. Cleo H. Cherryholmes and Michael J. Shapiro, *Representatives and Roll Calls* (Indianapolis: Bobbs-Merrill, 1969); and Donald R. Matthews and James A. Stimson, "Decision-making by U.S. Representatives," in *Political Decision-Making,* ed. S. Sidney Ulmer (New York: Van Nostrand, 1970).

11. Duncan MacRae, Jr., *Dimensions of Congressional Voting* (Berkeley: University of California Press, 1958); Aage R. Clausen, "Measurement Identity in the Longitudinal Analysis of Legislative Voting," *American Political Science Review,* 61(1967):1020–1035; Clausen, *How Congressmen Decide* (New York: St. Martin's, 1973); Herbert Weisberg, "Scaling Models for Legislative Roll Call Analysis," *American Political Science Review* 66(1972): 1306–1315; Herbert Weisberg, "Dimensional Analysis of Legislative Roll Calls," Ph.D. dissertation, University of Michigan, 1968; Jerrold Schneider, *Ideological Coalitions in Congress* (Westport, Conn.: Greenwood Press, 1979).

12. For one paper which argues that ideology cannot be a useful guide to congressmen's decision-making, see Donald R. Matthews and James A. Stimson, "Decision-making by U.S. Representatives," in *Political Decision-Making,* ed. S. Sidney Ulmer (New York: Van Nostrand, 1970), pp. 20–21.

13. Charles E. Lindblom, "Decision-making in Taxation and Expenditure," in *Public Finances: Needs, Sources and Utilization* (Princeton, N.J.: National Bureau of Economic Research, 1961); Lindblom, "The Science of 'Muddling Through,'" *Public Administration Review* 19(1959):79–88; and Aaron Wildavsky, *The Politics of the Budgetary Process* (Boston: Little, Brown, 1964), pp. 13–16.

14. For example, see David Truman, *The Congressional Party* (New York: Wiley, 1959).

15. See the above discussion of ideology and footnote 11.

16. For example, see Julius Turner, *Party and Constituency: Pressures on Congress* (Baltimore: Johns Hopkins Press, 1951); and Gerald Marwell, "Party, Region, and Dimensions of Conflict in the House of Representatives, 1949–1954," *American Political Science Review* 61(1967):380–399.

17. Aage Clausen, "Measurement Identity in the Longitudinal Analysis of Legislative Voting," *American Political Science Review* 61(1967):1020–1035. See also Clausen, *How Congressmen Decide* (New York: St. Martin's, 1973).

18. Malcolm E. Jewell and Samuel C. Patterson, *The Legislative Process in the United States* (New York: Random House, 1966), p. 416.

19. See Harold Lasswell, *Politics: Who Gets What, When, How* (New York: Meridian Books, 1958); originally published 1936.

20. See Arthur Miller, "The Impact of Committees on the Structure of Issues and Voting Coalitions: The U.S. House of Representatives, 1955–1962," Ph.D. dissertation, University of Michigan, 1971 p. 15, for similar data drawn from the Miller-Stokes study of representation.

21. *Reading* is omitted here, because it often takes no position, and because it is simply a communication channel for another actor most of the time.

PART II

The Actors

2

The Constituency

In a discussion of legislative voting, one logical beginning is the legislators' constituencies. Congress is a representative body, with its members elected by popular vote in their respective districts. The recruitment process in those districts determines who the representatives will be, what kinds of people they will be, what major orientations and attitudes they will hold, and by implication, what the major distributions of these orientations and attitudes will be in the legislative body to which they are elected. The constituency is also the only actor in the political system to which the congressman is ultimately accountable. Every two years, members of the House of Representatives must face the electors in their districts to determine whether they will be allowed to continue in their posts. No other segment of the system has quite the same potential for negative sanctions as does the constituency.

There have been a number of recent empirical inquiries that have shed some light on such questions as the extent to which and the conditions under which constituencies can be said to influence legislators. Several studies have related demographic constituency characteristics to roll call voting. Other studies have considered various mechanisms that intervene between constituency characteristics and roll call behavior, such as role orientation, perception of constituency attitudes, and recruitment processes.[1] The study reported in this book complements the literature on relationships between legislators and their constituents in at least two ways. First, some of the literature on representation lacks the specific decisional focus of this study. One may find that a legislator has a certain role orientation, for example, without then having answered whether it has any appreciable effect on his behavior. One congressman in this study, who claimed at first that his constituency never affected him, was later clamoring for a way to get on the record in favor of impacted aid for school districts because of the heavy concentration of military installations in his district; he also said that if a payment limitation on agriculture subsidies hurt farmers in his district he would "have" to oppose it. In fact, many congressmen who did spontaneously enunciate some form of general role orientation toward their constituencies behaved unambiguously in a manner exactly opposite from their articulated orientation.

Second, other studies of representation do concentrate on the legislator's behavior, especially his roll call voting, but deal primarily with direct relationships between constituency characteristics and voting without taking much account of the mechanisms by which the translations are made. They also tend to use demographic variables or, at best, a survey of rank-and-file voters to measure constituency characteristics, which neglects the subgroups within districts having varied interests in governmental policy. The study described in this book is capable of inquiring into the effects of political elites, as well as investigating the mass public and its gross characteristics, and of exploring various mechanisms of constituency influence.

OVERALL CONSTITUENCY IMPORTANCE

There are some indications in the writing on legislative behavior that the importance of constituency in congressmen's voting behavior is rather limited. Since incumbents characteristically win reelection, constituents may usually be unable to sanction congressmen at the polls for votes which are out of keeping with their wishes.[2] The fact that voters know so little about their congressman's record, furthermore, can be said to indicate that they normally do not control his behavior.[3] Since the congressman rarely receives any kind of specific constituency guidance on how to cast a particular vote, another argument runs, he must fall back on his own devices and is left quite free to decide as he chooses.[4] Partly for these reasons, one model of legislative voting does not have a constituency factor explicitly built in as an influence on congressmen's voting decisions.[5]

This picture diverges somewhat from the obvious importance of constituency in this study. As reported in Chapter 1, if a congressman perceives a constituency position on any given issue, the probability that he will vote according to that position is .76, considerably better than a chance occurrence. The correlation between the perceived constituency position and the congressman's vote is .49. The only variable which noticeably reduces that correlation through partialing is the position of fellow congressmen, but even considering that powerful control, resilient constituency effects still show through.[6] To the extent that the congressman's informants among his colleagues come from similar constituencies, furthermore, even fellow congressmen may represent constituency influence. Controlling for other actors' positions has virtually no effect. In addition to this degree of agreement between constituency position and a congressman's votes, his constituency is also apparently much on his mind as he decides. Constituency was spontaneously mentioned 37 percent of the time, nearly as much as fellow congressmen and more than any other actor. It is also considered by the congressmen to be of major or determinative importance 38 percent of the time, again second only to the influence of freely selected colleagues within the House.

Constituency is thus by no means a complete explanation for congressmen's votes, but it still appears to have a substantial effect. While various intricacies and implications of this finding are explored throughout this chapter, one preliminary point might be made here. It could be that alternative interpretations of evidence about constituencies are possible. Simply because a congressman wins by a substantial margin, for example, he is not necessarily free to ignore the wishes of his constituents. Indeed, the fact that he abides by their wishes, at least in matters about which they have an attitude of some intensity, may be one *reason why* he wins by substantial margins and has little primary opposition. Even if constituents are rarely interested in the congressman's actions, furthermore, he may anticipate their possible reactions to his votes and take those potential reactions into account.[7] Indeed, his reasonably accurate anticipations could be one reason why constituents normally remain inattentive. His own behavior is not the sole explanation for his success or for constituency inattention, of course, but it may be an important contributing factor.

CONSTITUENCY COMPLEXITY

Much of the time, we are accustomed to thinking of a constituency in simplified terms. The congressman is thought to represent "his district," he adopts certain roles toward "his constituency," or he reflects the constituency's general characteristics. Actually, the constituency is an object of considerable complexity.[8] It is characterized by certain gross demographic features, to be sure, and

it is populated by a mass public with certain attitudinal distributions. But it is also a mottled collection of many subgroups. Some
constituents are attentive to political affairs, others are not.[9]
Within a congressman's constituency, there also are various oc-
cupational subgroups, various interest group leaders, party activists of varying persuasions, newspaper editors and other media
people, people who are especially involved in particular governmental policy areas—in short, a host of separate actors. To the
extent that these actors are politically active, they can be considered elites within the district. Some of these elites make up
the congressman's supporting coalition;[10] others are distinct
from it.

Congressmen themselves recognize this complexity as a matter of course. Indeed, the mass public may not be involved in an
issue at all, but the congressman may perceive a district opinion
among the elites, which may have a marked influence on his
behavior. One congressman put it this way in response to a question about the seating of Adam Clayton Powell:

Most of my constituents don't care. They don't wake up in the morning
and ask, 'Wonder how ――― will vote today?' But there is one group
that will notice—the black community. They'll take account of what you
do, and hold it against you if you go wrong. This is often the way it is.
Take the compulsory arbitration matter last year. Most of the people
don't have the vaguest notion about this, but labor groups will notice and
take account of it.

Other congressmen pointed out that while the bulk of their constituents were not aware of the issue, the school people were
actively interested in raising funding for education programs,
poverty workers strongly resisted changes in the program, and
large-scale farmers were interested in keeping the subsidy levels
high. Another congressman, in an exchange concerning the
House Un-American Activities Committee name change, said:

That's the big problem here. You're here to represent your people, but
you don't know what they want. The only way to really know is to take
a referendum. (Question: I realize you have imperfect information, but
given that, what do you think they wanted you to do?) I don't know of
any significant group who would oppose the committee. The same goes
for Powell—neither gave me any political problem.

This respondent started out by maintaining that he couldn't know, but ended by citing group evidence to the effect that there was no problem with the vote. It became clear that he could easily ascertain a constituency position.

Sometimes, then, the legislator makes his judgment about the constituency without thinking of elites in the district, either by considering the mass public or simply by not differentiating among elements within the constituency. On other occasions, he sees the mass public as not involved at all, and observes only elites. On still others, both are involved. While no standard question aimed at discerning perceptions of mass as opposed to elites was asked in the interview, whatever comments the congressmen made were coded according to elite and mass mentions. In 41 percent of the decisions, congressmen judged district opinion either by referring to the mass public alone or by citing a simple, undifferentiated view of the district such as "this was good politically," or "it is unpopular back home." This 41 percent, in other words, carried no mention of elites. In 28 percent of the cases, there was mention of elites, but not of the mass public. And in the remaining 32 percent, both the elites and mass public were taken into account.

Furthermore, the presence of elites in the congressman's perceptual map of his constituency, whether there because of overt elite activity or because he takes account of those groups independent of their activity, considerably enhances the importance of the constituency in his decision. There is more spontaneous mention of constituency when elites are involved, for instance, than when only the mass public is. Of those who mention the mass public only, 32 percent spontaneously mention constituency, while 44 percent of elite mentions and 55 percent of combination mass-elite mentions are spontaneous. The same picture is painted by the coding of constituency importance in the decision. Of those considering mass opinion only, 73 percent show the constituency to be of no more than minor importance, while the comparable figure for elite opinion only is 50 percent, and for both mass and elite, 44 percent.

To add further to the complexity of the constituency, differentiations can be made among types of elites, for example, according to whether they are "policy" or "process" elites. Policy elites would be those who have a direct expertise or interest in the governmental policy at issue, such as school people on education funding, conservationists on water pollution funding, farmers on farm policy, bankers on some tax matters, or municipal officials on poverty programs and bond taxation. Process elites are those such as newspaper editors and party activists who did not have any direct interest in the policy area, but who might be important in the more general political process in the district. One Republican said that part of his decision to vote for the surtax, for example, was that "the Republican organization back in the district would be upset if I voted against the administration." Policy elites are far more frequently mentioned in voting decisions than are process elites. Of the decisions in which constituency figured at all, 54 percent carried some involvement of policy elites, while only 9 percent involved process elites. In a sense, this result is only to be expected, since we are dealing with governmental policy decisions and not explicit campaign or electoral decisions. In view of the traditional importance of party in theories of the political process, on the other hand, there are rather few mentions of process elites.

A final differentiation among elites in the district is whether the elite in question is part of the congressman's electoral supporting coalition.[11] The congressman may pay close attention to elites that are not among his supporters. But it is likely that they will wield more influence if they have been political friends. One Republican, when asked what would have happened if the bankers in his district had opposed the surtax extension, replied, "That would have made it even tougher than it is. I don't know. It's an iffy question, and fortunately it hasn't happened." Another referred to "very close friends of mine" in the district poverty program. A city Democrat confided that he had "one pretty sticky problem" on tax reform: "A close friend of mine, who's been associated with me for years and is an important campaign contributor, is in the oil business. I had no idea how this bill would affect the oil people until I heard from him." Another Democrat referred to his strong political position by virtue of the fact that he has "the backing of the major power blocs in the district. I'm of the right ethnic and religious background, and I have close ties to the unions."

As for those groups that are not part of his supporting coalition, the congressman may take or leave them as he sees fit. While he may choose to pay them attention, he may also summarily dismiss their petitions. Two conservative congressmen referred to pressure against the ABM as coming from the "peace-at-any-price crowd." A liberal referred to support for the Internal

Securities Committee as the work of "a few right-wingers." Another said of those writing to oppose the seating of Adam Clayton Powell, "Oh you know, the usual nuts writing me a lot of crap." Several congressmen said that it did not make any political difference if a known opponent wrote. One remarked of labor unions, "They've never supported me, and I never support them, so I'm not listening."

On the other hand, a legislator often responds affirmatively to the requests of groups not in his supporting coalition. The politician apparently does so (1) when the request does not conflict with his own policy attitude and (2) when groups more central to his coalition than the group making the request would not be offended by acquiescence. If those two conditions are met, doing a favor for the group becomes virtually costless either in electoral or ideological terms, and in fact presents the opportunity to win further support or at least to neutralize potential opposition. Supporting even a numerically small group that might be expected to oppose the politician becomes virtually like casework for a constituent. The responsiveness which this sort of reasoning builds into legislators' actions can really be quite substantial.

INTENSITY

The intensity with which constituents hold their attitudes is of course not constant. With some issues they may be very intense about their preferences. With others, they may not care a great deal. It is an easy inference, then, that this constituency intensity will be reflected in congressional voting decisions. As constituents become more intense, the congressman will weigh their opinions more heavily. As they become less intense, he will feel free to let other factors come into play.

Many issues that come before the House, even in my core sample of issues, do not generate strong constituency feelings. A congressman can often guess reasonably well what most of his constituents would feel, but their opinions are not regarded as particularly intense, and are not taken as seriously as if they were. Said one liberal congressman about the House Un-American Activities Committee vote, "The bulk of my constituents oppose me on this, but they don't care enough about it to make a difference." A Republican who voted for an increase in the debt limit described his constituents thus: "This isn't a big issue with them. They probably oppose raising it, but it's not crucial." A midwesterner asserted, "Foreign aid has receded as an issue. But in a straight political sense, it would be better to oppose it."

Earlier in this chapter, the importance of the constituency in the congressman's decisions and the level of agreement between his vote and perceived constituency opinion was found to be quite high. One reason why these figures were not even higher is shown in these judgments about constituency intensity. Several of these congressmen perceived the constituency to be against them, but felt they could vote against this district attitude without fear of the consequences. This option is often not open with many other actors in the system. Fellow congressmen, for instance, generally care a great deal about an issue on which they have worked for months. Interest groups will not contact the congressman unless they feel fairly intensely about the issue. But constituency intensity is more variable than is the intensity of many other actors, and one can violate an actor's preferences if he is not intense about them.

On other issues, however, congressmen perceive much higher constituency interest. During the session of Congress studied, for instance, tax matters were cited by respondents as particularly arousing constituents, a perception which clearly affected the surtax and the tax reform bills. Even in interviews that were not directed to the surtax extension, congressmen would spontaneously bring up the subject. And the tax reform measure, which made many economists acutely unhappy because of its revenue losses, was described by one congressman as "a motherhood bill under the circumstances." The congressional pay raise was another issue which was seen as arousing constituents. As one congressman put it: "We got tremendous flak on it and it's still coming. I spoke out against it and letters I got said, 'Why don't you refuse to accept yours?' And these postal employees, if we wouldn't vote them an increase, they would say, 'You fat sons-of-bitches, how the hell can you take a 40 percent raise and then deny us the opportunity?' " Constituents were described as "mad as hell" about college disruptions, and the subject produced thoroughly angry exchanges and introduction of heavily punitive legislation. Matters having to do with race, such as open housing, bussing, and school desegregation, were also thought to produce intense constituency reactions.

One type of intensity deserves special mention, that related to an important industry in the district. If there is a piece of legislation pending that would help a district industry in a direct way, or especially one that would hurt it, nearly all congressmen defend that industry's interests. They do it because they see the whole economy of their area at stake, and when the economy is at stake, jobs are on the line. One tobacco-state congressman summed up the prevailing sentiment particularly well:

I've got many, many families in my district who make a living on tobacco. Now, I never argued that cigarettes are good for your health. I guess I was ridiculed in some quarters for what I did. If you could show me some way my people are going to eat if I vote against cigarettes, I'll do it. (Kingdon: So you start with this constituency factor.) It starts there and it ends there. That's all there is to it. If you don't, you aren't going to be around here very long. Not on something like this, where their livelihood is involved.

Many examples of this kind of protection for constituency industries can be found. For one congressman, it is agriculture: "I'm from an agriculture-producing area, and I'm concerned for farmers' welfare and will look out for them. If New England consumers are suffering, why the hell should I care?" For another, it is the oil industry; for another, insurance; for another, shoe manufacturers' problems with foreign competition; for another, mineral interests. Every area has its important industry, and every congressman is expected as a matter of course to defend these interests. Said one congressman about defending a major industry in the district, in his case, steel producers, "It's the only thing that really puts the crunch on you."

There are several reasons why congressmen adopt this kind of posture toward major industries in their districts. One is the sheer intensity of the interest. It would be extremely difficult to resist a man pleading for his job. Another is that the congressman may positively be convinced of the industry's point of view. One coastal area congressman spoke this way of his vote for a billion-dollar increase for the navy, which showed many seaboard members walking up the aisle for the amendment: "I don't have much in the way of navy yards and things in my district. But let's face it, I'm navy-oriented. Most of us are. We're men of the sea, all interested in ships and fish and that sort of thing. It's natural to support the Navy, coming from where I come from." Finally, a congressman can create something of an advantage politically by vigorously supporting a major industry. Generally speaking, there is little opposition in the district to the industry's interests, so that there is nothing to lose and everything to gain by defending them. It is almost like casework for an aggrieved constituent.

The natural protection of constituents' pocketbooks extends from their means of livelihood into other types of policy. Many congressmen, for instance, look upon impacted aid to school districts in much the same way as they would view a major industry in the district. One with a heavy concentration of federal installations in his district exclaimed:

Some of these school districts have a quarter of their budget in impact aid. The subcommittee cut out all aid for Category B students, and of course these school people came screaming to me. When you've got a quarter of your budget involved, you bet your life you'll scream. . . . There were very conservative members of the House who could never be accused of fiscal irresponsibility or overspending, who just said, "Damn it, home comes first." It was as simple as that.

Another such policy area is social security, since millions of people depend directly on the government for the checks. Another area, which is somewhat similar in its direct impact on the congressman's constituency, is public works. One staffer mused when asked why congressmen were so interested in public works projects, "I don't know. My boss is too. They like concrete, I guess. You know, there's a ribbon to cut."

Weighing of Intensities

In our consideration of constituency intensity, we have assumed to this point that the problem is one of simply responding to intensity. Actually, a congressman's decision is more complicated than simple response, since he must weigh his own intensity into the picture. If a segment of his constituents feels strongly about a given course of action, and he does not feel strongly about it, then he finds it convenient to go along with them. If, on the other hand, he does feel strongly as well, and in the direction opposite from his constituents, then he has something of a decisional problem. He must then weigh his intensity against that of his constituents. Schematically, the situations of conflict between constituency position and congressman's attitudes are presented in Figure 2–1.

The cases of mismatched intensities are relatively easy to predict. When the congressman feels strongly and his constituents do not, he will prefer his own feeling, since his constituents, while having an opinion contrary to his, do not feel particularly strongly about the matter. When the congressman does not feel very strongly about the matter but his constituents do, he is likely to

Figure 2–1 Weighing Intensities

CONSTITUENCY INTENSITY

		HIGH	LOW
OWN INTENSITY	HIGH	Redefine conflict and/or consider other actors	Prefer own position
	LOW	Prefer constituency position	Consider other actors

go along with them. Said one staff member, "Sometimes he goes against his constituents. But take maritime stuff. Now there may be a bad bill on that sort of thing, it's just a bad bill, but he doesn't care a great deal about maritime legislation and it isn't worth it to oppose them. So he goes along." A congressman said that he was not happy about direct popular election of the president, but that he voted for final passage because "my people want some reform." Another claimed that many of his colleagues are not pleased about postal pay increases, but that when the postal workers demand them, "They get scared and run." Another congressman, citing his vote for an appropriations amendment against college disruptions, about which he did not feel strongly, summed up this situation very well:

People are terribly upset about the colleges, and Congress has been getting a lot of complaint. "What are you characters doing down in Washington, anyway?" That's a potentially dangerous situation for the country, when people feel this way about their representatives. This was one way to show them that we have noticed what's going on. It was a bit of demagoguery, if you will, but I think that has its place. It lets people know that Congress cares. I wouldn't do it if it would really do some damage. But it wasn't going to do any damage. It was pretty innocuous. So my conscience is clear on this.

The college disruption case presented other congressmen the much more difficult conflict between two strongly held attitudes, their own and that of their constituents. In contrast to the legislator who did not believe the amendment in question would seriously hurt the colleges, these congressmen were more concerned. Their decision then becomes more unpredictable, and may go either way. They may decide, as one congressman did, to "rise above politics and take my lumps," or they may decide they just cannot do so, as the following congressman did on campus unrest:

The college amendment I really agonized over. It's all very well to say that we need to resist incursions on academic freedom, and I agree with that. But the local newspaper has been beating this thing to death and they'd really go after me. And there are officeholders there who have made whole reputations by hollering about this. They'd eat me alive. I finally decided, damn it, if I'm going to put my head in the meatgrinder it's going to be for something more important than a bunch of revolution-playing, scatter-brained militants. That may not be much of a way to make laws, but what the hell can I do?

Often this sort of decision turns in part on the congressman's feeling about how long the constituency intensity will last. If he feels it will be a fleeting thing, that the situation later on will be more like the case of weak constituency intensity, he can vote according to his own attitude. But if he feels that constituency intensity will persist, then he may adjust his own attitude to revise his intensity downward, and vote according to constituency feeling. It can be hypothesized that the decisional dynamic in high-conflict situations involves cognitively restructuring or redefining the situation to make it look like a case of mismatched intensity, which simplifies the choice.

On occasions in which neither the congressman nor his constituents feel intensely about the matter, he is quite likely to turn for guidance to other actors in the legislative system, such as fellow congressmen or the administration. Or the cases in which no conflict at all exists between the congressman and his constituency present him with a happier situation. One can almost sense the emotional release the following respondent feels:

Most people back home don't realize it, but it's very easy to influence a congressman. The only problem is that we can't respond to the pressure some of the time. There are other things we have to consider that prevent us from going along with it. That's why when you get something like funds for education or water pollution, it's just about irresistible. There's no reason to vote against education or for pollution. So you look at the pressure and say, "Here's my chance," and Zoom! you leap in with both feet.

Just how often each of these intensity situations arises is a function both of how often constituency and congressmen are intense, and of how often they conflict. It is not difficult to argue that constituents are rarely intense in their preferences, though when one takes account of elites in a district, the frequency of constituency intensity must rise. It is also possible that a congressman's "zone of indifference"[12] is quite wide, that he does not feel intensely about his votes on many issues. If he does not feel strongly, then the best thing for him to do is to play it safe and preserve the occasions on which he will anger constituents for those votes which mean something to him.

This may be one reason why surveys have discovered that constituents are usually not well informed about the performance of their congressman. If constituents were better informed, it would probably be a mark of arousal over something that the congressman did which was out of keeping with their strongly held beliefs. In fact, Miller and Stokes[13] found precisely this situation in the case of Brooks Hays, an Arkansas congressman and racial moderate who was defeated by write-in votes in a primary. The congressman does not need to vote in agreement with everything his constituents say, but only on matters about which they feel intensely. It is probably true that one rarely finds instances in which a legislator votes against the intense feelings of any significant group of constituents, and it is even rarer to find him voting against an intense majority of them. Their apparent lack of interest in him, in short, far from being testimony to their inability to control him, may in fact be testimony to his ability to discern the matters on which they feel intensely and vote according to their preferences.

The String of Votes
It can be argued, and many congressmen do argue, that even when constituents feel intensely about something, the congressman can generally afford to vote against them, on the grounds that one vote will probably not ruin his whole career. One said, "This is the sort of thing where you could vote either way and be safe. Most votes are, as you know." Of course, there are matters on which only one vote could cost the congressman dearly. A congressman cited one such instance as being "something that directly affects their pocketbook, like farmers on an agriculture bill or something like that."

Even if it is granted that one vote out of the ordinary will not create lasting political damage, that fact alone is not all that congressmen must consider. It is possible to cast what one congressman called a "string of votes" against various elements of the constituency, the cumulative effect of which could be very serious. Even if each of them singly would create no great electoral problem, the string of them taken together would. As one congressman perceptively put it when explaining his vote in support of the House Un-American Activities Committee:

I suppose this one issue wouldn't make much difference. Any one issue wouldn't swing it. But you get one group mad with this one. Then another group—much more potent, by the way—gets mad about gun control. Then unions about compulsory arbitration. Pretty soon you're hurting. It doesn't take too many votes like this before you've got several groups against you, all for different reasons, and they all care only about that one issue that you were wrong on. A congressman can only afford two or three votes like that in a session. You get a string of them, then watch out.

Another congressman, this one a Republican who had voted for several unpopular administration measures, allowed that he was taking a "calculated risk": "I don't think this one vote will be decisive. But I have a string of them. There are several votes where I'm supporting the administration that are unpopular back home. If I were my next opponent, I could put it together and mount a terrific campaign against me. I would wipe me out. I hope he isn't smart enough or mean enough to do it."

The rapid increase in the number of single-issue interest groups during the 1970s only serves to reinforce congressmen's concern with the string of votes. Observers of recent congressional change have been impressed, and in some cases alarmed, by the increasing number and vigor of groups whose members seem willing to act and to mobilize others in the electoral arena solely on the basis of a single, intensely held preference. Examples include abortion and antiabortion advocates, the gun lobby, taxpayer groups, bussing opponents, and even snowmobilers whose opposition to Donald Fraser's Senate candidacy in Minnesota was partially responsible for his defeat. The emergence of this welter of groups during the 1970s adds a mechanism by which public dissatisfaction over a string of unpopular votes might be expressed. The potential for alienating a series of constituency groups, each passionately devoted to their single cause, is much enhanced by the presence of this lobbying force.

The congressman, then, must not only take account of constituency reaction on the vote at hand in isolation, but must also consider the place the vote has in his total voting record. This consideration provides something of an incentive to vote with the constituency most of the time, in order to save deviance for matters that count.

Salience Effects

Quantitative evidence on the effects of intensity is difficult to obtain in any study, since people's intensities are so hard to measure.[14] In this study, it is doubly difficult, since no measurement was expressly designed to tap intensities. We can, however, use the classification of issues according to salience (see Appendix D). It is likely that salient issues—those which aroused considerable attention inside and outside of Congress and were much on congressmen's minds—are also those on which constituency intensity is the greatest, at least for congressmen in general. If the intensity effects which we have been describing actually obtain, one should thus find greater constituency importance on the most salient issues.

In fact, one does find exactly that. Table 2–1 relates issue salience to the subjective importance of the constituency in the congressman's decision. The high-salience issues like the surtax and ABM are distinctive. There was only one such decision in which the congressman indicated that the constituency was not at all involved, and in over half of these cases, the constituency was at least of "major" importance. When one retreats from the issues of highest salience, one finds the more "normal" case.

It is also interesting that salience is associated with a relatively complex view of the constituency, as Table 2–2 demonstrates. Congressmen apparently define issue salience partly by the involvement of elites in the issue. Issues of low salience tend to be characterized by mass public involvement only, a kind of vague perception of constituency mood. Medium-salience issues involve elites in the district to the exclusion of the mass public, more

Table 2–1 Salience and Constituency Importance

constituency importance	issue salience low	medium	high
No importance	18%	18%	1%
Minor	52	52	47
Major	25	22	45
Determinative	6	8	7
Total %	101%	100%	100%
Total *n*	73	73	76

Table 2–2 Salience and Complexity

constituency actor	low	issue salience medium	high
Mass only	61%	31%	31%
Elites only	10	49	26
Both mass and elites	29	20	43
Total %	100%	100%	100%
Total n	62	59	74

than other issues. High-salience issues find both mass and elite involved, more than other issues do. Apparently, elite involvement is generally necessary to move an issue into the categories of higher salience in the minds of the participants.

Moving from the subjective frame of mind of the congressman to the objective agreement with his constituency, salience effects are noticeable there as well. As Table 2–3 shows, high-salience issues occupy a special place. The probability that a congressman will vote with his constituency, given a constituency position, is greater with high-salience issues than with the other two. The correlation between constituency position and vote is really quite high in the case of high-salience issues, and the difference between high-salience and the others persists when the other five variables in the correlation model are controlled for, using the partial correlation coefficient. In view of the probable low constituency intensity on low- and medium-salience issues, it is interesting that the agreement between vote and constituency position is as high on such issues as it is. But the main point of the figures is that issues of high salience produce a dramatically better chance that the congressman will vote with his constituency.

The figures clearly show, then, that on high-salience issues the constituency is more important in the congressman's decision than it is on other issues. He subjectively considers constituents more important, and he votes more in accordance with their

Table 2–3 Salience and Agreement Between Constituency Position and Vote

salience	conditional probability	correlation coefficient	partial correlation
Low	.70	.42	.32
Medium	.72	.43	.29
High	.86	.73	.56

wishes, to the point that the predictive capability of a constituency position is really quite remarkable. We have also seen that it apparently does not matter a great deal whether one is talking of low- or medium-salience issues. Once one leaves the exalted place of the high-salience issues, the constituency effects are similar. It is also important to note, however, that constituency still has a substantial impact even on low-salience votes.

MECHANISMS OF CONSTITUENCY INFLUENCE

Recruitment

The simplest mechanism through which constituents can influence a congressman is to select a person initially for the office who fundamentally agrees with their attitudes. The recruitment process is partly a phenomenon involving the mass public.[15] Congressmen are elected by the mass of the voters and their continuation in office is ultimately a function of their continued reelection. But recruitment is also, and perhaps more importantly, an elite function.[16] Party activists, campaign contributors, interest group leaders in the district, and other such political actors decidedly play a major role in determining what sorts of people will be nominated and elected in a given district. Therefore, whatever strictures are placed on the types of politicians that can or cannot be recruited are not only mass public strictures, but also elite strictures. In particular, the prevailing coalition in the district, the congressman's supporting coalition, is in part responsible for the kind of politician who is eventually elected.[17] Thus when a congressman speaks of "agreeing" with the fundamental attitudes of his constituents by virtue of the recruitment process, he is referring only in part to mass attitudes, but also to elite attitudes.

Congressmen fully recognize the importance of this recruitment process. One pointed out, "Most of the time, the congressman and his constituency agree. That's why we're here." Said another, "If you have a conflict between you and your district very often, you don't belong here anyway." On some policy matters, the basic values of the constituency have been ingrained in the congressman practically from birth. One farm congressman emphasized his feeling for agriculture: "I understand farm problems. I have one of the most heavily agricultural districts in the country. I grew up with these people and I guess I reflect their thinking."

This simple, elemental point has profound implications for any consideration of constituency influence in the legislative process. Congressmen are often fond of saying that "political" considerations don't sway them. As one put it, "You'll find congressmen most of the time will want to vote according to their obligations and principles as they see them. The political considerations are less important." Another emphasized the point, rather personally I thought: "One trouble you scholars and students have is that you're always looking for some other motive. What's behind it? Well, most of the time, nothing is." Even if these respondents are basically right, the recruitment process that brought them rather than someone else to the Congress still profoundly affects the kind of representation the district will have. It often happens that a congressman never feels pressured by his constituency and in fact never even takes them into account, simply because he is "their kind of people" anyway. But because he is, the constituency has exercised a profound influence upon him. The real test of the proposition that he "doesn't take account of politics" would come if he were to begin consistently voting against their wishes. He would undoubtedly hear from them then. But this unhappy event almost never springs up to haunt the congressman, since he normally has no inclination to vote against his constituents' wishes on anything fundamental, or with any frequency.

In the sample of voting decisions used in this research, the congressman's attitude on the matter before him and his perception of the constituency attitude agreed in 61 percent of the cases. In another 13 percent, the congressman saw no constituency position. Approximately three-quarters of the time, in other words, there was no conflict between the constituency position and the legislator's own attitude, at least in the congressman's mind. There was even less conflict among Northern Democrats, congressmen from urban areas, and congressmen with safe seats. Eighty-four percent of decisions made by Northern Democrats, 88 percent of decisions involving urban districts, and 84 percent of those involving safe seats[18] saw no conflict between constituency and congressman's attitude. Especially among these particular subgroups, therefore, but also among all congressmen, agreement with constituency is the normal state of affairs. Many cases of disagreement, furthermore, are on issues of low constituency intensity.

That the recruitment process affects congressmen's voting is an elemental, easy-to-understand proposition, but its profound importance cannot be emphasized too strongly. If one starts to explain variance in legislative voting, the mechanism that probably explains the most variance is the recruitment process which brought a legislator of one set of attitudes to the Congress rather than another. It is fair to say that a John Stennis would not have been elected in New York City, nor would a Bella Abzug have been recruited in Mississippi. Different districts simply recruit people of different attitudes to run for Congress. Before the congressman casts a single vote, the broad pattern of his voting has already been determined by this process. As one journalist put it in a most elegant summary statement: "They just reflect where they come from."

Explaining

Congressmen are constantly called upon to explain to constituents why they voted as they did. In the process of answering mail and talking with constituents, questions asking them to justify their votes are put to them repeatedly. They not only actually experience being called upon to explain their vote, but they also anticipate that the situation will arise. This problem of "explaining" the vote, as congressmen call it, has a subtle but important effect on their voting behavior.

Some of the time, the process of justifying his vote does not alter the congressman's behavior. He decides to vote on whatever grounds he happens to think are important, and then finds he must construct a justification. As one congressman said: "It's more a question of devising a way of explaining what I decided to do after the fact, rather than having my constituency affect my original decision." Another said he had called his district office to find out what constituents had been saying about his vote to seat Adam Clayton Powell, because "My district is strongly against Powell and against civil rights, and I just wanted to be prepared to defend myself." Another congressman has explained votes for foreign aid to his rural constituents by pointing out that most of the money is spent within the borders of the United States. Edelman, drawing on Steiner and Gove, also speaks of the importance of providing a "cover" for legislators, a rationalization that they can use to explain their votes.[19]

But there is more to the phenomenon of explaining than simply devising a justification for a vote. Congressmen sometimes find themselves in the position of being unable to devise an acceptable explanation. In such a situation, especially if they do not feel intensely about the matter, they often vote so as to avoid the predicament. In such an instance, it can be said that the necessity to explain one's vote has had an impact on the congressman's behavior.

Instances of this impact were plentiful in the interviews. One liberal congressman, in telling why he will never vote to abolish the Internal Security Committee, put it well:

The right-wingers in the district are active enough as it is. I don't want to give them anything more. I vote against HUAC, and they'll raise a helluva hooraw about it. They'd write letters to the editor, and every time I'd go back there, I'll be explaining my position. It just isn't worth the fuss. I guess about 50 percent of the House really believes in the committee. The rest of us know we won't win a fight, and if you won't win it, why create this problem? It just isn't worth the trouble.

Another, considering the supplemental bill, which contained the spending ceiling and a college disruption provision, made a very similar commentary:

I could have voted against it, but frankly, I'd have to be running around explaining why I did it, and it just isn't worth the bother. It's much more simple this way. I don't stick out, and nobody is puzzled by what I did. And again, suppose I vote against the college disruption amendment. Then I have to explain to everybody why I voted in favor of riots. There we are again.

A farm-area congressman, voting for the limitation on agriculture payments, confessed: "It's a damn bad vote. But I'll never live long enough to be able to persuade these farmers of that." An opponent of direct election of the president voted for it, saying: "Very frankly, if I had a chance to sit down with all of my constituents for 15 minutes and talk to them, I'd have voted against the whole thing. But I don't have that chance. They wanted to change. If I voted against it, it would appear to them that I was against change, and I wouldn't have a chance to explain myself."

The effect of this need to explain oneself is somewhat related to the weighing of intensities discussed earlier. If the congressman feels intensely about the matter, he will take the trouble to explain his position. If he does not feel so strongly, it is likely that he will avoid the situation in which he is obliged to explain by voting with his constituents. Because there are many occasions on which a segment of his constituency has strong preferences and the congressman's preferences are not so strong, this ten-

dency to avoid the uncomfortable confrontation probably contributes a good deal to effective representation of such interests.
One sympathetic staff member pointed out: "If you vote wrong,
people start to ask you. They come up after a meeting or something and ask why. That's wearing on a guy. They're under
enough pressure as it is, without causing more." As a congressman summarized it, "It's a question of risk. Why cause trouble
that you can avoid?"

No standard question was asked about this concept in the
interviews. But by counting the number of interviews in which
explaining or some similar concept was mentioned, the notion
appears slightly more than one-third of the time. Those from safe
districts are apparently less concerned about explaining their position than are those from competitive districts, and congressmen
with higher seniority refer to it less than more junior members.[20]
Urban congressmen also mention explaining less than small-town
congressmen, and Democrats less than Republicans, probably
because small-town, Republican congressmen more often found
themselves asked by the administration and interest groups to
support legislation which they did not favor. At any rate, in view
of the fact that it was not a standard part of the interview schedule, there was a good deal of reference to the problem.

Explaining one's vote has several interesting implications for
the behavior of actors in the legislative system other than the
deciding congressman. Part of the process of building a coalition
around a given piece of legislation, for instance, is providing
potential members of the coalition with handy explanations that
they can use in case the vote gives them some trouble back home.
They may not join the coalition without such an explanation. For
instance, one Republican staffer said of Republicans who voted
for a Nixon-requested increase in the debt limit when they had
consistently voted against such increases before, "They were
really floundering around, and they needed to be provided with
some way that they could explain this vote." The standard explanation which evolved, which emerged in interview after interview with Republicans, was along the lines that the Nixon administration inherited the deficit from the previous administration
and that Republicans could have more faith in this administration's fiscal responsibility. Without being provided with such an
explanation, it is unlikely that as many Republicans would have
voted for it, since they would have no way to face their constituents gracefully.

Other instances of this attention to the explaining problem by coalition builders came up frequently. Those trying to resist the most punitive measures against universities, for example, used the potent argument that they would play into the hands of the Students for a Democratic Society (SDS), an argument which could then be used on constituents who questioned the congressman's willingness to take a hard line against riots. Tobacco-area congressmen spent great effort in discrediting research on the link between smoking and cancer, so that their colleagues could then tell constituents that the hearings showed that the link was not conclusive. A ritual reduction in the foreign aid bill was proposed, in order to provide congressmen with the argument that they voted to cut the program, "Just a chance to get on the record," as one put it. Liberals voted to transfer the functions of the House Un-American Activities Committee to the Judiciary Committee, a position much easier to defend than a vote to abolish the committee outright. Or votes to seat Adam Clayton Powell were obtained by fining him because, as one congressman put it, "A lot of members thought that the wrath of the gods would really come down if they just seated him. So they had to find some formula." In fact, the failure of legislative leaders to structure a parliamentary situation to provide members with the ability to explain their votes rather upsets those congressmen, to say the least. Several conservative Republicans were very unhappy with their leadership over the Health, Education, and Welfare appropriation, for example, because they were never provided with the opportunity to be on the record for impacted aid to schools only, and were forced to vote for the entire education package which included higher spending for less popular programs.

The need to explain is also used to blunt potential opposition. It is often alleged, for instance, that the proper packaging of a legislative proposal has a great deal to do with its success. Education programs are titled "national defense." A new name is found for "welfare." Diverse programs are subsumed under the title "poverty." The National Institutes of Health are organized according to disease, rather than by some other mode. One reason that these strategies are employed is that congressmen find it difficult to explain votes for cancer, for hunger, or against the national defense. If one can maneuver a number of congressmen into a position in which they feel they cannot satisfactorily explain themselves, one might gain sufficient votes to make a difference.

Thus far, in the case of conflict with constituents, we have been discussing only two of the congressman's options: he may either decide that explaining the vote is too much trouble and vote with his constituents' wishes, or he may decide to vote according to his own attitude and defend his position on substantive, public policy grounds. These two alternatives, however, are not the limit of his options. There are also a number of strategies for "taking legislators off the hook," as one congressman put it, which do not avoid the problem but do provide additional aids to explanation. Among these strategies for getting off the hook are the following:

1. Taking advantage of the Senate, conference committee, or the executive branch. On occasion, it is possible when faced with a voting dilemma to vote according to one side of the dilemma, on the assumption that the other side will be looked after in another part of the governmental process. The congressman can thus take care of himself and be better able to explain his vote, while at the same time believing that little harm will be done because the Senate, president, or someone else will redress the balance. Several congressmen, for instance, told me that it was easier to vote for the payment limitation on agriculture subsidies partly because the Senate was expected to kill it. One bluntly put it: "This limitation is a good chance to demagogue, because you know the Senate is going to knock it out anyway. Even if everything Secretary Hardin said is true—that there would be increased cost and this would ruin the program—you don't have to worry about it. The Senate is going to take care of him anyway, so take care of yourself, buddy."

2. Pleading the parliamentary situation. The structure of the House rules—the committee system, a closed rule, infrequency of record votes, and the like—sometimes provide congressmen with graceful ways of getting off the hook. Respondent after respondent on the tax reform bill, for example, told me that the closed rule, which prohibited amendments, helped them to handle the pleas of groups seeking to maintain their favorable tax position. When asked what he told people trying to protect themselves, one congressman said, "I said I didn't agree with all the features of the bill, but it came up under a closed rule and there was nothing I could do." Another sharpened the picture by saying, "The closed rule completely takes the heat off. What it means is that the pressure is transferred to the committee and to the Senate." One Ways and Means Committee member acknowledged

the effect: "God, I heard from everybody. The oil guys, foundations, were in here, real estate people, municipalities—you name it, I saw them." Another instance of committee action taking congressmen off the hook was evident in the pay raise bill, when the Rules Committee voted not to take the bill to the floor. One congressman noted, "It often happens that members will quietly go to the Rules Committee members asking them to kill a bill and transfer the pressure to them. They do it all the time."[21]

The infrequency of votes on which congressmen are recorded aye or nay was another feature of the parliamentary situation used to get off the hook, at least in the late 1960s. If the vote is not recorded, then the congressman is able to miss the vote or even to vote contrary to the way he votes on the record. One metropolitan congressman told me of his actions on the Whitten amendment to restrict HEW desegregation guidelines:

The bussing thing was hard. Bussing has created a lot of trouble in my city. People are mad about it. Damn good thing it wasn't a roll call vote. I just didn't vote on the Whitten amendment. I sat it out. (Question: What if it had been on the record?) That would have been a very tough decision. I don't know what I would have done. But a nonrecord vote made it easy for me.

Another congressman said he sat out a teller vote on an amendment concerning college disruption. Another even voted with the leadership on the agriculture payment limitation and the opposite way on the roll call vote.

A rules change which took place subsequent to my interviewing has made it easier for the House to obtain record votes on amendments. Under the new procedure, teller votes which were previously cast anonymously can now be recorded. Many congressmen, despite the convenience of nonrecord voting in terms of explaining their votes, found it frustrating on several occasions in which they would have preferred a clear-cut, easily interpretable vote on a crucial amendment. ABM deployment, for instance, never did come to an unambiguous vote for or against. So the House, in response particularly to liberal pressure to let the sun shine in on the legislative process, changed the rules to allow 20 members to insist on record votes on amendments.

It is likely that the greater frequency of record votes makes a considerable difference. Members are more obliged to pay attention to floor proceedings and to constituency reactions to their votes. Committee leaders managing legislation probably also find it necessary more frequently than in the past to anticipate what will happen on the floor and to revise a bill in committee to head off potential floor opposition, because they have been stripped of their ability to defeat amendments on nonrecord votes. The impetus toward opening up the legislative process by such measures as recorded teller voting, open committee markup sessions, and less frequent closed rules may have increased the degree to which congressmen take constituents into account. But following from our earlier discussion of constituency elites, because the constituents who are paying attention are often the organized interests, these procedural changes may also have resulted in more attention to narrow interests, more parochial voting, and less ability or willingness to structure the legislative situation to look after collective interests. Stripping legislators of the ability to conceal votes may have increased their responsiveness to constituents at the same time that it has decreased their ability to rise above narrow or parochial constituency interests.

3. Avoiding commitment if possible. Closely related to sitting out nonrecorded votes is a more general strategy, that of avoiding a commitment if it is possible to do so. This is done partly on the chance that whoever is asking the congressman for a commitment will forget his vote later on, that he can mollify several groups by hedging, that he may want to change his mind, or that the vote may never come up at all. One congressman said: "I'm sure I'll vote for the surtax package. It would take something just revolutionary happening between now and tomorrow to change my mind. But I haven't told my constituents. (Question: Why?) Because there may not be a record vote. Why should I be out on a limb until it's necessary?" Fortunate for the man that he did stay uncommitted, since something did come up in the interim which changed his mind, and he voted against the surtax. Another respondent chuckled that he had told tax reform opponents that he would "consider their view and then make a judgment," even though he had decided a week before to vote against them.

4. Citing other votes or actions. Congressmen sometimes attempt to divert the attention of a concerned constituent from the issue at hand by citing some other vote or action they have taken. One said he could justify his vote for the surtax by his vote in favor of tax reform: "I can always point to this vote and say I voted to cut your taxes." Another felt his support of the pay raise would not hurt him, stating, "They know I'm a budget-cutter anyway, so they usually understand." Others make such a point of

constituency service and nonpolicy favors to constituents that they feel they can afford some votes that are not in accord with their constituents' wishes. A liberal Democrat grinned, "I have built up pretty good rapport with bankers and now they're practically embarassed to call me."

This strategy of pointing to other votes or actions is prevalent enough so that many congressmen importune the leadership to provide them with votes to which they can point, if none are available. During the time at which college unrest was most salient, congressmen were asking Education and Labor Committee members to report some bill or to support some floor amendment aimed at disrupters, even if it might not cause any serious dislocation to the universities, so they could have some vote on the record to which they could point and claim that they had voted to "get tough."

5. Citing respected authority. One way to defend an unpopular vote is to cite some authority whom the dissatisfied constituents respect. One Democrat, responding to businessmen who opposed repeal of the investment tax credit, said, "I quoted their president to them. Most of them would be supporters of his administration anyway." Another thought, regarding his vote against a college disruption amendment, "I can defend myself pretty well," by citing Attorney General Mitchell's testimony that no more restrictive legislation was needed.

6. Citing other constituents. A final strategy for getting off the hook is quoting other constituents to the aggrieved party. The congressman can then claim that he is at least representing part of his constituency. One even went so far as to carry his constituency poll around in his pocket: "Then if someone asks, 'Why didn't you vote so and so?' I'll say, 'Because two-thirds of your neighbors told me to vote the other way.'"

Direct Communication
Another mechanism of constituency influence is some form of direct communication from constituents to congressmen. This communication often takes the form of mail,[22] though as we will discover, it is not always so.

The direct communication serves a number of functions for the congressman. The first is that it simply serves as an attention-focusing agent. Problems of which the congressman might not have been aware, or even problems of which he was aware but had not placed in the forefront of his thinking, are brought to his attention by mail, especially if it comes in any volume or intensity. Several congressmen referred to mail from educators as having "alerted" them to the size of the proposed appropriation cuts that had been made by the Bureau of the Budget and the House Appropriations Committee. The heavy mail regarding taxes served to focus attention on tax inequities of which congressmen had always been aware, and also informed them about rationales for various "loopholes" in the code. Mail and other communication from constituents focused attention on pollution problems: A New Yorker talked about the East River; a midwesterner, about drinking water in his hometown; a Great Lakes congressman, about pollution of Lake Erie.

The second function served by mail is that it offers some indication of the direction of the constituents' thinking.[23] Repeatedly in the interviews, when asked what his constituents thought about the issue at hand, a congressman would give an answer and then add something to this effect: "if I can judge by my mail." In fact, respondents spontaneously brought up the subject of the mail from the constituency in one-quarter of the interviews, without having been asked a question about it. Respondents also replied that they had received no mail only 29 percent of the time.

Of course, many of the issues in this sample would be ones on which mail would be forthcoming. Indeed, the volume of the mail is clearly related to issue salience, as Table 2–4 demonstrates. One possible interpretation of this table is that congressmen in fact define issue salience partly according to whether they are getting heavy mail or not. Tax matters, gun control, education

Table 2–4 Issue Salience and Mail Volume

mail volume[a]	low	salience medium	high
No mail	56%	29%	4%
Very little: one or two letters	13	15	7
"Normal" volume	15	45	30
Heavier than normal	14	11	44
Very heavy	3	0	16
Total %	101%	100%	101%
Total *n*	72	65	71

[a] This is the congressman's subjective definition of what is "normal" or "heavy," not a count of pieces of mail.

funding, ABM—the issues which were particularly salient to congressmen—were also those on which the mail had been heavy. Incidentally, there was no difference in reported mail volume between urban districts and small-town districts.

In addition to indicating to some congressmen the direction of constituency opinion, mail also is used as an index of the intensity of that opinion. Congressmen reason that it takes some trouble to write, and hence some degree of intensity. Thus, the volume of mail is taken as a rough index of constituency intensity. One respondent, when asked if his constituents cared about the electoral college issue, replied, "We've received very little mail on it." Some congressmen also notice the ways in which the letter-writers express themselves, in addition to the volume of mail received. One, when asked if he had received more mail on taxes this session than before, replied, "Not more, but they're madder." This kind of qualitative judgment, as well as simple mail counts, came up quite often in congressmen's assessments of mail.

A third function of communication from the constituency has to do with congressional oversight of administration. It is often argued that Congress is a decidedly weak sister to the executive branch when it comes to information about the operation of federal programs. While the information problems of Congress are of course well known, the districts do provide legislators with some feedback about the execution of federal programs straight from the operating levels of bureaucracy, particularly negative feedback. If constituents are personally aggrieved by an administrative agency, many write their congressmen, and in the process of handling this volume of casework and other complaints, the congressmen obtain valuable information. They can then use this information either to attack the executive agency or to amend the law.

A final function of the mail is for use as an intra-House bargaining tool. A congressman is sometimes in a position to generate a volume of mail from his district and then use it as an argument for his position, either in convincing other congressmen or in pleading that he cannot go along with party policy because his district demands the reverse. One congressman, skeptical of others' claims about volumes of mail for tax reform, stated it in his own inimitable style:

You know how members get that mail. They go back to their districts and talk up something, and then they get the letters. Then they slay the dragon. But they've created the dragon that they're going to slay. I could go back to my district and holler about something, and then come back here and say my constituency was all hopped up. I could go back there and make speeches saying that the defense budget is wasteful, that two billion was lost on the C-5A, that the generals are pissing your money away, and the army this and the air force that, and I'd get floods of mail. There are a lot of good actors around here. That's the size of it.

Mail has a number of origins. Much of it comes to the congressman because the letter-writer is personally involved in an aspect of the issue. Several congressmen said that the mail on taxes was heavy partly because state and local taxes, as well as federal taxes (the surcharge), had been raised all at once, and people resented it. Or mail on social security payments or college loans comes from those directly affected. The coverage of issues in the mass media contributes to mail as well. One congressman, for instance, received "a great deal of mail" favoring electoral reform at the time that the Judiciary Committee was holding hearings that were reported in the press in his district.

Other mail is organized by a more or less formalized communication system based in Washington, when an interest group headquarters asks their members to write. Congressmen say that they can readily spot this "inspired" or "stimulated" mail.[24] One showed me letter after obviously stimulated letter supporting the poverty program, saying the same thing in the same phrases. Another spoke of a thousand mimeographed letters simply signed at the bottom, including one man who signed his upside down. This sort of mail is seen very differently from, for instance, the mail on taxes which congressmen received during the session. The tax mail, in the words of one congressman, "just sort of welled up." Another instance was mail against Adam Clayton Powell in 1967. In these sorts of cases, congressmen judge that a substantial number of people are intense about their preferences. Stimulated writers, however, are usually seen as being neither intense about their preferences nor numerous enough to count much. One congressman summed up the prevailing attitude when asked if he discounted inspired mail: "No, you just evaluate it and avoid getting stampeded by it."

Regardless of its origins, it is possible to classify the mail as coming from elites, the bulk of the people, or both, much as we used this classification earlier in this chapter. Even though we discovered then that in only 28 percent of the time were congressmen making generalizations about their constituencies on the basis of elite judgments only, it develops here that in 59 percent of the cases, mail comes from elites only. In 28 percent, it is judged to be from the mass public, and in 13 percent it is from a combination of mass and elite. This elite emphasis in the mail is of course to be expected, since those most directly involved in a given policy, such as school people on education or municipal officials on tax-exempt bonds, would be writing.

So far as the ideological direction of the mail is concerned, constituency mail agrees with the congressman's position 64 percent of the time. Twenty-four percent of the time, the bulk of it is more liberal than the congressman is, and in 8 percent of the cases, it is more conservative. The remaining 5 percent finds the mail split evenly between liberal and conservative. The more conservative mail comes almost exclusively on low-salience issues, and also tends to come from the mass public rather than from elites: 85 percent of the more liberal mail comes from elites only, while over half of the more conservative mail is from the mass public only. The issues and moods of the 1970s may have slanted the mail in a more conservative direction than these figures indicate.

Agreement of the mail with congressmen might vary according to seniority.[25] More senior members, the argument would run, would establish a well-known position on most issues, and thus would get less mail in total volume, since people would not feel their letters would make a difference either way; they particularly would get less mail from those who disagree with them. These hypotheses, however, do not find support in my data. Senior members receive easily as much mail by volume, and their mail disagrees with their position as much, and in fact somewhat more than it does at other seniority levels.[26]

What really accounts for differences is party affiliation and "urbanness" of the district. The mail agrees with the Northern Democrats' positions in 89 percent of the cases, and with the urban congressmen's positions in 92 percent. But mail agrees with Republicans in less than half of the cases (43 percent), and with small-town representatives, 59 percent of the time. Southern Democrats find a 68 percent agreement. Liberals (in Americans for Democratic Action terms) also receive more "agree" mail than conservatives, whose mail is more liberal than they are. It is clear from these data that letter-writers tend to be relatively liberal. On any given issue up for floor consideration, people will generally write to obtain action from government, rather than to obtain inaction; hence, mail comes largely from a liberal direction. School people and pollution opponents want more funding, people write to support direct election of the president more than they urge maintenance of the electoral college system, and so forth. People appear to write according to what moves them, regardless of some calculus about whether it will affect the congressman. And because the mail coming from the attentive people tends to be liberal, it agrees with liberal Northern Democrats and those from urban areas, and disagrees with conservative Republicans. This finding has the further implication that for Northern Democrats, their political environment is more homogeneous and less conflict-ridden than it is for Republicans, which we will find to be true in other contexts as well.

Finally, and very important, mail is not the only type of direct communication that a congressman has with the district. It is obviously an important type, judging by how often congressmen spontaneously bring it up. But there are alternative sources of information.[27] Many congressmen pointed to their frequent trips back to the district and the conversations they had with constituents during those trips. As one said, "At times, you don't get a letter, but people do feel strongly about it. I judge their feelings by going back there every weekend. I have talks with wide varieties of people." At other times, the trips are combined with the mail, as in the case of taxes: "You'd go back to the district and all they'd talk about was taxes, taxes, taxes, and cost of living too. The pressure from the public was really on."

Another source of information is the questionnaire that many congressmen send to every boxholder in the district. While this is used for argument and other purposes, of course, it is also used for information. If one is measuring the opinions of the attentive public, furthermore, it probably is not without virtue. One congressman voted for direct election of the president, even though he was not happy about it, partly as a result of his questionnaire. Another noted that his respondents would stand for higher taxes if tax reform were included. As one congressman summarized it, "I don't go by these questionnaires, but I regard them as another interesting bit of information."

It is also possible for a congressman to judge constituency opinion without any communication whatever. This is partly by way of anticipating what constituency reaction would be if he voted a given way. One referred to unpopular votes, commenting, "You're more likely to hear about it afterward, not before." Even when not attempting to anticipate reactions, however, congressmen often are able to make a judgment about constituency opinion. One told of their attitudes on ABM: "I know my people very well. They would overwhelmingly support it. I don't have to hear from them."

Electoral Consequences

The classic enforcement of constituency control over the representative is through retribution at the polls. Actually, electoral consequences are not solely limited to the ultimate sanction of loss of the seat, or even significant loss of votes. Politicians simply anticipate possible campaign occurrences and take them into account as they vote. One possibility is that a given vote can be used as a good campaign talking point. One congressman voted for full funding for water pollution abatement, had his staff check how it would affect each governmental unit in his district, and then used it extensively: "I've used it in publicity releases. I'm running hard on it. I mention it every time I make a speech. It's a good issue." The same use was made of full funding for education.

Congressmen more often mentioned issues which might be used against them. If nobody in the district notices a vote at the time it occurs, an opponent in the next election still might pick up an unpopular vote and use it against the congressman. Even though it doesn't affect the election outcome, legislators often simply try to avoid such an embarrassing situation if they can. One congressman who "agonized" over an amendment against college disruptions, when asked if anybody would actually notice his vote, replied:

No. I know that nobody will notice it right now. People never do. But it may be used against you in the next campaign. I learned that lesson in my first campaign for reelection. About five days before the election day, they hauled out the charge that I was prohomosexual because I cast a vote against some ridiculous District bill. You see, most people don't notice it. But your opponent will comb down through every aspect of your record, every vote you've ever cast, looking for dirt and using it.

Another discussed his vote for the tax reform bill in these terms: "If you vote against this bill, you'd be blamed. Some demagogue would take you on and beat you to death over it. Politically, you just about have to vote for it." Another exclaimed, concerning his vote for foreign aid, "My opponent next time will seize on this if he's got a brain in his head, because it's a beauty."

Whether such a consideration about avoiding campaign trouble sways the congressman in the direction of voting to avoid that trouble becomes once again a question of balancing his intensity against the intensity of his constituents. Many of these mechanisms for constituency influence involve the same calculus. If he doesn't feel strongly about it, then he may opt to avoid the trouble. If he does feel strongly, then he will take the heat.

Potential election consequences, of course, are not ended by anticipation of the opponent's actions. The congressman also pays some attention to his supporting coalition.[28] Active supporters, including campaign contributors, may be as important as votes. If the mass of citizens are not watching the congressman's votes, then more active people may be. A congressman at least attempts to hold his previously existing coalition together. One who depended on organized labor said, "When some labor matter comes up, it's pretty much automatic with me. I'll go along with them." On occasion, he may see the opportunity to enlarge his coalition, as did another respondent in discussing his support of greater education funding: "The result is that back in my district there are now a bunch of education people who will be very active supporters of mine for years. They never were before. They voted for me, but weren't active. It will be different now. This thing has had nothing but good political effects as far as I'm concerned." Even if he cannot obtain the support of a given group, his actions may serve to neutralize the group politically. He can on occasion satisfy them enough so that they will not join an opposing coalition and fight him actively.

In any discussion of electoral consequences of votes, it must be remembered that there is a good deal of uncertainty which surrounds elections.[29] This uncertainty is not simply limited to unease over the outcome of the general election. The congressman may also face primary opposition, his district's boundaries may be redrawn to his disadvantage, or he may fall victim to national trends. So many things could conceivably happen to damage or even ruin a carefully built political career that congressmen engage in many kinds of activities designed to build support as a hedge against uncertainty, such as trips to the district and meticulous attention to casework. They also take some account of the district as they vote, especially on the more salient issues. As one senator said when the Haynsworth nomination to the Supreme Court was the current hot issue, "That vote may decide the outcome of elections to ten Senate seats. But then again, it may not. Something else may come along and everyone will forget how you voted on Haynsworth. The trouble is, you can never be sure."[30] In a congressman's calculus, the probability of losing an election may be quite low, but the cost (the end of his career) is extremely high. Balancing that cost against the probability of losing, a politician may well opt to vote in an electorally safe way, even though he reasons that the loss of a significant number of votes in the next election really is not at issue.

Thus drawing conclusions about simple election returns can be a rather complicated business. It is not enough to observe that because congressmen win in general elections by large margins and because they rarely face primary opposition, they therefore need not be concerned about constituency reaction to their behavior. Such an argument neglects the possibility that they may be so seemingly secure partly *because* they were careful about catering to their constituencies. One cannot fail to notice that even congressmen from safe seats spend a great deal of energy looking after constituents and taking account of them as they decide. One congressman, who won reelection by about 65 percent of the vote in 1968 and who had been unopposed before, astonished me by saying, "I have to run the cocktail circuit and go back to the district every two or three weekends just to stay in office." Marveling at such statements from even very "safe" congressmen, I asked a staffer why a politician from a safe district should be worried about how constituents will react. His answer was as simple as it was profound: "They're safe *because* they vote that way."

Several scholars have commented on the increased electoral margins by which incumbents have been winning reelection during the decade of the 1970s.[31] By a number of measures, the advantage of incumbency seems to have increased. Various explanations for this trend have been discussed in the literature. It is possible that redistricting may have contributed to increased incumbent safety as boundaries were redrawn to benefit current office holders. Weakened party identification in the electorate may have produced a greater advantage for incumbents as voters use incumbency as a guide to voting in the absence of strong party attachments. Incumbents may have capitalized on such greater perquisites of office as mailings and trips home and on their ability to perform casework services for constituents, to produce formidable advantages in advertising themselves, and gaining constituents' gratitude for favors done. Whatever the mix of causes, the increased electoral margins enjoyed by incumbents may have the consequence of making it less necessary to respond to constituency wishes.

For a number of reasons, however, I would maintain that representatives have not fundamentally altered their stance toward constituents.[32] It seems likely, first, that they themselves have played a part in producing their advantages through increasing advertising and assiduous attention to constituent requests. One of the factors over which they have control is their own voting record. Thus among the contributions to incumbency advantage may be their attention to constituents' wishes when casting votes on the floor as part of the package of actions and qualities that they present to the electorate every two years.[33] There is no necessary reason, in other words, that the responses reported above that members are safe *because* they keep their records free of unpopular votes would not still hold true. Second, the apparent increasing influence of single-issue interest groups discussed earlier in this chapter lends some support to the argument that responsiveness to constituents may be increasing at the same time that incumbency advantage is increasing. If these groups' major stock in trade is their ability to mobilize constituents, then members' responsiveness to those groups implies a responsiveness to those constituents. Third, such recent instances as the tremendous pressure for tax relief and a balanced federal budget in the face of California's Proposition 13 and similar indications of a taxpayer revolt in other states would seem to indicate that legislator concern for constituency reactions remains undiminished. If anything, the relatively low seniority of the House membership of the late 1970s might accentuate their attention to constituents' wishes, as we shall see presently.

The topic of electoral uncertainty leads directly to a consideration of the competitiveness of the district. It could be, on the one hand, that congressmen who come from competitive districts are obliged to be more concerned about constituency reaction than are those from safe districts. One staff member of a congressman from a relatively safe, urban district said that his boss was "simply splendid on civil rights, and does get trouble on that. But it's the difference between 70 percent and 60 percent. We had quite a drop last time, but we have the margin." But a congressman from a competitive district, dealing with an issue on which an important segment of his constituency felt strongly, exclaimed, "I won by a razor-thin margin last time. If I had won by a larger margin, frankly, I'd have gone back and told them to stick it. But it's nip and tuck in my case, and on something like this, I'd better be with them." On the other hand, Miller has discovered that those from safe districts actually vote with their constituency more often than do those from competitive districts, partly because it is easier to discern a constituency attitude in the more homogeneous safe district.[34]

By several measures in my data, constituency initially appears to be more important in the decisions of congressmen from both competitive and safe districts than it is for those from medium-competition districts. But controls for party and for seniority render this originally rather novel relationship nearly meaningless. Once the controls are introduced, no consistent or clear picture of the effects of district competitiveness is discernible. It appears that to the extent that electoral considerations affect congressmen's voting decisions, they affect congressmen from safe as well as competitive districts.

Another electoral effect is associated with seniority. Independent of their margins of victory, senior members of the House appear to be less preoccupied with their constituencies than are junior congressmen. Congressmen at all seniority levels vote in accordance with their constituencies' positions with about the same frequency. But the junior congressmen pay more careful attention to constituency opinions. Relatively junior congressmen considered their constituency to be of major or determinative importance 45 percent of the time, while middle-seniority members did so 38 percent of the time, and senior congressmen did so 28 percent of the time. These differences, unlike those for competitiveness, persist while controlling for other third variables.

One reason for this seniority difference is that as he accumulates years in Congress, a House member is likely, through years of constituency service and exposure, to feel more safe electorally. His election margins may improve, but even if they do not, he will gradually build elite allegiance and frighten away potentially formidable opponents. Two congressmen who had been in office for a few terms and had won by percentages in the lower sixties, discussed a vote against the House Un-American Activities Committee in just such terms:

I agonized over HUAC a while ago. I wasn't in Congress very long at the time, so there was a political problem. As I've been here longer and gotten larger margins of victory, I've felt I could exercise greater freedom.

This would have been a greater problem if I had been a freshman or sophomore here. But after several terms, I don't give a damn any more. I'm pretty safe now, and I don't have to worry about reaction in the district.

A second reason is that as a congressman accumulates seniority, he has the opportunity over the years to confront a number of situations in which he has been obliged to cast votes that were difficult politically. Perhaps in a few of these situations, he has cast his vote against what he sees as the wishes of his constituents, fully expecting a vigorous reaction. But the reaction has not materialized. Finding that he can cast such votes without fear of such a reaction, or at least finding that he can gracefully handle the reaction that does occur, the congressman is less hesitant the next time to try an unpopular vote. As he tries several of them, which probably takes a number of years, he develops a fund of experience with such situations and develops more confidence in his ability to handle his constituency. A more junior legislator simply has not had enough of those tough situations to have learned from them and adapted to them.

This tendency for relatively junior members to take particular note of constituency opinion may have affected outcomes in the 1970s rather substantially. Many observers noticed a marked trend in those years to vote with the perceived district interest, certainly at the expense of party or presidential support, and sometimes at the expense of a common national interest, on such issues as energy and taxation. In many of those cases, of course, the legislator may not have seen any conflict between his constituency opinion and his own principles or conception of the national interest. But to the extent that members were placing unusual weight on district opinion or on interest group pressure, it may have been because the Congresses of those years were composed of extraordinarily low-seniority members. In 1979, for instance, over half of the House of Representatives had been in Congress for four or fewer years. As the findings from a decade earlier would have indicated, these low-seniority members would be particularly prone to weigh constituency opinion heavily in their decision-making because of their lesser experience with constituency pressure and their particular attention to reelection considerations.

Several relatively senior congressmen told me in 1969 of instances in which they did learn from experience which sorts of issues cause political trouble and which do not. One said he had voted for the farm payment limitation the previous year, and "it didn't have any adverse reaction, so it must be okay." Another discussed his first vote against military appropriations: "When I first did it, I thought the heavens and sky were going to fall in on me. Much to my surprise, they didn't. I got many letters and a few editorials supporting my position, and practically no opposition. It was very lonely at first, and I thought quite courageous. But after the favorable response, it's been much easier." Several congressmen referred to the fact that election opposition was beaten back, with the result that they need not heed the wishes of the opposing faction. One voted against labor's wishes on the surtax extension, adding, "They made a concerted effort to dump me, but I survived that." Another, when asked about the possible reaction of Wallace supporters in his district to electoral college reform, erupted: "Look, I won by a smashing margin. I took on the Wallace people and whipped their ass good. Why the hell should I give a damn about them?"

Of course, the opposite may happen. A vigorous constituency reaction to an unpopular vote may surprise and possibly alarm the congressman, and cause him to be more cautious subsequently. Said one:

When I first came here, I voted on principle, and I got beat over the head for it. That made me take a second look. You'll find most guys operate this way. If they vote one way, and it's used in the next campaign to beat them over the head and about the ears, they'll be pretty cautious about doing it again. I came here with a lot of idealism, but I've sure lost it.

Another backed away from a pro-civil rights stance because of reaction from home.

There is also a process of natural selection at work. A few congressmen who have been out of step with their constituency on a few votes find themselves faced with an election challenge serious enough to cause them either to retire or to go down to defeat. Such former congressmen were neither in my sample nor in many studies of Congress, but comments of several incumbent congressmen illustrated the process. One showed me, election by election, how his margins of victory noticeably suffered when he took a highly visible stance against the Vietnam war. In fact, had his margins suffered slightly more than they did, he would have been "naturally selected" out of Congress. Thus, those who survive to become senior members either have cast unpopular votes and have learned that they will survive them or have adapted to their constituents' wishes. Those who have neither adapted nor survived do not populate the senior ranks, and are replaced with the more constituency-oriented junior representatives.

CONCLUSIONS

Few would expect the congressman's constituency to be the sum total of influences on his votes. But by several measures used in this study, constituency does appear to be quite important. While it has a greater impact on high-salience votes, there is still substantial evidence of distinct influence even on low-salience votes in which constituents' interest is probably virtually nil. Liberal Northern Democrats from urban areas, though not more prone than other congressmen to take account of constituents subjectively, appear to experience less conflict with constituents. Senior congressmen, while voting in agreement with district positions as often as junior congressmen, apparently take less subjective account of their constituencies. Interestingly, no important differences according to district competitiveness emerge. Safe congressmen take as much account of their constituents as do insecure ones.

The importance of constituency is rooted in several mechanisms of influence. The recruitment process, which brings a congressman with certain attitudes to the House and keeps him there, first of all, determines the major directions which his voting decisions take. Congressmen's apparent preoccupation with graceful ways of explaining potentially unpopular votes, furthermore, often results in votes cast in accordance with constituents' wishes. Particularly in those instances in which some segment of the constituency feels intensely about the issue, but on other votes as well, the congressman concludes that attempting to explain an unpopular vote would be more trouble than it would be worth. Potential campaign or electoral consequences and the many uncertainties of primary and general election politics, finally, prompt congressmen to keep their constituents in mind as they vote.

It is thus likely that the constituency imposes some meaningful constraints on congressmen's voting behavior. It may not be possible for social scientists to pinpoint what "causes" a congressman *to* vote in a given way, but it may be somewhat easier to say what makes certain votes highly *im*probable. In the case of the constituency, the mass public probably imposes rather vague constraints on the congressman's behavior most of the time. Elites within the district which are even numerically quite small, make some voting choices improbable that would be allowed by the mass public. Even if a congressman transgresses those boundaries for isolated votes, he feels uneasy about doing so for a series of votes.

NOTES

1. The use of constituency characteristics include Julius Turner, *Party and Constituency: Pressures on Congress* (Baltimore: Johns Hopkins Press, 1951); David B. Truman, *The Congressional Party* (New York: Wiley, 1959); Duncan MacRae, *Dimensions of Congressional Voting* (Berkeley: University of California Press, 1958); Lewis A. Froman, Jr., *Congressmen and their Constituencies* (Chicago: Rand McNally, 1963); and John E. Jackson, "Statistical Models of Senate Roll Call Voting," *American Political Science Review* 65(1971):451–470. On role orientation, see John C. Wahlke, Heinz Eulau, William Buchanan, and Leroy C. Ferguson, *The Legislative System* (New York: Wiley, 1962). On perception and communication, see Lewis A. Dexter, "The Representative and his District," *Human Organization* 16(1957):2–13, reprinted in *New Perspectives on the House of Representatives,* ed. Robert L. Peabody and Nelson W. Polsby (Chicago: Rand McNally, 1969). See also Warren E. Miller and Donald E. Stokes, "Constituency Influence in Congress," *American Political Science Review* 57(1963):45–56. Studies of recruitment include that of Donald R. Matthews, *The Social Background of Political Decision-Makers* (New York: Random House, 1954); and Leo M. Snowiss, "Congressional Recruitment and Representation," *American Political Science Review* 60(1966):627–639. For a review of this representation literature, see John W. Kingdon, *Candidates for Office* (New York: Random House, 1968), chap. 1. Recent works include Morris P. Fiorina, *Representatives, Roll Calls, and Constituencies* (Lexington, Mass.: D. C. Heath, 1974); David Mayhew, *Congress: The Electoral Connection* (New Haven: Yale University Press, 1974); and Richard Fenno, *Home Style* (Boston: Little, Brown, 1978).
2. Charles O. Jones, "The Role of the Campaign in Congressional Politics," in *The Electoral Process,* ed. M. Kent Jennings and L. Harmon Zeigler (Englewood Cliffs, N.J.: Prentice-Hall, 1966), chap. 2.
3. Warren E. Miller and Donald E. Stokes, "Constituency Influence in Congress," *American Political Science Review* 57(1963):45–56.
4. John C. Wahlke, Heinz Eulau, William Buchanan, and Leroy Ferguson,

The Legislative System (New York: Wiley, 1962), p. 281. Another argument for the proposition that the representative is quite free is found in Raymond A. Bauer, Ithiel de Sola Pool, and Lewis Anthony Dexter, *American Business and Public Policy* (New York: Atherton, 1964), chap. 30.

5. Donald R. Matthews and James A. Stimson, "Decision-making by U.S. Representatives," in *Political Decision-Making, ed. S. Sidney Ulmer* (New York: Van Nostrand, 1970); see also Matthews and Stimson, *Yeas and Nays* (New York: Wiley-Interscience, 1975).

6. The partial correlation coefficient between constituency position and vote, controlling for fellow congressman position, is .36.

7. On the notion of anticipated reactions, see Carl J. Friedrich, *Constitutional Government and Democracy* (Boston: Ginn, 1950), p. 49. Empirical support for the concept of constituents' potential sanctions is found in Warren E. Miller and Donald E. Stokes, "Constituency Influence in Congress," *American Political Science Review* 57(1963):55.

8. Lewis A. Dexter, "The Representative and his District," in *New Perspectives on the House of Representatives,* ed. Robert L. Peabody and Nelson W. Polsby (Chicago: Rand McNally, 1969, 2nd ed.), pp. 9–11. Constituency positions can often be defined by a rather small segment of the constituency; see Raymond A. Bauer, Ithiel de Sola Pool, and Lewis Anthony Dexter, *American Business and Public Policy* (New York: Atherton, 1964), pp. 292–293, 315–316. For a recent statement of constituency subgroups, see Richard Fenno, *Home Style* (Boston: Little, Brown, 1978), chap. 1.

9. One interesting study of the attentive public is found in G. R. Boynton, Samuel C. Patterson, and Ronald D. Hedlund, "The Missing Links in Legislative Politics: Attentive Constituents," *Journal of Politics* 31(1969):700–721.

10. Work on supporting coalitions of politicians includes that of John W. Kingdon, *Candidates for Office* (New York: Random House, 1968), chap. 3; and Frank J. Sorauf, *Party and Representation* (New York: Atherton, 1963).

11. *Ibid.*

12. Manley uses the concept of the zone of indifference when discussing Ways and Means Committee members' tendency to leave many matters to the discretion of Chairman Wilbur Mills. See John F. Manley, *The Politics of Finance* (Boston: Little, Brown, 1970), pp. 129–130. The concept was earlier developed by Chester I. Barnard, *The Functions of the Executive* (Cambridge, Mass.: Harvard University Press, 1966; first published 1938), pp. 167–170.

13. Warren E. Miller and Donald E. Stokes, "Constituency Influence in Congress, *American Political Science Review* 57(1963):55.

14. On the concept of intensity and its problems of definition and measurement, see Robert A. Dahl, *A Preface to Democratic Theory* (Chicago: University of Chicago Press, 1956), chap. 4. Another discussion of the concept is Willmoore Kendall and George W. Carey, "The 'Intensity' Problem and Democratic Theory," *American Political Science Review* 62(1968):5–24.

15. Studies of recruitment include those by Matthews and Snowiss, cited in footnote 1 above. See also Kenneth Prewitt, *The Recruitment of Political Leaders* (Indianapolis: Bobbs-Merrill, 1970).

16. See William J. Gore and Robert L. Peabody, "The Functions of the Political Campaign: A Case Study," *Western Political Quarterly* 11(1958):55–70.

17. John W. Kingdon, *Candidates for Office* (New York: Random House, 1968), chap. 3.

18. For the definition and measurement of independent variables such as urbanness and competitiveness of the district, see Appendix D.

19. Murray Edelman, *The Symbolic Uses of Politics* (Urbana: University of Illinois Press, 1964), p. 136. The original study was from Gilbert Y. Steiner and Samuel K. Gove, *Legislative Politics in Illinois* (Urbana: University of Illinois Press, 1960), p. 77.

20. The figures are, using the percentage of each category which mentions the notion of explaining, for seniority levels: senior, 26 percent; middle, 37 percent; junior, 43 percent; for competitiveness of district, safe, 27 percent, middle, 42 percent; marginal, 39 percent; for urbanness, urban, 23 percent; middle, 42 percent; small-town, 38 percent. See Appendix D for an explanation of these variables.

21. This point is made by Robert L. Peabody in, "The Enlarged Rules Committee," in *New Perspectives on the House of Representatives,* ed. Robert L. Peabody and Nelson W. Polsby (Chicago: Rand McNally, 1963, 1st ed.), pp. 143–145. The point that the parliamentary situation can be used to obfuscate stands on issues is also made in Raymond A. Bauer, Ithiel de Sola Pool, and Lewis Anthony Dexter, *American Business and Public Policy* (New York: Atherton, 1964), pp. 424–432. Leites's discussion of "The Struggle Against Responsibility" is also analogous to these strategies for getting off the hook; see Nathan Leites, *On the Game of Politics in France* (Stanford, Calif.: Stanford University Press, 1959), chap. 2.

22. On the importance of the mail, see Lewis A. Dexter, "What do Congressmen Hear: The Mail," *Public Opinion Quarterly* 20(1956–1957):16–27. See also Donald R. Matthews, *U.S. Senators and Their World* (Chapel Hill: University of North Carolina Press, 1960; also Vintage Books), pp. 219–228.

23. *Ibid.*

24. On inspired mail, see Donald R. Matthews, *U.S. Senators and their World* (Chapel Hill: University of North Carolina Press, 1960; Vintage Book edition), pp. 184–186.

25. Dexter maintains that a congressman receives communications more from those who support his position than from those who do not. If this is true (and the evidence in my study is mixed on that point), then as a congressman's reputation gets better established with the years, the amount of mail which disagrees with his point of view might be expected to decrease. See Lewis Anthony Dexter, "The Representative and his District," in *New Perspectives on the House of Representatives,* ed. Robert L. Peabody and Nelson W. Polsby (Chicago: Rand McNally, 1969), pp. 11, 17–19. See also Raymond A. Bauer, Ithiel de Sola Pool, and Lewis Anthony Dexter, *American Business and Public Policy* (New York: Atherton, 1964), p. 420.

26. The percentages of agreement are: junior, 62 percent; middle, 74 percent; and senior, 53 percent;

27. See Malcolm E. Jewell and Samuel C. Patterson, *The Legislative Process in the United States* (New York: Random House, 1966), pp. 343–352.

28. See John W. Kingdon, *Candidates for Office* (New York: Random House, 1968), chap. 3; and William J. Gore and Robert L. Peabody, "The Functions of the Political Campaign: A Case Study," *Western Political Quarterly* 11(1958):55–70.

29. Kingdon, *ibid.,* pp. 84–89.

30. Sen. George Aiken, quoted in the *Washington Post,* November 9, 1969, p. A-1.

31. A sampling of that writing includes David Mayhew, "Congressional Elections: The Case of the Vanishing Marginals," *Polity* 6(1974):295–317; John Ferejohn, "On the Decline of Competition in Congressional Elections," *American Political Science Review* 71(1977):166–176; Morris P. Fiorina, "The Case of the Vanishing Marginals: The Bureaucracy Did It," *American Political Science Review* 71(1977):177–181; and Albert Cover, "One Good Term Deserves Another," *American Journal of Political Science* 21(1977):523–541.

32. Some scholars suggest that incumbents are not in any event as safe as their margins suggest. See Thomas Mann, *Unsafe at Any Margin* (Washington: American Enterprise Institute, 1978), and Robert Erikson, "Is There Such a Thing as a Safe Seat?" *Polity* 8(1976):623–632.

33. On the concept of presentation of self to constituency, see Richard Fenno, *Home Style* (Boston: Little, Brown, 1978), chaps. 3 and 4.

34. Warren E. Miller, "Majority Rule and the Representative System of Government," in *Cleavages, Ideologies, and Party Systems. Contributions to Comparative Political Sociology,* ed. E. Allardt and Y. Lithunen (Helsinki: Transactions of the Westermarck Society, 1964), pp. 343–376. For a discussion of the subject, see Morris P. Fiorina, *Representatives, Roll Calls, and Constituencies* (Lexington, Mass.: D. C. Heath, 1974).

3

Fellow Congressmen

One can think of a congressman's constituency as setting the general policy boundaries within which he must operate. Constituents recruit representatives of one general persuasion rather than another; they hold opinions on questions of governmental policy to which most congressmen feel they should pay some degree of attention; and on certain questions, constituents and especially elites will express attitudes concerning specific pieces of legislation upon which legislators must vote.

Despite the importance of the constituency to the congressman, however, it is fair to say that the constituency rarely gives him all the detailed guidance which he requires in order to vote. Scores of matters reach the voting stage on which constituents have neither expressed an opinion nor even held one with any significant degree of intensity. Out of these matters, there are many on which the congressman himself holds no strong opinion one way or the other. Even on issues of relatively high salience such as those that form the core sample of this study, congressmen may find themselves lacking the information they need in order to vote even semirationally.

It has long been held that in providing themselves with cues for voting, then, congressmen turn to each other for information, guidance, and even direct yes-or-no advice on how to vote. Literature on legislative behavior, particularly on Congress, has traditionally emphasized the importance of fellow congressmen in the voting decision.[1] At least since the time of Woodrow Wilson, studies of Congress have acknowledged the great importance of committee action in the legislative process. Stated in terms of legislative folkways, congressmen are expected to specialize in given subjects and then to rely on each other's specialized knowledge in areas that are not within their particular competence. This specialization, of course, is closely tied to the committee system, though not exclusively identical to it. The emphasis placed on fellow congressmen as an influence on voting is not limited to literature on committees and on congressional norms, but is prominent in writing on the act of voting itself. The technique of cluster-bloc analysis, for instance, which seeks to discover blocs of congressmen who regularly vote together, has been used to make inferences about the cues on which congressmen rely.[2] The communications patterns among legislators have been directly explored.[3] Simulation of voting behavior has relied heavily on fellow congressmen of various descriptions as predictors of the vote.[4]

There are a number of persuasive reasons why one would expect a fellow congressman to be an excellent source of voting cues.[5] He is a professional politician, and will give advice appropriately tailored to the congressman's political needs. His past performance as a cue-giver, including his judgment, his knowledge of facts, and his trustworthiness, is known to the congressman. He is readily available at the time of voting, a consideration of paramount importance. He is also of equal status with his fellows, so that a colleague feels comfortable about discussing legislation with him.

This chapter, then, concerns the fellow congressman as a possible influence in legislative voting. The fellow congressmen to whom we will refer are those to whom the decision-maker may *informally* turn for information or advice. Holders of certain formal positions are discussed in Chapter 4, when we deal with the party leadership and ranking committee members. Of course, these "informants" within the House, as we will call them, may occupy such formal positions as well, but they may just as easily not. Regardless of their position, those discussed in this chapter are any fellow congressmen whom respondents cited as being of any importance in their decision.

OVERALL IMPORTANCE OF FELLOW CONGRESSMEN

The voting decision for the congressman has often been portrayed as one in which there is either very little information available to the congressman upon which to base his decision, or a plethora of information which is undistilled and hence useless—either because it is too cumbersome in sheer volume or because the source of the information is of unknown reliability. Given this situation of a time constraint on the decision and the existence of an input deficiency or an input overload, the congressman must turn to someone for cues on how to vote. Fellow congressmen might constitute one excellent source.

In this study, indeed, the position of the fellow congressmen to whom the deciding congressman turns is a perfectly splendid predictor of his vote. Given that the congressman turned to such informants, the probability that he will vote with their position is fully .96, almost perfect prediction. The correlation coefficient between informants' positions and congressmen's votes is .78, also very high for any single predictor, and the partial correlation when one controls for all the other five variables in the model reads a scarcely reduced .71. Prediction remains high within all categories of congressmen, within party, type of district, seniority, and several other categories. By any account, this must be taken to be impressive evidence for the importance of informants among the House membership in voting decisions.

It must be remembered, however, that in one sense such a result is to be expected. Congressmen have a completely free choice within the House membership concerning which informants they will pick on any given issue. The informants vary from one issue to another, in the first place, so that this fellow congressmen factor must yield greater prediction than, say, the party leadership, because of this fluidity alone. Furthermore, there are no ideological strictures on the choice of informants. In other words, congressmen are not obliged to follow the advice of colleagues with whom they disagree. Within the ideological range presented to them in the House, they are free to choose anybody. Not surprisingly, they overwhelmingly choose those with whom they agree.

Another way in which we have evaluated the overall importance of each actor in the system is to note how often congressmen spontaneously mention the actor in the interview without being prompted to do so by a question, and to code how important the actor appeared to be in the decisions. By these measures, fellow congressmen again appear to be more important than the other actors in the legislative system, though the gulf between their importance and that of others is not as great as one finds in the agreement scores.

Fellow congressmen were mentioned spontaneously as being of some importance in the vote 40 percent of the time, more so than any other actor, but only slightly more than the constituency's figure of 37 percent. In response to the question, "Were there any fellow congressmen that you paid attention to?" informants among colleagues were cited in an additional 27 percent of the decisions. In case some respondents felt uncomfortable about admitting that they were "bossed" by anyone, the further probe, "I don't mean just following them; I mean looking to them for information and guidance," was posed. This probe elicited another 8 percent of the decisions in which fellow congressmen were of some importance. For the remaining 25 percent of the voting decisions, fellow congressmen were reported to be not involved at all. In the standard importance coding, fellow congressmen were classified as being of determinative or major importance in the decisions slightly less than half the time, in 47 percent of the cases. Again, this shows informants within the House to be the most important of the actors, but again, not by a large margin. The comparable constituency value is 38 percent. Fellow congressmen were seen to be not important in a quarter of the cases, and the remaining 28 percent showed them to be of minor importance.

It is possible, of course, that my questions did not tap some of the discussion which took place among colleagues, but it is also likely that such discussion made little difference to the congressman if he neglected to mention it after two questions on the subject. In any event, there is a good bit of previous work which indicates the preeminent place of informants within the House in voting decisions. The extraordinary performance of informants' positions as a predictor in my own data lends additional support for that picture. Thus, the fact that congressmen report that their colleagues were not involved in fully a quarter of the decisions and that much of the discussion which does take place is of a minor nature suggests that while cue-passing within the House is of course important, it is clearly not all-important.

CHARACTERISTICS OF INFORMANTS

Considering now only the cases in which congressmen did turn to their colleagues within the House for information or advice, what are the characteristics of these informants? What is their ideological bent as compared to that of the deciding congressman? Are they experts in the legislation? Are they from the same state delegation or region? Have they greater seniority?

Agreement
In selecting congressmen upon whom to rely, the first rule appears to be, as one respondent put it, "Choose those you agree with."[6] Another said, "For advice on how to vote, I go to someone whose voting record is like mine." A virtual flood of issue-by-issue exam-

ples could be added. One liberal voted for a long extension of the Elementary and Secondary Education Act because, "All the people I trust on education matters were for it." Another congressman from a large city said, "I always talk to ———— on conservation things. He has a sensible attitude on conservation. I mean, he doesn't want to have areas where you can only get in there on mule or something."

The quantitative evidence for this agreement being a fundamental decision rule is very strong. Comparing the congressman's attitude on the issue at hand with those of his informants, in 39 percent of the cases on which congressmen did consult their House colleagues, they consulted exclusively those who agreed with them on the issue, with no dissenters from that attitude. In an additional 47 percent, there was some mixture of opinion, but the informants were mostly of the same bent as the congressman himself. Only 8 percent showed a true mix of attitudes on the issue, and congressmen talked to those of predominantly opposite persuasion in only 6 percent of the cases. In a full 86 percent of the cases in which fellow congressmen were consulted, therefore, informants were largely of the same opinion as the decision-maker, and in nearly half of those cases, there was no disagreement among the informants at all.

The tendency to consult exclusively with those of the same attitude on the issue is particularly strong in the case of urban, liberal, Northern Democrats. Northern Democrats turned exclusively to those of the same attitude in a full 59 percent of the cases, compared with 29 percent for Southern Democrats, and 30 percent for Republicans. Similar figures obtain within categories of urbanness of the district and liberalism, as measured by Americans for Democratic Action (ADA) score.[7] In Chapter 2, we discovered that there was less mail in disagreement with the congressman's position coming from urban Northern Democratic constituencies than came from others. The same pattern of agreement is evident here. We are gradually confirming a finding that Northern, urban Democrats operate within a relatively closed political environment, relatively isolated from cues or pressures that would push them in different directions. This isolation occurs partly because of the nature of their districts, but also, as is apparent here, partly by their own choice. The relative lack of conflict for Northern Democrats was also due to the presence of a Republican administration, a fact which we examine in Chapters 4 and 6.

Some of the natural tendency to seek out those with whom the congressman agrees is regularized by organizing more or less formal subgroups of like-minded legislators within the House for periodic gatherings. These groups can range in institutionalization from the informal group that simply sits together on the floor as debate progresses, through the somewhat more regularized luncheon or dinner gatherings, to groups like the Wednesday Club among Republicans and the larger Democratic Study Group among Democrats.

There are at least two reasons why congressmen consult so heavily with those who hold similar attitudes. First, the congressman is unable, even superficially, to inform himself on many matters upon which he is obliged to vote. He wants to evolve some decision-making procedure which allows him to vote *as if* he were informed. He thus picks sources who, like him, are congressmen and who share his general policy attitudes, but who know the legislation as he does not. Said one, "On something like banking and currency, I don't pretend to be acquainted with it, so I just ask ——— or ———. These are people who think exactly like I do, and I don't need to be an expert." Second, the congressman presumably adopts the device of consulting with like-minded congressmen because it is extremely helpful in simplifying his decision. If he were to take in too many diverse points of view, his decision would hardly be simplified; it might even be made more difficult. As one respondent pointed out, "Some congressmen never learn it. One man on our delegation samples too widely, and ends up utterly confused. He has the hardest time of anybody in the Congress making up his mind."

It is important not only to notice that some sort of communication among congressmen takes place but also to consider what kind it is.[8] In the context of agreement, much of the contact is simply reality-checking. The congressman looks at a given measure or amendment, has an initial reaction to it, and then does some checking among those whose judgments would be likely to be similar, in order to be sure that he hasn't missed anything significant or failed to consider something important. If he turns up something through this process that is unexpected, he checks further. The following examples illustrate this phenomenon:

There's always a lot of talking among members. "What are you going to do on this? Why is that?" Just checking around, getting ideas, making sure you're not missing something important that you haven't thought of.

You do a lot of talking on the floor. This is mostly to confirm that you have your facts straight. Like I talked to ———, to make sure whether his amendment was the same as last year's. You do this sort of thing. But I knew where I stood on principle. It was just a matter of getting the facts straight.

One congressman said, "I just asked him how he was going to vote, just to check in." Another said, "I checked a few wrinkles with ———, but that's all." Another answered, "You talk around, but it was nothing important."

The importance of this reality-checking is difficult to assess. Many of the respondents clearly thought it was not important. But that is the conclusion which one would reach if one considered only attitude conversion as important. While this kind of communication probably does not change many minds, other types of effects are also important in the legislative process. One of these is reinforcement. Even if the net effect of the communication is simply to reinforce an original feeling, in a confusing situation with so many contradictory cues flying about, reinforcement is of no mean importance. Another communication effect is opinion formation. It may often be the case that a congressman holds a rather general view as to what the government should be doing in a given area, but has not formed an opinion about a specific proposal upon which he is called to vote. He may then turn to fellow congressmen with whom he agrees in general terms, in order to connect his policy views to the proposal at hand.

The elemental fact that congressmen turn most of the time to those with whom they agree has a number of significant possible implications. First, we are accustomed to concluding, when observing the high predictive value of the position of potential cue-givers in this study and in other studies, that fellow congressmen influenced the decision-making congressman. Actually, the causal chain may often be the reverse: The congressman's general policy attitudes affect his choice of informants. Such a self-confirming selection of cues would go a long way toward accounting for the extraordinary performance of fellow congressmen in the correlation model presented earlier. But it is important to emphasize that the congressman's own attitudes on public policy, not those of his informants, ultimately control his vote in many cases. His informants simply provide him with one means among several by which attitudes can be translated into votes.

Schematically, the process can be represented thus:

Attitude → Choice of Informant → Vote.

A quantitative test of this hypothesis is difficult to devise. The test would be to observe what happens when the congressman's attitudes come into conflict with the advice of a congressman who would normally be an informant. Does he go along with the fellow congressman, or does he change informants? It is likely that some of each takes place, depending upon the intensity with which the congressman holds his attitude. But the interview material suggests that on matters of any importance, the congressman shops for cues or switches informants.

At least, most congressmen do some cue-shopping. Among the potential informants whom he might very well follow, he selects those he will follow according to his policy attitudes. Many congressmen referred to excellent presentations made by those whose competence they respected and whose ideology was generally like theirs, but then told of how they decided to vote against these informants because other advice, more in tune with their own attitudes, was available. One noted the heavy committee majority in favor of foreign aid, but decided to go along with a three-person minority because "I read the minority views and felt they made some good points." Another said of a colleague with whom he disagreed: "He's always well prepared and he really delves into something. He's one of the top two or three members of the House when it comes to being prepared and having an impact when he speaks out on something. I told him that he'd done his usual good job, and he asked me if it was good enough to bring me along. I said, 'No, not quite that good.'" Another, a Republican referring to "long talks" with several ranking members of the Judiciary Committee dealing with electoral college reform, in answer to my question, "Which did you find most persuasive?" replied, "I found ——— especially persuasive. It's the old story. You find the man who agrees with you the most persuasive. That was true here."

In addition to cue-shopping on any particular issue, the congressman may change informants more permanently if he finds an habitual cue source increasingly out of keeping with his general policy preferences. Several senior Democrats referred to their resignations from the Democratic Study Group after having been actively involved, when they perceived it as taking a more liberal and antileadership tack. Another congressman said, "I don't follow ——— much any more. He's done this sort of thing before, and I don't understand his position. He's very capable, but I just don't understand. He must have some kind of axe to grind." A final option is that of relying on no informants within the House at all. A congressman with a business background said that if Republicans on the Ways and Means Committee disagreed with his position on the surtax extension, "I'll vote as I please. I know as much about these matters as they do."

Therefore, our admittedly nonquantitative information suggests that at least on issues such as those that form the core sample of this study, congressmen will choose informants with whom they agree, and when confronted with situations in which a potential or habitual informant disagrees, will shop for reinforcing cues, sometimes even switching informants in order to vote according to their own attitudes. Because such a plethora of cues is available from which to choose, such a procedure is not at all difficult to carry out. Such a dynamic reinforces both the point that congressmen fairly freely choose their informants rather than having informants simply influence them, and the implication that high-agreement scores between fellow congressmen and the vote are due to this self-confirmation.

A second implication of the tendency to pick informants with whom one agrees relates to the structure of legislative voting. Analyses of roll call voting have discovered two rather different fundamental patterns. On the one hand, some studies have pointed to the bloc structure of voting, that is, the pattern of a set of congressmen regularly voting together on a wide variety of issues.[9] Other studies have discovered that congressmen cast their votes along a relatively small set of dimensions, which can be interpreted as ideological dimensions.[10] These two models— the interpersonal relations and the ideological—have largely stood beside one another in the legislative literature without being particularly related. But the decision model which specifies that congressmen start with a general policy attitude and then vote with informants of the same persuasion provides a link between the two complementary voting models. The congressman does see issues in terms of dimensions or continua (e.g., a stronger or weaker defense system, more or less for education), and these general policy preferences determine his pattern of interpersonal relations. Hence, one finds both dimensions in legislative voting which can be interpreted ideologically, as well as a bloc structure or a pattern of cue-passing in the voting.[11]

A third implication, considered more fully in Chapter 4, is

that these agreement patterns in selecting informants provide a convincing explanation for the party cohesion which has been repeatedly found in studies of legislative voting. If congressmen turn to informants with whom they agree, it is only natural that they turn to those within their own party. Table 3–1 shows that this is decidedly the case. Considering the House as having a three-party system for all practical purposes,[12] congressmen overwhelmingly pick informants from within their party grouping. Once again, the most "inbred" group is the Northern Democrats. In keeping with their pivotal position between the two major parties and their small numbers, the Southern Democrats turn to informants in other parties more often than do the Republicans and Northern Democrats.[13]

This pattern of intraparty discussion varies according to seniority and ideology. Senior congressmen turn to informants outside their party group more than others do: Of the voting decisions in which fellow congressmen figured at all, made by the congressmen with the greatest length of service in the House, 54 percent showed the informants to be concentrated in the same party grouping as the respondent; the comparable figure for junior legislators is 83 percent; and for middle-seniority members, 75 percent. Apparently, congressmen widen their circle of informants as they accumulate years of service. This is true within all party groupings—Northern Democrat, Southern Democrat, and Republican. Middle-ideology congressmen also go outside of their party group more often than either liberals or conservatives, in keeping with their probable greater receptivity to others' points of view.[14]

Table 3–1 Party of Informants

informants' party	respondents' party Northern Democrat	Southern Democrat	Republican
Northern Democrat	85%	14%	3%
Southern Democrat	4	51	1
Republican	0	6	71
Mixed[a]	11	29	25
Total %	100%	100%	100%
Total *n*	54	35	75

[a] When it was not possible to classify a set of named informants, even in terms of a general tendency to be in one party grouping or another, the responses were coded as "mixed" party.

A final implication of the heavy tendency to consult fellow congressmen with whom one agrees is that this decision rule probably builds a good deal of inertia into the legislative process. If one major effect of the process of consultation among fellow congressmen is reinforcement of preexisting attitudes, and if, in the face of a flurry of conflicting cues, a congressman can shop for the cue which will reinforce his own attitude, then it becomes quite difficult to change him. A continuous cycle of reinforcement sets in. Even changing the opinions of key informants will not necessarily produce change, since congressmen may simply shift to other informants. Agents that produce change in the legislative system under these circumstances are not likely to be within the House itself. It takes either a change in the House membership such as the 1964 or 1974 elections so that a different set of attitudes is represented, or some gross change in the legislative environment such as expressed taxpayer anger, *Sputnik,* a mine disaster, or a new administration. Congressmen can do a good deal by focusing attention, getting publicity, and the like, to speed along changes once they have been initiated. But without changes in the membership or in the environment, inertia is a powerful force with which to contend.

Credibility

Closely linked with attitudinal agreement is credibility. The congressman wants someone for an informant who not only shares his attitudes, but who also can be "believed." Part of this has to do with the informant's reputation for being well prepared and careful of his facts before speaking. One congressman said of such a person, "He's responsible, he's well informed, and he never says anything he hasn't thoroughly considered." Another admitted that an opponent's well-researched and well-delivered speech had been "just devastating." A congressman loses his credibility by not being thoroughly prepared. One said of a committee leader from his own party, "Oh, he's inept and everybody knows it." Another said of a committee chairman with whom he actually agreed, "He really isn't that effective. When he makes a presentation, he kind of bumbles around; he isn't very well prepared." Aside from preparation, certain personal qualities recur in the interviews as being important: the informant's approachability and likable personality, his political astuteness, and whether one can trust him not to "con you" or "pull a deal." One floor manager may pick up votes just because he's "good ol'

Joe," or people want to "help him out." But another was unable even to get enough members to ask for a roll call vote on an amendment, because, as one supporter of his put it, "Frankly, he's a crashing bore. Members won't give him the time of day."

Even though much of the talk about who is influential and who is not is couched in terms of preparation and personal qualities, and even though these are actually important on occasion, still a good deal of credibility comes back to substantive agreement. An informant is a credible source for a congressman because he has a record of votes and actions with which the congressman agrees. In fact, the informant may have consciously built his record in order to remain credible to his colleagues. One younger congressman said, "You get pigeonholed very quickly. You get an image, as a burning liberal or as a conservative or something, and you can't do much about changing it." Furthermore, congressmen tolerate a good deal in the way of breeches of accepted ways of operating if the informant is on the same side. Despite not liking the fact that the Sikes (D.–Fla.) amendment to add planes for Nationalist China to the foreign aid bill was sprung without notice, for instance, many lined up to support it. The personality and style aspects of choosing informants, then, may be less important than the substantive agreement. They even get highly tangled conceptually: "There's another thing about this: personality. ——— is personally quite popular. They knew that he tried to get more out of his committee and didn't have the horses. He's on their side, see, and he's a good guy. Enough of them to make the difference will say, 'Let's stick with ol' Joe.' "

Building credibility can turn out to be highly important, partly because congressmen look for something unexpected from sources of information. A given argument or piece of information from a perfectly predictable source is less noticed than the same argument or information coming from an unexpected source. When Richard Poff (R.–Va.) argued against a provision which would have placed the Office of Economic Opportunity's legal aid program more directly under a governor's control, for instance, it had more effect among Republicans than if Emanuel Celler (D.–N.Y.) had been making the same case, because Poff was well known as a conservative. When Edith Green (D.–Ore.) argued against a bill punishing universities, it had more effect than if, say, John Brademas (D.–Ind.) had been making the same argument, because of her previous record of supporting education causes with which southerners and Republicans were in more accord. Or when several Judiciary Committee Republicans went into hearings against direct election of the president and came out favoring direct election, many Republicans noticed that shift and it had an effect. Several Republicans, finally, supported a hike in the debt limit because certain of their very conservative colleagues supported it and this first jarred them into thinking of going along. As one said, "In the caucus, ———— and ———— both spoke in favor of it. When you get conservatives like that supporting it, you're bound to think twice."

One consequence of the importance of credibility is the well-known tendency for the sponsor and backers of a measure to make some difference in the outcome. If a member with some credibility and standing among his followers offers an amendment, it stands a better chance than if someone who does not have their respect offers it. One Southern Democrat who could have voted for a budget-cutting amendment which he actually favored voted against it, saying, "He's the wrong guy to offer the amendment. If it had been a committee Republican, I'd vote for it." Another said, "I look at the minority views and I especially note who wrote them. If it's ————, forget it." Another dismissed a fellow congressman: "I'll oppose just about anything he does. It makes me feel funny just to be around him."

It appears to be very important to be identified with the "right crowd" and to avoid the "wrong crowd." One congressman told me that he took a little intra-House poll to find out how many people would vote with him, "because I wanted to assure myself that I wasn't going to be out in left field with only four or five guys with me." When asked about avoiding the wrong crowd, he replied, "It's very important. You're judged by the company you keep." This is partly a matter of maintaining one's own credibility, but also partly a question of having one's actions interpreted properly. Much of the time, such interpretation is done according to which bloc is supporting which position. For example, how will a vote against the surtax extension be interpreted: as a vote for tax reform, for fiscal irresponsibility, against taxation, against this particular tax, or what? Much of the answer depends on who is backing a movement to vote against the tax. If it is a group of liberal Democrats, it can be presented as a vote for tax reform; if they are conservative Republicans, it can be a vote for lower taxes.

The wrong crowd, of course, comes in for some scorching criticism, particularly if there is some reason to expect that an antagonist on a given issue should be on one's own side. The norm of courtesy[15] barely conceals from public view the bitter commentary which boils readily to the surface in interviews:

He's practically a psychopathic personality and he was lying like a rug.

A fellow party member called him a son-of-a-bitch to his face.

He's an awful demagogue. Everybody will tell you that.

He's regarded as a sort of lightweight, joke-making pip-squeak.

Things got a lot rougher and there was more blood around on the floor by the time it was over. People got hot under the collar. You'd hear it back by the rail.

Expertise

There is a good deal of writing which would suggest that congressmen pick informants with some expertise on the legislation in question.[16] My interviews are also filled with commentary extolling the virtues of the committee and specialization system, and indicating that one reason for turning to a given informant is his expertise. Says one, "You always turn to someone on the committee for information." Another said, "You seek out fellow members who are on the committee that heard the experts and considered the legislation." A lobbyist commented, "They try to follow the committee if they can. That way they feel assured of getting expert advice." When the congressman is himself on the committee that reported the bill, he feels at something of an advantage in terms of his own expertise: "I know that in great detail, having attended the hearings and sessions." This advantage can be used on the floor, as one committee member who had a constituency problem explained his action: "What I did was go around and round up three votes against the amendment—guys who were on the fence—and then voted for it myself."

There are several reasons for this reliance on fellow congressmen with expertise. One is their sheer knowledge of the subject. In this connection, it appears that the hearings on a bill are highly important. Of course, hearings do represent an exercise in publicity, but they also represent a valuable source of information.[17] Congressmen often refer to the opportunity that their colleagues on the committee had to attend the hearings and "listen to the experts." One referred to them as "people who have sat through the hearings and are acquainted with the legislation." And on occasion, the hearing process changes the views of a number of congressmen, as it did on electoral college reform, or at least (more frequently) helps them to form an opinion.

Even congressmen on the committees, of course, may not be as well informed and as conversant with their subjects as are several sources external to the Congress. But unlike other sources of expertise, they are fellow congressmen and can be expected to share similar political and substantive outlooks. Information from committee members, unlike other information, also comes in a usable form: It is condensed and easily understandable. One congressman commented on short speeches during the debate; "Their five minutes represents months of study and work."

The special place of committee members is recognized, not only informally, but also in the rules of the House. They speak first, introduce amendments first, can ask to have the committee position sustained in the Committee of the Whole, and generally lead the debate.[18] These advantages in the rules generate an even greater importance for the committee. One lobbyist, finding himself unable to find a committee sponsor for his amendment, abandoned the effort. Another, needing someone on the committee who would be recognized by the presiding officer ahead of other congressmen, exclaimed: "We were getting desperate. We had to get somebody to put his name on it, and soon. We called around, and this is true I swear, ──── was the only guy in town. He's not exactly a heavy up there, but we needed somebody."

In agreement with the strong expectation that congressmen turn to informants with expertise, of those cases in which fellow congressmen are involved in the respondent's decision, the informants have some claim to expertise 82 percent of the time. An alternative way of viewing this finding, however, is that if one adds the remaining cases to those in which fellow congressmen were not involved in the decision at all, it develops that turning to informants with some claim to expertise is *not* the rule a full 40 percent of the time. In view of the emphasis placed upon specialization and the committee system in other literature, this must be considered a rather high figure.

It is conceivable that there would be sources of expertise among fellow congressmen, other than from those members of the committee who considered the legislation. A former member of the committee, for instance, is a likely source. Or because of some constituency factor or simple general interest, a member may take it upon himself to become an expert. When congressmen name their informants, however, listed among them are nearly always members of relevant committees. Of those cases involving informants with expertise, indeed, 98 percent are on the committees. Expertise, then, is seen in these formal terms of committee membership, partly because congressmen gravitate toward committees in which they are interested, leaving rather few interested congressmen who are not on the committee. Congressmen also feel that they need information, not just from someone who knows a given field in general, but also from someone who knows the specific piece of legislation; such a person is most likely to be sitting on the committee. Such a state of affairs also is likely to discourage congressmen from developing expertise outside of their committee assignment, since the effort will largely be wasted on their colleagues.

There are several reasons why there is not an even higher frequency of reliance on legislative experts than one finds. Committee members, for all their expended time and effort, may not be viewed as experts. This is partly because many congressmen, especially those who are inclined against the prevailing committee view, come to believe that the committee is biased in a given direction. One congressman who opposd ABM spoke of the Armed Services Committee in these terms: "I don't hold to the view that just because someone got a committee assignment that he's an expert. He'll learn something through absorption, just by sitting there, but he learns biases too, and you end up getting prejudiced information. I don't think Armed Services Committee members are especially experts, and they're certainly biased." The same respondent in another interview spoke of the Judiciary Committee as a "representative committee," that is, one that he did not view as being as biased. Another congressman, recognizing the same point, said, "I know a few people on Ways and Means, and they're human too. They have their biases, and they're not the source of all wisdom." Another, a conservative Republican, said he was "always suspicious" of anything reported from the relatively liberal Education and Labor Committee.

Of course, it may also be that the congressman does not see bias in given committee members, but rather a simple lack of knowledge. This problem often plagues the Appropriations Committee, because they can always be challenged on the grounds of expertise by members of the authorizing committees. One congressman referred to the Education and Labor members as the

"real experts" on funding for schools, even though the bill origi-
nated in Appropriations. In the appropriations bills in this study,
congressmen combined informants from the authorizing committees with Appropriations members as much as they relied
upon Appropriations Committee members alone. Another congressman, speaking of the very Armed Services Committee majority that he had voted to support on the antiballistic missile
(ABM), said, "I've talked to a lot of them, and frankly, I don't
think they know shit from Shinola. I know more about some of
these weapons systems than they do."

If one views committee members as being either biased or
not knowledgeable, it is generally possible to shop for cues. If
the chairman or ranking member does not agree with the congressman's position, he can move further down the committee
roster until he finds someone who does. Or if the committee
majority disagrees with him, he can find a minority that suits
him. If he finds nobody on the committee in agreement with his
views, and still feels inclined to vote the other way, colleagues
who are not on the committee are also available. Expertise is
sufficiently diffused, in short, so that congressmen are not obliged
to rely on any given source.

State Delegation

Another conceivable characteristic of an informant is geographical. He may be from the same general region as the congressman, or especially from the same state delegation. Several writers
have pointed to potential delegation importance.[19] There are a
number of reasons to expect consultation within state delegations. One is that the congressman simply knows the colleague
from his state delegation and feels he can trust him. Within the
same state party delegation, members have been through many
political wars together and they probably largely share the same
general attitudes. One congressman, when asked why he turned
to delegation colleagues, replied, "Because I know them and can
trust them not to feed me a line." Another said, "We just think
alike on this." This kind of reason simply involves getting good
information from a trusted source. Many congressmen combine
state delegation with committee membership in choosing informants.

A second reason for delegation consultation is that on occasion, a state's direct interests may be involved. A public works
project, a measure involving the state's economy, a governmental

program with a statewide impact, all these furnish natural occasions for consultation.

A third reason for talking to fellow delegation members—one which is true especially for members of large delegations—is that holding the delegation together gives greater leverage in intra-House bargaining. Those very words were used by two members of a large delegation: "On some matters, we get together and decide what to do, so that we have greater bargaining leverage with the leadership." Said the other, concerning the surtax extension:

I was against the tax. The only time I had any qualms was last week, when ——— called me. He wanted to keep the delegation solid on this and wanted to know if I'd go along with the bill if it included meaningful reforms. We like to keep the delegation solid whenever we can. (Question: Why?) Because it gives you more leverage in the House. He could say he was trading with a substantial bloc of votes, not just his own.

Finally, delegation solidarity is extremely useful in dealing with constituency problems, particularly in explaining one's vote. If a segment of the constituency will be unhappy about a given vote, the congressman can use delegation solidarity as an argument for his position. One congressman said he would use it in explaining to teachers his position against a five-year extension of the Elementary and Secondary Act: "Our delegation was solid for the two-year extension, and when all the votes go one way, it's bound to give them some pause." In another instance, after the administration substitute on the Voting Rights Act narrowly passed with southern help, Northern Democrats decided to vote against its final passage, leaving southerners in a quandary about whether to let the bill die or to cast a vote in favor of a civil rights bill. Knots of them gathered in delegation groupings, intensely talking to find their collective way out of the dilemma. They finally decided to vote for final passage, and a highly convincing explanation for such a vote back home, as several acknowledged to me, would be that all the southerners did it. Being with the right crowd can be extremely useful as an explaining device, and even crucial in avoiding political embarrassment.

Many congressmen feel uncomfortable about voting out of step with the rest of the delegation. Newspapers all over the state regularly print delegation box scores, and it can be something of an embarrassment to find oneself voting against the rest of the state's congressmen. Such occurrences can also be used against one in the next campaign. One congressman, discussing emergency college loans, cited the experiences of a colleague on his delegation:

We happened to be meeting on another matter, and guys started asking each other how they'd vote. I said I'd vote for it, and ——— said he'd be against it. Then most of us, as we talked around the room, said we'd vote for it. When we came back, ——— had voted for it. There is some tendency to try to stick together. (Question: Why?) Look what happened to ——— last time. His opponent put ads all over the district, saying, "Look at education: All [the state's] congressmen voted aye; ——— voted no. Stand up for education." Education is a kind of sacred cow. You look funny if you're not with the rest of the guys on it.

Another congressman was in a quandary trying to decide whether to introduce what he regarded as a "bad bill," when several other delegation members enthusiastically supported it, so that it would be uncomfortable if he balked. Another, referring to voting in opposition to a highly respected senior member of his state delegation, said, "I have on occasion, not on his specialty, but I try to keep it quiet." Not only is there safety in numbers, but there is also less anxiety in numbers. One respondent summarized, "It helps if you stand together."

A congressman often does not know just what his constituents think about a given issue. Given such uncertainty about such an important actor in the system, congressmen can use the state delegation as a convenient constituency substitute. At least one can check with fellow congressmen who are from the same delegation and have "similar problems," as one aide put it. One Northern Democrat said he particularly respected informants with "political judgment," defined as "their willingness to take electoral problems into account. I could talk to visceral liberals, but they wouldn't help me much." A Republican said of a colleague from an adjoining district: "That's a new part of my district, and I'm not so familiar there. So it's important to know how he is going to vote. I'm not saying that I'll always go along with him, but it is important to get his views so I know what I'm getting into."

Despite all these persuasive reasons for delegation consultation, region or state delegations are not nearly as important criteria for informant choice as are agreement or expertise. Of the decisions in which informants were involved, the named informants included nobody from the same region of the country nearly half of the time (49 percent). Fellow congressmen included people from the state delegation in 36 percent of the cases, and from the same region of the country, but not on the state delegation, an additional 15 percent of the time. These general regional mentions are particularly true of Southern Democrats, who caucus and consult regionally more often than either Northern Democrats or Republicans. Among Southern Democrats, selection of informants generally from the same region occurs 23 percent of the time, compared with 9 percent for Northern Democrats and 8 percent for Republicans.

Congressmen from large state delegations are more likely to consult within their delegation than are those from small delegations, as Table 3–2 shows.[20] Large delegations are more likely to have a good distribution among the committees, so that a committee member for the legislation at hand is likely to be one of the delegation. The larger delegations can also be used as blocs of votes for bargaining leverage within the House, in a way that small delegations cannot. Table 3–2 also suggests that given the problems with delegation consultation that small delegations have, they attempt to make up for the deficiency by at least consulting within their region. There is no greater tendency for congressmen from large delegations to consult fellow congressmen in general, but when they do so, they talk within the delegation. This is true of both Democrats and Republicans.

Seniority

A final characteristic of informants is that they might be more senior than the deciding congressman. This would presumably be true partly because of the seniors' greater experience and information, as one junior congressman said: "That's the beauty

Table 3–2 State Delegation and Informants' Region

informants' region	respondent's delegation		
	small	medium	large
Respondent's state delegation	17%	33%	60%
Same region	26	17	2
No regional effect	57	50	39
Total %	100%	100%	101%
Total *n*	58	54	52

of the seniority system—there are informed, experienced people on each committee you can consult." The members with seniority are also in a position to withhold desired favors from those who do not go along. One congressman said that he couldn't lead a fight against an amendment because "you have this relationship with the senior members of your committee to protect," although another respondent told me that this congressman had urged him to vote against it even though he could not do so publicly. In another instance, a congressman said that one reason the cigarette bill passed was that "you had some pretty powerfully placed people who were lobbying for the bill, like ———, a power on appropriations and public works. It's pretty hard for a congressman to turn a guy like that down, without risking losing a good deal. When in doubt, be safe."

Quantitatively, it turns out that congressmen turn to someone of lower seniority than themselves in only 12 percent of the cases in which informants were used. In slightly over half of the cases (52 percent) informants were more senior than the congressmen themselves, while in the remaining 36 percent, informants had roughly the same seniority. The seniority system, it appears, is built into this pattern of interaction. This deference to seniority, however, is much less noticeable among Northern Democrats than among either Southern Democrats or Republicans. Northern Democrats turn to informants more senior than themselves 32 percent of the time, compared with 59 percent for Southern Democrats and 64 percent for Republicans.

For a number of reasons, one would expect junior congressmen to look upward on the seniority ladder for advice more often than their senior colleagues, aside from the fact that it is simply arithmetically more conceivable (since the most senior cannot look up). As already argued, junior members would be relatively inexperienced and, thus, might feel the need to turn to their more knowledgeable and experienced senior colleagues in a rational attempt to obtain more information. The junior members would also be in a relatively poor bargaining position, and would be somewhat at the mercy of senior legislators who were in formal positions of authority. And so far as the congressmen with long service in the House are concerned, several of them pointed out to me that they had been around long enough to have obtained enough knowledge that they did not need to consult much any more. Said one, "I've been here long enough to know what to do." Said another:

After you've been around for several years as I have, you've plowed the ground before. You've read and studied on it, and you develop a pattern. When I was first here, everything was fresh and often I had to turn to others for advice. Now that I've been here a while, I've been over that ground several times. You're not coming to it fresh any more. We've taken up these things over and over again.

For the occasions on which they do use informants, indeed, this seniority pattern develops, as Table 3–3 attests. Relatively junior legislators decidedly tend to look up the seniority ladder, although Northern Democrats do so less than either Southern Democrats or Republicans.[21] Middle-seniority congressmen have developed some expertise and status within their own ranks, and thus consult either among themselves or with more senior colleagues. Senior members, naturally enough, rarely look higher than themselves, but also interestingly enough, apparently feel little compulsion to look at consultation in status terms—they are nearly as likely to consult informants of lower seniority as to turn to senior colleagues.

Despite this clear seniority pattern, however, fellow congressmen are decidedly not more important in the voting decision for junior legislators than they are for their senior colleagues. In fact, if anything, the opposite applies. The most senior congressmen spontaneously mention fellow congressmen as being part of their decision-making 51 percent of the time, compared with 35 percent for medium-seniority and 36 percent for junior members. And as Table 3–4 shows, junior congressmen are actually somewhat less likely than are senior congressmen to exhibit influence on their decisions by fellow congressmen. The contacts they have with colleagues are more likely to be of minor importance in their decisions, and the correlations between fellow congress-

Table 3–3 Informant and Respondent Seniority

informant seniority	respondent seniority		
	junior	middle	senior
Higher than respondent	83%	51%	15%
Same as respondent	16	46	48
Lower than respondent	2	3	37
Total %	101%	100%	100%
Total *n*	57	59	46

Table 3–4 Seniority and Fellow Congressmen's Importance

importance of fellow congressmen	junior	seniority middle	senior
None	24%	29%	21%
Minor	37	21	25
Major	35	46	46
Determinative	4	4	8
Total %	100%	100%	100%
Total n	75	85	61
Correlation	.71	.80	.83
Partial correlation	.64	.67	.80

men's positions and their votes are lower, both the overall correlation and the partial correlation which controls for other influences on the vote. It is also true that the junior congressmen are the most prone to ignore expertise in the selection of informants, which contradicts the notion that they turn to fellow congressmen because of their inexperience and lack of substantive knowledge of the legislation. Their informants are devoid of expertise 32 percent of the time, compared with 10 percent for middle-seniority and 13 percent for senior congressmen.

We were originally led to the hypothesis that junior congressmen would turn to their fellow congressmen more than would senior congressmen, by a kind of model of rational decision-making. The younger House members, this model would postulate, are in greater need of good information to make rational voting decisions, having had less experience with the issues and less time to build a habitual voting pattern. But the data suggest that not only does this difference fail to materialize, but if anything, the reverse is true. This development leads one to an alternative hypothesis, which we may label the "lengthy interaction" hypothesis. As one accumulates years in the House, this argument would run, one has an opportunity to build up a larger set of acquaintances. One widens his circle of informants, and comes to know which colleagues one can trust as useful sources and which one should discard. The relatively junior member, by contrast, simply knows fewer people, has a narrower circle of acquaintances, and has not yet had the time to ascertain which sources will be trustworthy. He thus gets along as best he can, relying on fellow congressmen less than do his more senior colleagues.[22] This tendency to accumulate useful interaction with colleagues through the years is reinforced by the tendency for senior congressmen to be highly preoccupied with their committee business, necessitating greater reliance on informants than is necessary for a congressman with more time at his disposal.

There is another piece of information which is consistent with this lengthy interaction hypothesis. The contacts of junior congressmen are much more heavily within their own party than is the case for senior legislators, indicating again that they have had less time to develop this wider circle of informants. Fully 83 percent of the time, junior congressmen name informants who are predominantly within their own party group; whereas this figure drops to 75 percent for middle-seniority, and down to 54 percent for senior congressmen. This pattern is true of all party groups, Northern Democrat, Southern Democrat, and Republican. It also apparently takes a considerable period of time to begin to consult outside one's own party, judging by the fact that middle-seniority congressmen are more like their junior than their senior colleagues.

These observations help us to understand legislative change as well. The House of the late 1970s was younger than that of the 1960s. Over half of the House in 1979 had been in the body for four or fewer years. We noticed above that junior members rely on colleagues somewhat less than senior members, not because they have less need for advice but because they have had less opportunity to develop a set of trusted informants. If that pattern were to hold true of the junior members of the late 1970s, then simply because there are larger numbers of them, there would be less deference to senior leaders in the House of the late 1970s and early 1980s than in the 1950s or 1960s. Many observers have maintained that members do in fact seem less deferential than before, which would be consistent with junior representatives' cue-taking.

OCCASIONS FOR INFLUENCE OF FELLOW CONGRESSMEN

We have already considered, to an extent, the occasions on which fellow congressmen are likely to be called upon to aid in a voting decision. Much of the contact with fellow congressmen, for instance, is reality-checking, in which the congressman takes an initial position and then enters into a degree of communication with trustworthy colleagues simply to be sure that they see the matter as he does. In this section, without attempting to be exhaustive about the occasions for influence, we consider two situations in which it appeared from the interviews that congressmen would find their colleagues particularly important: "minor" matters and bargaining situations.

Minor Matters

Congressmen, like the rest of us, search for information only when they have a problem that needs to be solved. This "problemistic search"[23] is likely to occur particularly on relatively minor matters. One category of such matters is composed of bills on which information is scanty, bills of low salience. Public attention to such measures is very low or nonexistent, which means that congressmen have little information about the measure which is not obtained from their colleagues, and are subjected to little in the way of public pressure to vote one way or the other. As issues become more salient, however, congressmen obtain more information in the relatively information-rich environment, and they also have less room to maneuver in a political sense. This leads to the hypothesis that as salience increases, reliance on fellow congressmen decreases. As one congressman commented on the surtax extension, when asked about paying attention to fellow congressmen, "Not on an issue like this. On your run-of-the-mill vote, on an obscure bill, you need some guidance. You don't know what's in it, and don't have time to find out. But on this, you sure know about it." Another said regarding the ABM, "This was the sort of issue that there was so much information about that I didn't have to rely heavily on colleagues."

Aside from relatively rich information, the congressman is also more likely to have a well-formed, fairly solid opinion on a more major, salient matter. He has either established a well-known voting record on it, or he has heard enough to have formed an opinion. As one congressman said, when asked if he had paid attention to fellow congressmen on the measure involving the House Un-American Activities Committee, "No, I had my mind made up." Said another, "I didn't need any coaching on this one." We concluded earlier that much of the communication among colleagues in the House has the effect of reinforcing preexisting attitudes. In the case of a minor bill on which there is little information or pressure, however, it may also have an attitude-formation effect. The congressman may have no well-formed attitude on the specific measure at hand, and be relatively indifferent as to its outcome.[24]

With the data in this study, it is difficult to obtain a clear-cut test of the proposition that as salience increases, reliance on fellow congressmen decreases. For reasons set forth in Chapter 1, all of the issues in the core sample were relatively high-information issues. While they had sharply different saliences in the public, their preexisting information content for congressmen was somewhat more similar. Within this core sample, the results are in the predicted direction, though the differences among salience levels are not substantial. Respondents saw fellow congressmen as being of either major or determinative importance in their decisions 51 percent of the time with low-salience issues, 50 percent with medium-salience issues, and 41 percent with high-salience issues. We might speculate that if one were to go further down salience levels from those covered in this study and find truly obscure pieces of legislation, the importance of fellow congressmen would markedly increase.

Akin to the minor bill is the "detail" on a major bill. Congressmen often take a general attitudinal position on major legislation and then leave the details to be worked out by committee members, whom they then follow. Many congressmen viewed the electoral college reform bill in this light. They were for direct popular election, say, and never bothered to look into the extremely crucial question of whether the winner should be required to obtain a majority of the vote, 40 percent, a plurality, or what. Said one, "I don't think it makes much difference where it's set. Any figure is fine with me. I'll go along with the committee on that. Forty percent sounds about right." Another remarked, "The main thing for me is the broad principle involved. If they decided to compromise on 40 percent, that's fine with me." Appropriations Committee bills are in a particularly strong position on this question, since the differences between given dollar amounts are difficult for the noncommittee congressman to sort out. Even after detailed analysis, it is difficult to determine whether a given amount is too much or too little.[25] One congressman said, "On the specific dollars and cents, you have to go along with the committee. How else could you do it?" Another kind of detail often left to the committee is something which is technical in an engineering sense. Military hardware or space flight appropriations fall into that category, as this congressman said: "On things like this—ABM, anything having to do with the space program, or atomic energy—I rely on the committee. You have to be a nuclear physicist or a Ph.D. or something to even understand what's involved. A common member of Congress can't make an independent judgment on it no matter how hard he tries." Another, referring to the Armed Services Committee's report on aircraft, said, "On technical things like whether we need eight wings or nine wings, their judgment is as good as anybody's."

On occasion, decision-making on the "details" or the "minor" bills can be a nearly blind following of a fellow congressman. The following illustrate:

I've been so busy on my committee meetings that I just went in when the bells rang, asked somebody what this was all about, cast my vote and left.

We've been so tied up with the surtax that I haven't had a minute to look into it. I just went along with the majority of the committee. I figured they knew what they were doing.

A lot of votes come up that you know absolutely nothing about. On major issues, you will think about it beforehand. But on other things—scores of votes, really—many members rush on to the floor, seek out someone on the committee they know, have a 3- or 4-minute talk, and make up their mind on the spot.

[From a staffer] They may rush in from the cloakroom, look who is in the teller line, and if there are three or four people they know in the line, they'll just join it. They may not even know what they're voting on.

There is also the question of the type of cue which congressmen receive from informants. Up to now, we have assumed that the cues were all substantive—whether major or minor, philosophy or detail, they had to do with the substance of the legislation. But many cues may not be substantive at all, but rather procedural or strategic.[26] They are simply ways of sorting out a sometimes confusing parliamentary situation. Or a congressman may decide substantively while leaving the strategic decisions to his more involved colleagues. The following illustrate the case in which the congressman has his course well charted, and uses fellow congressmen simply as a means of doing the correct thing procedurally or strategically:

On the Powell vote, I can't tell you how I will vote on each question, because I can't interpret the procedural points. I don't know what they will mean in context. But I know what I will do in the end. I will vote to seat him, even without the fine.

I'm for the strongest poverty bill possible. What's to decide? It's ridiculously simple. The only thing I need to do is straighten out the strategy questions. (Question: Like what?) You know, like where we're making the compromises, who's for so-and-so amendment, should we try to strengthen it—the normal horse-trading.

I was in another meeting, and arrived on the floor when the teller bells rang. I had thought it through beforehand, and knew what I was going to do. I went in, saw ——— on the tellers, asked somebody what the vote was, and joined the right line.

This distinction between substantive cues on the one hand, and procedural or strategic cues on the other, is highly important to an understanding of cue-passing in the House. When one says that a congressman "follows cues," it is difficult to interpret such a generalization without knowing the sort of cue. Is he reality-checking and largely looking for reinforcement? Is his attitude being formed or changed? Or is he straightening out the parliamentary or strategic situation, devoid of substantive implications? If the latter, it cannot be said that the cue influenced his thinking or his vote in any meaningful way. Whatever influenced his position has already happened, and he is simply using the cue to be sure he is recorded appropriately.

An attempt was made in this study to distinguish between substantive and procedural (including strategic) cues. The full coding and reliability checks are described in Appendix D. Of the cues which respondents reported receiving from fellow congressmen, 31 percent were coded as being primarily procedural. The cue-taking was procedural more heavily for Northern Democrats than for other party groups, and for junior congressmen more than their senior colleagues.[27]

Bargaining

Another occasion on which fellow congressmen loom large in the voting calculus is in a bargaining situation.[28] On one basis or another, a trade between congressmen is involved. It may be a simple acknowledgment that one specializes in a given area and reciprocity dictates that one should turn to specialists in other areas. One senior congressman said of his colleagues on other committees, "They trust us to report a good bill, so I trust their judgment in this case."

Aside from simple reciprocity in specializations, bargaining may involve policy trades on given bills. A group of congressmen agrees to support the Appropriations Committee on increased funding for alleviating water pollution if the committee will raise its figure. Congressmen interested in education funding, said one, "put together a package that we could all support. Everybody has his own interests in this area. There wasn't nearly enough in the amendment for my interest, but I did get some." The Rules Committee held up a rule on gun control in the previous session until the Judiciary Committee took out registration and licensing provisions. When these kinds of policy trades are not forthcoming, coalitions behind given pieces of legislation begin to break down. An urban congressman presented his point of view on agriculture legislation in these words:

Big-city people have always supported farm subsidies and were responsible for getting them passed. But there's no reciprocity. When we vote for farmers, it's a subsidy. But when it's a poverty program, it's a dole. OK, if they don't go along with things we need, then why should we go along with them? That's the reason many of us have shifted over the years.

Bargaining may not involve exchanges on policy, but rather personal favor-trading. These favors are likely to be constituency-connected projects, a vote on a matter that has a direct impact in a colleague's constituency or a grant of such a favor by a well-placed committee chairman, which then becomes a credit which can be called in later. One Appropriations Committee member said of the public works subcommittee's funding of a project in his district: "Now, when they've done this for me, why raise a fuss? They've helped me, and now I'll try to see my way clear to help them. This favor-trading builds good will. We frankly play politics with our bill, like letting congressmen announce projects in their districts. Congressmen remember this sort of thing, and you have a smoother time later." Another said of his vote for the bill that would prohibit regulatory agencies from banning cigarette advertising: "This will be sort of a buddy vote. I know cigarettes are harmful and I wouldn't touch them myself. But a lot of my friends are concerned about this, because tobacco means a lot to the economy of their areas. They do things for me when I need it, and I'll do this for them. Frankly, it's just a matter of helping out your friends."

This kind of bargaining is especially noticeable when congressmen are attempting to protect a major industry in their district, an acute constituency problem discussed in Chapter 2. It is the classic case of logrolling, because the congressmen concerned do not have a majority and the only way to get one is for them to trade, explicitly or implicitly, for support on a colleague's district problem. It often is an implicit bargain, simply understood by the parties without being discussed, or part of "building good will." One respondent put it well:

There isn't any definite exchange of favors. Like ———— may come up to me and say that this thing means a lot to him and to his district and ask for my support, but when I need him, I'm not going to go back and remind him that I voted with him and now I want him to vote with me. And if I were to say something like, "Remember this when I need you," it would be like questioning his integrity. But I do think that if I ask him for something in the future, he might remember. And if I would have fought him on this, then he'd say, "Where was ———— when I needed him?"

Of course, some congressmen are in excellent positions to grant favors, and then to call on their largesse on other occasions when requesting support from the recipient. A committee chairman appealed to a congressman, "I've done a lot of favors for you over the years, now how about doing me one?" An Appropriations Committee member reminded a party colleague of a public works project pending in his district just before a crucial vote. A congressman referred to a ranking committee member in these words: "He's helped me out before. He's a friend, and when he came to me and asked, I said yes." Committee chairmen are in an especially strong position when dealing with their own committee members, since they dispense subcommittee assignments, assign staffs, and schedule the committee agenda. One congressman said of his chairman: "Don't vote against him if you can help it. I voted against him on something he cared about a while ago, and I know what can happen to a guy who does that. There's been a real coolness since, and it will take a long time to overcome it. If I ever needed something from him, I probably wouldn't get it." Said another, in apologizing for the position of a state delegation colleague, "It's understandable that he would want to go along with his chairman now and then. Everybody will permit that."

CHANNELS OF COMMUNICATION

We will consider now the channels by which congressmen learn attitudes and information from their colleagues in the House. It is common to think of interaction with fellow congressmen as being a face-to-face conversation. Of course, such contact is highly important. But actually, the means of communicating among fellow congressmen are much more varied. In fact, direct contact may be much less frequent than other forms are.

First, there are several written sources which convey fellow congressmen's positions, arguments, and information. It is a common practice to send a "Dear Colleague" letter to all congressmen, setting forth an action which the congressmen will take on the floor and soliciting support. By this means, a floor manager will argue for keeping the bill intact, while others will discuss their amendments to the bill. Other written sources include the printed committee report and the *Congressional Record,* routinely available to all congressmen. When a congressman desires condensed, readily usable information, he can read the committee report, which contains major facts, major arguments, and the dissenting views of the committee minority. This written report, plus the debate on the bill, is an extremely efficient way for committee members to reach large numbers of their colleagues. Many conservative congressmen, for instance, spontaneously brought up a chart in the minority views on electoral reform which purported to show how their states would lose power under a direct election plan, and how there were enough states that would so lose that the plan could not be ratified. For the member who wants more information, the *Congressional Record* is available. There is a wealth of statements from their colleagues about nearly everything. Members often at least scan the *Record* to find out what transpired the previous day.

Aside from these important written sources, there is a good deal of oral communication. One such means is the debate on the bill. It is common to claim that debate rarely changes votes, which may be true. But it is still a regular occurrence that a quarter or so of the House membership will spend hours in the chamber listening to the debate; if not to change their minds, then at least to gain more information, to listen for new arguments, or perchance to formulate an opinion when they do not hold a strong view. On a close vote, furthermore, the debate may influence several members at least to stay away, perhaps enough of them to make a difference. One congressman told me that he had been prepared to speak against the extension of the west front of the Capitol, but the debate shook his convictions enough that he decided against it. Another said that he listened to debate, "not for the merits of it, but for the political questions that will help me with political problems." Indeed, it was common for the explanations given by congressmen to their constituents to be couched in terms very similar to those prominently used in the debate on the bill.

Since the field work for the study was done in 1969, another twist on the use of debate as a channel of communication from colleagues has been added. Starting in the late 1970s, the House floor proceedings were carried into members' offices via closed-circuit television. It has become common for members or their staffs to listen to the debate on the set in the office, keeping one ear on the proceedings while attending to other kinds of work. The advent of this circuitry has not so much changed the generalization that legislators rely on colleagues for information and advice as it has added another way for them to receive that communication more efficiently. In an environment in which the sheer number of votes has increased dramatically, a fact to which we will return in Chapter 9, televised debate has proven to be a rather important way to keep abreast of developments.

Electronic voting was also introduced in the 1970s since this study's interviewing. Instead of shouting aye or nay, a member now inserts an identification card into a station in the House chamber and presses a button which records his vote. When congressmen enter the chamber, the votes of all members who preceded them are displayed on boards at the front of the room. It becomes fairly simple to glance at the display panels, pick out several members with whom one would be likely to agree, discern a pattern among them, and vote with that pattern. This procedure does not represent a departure from the situation before electronic voting. In fact, it is precisely the same as joining a teller line in which one's friends are standing. The same decision-making procedure can simply be executed with greater efficiency than before.

The debate or quorum calls also provide the occasion for a good deal of conversation in the chamber. Members wander in and out of the cloakrooms, stand behind the rail, sit together, and converse while the debate progresses. As one said, "As the debate goes on, a lot of talk among the members takes place. This discussion in the chamber is extremely important." Members form patterns of sitting in given places with people of like philosophical persuasion. Southerners, for instance, sit in a particular part of the chamber, a given state delegation will have its own special corner, or a few congressmen of conservative persuasion sit together in another corner. Another congressman told me, "You get more information in the cloakroom than you do out on the floor." This conversation is especially important in the minor matters or the procedural or strategic decisions which are often made, and on occasion must be made, quickly on the floor as the parliamentary situation develops. Civil rights advocates decided while on the floor, without prior planning, to vote against the voting rights bill after the administration's substitute passed. When the form of the motion to recommit the military procurement bill failed to provide a clear-cut vote on ABM deployment, anti-ABM congressmen "went into a huddle," as one said, deciding collectively what to do. The unexpected or the low-information situations especially call for this kind of readily available consultation.

The communication may be even more informal. One staffer expressed his amazement at just how informal it may get: "A lot of information is rumor-passing. As a newspaperman, I wasn't used to this. If a newspaperman wants to know what Wilbur Mills thinks, he'll call up and ask. But members won't. They'll wait to read about it, or they'll hear a Ways and Means Committee member say that Mills raised his eyebrows or coughed or something." Said another, "The word just gets around." Apparently, too much personal contact can be harmful. The recipient congressman does not care to do it, because it means bothering his busy colleagues and then being obligated to them because of the time spent. And the leaders of the fight may shy away from too much personal contact, because, as one aide put it, "If you do too much, then it looks like pressure." It is better to rely as a normal matter on the more impersonal kinds of communication, and save the personal contact for occasions on which it is really needed. Communication may sometimes be even more subtle. What a congressman fails to do attracts the attention of his colleagues easily as much as what he does do. One respondent illustrated such highly subtle cues: "He didn't address the caucus on it, and we assumed he was just doing a favor for his chairman. (Question: Did he say anything like that?) No, but he didn't have to. The fact that he didn't do anything in caucus was enough."

CONCLUSIONS

By any measure, fellow congressmen turn out to be highly important influences on votes. Congressmen find that their colleagues in the House possess several particularly useful attributes as sources of information and guidance. They are readily available at the time of decision, and able to furnish the kind of information which is most useful: digested, explicitly evaluative information which takes account of political as well as policy implications of legislative issues. They are also known quantities, and members develop notions about whom they can and cannot trust. To be sure, fellow congressmen are not all-important by any means; respondents report they were of minor or no importance slightly more than half the time. It is a reasonable conjecture that they are more important on measures that are less visible than on those in the core sample of this study. While these sampled votes may have had sharply varying saliences in the general public, they were all relatively information-rich to congressmen, who then had less need to turn to their colleagues for guidance.

The foremost criteria for selecting whom to consult among fellow congressmen are the informant's agreement with one's own point of view and expertise, the latter being defined as membership on the committee that considered the bill. Liberal, Northern Democrats from urban constituencies are particularly prone to turn to congressmen with whom they agree. A less frequently used criterion is that the informant be from the congressman's state delegation or region. Congressmen from large delegations consult colleagues from their states more than do those from small delegations, and Southern Democrats consult more heavily within their geographical region than do others. Seniority, finally, is of some importance in the choice, but not as important as the other criteria. In choosing informants, relatively junior congressmen—particularly Southern Democrats and Republicans —do tend to look up the seniority ladder, but do not necessarily weight the advice of their informants more heavily than their senior colleagues do; if anything, the reverse is true.

The use of these criteria leads to some speculation about their implications. The tendency to associate primarily with those of one's own persuasion may result in great inertia in the legislative process, since the opportunities for reinforcing one's general policy attitudes are plentiful. This tendency also contributes toward an understanding of why there is a good deal of party voting in Congress, since consultation is likely to take place within party groups. Third, it explains why roll call analyses have been able to find both bloc and dimensional voting, since policy attitudes and interaction are connected in patterns of consultation.

Finally, it is possible that a social psychological model may contribute as much to an understanding of legislative decisions as a rational cognitive process model. Many writers on decision-making are accustomed to assuming that decision-makers are rational, that their decision rules are products of the inevitable press of business upon them and the severe time constraints within which they must operate. Thus the congressman would ask himself, "If I had the time and information, how would I decide?" and turn to committee members with whom he agrees for guidance. Perhaps the congressman as easily asks himself, "How are 'the boys' going to vote?" Consistent with a model which would emphasize interaction as well as information needs is the fact that the very congressmen who presumably need information the most, the relatively junior members of the House, turn to their colleagues the least, apparently because they simply have not yet had time enough to build up a set of reliable acquaintances. That model is also consistent with the emphasis placed upon the political importance of being with the right crowd. It has been found in many contexts that people seek social reinforcement,[29] and congressmen are apparently no exception.

NOTES

1. Woodrow Wilson, *Congressional Government* (New York: Meridian, 1956; originally published 1885), chap. 2. On the folkway of specialization, see Donald R. Matthews, *U.S. Senators and their World* (Chapel Hill: University of North Carolina Press, 1960; Vintage Books), chap. 5. Two works which consider fellow congressmen as sources of information are Raymond A. Bauer, Ithiel de Sola Pool, and Lewis Anthony Dexter, *American Business and Public Policy* (New York: Atherton, 1964), p. 437; and Edward Schneier, "The Intelligence of Congress: Information and Public Policy Patterns," The *Annals* of the American Academy of Political and Social Science, 388 (1970):18.

2. David Truman, *The Congressional Party* (New York: Wiley, 1959).

3. David Kovenock, "Influence in the U.S. House of Representatives," *American Politics Quarterly* 1(1973):407–464. See also several studies of sources of information in state legislatures, including Wayne L. Francis, "Influence and Interaction in a State Legislative Body," *American Political Science Review* 56(1962):953–960; Robert Huckshorn, "Decision-making Stimuli in the State Legislative Process," *Western Political Quarterly* 18(1964):164 ff.;

and Hubert Owen Porter, *"Legislative Expertise in Michigan,"* Ph.D. dissertation, University of Michigan, 1972).

4. See Cleo H. Cherryholmes and Michael J. Shapiro, *Representatives and Roll Calls* (Indianapolis: Bobbs-Merrill, 1969); Donald R. Matthews and James A. Stimson, "Decision-making by U.S. Representatives," in S. Sidney Ulmer (ed.), *Political Decision-Making* (New York: Van Nostrand, 1970); and Matthews and Stimson, *Yeas and Nays* (New York: Wiley, 1975).

5. These reasons are nicely discussed in Donald R. Matthews and James A. Stimson, "The Decision-making Approach to the Study of Legislative Behavior." (Paper prepared for delivery at the Annual Meeting of the American Political Science Association, 1969), p. 16; see also Matthews and Stimson, *Ibid.*

6. The same point is made in Arthur Miller, "The Impact of Committees on the Structure of Issues and Voting Coalitions." Ph.D. dissertation, University of Michigan, 1971, pp. 19–20.

7. The figures are: urban, 54 percent; middle, 44 percent; smalltown, 25 percent; according to ADA score: liberal, 59 percent; middle, 27 percent; conservative, 35 percent.

8. One argument for the importance of recognizing different types of information is to be found in Norman Ornstein, "Information, Resources, and Legislative Decision-Making: Some Comparative Perspectives in the U.S. Congress." Ph.D. dissertation, University of Michigan, 1972, chap. 2.

9. See, for example, David Truman, *The Congressional Party* (New York: Wiley, 1959).

10. See, for example, Duncan MacRae, Jr., *Dimensions of Congressional Voting* (Berkeley: University of California Press, 1958); Aage Clausen, "Measurement Identity in the Longitudinal Analysis of Legislative Voting," *American Political Science Review* 61(1967):1020–1035; Clausen, *How Congressmen Decide* (New York: St. Martin's, 1973); and Jerrold Schneider, *Ideological Coalitions in Congress* (Westport, Conn.: Greenwood Press, 1979). Clausen finds five different dimensions in congressional voting; Schneider argues for essentially one liberal–conservative dimension.

11. Miller combines cue-taking and dimensional structure in a similar fashion. See Arthur Miller, "The Impact of Committees on the Structure of Issues and Voting Coalitions." Ph.D. dissertation, University of Michigan, 1971, pp. 28 and 242. See also Clausen, *Ibid.*

12. See Clem Miller, in John W. Baker (ed.), *Member of the House* (New York: Scribner's, 1962) pp. 123–125.

13. Actually, the relationship would be even sharper than it is, were it not for the influence of Edith Green (D.-Ore.) among Southern Democrats and Republicans on Education and Labor Committee matters.

14. By ADA score, the figures for the percentage of cases in which respondents stayed within their party are: conservative, 74 percent; middle, 57 percent; liberal, 88 percent.

15. On legislative folkways, including courtesy, see Donald R. Matthews, *U.S. Senators and their World* (Chapel Hill: University of North Carolina Press, 1960; also Vintage Books), chap. 5.

16. See Woodrow Wilson, *Congressional Government* (New York: Meridian, 1956), chap. 2; Matthews, *ibid.;* and Arthur Miller, "The Impact of Committees on the Structure of Issues and Voting Coalitions." Ph.D. dissertation, University of Michigan, 1971.

17. Huitt emphasizes their publicity role. See Ralph K. Huitt, "The Congressional Committee: A Case Study," *American Political Science Review* 48(1954):340–365. Schneier discusses the use of hearings as sources of information for committee members. See Edward Schneier, "The Intelligence of Congress: Information and Public Policy Patterns," The *Annals* of the American Academy of Political and Social Science, 388(1970):19.

18. For a discussion of the rules and the advantages they confer on committee members, see Lewis A. Froman, Jr., *The Congressional Process* (Boston: Little, Brown, 1967), chap. 4.

19. Alan Fiellin, "The Functions of Informal Groups in Legislative Institutions," *Journal of Politics* 24(1962):72–91; John H. Kessel, "The Washington Congressional Delegation," *Midwest Journal of Political Science* 8(1964)1–21; David Truman, "The State Delegations and the Structure of Party Voting in the United States House of Representatives," *American Political Science Review* 50(1956):1023–1045; Arthur Stevens, "Informal Groups and Decision-making in the U.S. House of Representatives." Ph.D. dissertation, University of Michigan, 1970; and Barbara Deckard, "State Party Delegations in the U.S. House of Representatives," *Journal of Politics* 34(1972):199–222; and Donald Matthews and James Stimson, *Yeas and Nays* (New York: Wiley, 1975).

20. Stevens finds the same. See Arthur Stevens, "Informal Groups and Decision-making in the U.S. House of Representatives" Ph.D. dissertation, University of Michigan, 1970.

21. Junior Northern Democrats consult congressmen with greater seniority only 60 percent of the time, compared with 91 percent for both Southern Democrats and Republicans.

22. Asher also finds that freshman congressmen take a period of time to build a set of informants in the House. See Herbert Asher, "The Freshman Congressman: A Developmental Analysis," (Ph.D. dissertation, University of Michigan, 1970), chap. 5. The same point is made in Donald R. Matthews, *U.S. Senators and Their World* (Chapel Hill: University of North Carolina Press, 1960; also Vintage Books), p. 252.

23. A discussion of the concept of problemistic search is found in Richard M. Cyert and James G. March, *A Behavioral Theory of the Firm* (Englewood Cliffs, N.J.: Prentice-Hall, 1963), pp. 120–122.

24. In other terms, the congressman's "zone of indifference" might be quite wide on minor legislative matters. On this concept, see Chester I. Barnard, *The Functions of the Executive* (Cambridge, Mass.: Harvard University Press, 1966; first published 1938), pp. 167–170; and John F. Manley, *The Politics of Finance* (Boston: Little, Brown, 1970), pp. 129–130.

25. Aaron Wildavsky, *The Politics of the Budgetary Process* (Boston: Little, Brown, 1964), p. 43.

26. For a somewhat different categorization of types of information, see Norman Ornstein, "Information, Resources, and Legislative Decision-making: Some Comparative Perspectives on the U.S. Congress." Ph.D. dissertation, University of Michigan, 1972, chap. 2.

27. The figures for the proportion of the cases which are primarily procedural are: Northern Democrat, 42 percent; Southern Democrat, 26 percent; Republican, 26 percent; and junior, 39 percent; middle-seniority, 28 percent; and senior, 26 percent.

28. There is an extensive literature on bargaining. For a few references, see Charles Lindblom, *The Intelligence of Democracy* (New York: Free Press,

1965); Thomas Schelling, *The Strategy of Conflict* (Cambridge, Mass.: Harvard University Press, 1960); Lewis A. Froman, *The Congressional Process* (Boston: Little, Brown, 1967), chap. 2; Roger H. Davidson, *The Role of the Congressman* (New York: Pegasus, 1969), chap. 1.

29. For one political example, see Raymond A. Bauer, Ithiel de Sola Pool, and Lewis Anthony Dexter, *American Business and Public Policy* (New York: Atherton, 1964), p. 350.

4

Party Leadership and Ranking Committee Members

Among fellow congressmen, those who occupy formal positions in the elected party leadership or on the standing committees might have a special place in voting decisions. If a congressman is elected by his party caucus to a leadership position, it is possible that either because of the personal esteem in which his colleagues hold him or because of his pivotal position in the balance of coalitions within his party, he would be a likely source of influence on party members. The committee chairman for the majority party and the ranking minority members might also influence their party colleagues, because of their accumulated years of expertise, their public exposure, and their influence on such vital House prerogatives as scheduling and agenda.

Writers on Congress and on legislative behavior in general have long been interested in the party as a source of cleavage in legislative voting. This interest was exhibited in the vigorous argument over the degree of party responsibility in the United States, which saw some arguing that American parties should be more like the British model of cohesion and accountability, and others arguing that they should not.[1] Other literature has examined empirically the degree to which it can be said that the parties are different in legislative voting. With high regularity, using diverse roll call analysis methods, these studies have come to the conclusion that despite the absence of the kind of party cohesion one finds in a parliamentary system, party differences in the U.S. Congress are still substantial.[2]

The data used in this study clearly present no argument with this conclusion. It reflects the reality of House voting to treat the House membership as a three-party system, with the Democratic party split into South and non-South. In the votes which form the core sample of this study, Northern Democrats voted on the liberal side 84 percent of the time, compared with 29 percent for Southern Democrats and 33 percent for Republicans. It must be remembered, of course, that the differences between a liberal and conservative position on any given issue are not necessarily great when considered as a subset of a broader left-right ideological space. The difference on the water pollution appropriation, for instance, amounted to a relatively narrow $400 million, rather than disputes over the very existence of the program or its fundamental features. But within the context of legislative voting, the party differences are quite sharp. Northern Democrats are heavily on the liberal side of the vote, and Southern Democrats and Republicans slightly less heavily on the conservative side.

A part of an explanation for these party differences might conceivably reside in the influence of the party leadership and ranking party members on the committees. One staff member even went so far as to say, "Some follow the leaders without question. The leaders post their staff at the door, and as members walk in, the staff will say, 'Poverty amendment, vote yes,' or something. They'll do it."

One might expect party leaders to be a potential source of influence on legislative voting for a number of reasons.[3] One is that they control a number of sanctions which can be used against dissident party members, such as committee assignments, passage of pet pieces of legislation, favorable or unfavorable scheduling of bills, and a host of minor favors. Party leaders might also be expected to possess vital brokerage and other interpersonal skills, as attested by their election by their party colleagues. Both party leaders and ranking committee members, furthermore, have considerable potential for public exposure, which might be expected to enhance their influence in the House.

Previous studies of legislative voting have discovered that the party leadership tends to vote with the ranking members of the committee which reported a bill under consideration.[4] In my interviews, congressmen said that both leaderships heavily tended to go along with their ranking members. One Southern Democrat said, "They go along with the committee," and even told of one instance in which a party leader was publicly "committed" by a chairman much against his desires. A Northern Democrat agreed, charging, "They let party policy be made by the committee chairman. Whatever the chairman says, that becomes the policy. You and I can agree that's the fact. I don't know what you think about it, but I think it's outrageous." The same pattern developed on the minority side, perhaps because of a desire to forge common cause with the Republican administration. Whether this pattern of party leadership deference to committee leadership persisted into the 1970s is difficult to determine. On the one hand, there seemed to be more press accounts of Speaker O'Neill's activism and pressure on committees than there had been with previous speakers. On the other hand, there also appeared to be few instances of public conflict between party and committee leaders at the time of floor decisions, and many instances in which neither kind of leadership could control the behavior of its party members.

In the votes comprising the core sample of this study, in any event, the position of the party leadership of both parties was always the same as that of their party's ranking members on the committee that had reported the bill. In the correlation model, therefore, the importance of the party leadership position as a predictor of the vote can be taken as being equivalent to the importance of the ranking committee members of the congressman's own party. Though we do not have any direct measure of the subjective importance which congressmen place on the committee leaders as distinct from the party leadership, it is my impression that they would also be roughly the same. Informal following of fellow congressmen of like persuasion on the committee, whether leaders or not, is probably far more important than following the committee chairman or ranking minority member simply because of his position. For these reasons, we will consider the party leadership and the ranking committee members together in this chapter.

OVERALL IMPORTANCE

As an actor that might have some weight in the decisional calculus of congressmen, their party leadership is singularly unimportant. The congressmen in my sample spontaneously mentioned the party leadership only 10 percent of the time, indicating that the leadership was decidedly not much in their minds. The party leadership was never coded as being of determinative importance in a respondent's decision, was of major importance in only 5 percent of the decisions, and of no importance at all 63 percent of the time. This is the weakest performance of any actor considered in this study.

It is traditional to consider minority or majority status in the House as a variable which might affect the importance of the party. Actually, control of the presidency is probably far more important. The president, being the public focal point in the system and the author of a legislative program, has a degree of influence among his party adherents, regardless of their House numbers. We will consider this point further in Chapter 6. But the pattern is also noticeable here. Of the 23 spontaneous mentions of the party leadership, 19 were from Republicans. And all of the instances in which the party leadership was of major importance in the decision were Republican.

Indications that this party difference has to do with control of the administration came from the fact that many respondents would refer to the change in party leadership behavior which occurred with the change of administrations in January of 1969. One Southern Democrat said, "The party leadership was more active last year, when it was the Johnson administration and they had a program to get through. They'd contact me once a day sometimes. This year, it's entirely different." Critics of the Democratic leadership would blame their inactivity on their former reliance on administration lobbying. As one liberal Democrat said, "Now that they're on their own, they don't know what to do." So the loss of the White House results in lack of an administration legislative program and consequent inactivity by that party's leadership. But the party which acceded to administration control finds itself with a need to close ranks behind its administration and a greater party leadership activity. One Republican could recall only one case during the previous session in which the party leadership had made a bill a party matter, whereas it happened repeatedly during the first session of the Nixon administration. Indeed, it was quite common for Republicans to mention their party leadership and the administration in one breath, thinking of the two as virtually interchangeable. As one Republican replied when asked if the party leadership had contacted him about electoral college reform, "I don't think the administration really cares about this."

Granting these party differences, however, the party leadership is still not of great importance, even among Republicans. Fully half of the time, Republicans report that the party leadership was not involved in their decisions at all, compared with a 69 percent incidence for Northern Democrats and 77 percent for Southern Democrats. Some of the time, of course, the party leadership may not have made its position known. But even taking account of that possibility, the leadership still appears to be of minimal importance within the party that controls the White House. It is possible that different administrations, such as the Johnson administration in 1965, would produce different results.

In his classic cluster-bloc analysis of congressional roll call voting, Truman discovered that junior members formed a distinctive grouping around the party leadership,[5] and hypothesized that, because of their newness to the chamber, they would tend to stay close to the orthodox party position. I found the same tendency, but only in the Republican party. Among Republicans, the most junior congressmen ignored the party leadership 41 percent of the time, compared with 55 percent for middle-seniority and 62 percent for senior Republicans. But for Northern Democrats, junior members demonstrated a positive disdain for the party leadership, rejecting it a full 74 percent of the time. The explanation for this finding, again, lies largely in administration control. Junior congressmen of the party that controls the White House appear to pay more attention to their party leadership than do those of the other party.[6]

Electoral competition also has something to do with party allegiance. There are minimal differences among congressmen according to the percentages by which they won in the previous election. But by the Index of Comparative Margins[7] those who are least secure electorally are substantially less likely to consider party leadership in their decision than those who are secure. Fully 71 percent of the insecure congressmen show party leadership as unimportant, compared with 56 percent of the most secure. Apparently in the traditional case of party versus constituency, greater electoral security permits a congressman to pay more attention to his party leaders. This pattern, however, obtains only for Republicans and Southern Democrats.

So far as the objective agreement between the party leadership (and committee leadership) position and the congressman's vote is concerned, the party leadership fares no better as an influence on the vote. To obtain a good estimate of the party leadership position, we use here the vote that party leaders actually cast as the measure of their position, meaning that they are always involved in the correlation model. Given his party leadership position, the probability that a congressman will vote with that position is .57, which is only slightly better than a chance performance. The correlation between party position and vote is very weak, only .15, and even this relationship is wiped out by controls for the other variables in the model. Controlling for the other five actors makes the partial correlation coefficient −.08. Interestingly, controlling only for fellow congressman position, the partial correlation between party position and vote is −.02, which means that the party leadership and ranking committee members have no influence on the vote independent of the congressman's chosen informants within the House. But the partial correlation excluding fellow congressmen and staff is also nearly zero, .04. In short, the party leadership and ranking member position make virtually no unique contribution to an explanation of the vote.

Again, taking account of party, Northern Democrats are particularly prone to disregard the position of their leaders in the elected party leadership and on the committees, as Table 4–1 shows. The conditional probability that a Northern Democrat will vote with his party leadership is actually lower than a chance occurrence. In this Congress, the Democratic leadership's practice of following the committee chairman, therefore, put them markedly out of step with Northern Democrats, since so many chairmen were southerners. As for the Republicans, as Table 4–1 shows, the position of the party leadership is scarcely improved in the correlation model. They may pay greater attention to the party position, but this attention is not necessarily reflected in greater agreement with the leadership when voting.

The influence of people in leadership positions may have changed since the field work for this study was completed in 1969. In the case of committee chairs and ranking members, the changes seem to be unambiguous: The image of committee leadership as a weak influence on floor votes is even more true than it was in the late 1960s. As noted above, committee leaders might be consulted in the same fashion that one might consult a fellow congressman—because of expertise and philosophical agreement. But it seems likely that the influence that they might have wielded *because* of their positions has rather substantially

Table 4–1 Agreement between Party Leadership and Vote, Within Party Groupings

	conditional probability	correlation	partial correlation[a]
Northern Democrats	.38	.10	−.01
Southern Democrats	.63	.19	−.07
Republicans	.68	.25	−.12

[a] Controlling for the other five independent variables.

eroded. First, the choice of committee and Appropriations sub-committee chairs must be ratified by the majority party caucus; and three chairmen were denied reappointment in 1975. Second, subcommittee chairs are now selected by vote of the majority members of the committee of which the subcommittee is a part, which resulted, for example, in the election of a relatively junior member over one many years his senior to head the Subcommittee on Health and Environment of the Commerce Committee in 1979. The introduction of these election processes cannot help but curb the independent power of chairmen, as they all gain and retain their positions by performing in a way that will satisfy the majorities to which they are accountable. Beyond the selection processes, there have been several rules changes that have further curbed the powers of committee chairs.

The picture in the case of the party leadership is somewhat less clear; though on balance, it seems that the party leadership influence on members' voting decisions is no greater and, if anything, lower than these data from 1969 would suggest. On the one hand, the position of the Speaker has been strengthened in some respects through the rules changes of the 1970s. For example, the Speaker has gained greater control over referral of bills and more influence on committee assignments. The use of the Democratic caucus also might strengthen the hand of the leadership of that caucus, although the exent to which that might be true is not at all clear. On the other hand, the strength of single-issue interest groups which I discuss in Chapters 2 and 5 would tend to weaken party leadership. As members are pressured by increasingly vigorous and sophisticated groups with strong constituency connections, the relative influence of the party leadership is bound to suffer. Another weakening factor is the general orientation of the new legislators of the 1970s. More than half of the House of Representatives in 1979 had been in the House four or fewer years. Many observers have commented that these young members are much more independent of leadership and more constituency- and policy-oriented. A third force at work is the considerable decentralization of the House to the subcommittee level, which complicates party leadership attempts at coordination or control. Although it is difficult to sort out the net effects on these various changes, it seems reasonable to conclude that the combination of the interest group, member turnover, and subcommittee changes has resulted in a net weakening of party leadership, or at least not a net strengthening.

We have found, then, that party and committee leadership does not appear to be among the major direct influences on floor voting decisions. It is likely that this picture has not changed a great deal during the 1970s and, if anything, has been reinforced. None of these findings, of course, implies that the leadership is impotent in ways other than their direct influence on voting decisions. Such resources as control over scheduling, influence on the agenda, and the information and the rules advantages of the leadership might enlarge leadership importance beyond their evident weak position relative to other influences in terms of direct impact on voting decisions. I discuss several of these enlarged possibilities later in this chapter.

Some Classic Conflicts

The potential conflict between constituency and party is among the subjects which have long interested students of legislative behavior. It is captured in the title of Julius Turner's pioneering work, *Party and Constituency: Pressures on Congress,* and has been treated in other works.[8] The data in this study can be explicitly used to cast some light on the frequency with which this conflict arises, the proportions of the time the congressmen vote with party or constituency in cases of conflict, and the subgroups in which the conflict most often arises.

As Table 4–2 shows, when one contrasts the party leadership's objective position with the congressman's perception of his constituency's opinion, a conflict between the two emerges nearly half the time. But by virtue of voting themselves, the members of

Table 4–2   Extent of Three Classic Conflicts

conflict	percentage of vote decisions in which a conflict between the two actors emerges[a]	
	objective[b] measure	subjective[b] measure
Constituency–party	48%	17%
Administration–constituency	46%	21%
Party–administration	17%	4%

[a] Each cell entry's $n = 222$ minus a few cases of missing data.
[b] *Objective* involves the actual position of the party leadership and administration, rather than the congressman's perception of it and regardless of the degree to which they are involved in his decision. *Subjective* is the position of the party leadership or administration only if the congressman took account of that position in his decision.

the party leadership are often "taking a position" when, in fact, they either do not hold it strongly enough to push for it, or if they do, congressmen are not weighing the leadership position into their own decisional calculus. The result is that much of the time, the party leadership is simply not involved in congressmen's decisions. When not involved, there is no chance for conflict with the constituency position in a subjective sense; hence, the rather infrequent occurrence of a conflict between party leadership and constituency from the congressman's own subjective point of view.

The congressman's political party is related in some degree to the extent of conflict between constituency and party leadership. In the objective case, there are no substantial party differences, meaning that Republicans are just about as likely to find conflict between these two actors as are Democrats. But because there was a Republican president during this period, Republicans paid somewhat more attention to their party leadership than Democrats did. This greater attention was reflected in the degree of conflict, the result being that Republicans experienced "subjective" conflict between the party leadership and constituency positions about twice as often as did either Northern or Southern Democrats. Even for Republicans, however, this degree of conflict does not amount to a particularly high figure (23 percent).

In cases of conflict, the actor with which the congressman votes depends again on his party. In both the objective and subjective cases, Northern Democrats vote overwhelmingly with their constituencies and against the party leadership. Because the Democratic party leadership routinely opted for the position of the often-conservative committee chairmen, Northern Democrats regularly voted against them. Republicans in each case split about evenly, but tended slightly to favor their constituencies, which indicates the greater pulling power of a party leadership tied to their administration, but which also shows a substantial amount of constituency voting. Southern Democrats also split quite evenly, though the small number of conflicts in the subjective case makes generalization difficult.

A second classic conflict, particularly for the congressmen whose party is the same as the president's, involves the administration and the constituency. The congressman, rising as he does from his own particular district, sometimes finds this constituency in conflict with the requests from the president, who, it has been argued, represents a wider constituency.[9] In part, this potential conflict is strictly partisan, but in part it also represents the familiar conflict between national and district interests discussed by Edmund Burke.

Actually, this potential conflict parallels the one between constituency and party very closely. As Table 4–2 shows, first of all, the degree of conflict between these two actors is almost identical to that of the preceding pair. The party distribution of conflict is also similar. In the case of the pairing between constituency and "subjective" administration position, Republicans are almost twice as likely as Southern Democrats, and three times as likely as Northern Democrats, to experience a conflict between the administration position and their constituency position, because the administration is more often involved in their decision. But turning to objective disagreements between the actual administration position and the constituency, the party differences are minimal. Democrats find their constituencies in conflict with administration positions about half the time, while Republicans experience this 41 percent of the time. So their own president calls the legislators in his party to vote against their constituency nearly as often as this conflict is experienced by those in the opposition, but the conflict has more effect on his partisans because they are likely to pay him more heed.

As in the case with party-constituency conflict, the actor with whom the congressman votes depends upon his party affiliation. Northern Democrats again overwhelmingly favor their constituency position over the administration position, there being even less reason to vote with the opposite party's administration than with their own party leadership. Republicans, it is interesting to note, despite the fact that their president is calling them, actually somewhat favor their constituency over the administration in the cases of both objective and subjective conflict. Southern Democrats actually vote slightly more often with the administration than with their constituencies, and thus more often than Republicans do. This Southern support is probably on ideological grounds for the most part.

A final possible conflict is between the administration position and the party leadership position. Once again, we should have a classic case of conflict. The party leadership of the presidential party would be expected to work closely with the administration, and thus present members of that party with very little in the way of conflict. A vigorous opposition party leadership, by contrast, might present a good deal of conflict between its party and the administration.

Actually, as Table 4–2 indicates, this pair of actors comes into conflict far less often than do the previous two pairs. In the subjective case, because congressmen of both parties are highly prone to ignore the positions of at least one of these actors, we find conflict between them only 4 percent of the time, leaving virtually no conflict to analyze quantitatively. Surprisingly enough, the conflict between the objective positions of party leaderships and administration is not a great deal higher (17 percent). Democrats, furthermore, find their party leadership objective position opposed to that of the administration little more than Republicans do (19 percent to 14 percent), a finding which should be disturbing to advocates of increased party responsibility. Differences between the two parties which one finds in the roll call votes and in nonlegislative contexts are clearly not due to the activities of the House party leadership, at least with a Republican occupying the White House. The pattern with a Democratic president is presumably quite different.

There are very few cases of conflict to analyze. But in those that exist, Northern and Southern Democrats vote with their party leadership and the administration in about equal proportions. But Republicans vote more often with their party leadership than with their own administration (ten cases to three). One would guess that this party voting is simply the result of the more frequent and close contact between House party leaders and their members, as opposed to the more distant administration contact, heightened by administration liason difficulties at the beginning of President Nixon's first term.

Explanations for Party Voting

All indications are that the party leadership is a rather weak influence on congressional voting. But striking differences between Democrats and Republicans still persist. This anomaly leads one to search for alternative explanations for these party differences. One of these explanations has its roots in the constituencies of the congressmen. Party differences in legislative voting, such an explanation runs, are a function of differences in the constituencies from which the congressmen are elected. As I have argued elsewhere, the coalitions which support the major parties are different, with the result that the politicians recruited by these supporting coalitions will be different. Others have maintained that aside from supporting coalitions, the gross characteristics of the districts from which the Democratic and the Republican parties come are different.[10]

There is impressive evidence for such an argument in the present study, as Table 4–3 shows. Taking the size of the largest city in the district as an index of the urban-rural character of the district, and still using the voting decision as the unit of analysis, the party differences are striking, and closely parallel the differences in voting behavior presented earlier. Northern Democrats are heavily from urban areas, and Southern Democrats and Republicans tend to be from districts with smaller towns. Indeed, the relationship is so close that there are only seven decisions made by small-town Northern Democrats, four by urban Southern Democrats, and four by urban Republicans.[11] These small cells make it extremely difficult to sort out empirically the effects of type of district from party effects, even though the conceptual distinction is clear enough. At any rate, these constituency differences are reflected in party voting and in conservative coalition voting. The combination of party differences in constituency demography and in supporting electoral coalitions constitutes a convincing explanation for party voting.

A second explanation, working in conjunction with the first, centers on patterns of interaction within the House. Once congressmen with certain policy attitudes are recruited by these types of districts, we found in Chapter 3 that their cues from fellow congressmen tend heavily to be within their own party grouping, Northern Democrat, Southern Democrat, or Republican.[12] To the extent that cue-taking within the House is part of an explanation for party differences in legislative voting, this informal gravitation to colleagues of like persuasion and hence within one's own

Table 4–3 Party and Urbanness of District

size of largest city	party		
	Northern Democrat	*Southern Democrat*	*Republican*
500,000 or more	66%	8%	4%
76,000–499,000	24	40	42
75,000 or less	10	52	54
Total %	100%	100%	100%
Total *n*	74	52	96

party appears to be far more important than anything involving the formal party or committee leaders.

Third, common electoral experiences combine with the uneasiness about being with the "wrong crowd" discussed earlier, to produce a kind of compatriot feeling within each party. After all, back in their states and constituencies, Republicans and Democrats are political opponents. It is entirely to be expected that experiences with the opposition in campaigns should socialize congressmen into distrust of the opposition within the House, not only in remembrance of past campaigns, but also in anticipation of future ones. Examples of such thinking abounded in the interviews. On an increase in the debt limit, one Democrat described his party caucus: "We all felt that the Republicans should come through on this. They've voted 100 percent against it before, when there were Democratic administrations, but now they're asking us. They can't expect us to deliver the votes for them, and then duck out and leave us to take the rap." Another said of foreign aid, "This is an unpopular program. Why should we take the rap when the Republicans won't even support their own president?" Another complained of opposition use of the surtax: "With Nixon running around the country saying he'd abolish it, and then coming in here and asking for it, I'll be damned if I'll oblige him." Of course, Republicans had similar words for Democrats. One described his vote for the surtax extension: "I was dead set against it. But then the more I saw these big spenders and liberals trying to submarine the bill, the madder I got. I finally told Les Arends that if it came down to my one vote, I'd be there." Another said of tax reform, "The Democrats knew Nixon was going to do it, and they took the ball away from him. It was a smart move. We'd like to see it closer to election time, but they didn't let us." Another complained of liberal Democratic opposition to the surtax extension in these terms: "The stuff from the liberal Democrats was just demagoguery. Why are they so interested in reform right now? They had years and years under their own administration. Why not then? It's just a way to get at Nixon." The entire public exchange between Republican and Democratic leaders over whether Congress has been active or obstructionist is part of the same game. Congressmen not only characterize each other in these terms, but they also employ partisan strategies themselves. One Republican said he toyed with the idea of voting against the spending ceiling in order to blame cuts in congressmen's pet projects on the Democrats. A liberal

Democrat, angry at his leadership's failure to press for full funding for water pollution abatement, exclaimed, "Here was a beautiful chance to stick a finger in Nixon's eye again," as they had done with education funding.

Given this intraparty compatriot feeling which is forged in campaign experiences, congressmen like to "go along" with the leadership when they can. "When they can" apparently refers to occasions on which their constituency does not demand that they vote in a certain way and on which they have no strong preferences themselves. If they are free of constituency pressure and do not feel intensely about the matter, they may see a chance to curry favor with the leadership by going along, at little cost to themselves. One Republican said, "I've been off the bus so often this year that it's nice to be with them now and then." Said another, "I'm alone enough so that I like to go along when I can, just to keep with them on some things." Another had told me that he would definitely vote for the limitation on agriculture subsidies and in fact did so on the roll call vote, but voted against it on the teller vote. When I told him I had seen the inconsistency and was curious, he replied:

You have a sharp eye. (Question: Why did you?) I don't know. It was just one of those things. I guess the leadership was pretty insistent. (Question: Party or committee?) Both of them. They were insistent, and I said I'd go along, so that they could kill it on tellers and uphold the committee position. But I said that if it came to a roll call, I'd have to vote for it then. Anyway, if you can make any sense out of this in your write-up, I'd like to see it.

Of course, excluding cases of constituency or personal intensity leaves little room for party influence. One Republican congressman put it very well:

If it's nip and tuck and I don't know how to vote, I'll resolve my doubts by going along with the party. But the problem is that those are the very votes that they don't care about either. I'll go to Les Arends and ask what the party position is, and he'll say, "Do what you like." When they want something, it's an issue I've also got strong opinions on, and they know they can't get me.

LEADERSHIP RESOURCES

Examining the influence of the party leadership on congressmen's decisions, of course, does not tell the whole story of their influence in the legislative process. In the first place, the leadership may "save their powder" for the occasions on which their efforts are particularly needed and are likely to bear fruit. Such a strategy would make their influence appear numerically small in the entire population of congressmen's decisions, but would also imply their great importance in pivotal, crucial cases. Second, even if they do not influence congressmen's decisions directly, they do have some prerogatives which help them influence the outcome anyway. The authority to schedule legislation, for instance, allows them to take advantage of whatever forces do happen to be at work on congressmen's decisions when they themselves are not directly influential. Or being at the center of communications within the House, an advantage widely thought to reside in the leadership, would allow them to determine where, how, and by whom some pressure might be applied, even though they do not contact individual congressmen directly.

It is appropriate, therefore, to examine the resources at the disposal of the leadership.[13] I divide these resources into four categories: scheduling, parliamentary rules, potential sanctions, and communications.

Scheduling
Even after a bill is reported by the standing committee and granted a rule, the party leadership in the majority party still decides exactly when the measure will be scheduled for debate and voting. They may use this power of timing the bill as a way to obtain the result which they desire. On the agriculture bill, for instance, they scheduled the votes on a Monday, in order to catch many urban Eastern-seaboard congressmen out of town and hence to kill the amendment to impose a limitation on payments. (The amendment passed anyway, through strenuous efforts of liberals to notify their compatriots and urge them to return.) On the debt limit increase, the bill was put off for a week in order to give the Republican leadership time to obtain more Republican votes for the measure. On the poverty bill, liberals on the Education and Labor Committee forced the Speaker to delay consideration of the bill for a week, in order to allow time to organize opposition to the Quie-Green substitute. And the scheduling of the surtax extension went through a perfectly bewildering series of shifts on and off the agenda, as the leadership obtained changing estimates of their ability to produce the votes. Some of these attempts to affect the outcome by adjusting the

timing of the bill succeeded, some failed, and in some, timing probably did not affect the result in any event. But timing does at least have some potential for affecting enough votes to make a difference, and hence the potential for leadership influence.

In addition to the ability to affect the timing of a piece of legislation, the leadership may affect the appearance of the item on the agenda altogether. The majorities of standing committees and the ranking members of those committees especially are capable of preventing the matter from being considered at all. One of the hottest political issues of the session under study, college unrest, never did come to a clear floor vote, because bills which would have been aimed at college disrupters never left the Education and Labor Committee. A protracted, bitter fight within that committee, which saw virtual filibustering by liberals and angry retorts by conservatives, resulted in barely enough votes to block all bills. In another instance, a fundamental change in the selective service system was blocked by the Armed Services Committee.

The powers over timing and agenda appear to be more negative than positive. It is easier to block a piece of legislation in committee than it is to steer it through the legislative process. It is more convenient to delay a piece of legislation than it is to speed it up. Thus, decisions on timing more often involve delays than accelerations, and questions of agenda involve blocking an item. Such an observation has some interesting consequences. There are occasions on which a committee is simply not in a position to block a piece of legislation. When an old, established act comes up for renewal, for instance, some version of the bill must be passed, and congressmen on the floor have a chance to vote as they wish. The Appropriations Committee finds itself regularly in exactly this position, since their bills must come out of the committee, and do so under an open rule which allows amendments. This vulnerability could be one reason why Appropriations Committee members develop such well-defined norms about solidarity in the face of threats from the whole House.[14]

Parliamentary Rules

Several provisions in the rules or practices of the House give the party and committee leadership some advantage. First, the parliamentarian, operating under the Speaker's aegis, makes rulings which can materially affect the outcome. There was a real question, for instance, about whether the Joelson amendment which added funds to education appropriations was parliamentarily proper. Supporters of that amendment traced down an old precedent which allowed a package amendment to the appropriations bill, which is usually read line by line, and obtained the parliamentarian's assent. Without that much-disputed ruling, the amendment would have been ruled out of order, and many provisions of the package would have been defeated if brought up separately from impacted aid. One lobbyist said that up until the package was admitted, many had not taken them seriously, but then "they had to concede that these liberals had done their homework for a change and had looked up some precedents and stuff."

Second, the leadership controls the power of recognition on the floor. Who will be recognized and when is the leadership's prerogative. Sometimes, the order of recognition is crucial.[15] Again, in the education funding battle, supporters of impacted aid had no fallback position available; because of the order of the amendments, they could not vote against the Joelson package and then have a straight impacted aid amendment left for which to vote. Or the content of the motion to recommit the bill, one way to obtain roll call votes on matters of substance, resides in the minority party leadership, because the Speaker recognizes the person named by the Minority Leader. Or the Speaker declares when the voting has come to an end, to which one lobbyist on the surtax attributed some significance: "McCormack has a pretty quick gavel sometimes. But he sure didn't that day. You maybe noticed that he just waited and waited, gavel in the air, while more Republicans came into the well to change their votes. He could have waited there for a half hour until the thing sorted out like he wanted it." The electronic voting system in use after the mid-1970s made this tactic less available, due to limits imposed on the time for voting.

Closely akin to the power of recognition is the prerogative residing in the bill's manager to move to cut off debate. While it probably does not change many outcomes in the House, it still importantly shapes the nature of the discussion in the public at large. Those in the House who offered several cutting amendments to the military procurement bill, for instance, displayed public anger at the short time which Mendel Rivers (D.-S.C.) allowed for debate. The same was true of liberal opponents of the surtax extension, frustrated with Hale Boggs's (D.–La.) extended remarks which allowed little remaining time for discussion.

A final advantage under the rules is the entire Committee of the Whole procedure, the major result of which is to protect the committee bill. Amendments which are defeated in the Committee of the Whole may not be brought up again in the House proper, while amendments which are passed there may be voted on again. The committee majority, then, has two chances to defeat an amendment, while proposers have only one chance to pass it. The consequences are clear, as one aide to the majority leadership summarized them: "We often get commitments from Southern Democrats and even Republicans to just stay away and not vote. Then we'll get the amendment blocked on a teller vote and nobody gets hurt." This situation, used so often to protect Democratic administration bills, was often used in the session under study to block amendments from the liberal side. The importance of this advantage has been virtually eliminated by the rules change which allows for recorded teller votes on amendments.

Potential Sanctions

The party leadership is in a position to sanction negatively congressmen who do not behave as they would wish, by withholding certain favors over which they have control. These desired objects are well known to students of Congress. One of them which the leadership influences is committee assignments. As Masters points out,[16] assignments to the most desired committees of the House are done in part according to a criterion of "legislative responsibility," which translated into the vernacular may mean "going along." One congressman told me:

I've found out just in the last three years or so, not because of anything that has happened to me, but because of things that have happened to people I know, that the party leadership will punish you if you vote wrong too much. It especially happens on committee assignments. I don't mean run-of-the-mill assignments, but if you want a real plum like Ways and Means or Appropriations, the guys that vote against the leadership too much don't get them.

The leadership has a number of other favors which they are able to grant or withhold, depending on the willingness of the congressman to "go along." Committee chairmen can delay or expedite the progress of legislation of interest to congressmen.

Said one respondent, "There are some chairmen who keep lists, who eyeball you as you walk through the line, and check record votes the next day. If you're obnoxious, it will go hard on you." Several members pointed to the power of the committees dealing with public works, for instance, to grant or withhold approval of projects in individual districts. Said one, "There is almost no other area in which a committee has a direct, immediate, specific impact on an individual congressional district."

Given these possible leadership sanctions, it is significant that the party leadership and ranking committee members come out so poorly as influences on votes. If they have a number of prerogatives which allow them to sanction deviants, then why are they apparently so unimportant? The answer may be that the sanctions are not very effective. With committee assignments, for example, many House members already have an assignment with which they are reasonably contented, so that there is no threat. As one party maverick said, his current committee assignment "helps a good deal. I already have the assignment I want, I'm not bucking for another one, and that makes it easier." The sheer size of the House, for another thing, makes it difficult for the leadership to "keep book" on congressmen; as one respondent said, "There are so many people in the House that you get lost in the crowd." Furthermore, it may be that some leaders who are elected by their colleagues are elected for their skills at brokerage and ego-building, rather than for their toughness. Several Republican respondents expressed the opinion that Gerald Ford (R.–Mich.) was not "tough," would not use his power to punish deviants.

At any event, the sanctions apparently are not very effective, simply because many congressmen care more about voting as they see fit, either for ideological or political reasons, than about the risk of negative party sanction. Members repeatedly voiced perfect willingness to defy the leadership and take whatever consequences might come. It was a regular litany to declare that one is "independent" and will do "what I think is right." One staffer thought that there had been a change over the years: "You keep hearing that a chairman will cut you off at the knees, but actually members more and more are voting wrong and feeling no consequences. When you have over half the members coming in only seven or eight years ago [which by the late 1970s had been reduced to four years], things have changed a lot around here. There's more independence, and it's not Rayburn's 'get along, go along' thing any more." Whether there has been a change over time or not, the current situation was aptly summarized by another aide: "You can't just walk out there and persuade Members of Congress to go along. The fact is that you've got 435 prima donnas out there. They don't even want to have a Speaker, but they know somebody's got to chair meetings. So they elect him, give him the slightest smidgeon of power, and then the reporters say he's not effective."

Communications

The final leadership resource which we will consider is the leadership's position in the communications process.[17] Much of this central position is attributable to the whip system. That system is supposed both to keep the leadership informed of the wishes of the rank and file, and to communicate the wishes of the leadership down among the party members. Much of this process involves counting heads, to know how many votes there are for and against a given measure at any point in time. We will have a good deal to say about the importance of head-counting in Chapter 5, which concerns lobbying.

In this context, however, it is interesting to observe that head counts were not uniformly useful to the leadership, at least in the session under study. In the first place, head counts were often simply not taken. A staffer to the Republican leadership admitted that one reason that they were defeated on the Health, Education, and Welfare appropriation was simply that they had not been active at all, since all their energy at the time had been absorbed with the battle over the surtax extension. This was not the only instance. Leaders in legislative fights often told me that they were not sure exactly where they stood, since nobody had been doing any counting. One leader supporting the HEW funding amendment, in fact, said that they were operating on "just a feeling" rather than a hard count. Another, fighting for a straight extension of the voting rights act, said that they had taken no head count because they "would lose the momentum" if it turned out badly. Another, a leader in the poverty amendments, also told me that he was operating without a count. Part of this lack of counting may simply be lack of time and energy, but part of it may also be a reluctance on the part of the leadership, a fear that they might wear out their welcome.

In addition to simply having no poll at all, the leadership polls which were taken were often not very useful. It appeared to be quite common for members to reply that they were "uncommitted" at the time of the poll, either because they genuinely were or because they did not wish to cooperate in order to keep their options open. At the time the poll is taken, they often do not know enough about the structure of the amendments to be able to commit themselves. But if the whips were to wait longer, there would be less time to strike the compromises necessary to the attainment of their goals. Proper timing of a poll is obviously a delicate art.

Even if the count at a given time were correct and reasonably complete, there may still be changes between the time the poll is taken and the final vote. Members sometimes find themselves in an utterly unanticipated situation on the floor, and make up their minds on the spot, perhaps in contradiction to their earlier expressed intention. On the foreign aid bill, for instance, many congressmen who traditionally could be counted on to support the foreign aid bill, seeing the passage of the Sikes amendment which added planes for Nationalist China and the Adair motion to recommit, which cut economic aid, decided then and there to vote against the whole bill. One even felt obliged to apologize to his regional whip for going back on a commitment. But it is exactly this sort of situation which makes many congressmen reluctant to commit themselves in the first place.

Fragile as they are, however, a good many important leadership decisions are based on the whip polls. The Speaker decides when to take up a bill according to how he sees the vote turning out at a given point in time. On one occasion, the surtax extension, Minority Leader Gerald Ford led Speaker McCormack into taking up the bill according to a schedule which he preferred by announcing a poll result on the Republican side which was wildly inflated. Republicans felt it was important to take up the surtax before the impending Fourth of July recess, reasoning that if congressmen had a chance to get home and feel at close range the heat of their constituents' opposition to taxes, the surtax wouldn't stand a chance of passage. At a time when the Speaker was wavering about putting it off, Ford announced an estimate of the number of Republican votes for the bill which was simply far too high. On that assurance, the bill was scheduled for before the recess, and it was only through the most extreme persuasive efforts that it passed.

Decisions about where to concentrate such persuasive efforts are also made partly on the basis of the poll information. Congressmen often reported to me that after they had answered a poll in the affirmative, they were not bothered subsequently, since as one congressman put it, "They assumed I'd be with them." The contrary is also true. If a congressman shows that he is unalterably against the leadership position, he probably will not be contacted again. Said one, "I told them not to bother me because I wasn't going to change. I haven't heard a thing." It is the group which the leadership does not have supporting them, but who are good prospects, on which the attention is focused. Sometimes the sheer attention, devoid of anything else, is enough to persuade the congressman to go along. Said one staffer: "Just by virtue of activity alone, a congressman knows where the leadership stands and how important it is. Even if you don't try to persuade him at all, if you contact him two or three times, you get the message across that the leadership and the administration want this one badly." One Republican confirmed that impression on the surtax vote, saying that the leadership had been "on my tail every day." But the leadership effort can have a good deal of finesse, as a Hill aide described it:

They actually take a list of the members and go down it, marking them for or against, or undecided. Then they divide up the undecided ones, and figure out how they'll approach each one. ——— will say, "He just wants me to call so he'll think I'm obligated to him, so don't call him— he'll be all right without it." Or ——— will say, "OK, I'll talk to him, but I don't want to call him now. I'll just see him in the hall—that's the best way to approach him." Or for another guy, they'll know who in his district is important and could be used. Or they know if ——— falls, his whole delegation will go in with him. Who gets to him, and what is said, are both individually tailored to the congressman. These guys know their colleagues well enough to be able to do this.

Whether the leadership actually obtains the support of these members depends in part on the closeness of the vote. It is common, especially for the leadership of the party that controls the presidency, to have ready a group of congressmen who will cast their votes with the leadership, only in the event that their votes are absolutely needed. The Republican leadership had them ready on the surtax vote, the foreign aid final passage, and several others during the course of the session. Both supporters and opponents of the surtax extension, for instance, told me that they thought administration supporters could have pulled enough Republicans away from the ranks of surtax opponents to carry the day, almost regardless of how many Democratic votes had been delivered.

Finally, there are many alternative communications nets in the House, in addition to those maintained by the leaderships of the two parties; in fact, some of the former are more effective. It was quite common, for example, for Northern Democrats to heap praise on the communications system of the Democratic Study Group. The DSG staff prepares a weekly newsletter of information about bills that are up for floor consideration, including the parliamentary situation and the major amendments that are expected, a digest of the major provisions in the bill and amendments, a review of the considerations which a congressman might weigh as he decides on the amendments, and some commentary about how important each measure might be considered to be. DSG members characterized these materials as "extremely valuable," and one Northern Democrat told me that he still followed them closely, even though he could not agree with DSG much of the time. As a freshman Democrat said, "It's the best thing there is to keep me informed about what's coming up. I haven't seen anything else like it around here." On bills of major salience, the DSG material would be mostly a procedural cue,[18] but on others, it might very well play a greater part in a congressman's decision.

The Democratic Study Group also generates a whip system which parallels the party whip system, especially for the measures on which the party leadership does not agree with the DSG position. DSG members are assigned a list of legislators whom they have the responsibility to keep on the floor for amendments and keep in the fold as the parliamentary situation develops. And as one DSG leader pointed out to me, "We have a poorer attendance record than conservatives, because we take an activist view of our job and come from more competitive districts. Ask any liberal. We don't have time to legislate." Of course an extraparty whip system does not have to be institutionalized in the DSG or any other subgroup. On the education appropriation, for example, congressmen interested in impacted aid had their own whip system in operation for that one bill, since they were particularly interested in counting how many conservative congressmen would vote for increased funding for that type of education spending. Or a committee chairman may have his own system for getting information, quite independent of the party or of any other group.

Indeed, it appears that the supposed central position of the party leadership in the House communications net is not quite the advantage that it might be. There are so many alternative means of communication, both of information disseminated to the members and of head counting passed to the leaders of the fight, that the party leadership is hardly in a unique position. In some cases, these alternative means have been highly formalized, as in the case of the Democratic Study Group. In others, it is highly informal—a little meeting of friends, a chairman "walking and talking," or a whip system established for one bill only. The information of the party leadership is not only simply one kind of communication among many, but also may not be any better information than that possessed by others.

THE PARENT BODY

It has been traditional in literature on Congress, from the time of Woodrow Wilson forward, to emphasize the autonomy of the standing committees. Oft-cited aphorisms such as "Congress at work is Congress in committee," or the characterization of the committees as "little legislatures,"[19] are consistent with a general impression, current in the writing on Congress, that the "real decisions" are made in committee. Hence, the argument concludes, it is superficial and unimportant to be interested in either what happens on the floor or what the distributions of attitudes are in the House as a whole.

Other scholars offer an alternative view.[20] In his landmark work on the House Appropriations Committee, Richard Fenno lays great stress on the fact that even as august a committee as Appropriations finds it must act within the boundaries set by the parent body, the whole House. If the committee attempts to break those constraints, they find themselves being out-voted on the floor. The result is that most of the time, the Appropriations Committee acts within the constraints imposed by the whole House.

The major empirical problem confronting a political scientist who wants to test such a proposition is that, alas, as in so many other cases, practitioners rarely provide us with the opportunity of a clear test. A test of the notion that a committee cannot ride roughshod over the intense wishes of a House majority, for instance, comes so rarely, simply because committees as a matter of practice deliberately avoid placing themselves in such an untenable position. Unlike his colleagues in the laboratory sciences, who are able to create experimental conditions at their whim, the political scientist is obliged to wait until the conditions happen to present themselves in the real world.

Fortunately enough, at least for the progress of our knowledge about the workings of legislatures, a few tests of the proposition that committees must operate within the boundaries set by the parent body did present themselves in the session under study. These were cases in which the committee majority took a position contrary to the wishes of the House majority and attempted to defend it on the floor. Generally speaking, their defense was unsuccessful. When the whole House membership had a well-formed attitude on a given measure, the committee position could not prevail against it. One such case was the Elementary and Secondary Education Act extension. The committee majority voted a five-year extension of the act, and refused, until it was too late, to compromise on a shorter extension, despite early indications that they would be defeated. One committee Republican expressed his undisguised glee at the outcome: "On a nose-count basis, it never had a chance. I don't know how [Chairman] Perkins and the Democratic leadership got into this one. I always thought it was a rule of politics that if you're in charge, you should write the rules of the game to suit you. But they didn't. I just don't understand how they made this strategic mistake." The same thing happened with the passage of the amendment to limit farm payments, after the Appropriations subcommittee had reported a bill which did not contain the measure which was popular in the House at large.

The clearest test, however, came in the HEW appropriation bill and the package amendment for higher education funding levels, the Joelson amendment. The Appropriations subcommittee had decided to follow the recommendation of the Budget Bureau and cut back drastically on the existing funding levels, particularly the impacted aid funding. They were warned repeatedly, and they knew full well, that the impacted aid program was popular enough in the House that their bill would be increased, at least in that category. But they decided to stick by their original bill. This action was described by opponents of the committee in interviews as "terrible underfunding," "Appropriations Committee arrogance," and "absolute stubbornness." One active opponent admitted that if they had built in greater impacted aid, "it would have made our job much, much more difficult." Subcommittee members, on the other hand, stated their position differently: "There is no logical justification for Category B aid. It can't be defended by anybody. We considered it, whether to put more in or not, and then finally decided to do what was right. (Question: Couldn't you have saved yourself trouble by building it in?) It's as simple as the way I said it. No matter what happened, we decided to do what was right." Supporters and opponents of the committee alike, in short, agreed that the committee had reported a bill that was decidedly out of keeping with the wishes of the whole House. The stage was set for what happened on the floor.

Appropriations Committee members have a particularly pungent term to describe losing on the floor: They call it "getting rolled." In this case, they were rolled to the tune of approximately a billion dollars, one of the worst beatings in memory. The ranking subcommittee Republican, Robert Michel (R.–Ill.), prepared an amendment of his own which would raise the impacted aid funding, but not high enough to satisfy impacted aid advocates. When his amendment failed, partly because those who were supporting broader funding provisions voted against it, members of the House who were primarily interested in voting for impacted aid had no recourse but to vote for the package amendment sponsored by Charles Joelson (D.–N.J.), which included increases in many categories besides impacted aid. As one extremely conservative Republican who was anxious to be recorded in favor of impacted aid told me, "When there was no alternative, I swallowed my principles and walked up the aisle for the Joelson amendment. I didn't like to do it, but I did." A senior member of the Appropriations Committee summarized the outcome in this fashion:

Not only did the committee get rolled on impacted aid, but they got rolled on the whole thing. And the damndest thing is that they could have prevented it if they'd have had any sense at all. They could have put in more impacted funds and prevented these other parts of the package from being passed. They just didn't see that they were going to trigger this sort of reaction. I don't like to see the committee embarrassed like this any more than anybody else. But they put congressmen in a totally untenable position.

The lessons learned from this experience were not lost on Appropriations Committee members later in the session. A very similar situation confronted them on the public works bill, on which a majority of the House members signed a petition requesting that the committee increase funding for water pollution abatement to the authorized level of one billion dollars. The original budget figure was $214 million, a figure which, it was evident to everyone, would result in the same outcome if the committee tried to stick with it. With the Joelson amendment experience much in their minds, the full committee raised the amount to $600 million, using the argument that this was all that could be spent under the authorizing formula. They managed to beat back an amendment to add the additional $400 million by only two votes, on a teller vote. Committee opponents acknowledged, in the words of one of them, "One reason we lost was that the committee listened to us this time." Another said, "They were scared it would happen again." Committee supporters readily agreed that the former rolling had motivated the committee's action, and that the strategy paid off. An Appropriations Committee member, referring to the Joelson amendment experience, summarized the mood: "Over 200 congressmen had signed this petition asking for the full billion. Now we went through that before, on the impacted aid thing. The committee was hurt. This time, we told them, 'Now why spit in the face of the House and get clobbered again?' You get your head bloodied a couple of times and you start to learn a few things."

It is possible, in response to such case studies of the influence of the whole House on committee action, to reply that these are rare, isolated instances, and that the normal pattern is much different. Indeed it is. The "normal" pattern has the appearance of committee dominance, in part *because* committee members generally anticipate House reaction well enough that confrontations between House and committee are rare. On such occasions, it can be argued that the whole House has still had a profound influence on the committee action. Examples of such occurrences from the session under study are plentiful. One participant in the strategy sessions planning the package amendment which finally prevailed on the Elementary and Secondary Education Act said, "We first figured out what we would like to see in the bill. Then we decided what part of the list was salable—what we had the votes to pass." A Joelson amendment planner said, "We sat down with the figures and came up with a package that was frankly political. This is what we could win with on the floor." The leadership did not bring up a pension bill at the scheduled time because the subject was so closely tied to the hot pay raise issue that they believed the bill would be defeated on the floor. A farm-area congressman, noting the lack of sufficient votes against a payment limitation, said, "I know we're going to get run over, and the only thing we can do is figure out a way to get run over gracefully."

A prominent example in the session under study was the Ways and Means Committee and its chairman, Wilbur Mills. One Ways and Means member said that anticipation of floor reaction to the tax reform bill was "continually in the deliberations. If we put in this for oil, how will the oil boys react? Or if we hit farms, how will the farm bloc react? Will they be unhappy enough to vote against the bill? You think about it all the time." Another committee member said, "Mills is very careful about this. He checks with all the major groups in the House, to make sure that nobody important is offended." As John Manley has rightfully argued,[21] one secret to Mills's apparent power was his ability to anticipate the mood of his committee and of the whole House, and be responsive to it. Another committee chairman told me: "I try to anticipate what will happen on the floor and head it off if I can. I don't see myself as some kind of dictator, but as an instrument of the House. They were all elected just like I was, and ultimately it's their show. A chairman has to be a good judge of the temper of the House. That's his responsibility."

Whether a given chairman or committee majority choose to adopt such a posture in a given situation is, of course, not an easy choice.[22] It is simple to argue, as we have here, that in order to maintain his credibility, a chairman must anticipate what will happen and tailor his position to what he can reasonably expect to get. But on occasion, any chairman may decide to "do what's right," as the HEW appropriations subcommittee decided to do, in the hope that even if he is defeated in the short run, long-run success will vindicate his position. One congressman said, "If I were pragmatic about everything, I'd be immobilized. I have to suggest things in the hope that they'll be adopted ten years down the road." And a lobbyist replied when asked if it was important to preserve a committee's credibility, "That's almost a philosophical question. Sometimes it's best to adjust your goals to what you can get through. Other times, you want to set your goals high and see how much you can get."

Even if the decision to adjust to the whole House's wishes is basically a value judgment, a decision not to do so is very likely to result in at least a short-run loss, both on the substantive issue and in terms of one's more general credibility. That strain to credibility is manifested occasionally in deep bitterness on the part of those whom the leaders purport to lead. One Democrat described the attitudes of his colleagues toward the committee and party leadership on the HEW appropriation: "Democratic members don't see why they want to bail out Nixon. They sense that this is a very popular issue. Reaction all over the country has been extremely favorable. And here are their own Democratic leaders trying to blunt the effort." One of these very Democrats, when asked about the party leadership position on the HEW funding amendment, replied, "I assume they're out to screw us. That's my working assumption." Conservative Republicans were easily as angry at their own leadership for failing to build more impacted aid into the bill and saving them the embarrassment of being obliged to vote for a huge spending increase. One said that the leadership's failure to call for a record vote on the motion to recommit, which would have contained only impacted money and nothing else, meant that "I was stuck. On their assurance, I had voted against the Joelson amendment on a roll call. It was one of those things you sometimes get trapped into."

Examples other than the Joelson amendment experience abound, particularly on the Democratic side. Northern Democrats, angry that the leadership had traded support for a surtax extension for President Nixon's assent to taking the poor off the tax rolls, described the resulting "sweetener" variously as "that tidbit," "that gimmick," and "the phoniest thing yet." Or another conversation between two Northern Democrats over the Speaker's recognition of a Republican motion to recommit the military procurement bill without a clear-cut vote on ABM deployment went as follows: "You'd think the Speaker would help his friends once in a while." Answer: "What makes you think he's not?" Finally, the Democratic leadership's endorsement of the Wright (D.-Tex.) resolution, commending President Nixon for his search for a "just peace" in Vietnam, caused one Democratic dove to complain:

They should be defending the interests of the Democratic party. Presumably, there are differences between Democrats and Republicans, but you'd never know it by the way our leadership acts. They cozy up to Nixon, and that's a mistake. Nixon's intensely political, and he's using them. We know this Vietnam resolution will be used against Democrats. It just will. But our own leadership did nothing to protect us.

Occasions of Committee Power
In all this discussion about the importance of committee and leadership anticipation of the bulk of the House membership, it

should not be forgotten that the committees still have considerable influence on policy outcomes. The theoretical question is one of specifying the conditions under which committee influence predominates. We dealt with the cases of "minor" matters and "details" on major bills in Chapter 3. It is worth pointing out here, however, that in addition to affecting patterns of individual consultation, these matters also affect assessments of committee power.

The committee carries the day on bills about which the rest of the House membership does not feel intensely. These minor bills are characterized by low salience in the general public and press, and by low information dissemination in the House. Congressmen's "zone of indifference"[23] is wide enough in these cases to allow the committees wide latitude. Examples of such bills, curiously enough, include most appropriations bills. I deliberately asked respondents about the bills appropriating funds for the Interior Department and related agencies, and about the State, Justice, Commerce, and Judiciary bill. The responses were a collection of blank stares and shallow commentary, such as:

I guess they didn't do such a bad job, because I didn't hear anything about it.

They didn't cut so savagely, with the result that there was no controversy over it.

I just tend to throw up my hands and go along, I guess, unless something major comes along that's to the contrary.

There was no controversy over those, so I'm not acquainted with the details. Nobody brought up any objections to those bills.

This sort of situation is one major reason why the Appropriations Committee is considered to be so "powerful." The fact is that few congressmen care about their bills. When the State, Justice, Commerce, and Judiciary bill was up, attendance by my actual count in the House ranged from about 30 at the beginning of the debate to a high of about 70 when the final vote was imminent. House members just leave the bill to the committee, as they do in so many instances. In the case of appropriations, this neglect is probably due to several factors, including the dull nature of money as a subject of attention, the fact that marginal increments of money are generally at stake, rather than broad questions of public policy, and the tendency of the committee usually to anticipate the floor mood and come in fairly close to House wishes. But the consequence normally is that the committee writes the bill fairly free of House interference. One Appropriations Committee member used John Rooney (D.–N.Y.), the subcommittee chairman for the Justice Department, as an example:

Rooney's interesting. This year, there was more crap in his bill—funds for more staff for judges, more attorneys, and this and that—nothing really important, you understand, but just little things he's interested in. So what does he do? He spends all his time ranting and raving about a $13 thousand item for the University of Kansas theater group where they were putting on a play with four-letter words in it. He's a hell of an actor.

Congressmen also leave the decision to the committee in the case of the detail on the major bill. A standard operating procedure for many congressmen, for example, is to decide as a matter of principle not to instruct conferees, in order to leave them with room to bargain with the Senate. Or, to use an example cited in Chapter 3, it was very common for congressmen on the question of electoral college reform to adopt a highly general posture in favor of reform and leave the details, such as the plurality to be required for a win, in the hands of the Judiciary Committee. Said one congressman, "If you're not completely convinced of your points, you go along with the guys that studied it and thought it through."

Another matter left to the committee is the generation of the alternatives among which the congressman chooses on the floor. When he chooses among those alternatives, he may be quite free in his choice from external pressure and may very well make up his mind independently. But the posing of the alternatives in the first place is left to committee members, which is, of course, a considerable power over the final shape of the legislation. That committee members anticipate "what will go" on the floor, implies that the whole House is not entirely without its influence on the setting of the alternatives. But an individual congressman who is unhappy with the choice as posed considers himself almost powerless to change the alternatives. If committee members choose not to make a floor fight, or choose to exclude certain alternatives, the congressman on the floor rarely has a chance to change the situation. One respondent, for instance, unhappy at finding that a proportional plan for electoral college reform was not going to be proposed, replied, when asked why somebody did not offer one, "It has to come from the committee, and nobody on the committee offered it. You can't just take it on yourself."

Said another, regarding the water pollution abatement funding:

There was a group of congressmen working on it. They came up with a
figure that they thought was reasonable. I can't challenge their judgment.
I just have to take the amendment they offer me. Whether it's $800 mil-
lion, $1 billion, or $1.5 billion, I have to take it. I can't get up on the floor
and say, "I don't think it should be one billion; I think it should be $900,-
099,000." I just have to make the broad judgment and leave the dollar
figure to them.

A final condition under which committees tend to control the
outcome is on major legislation which they have the opportunity
to block in committee. If the bill does not have to reach the floor,
then the committee may block the legislation and prevent the
House from considering it, short of a difficult-to-obtain discharge
petition. It is important to emphasize that committees are often
not in this position: They must report a bill and let the whole
House have a chance to amend it. This is the case, for instance,
with the renewal of an established program or with an appropriations bill. But if no new legislation is legally required, then the
committee has the option of blocking the bill. The major example
in the session under study was the subject of campus unrest. Especially after the widely publicized appearance of guns on the
Cornell campus, congressmen felt a good deal of pressure from
their constituents to "do something." They in turn repeatedly and
forcefully brought up the subject with their colleagues from the
Education and Labor Committee. For a time, it appeared that some
sort of bill would be reported. But antilegislation congressmen
and lobbies were fearful that any bill, no matter how innocuous,
would provide a vehicle on the floor for amendments that would
do grave damage to educational institutions and, in the heat of
the moment, might have some chance of passage. So the committee blocked the legislation by a very narrow margin, and committee opponents had to content themselves with relatively harm-
less appropriations riders. In retrospect, there was some question
even here whether the most extreme of the measures proposed
would have passed. Some of the most conservative and outraged
members of the House told me that while they would vote for
anything aimed at the disrupters they would not vote for bills
aimed at colleges and universities as institutions. The committee,
on the other hand, paid a price for blocking the unrest legislation:
They found it extremely difficult to report out any legislation hav-

ing to do with higher education. Even an emergency loan provision for college students was brought up finally under suspension, a procedure which barred amendments.

CONCLUSIONS

The observation of high degrees of party regularity in roll call voting has led us naturally to the potential importance of the party leadership in voting decisions. We have found, however, that the leadership of neither party is particularly important, by any measure. These findings can be taken as roughly indicative of the influence of ranking committee members as well as the elected party leadership. The leadership of the president's party is more important in the thinking of their party members, particularly the junior members, than is that of the opposition party. Even among the groups of Republicans who turn to the party leadership the most, however, the importance of the leadership is not particularly impressive.

The fact that party regularity in voting remains, despite the apparent unimportance of the leadership, leads one to search for alternative explanations. Party voting seems to begin with constituency differences; the parties have very different demographic bases and supporting coalitions. Building on constituency differences are the patterns of interaction within the House. Congressmen rely heavily on informants within their own party grouping. Common campaign experiences cement the party regularity, since Democrats and Republicans are electoral opponents both nationally and locally.

Despite their paucity of direct influence, the party leadership and ranking committee members are not without some resources such as scheduling prerogatives and other advantages for influencing legislative outcomes in a more indirect fashion and in arenas other than floor voting. Many of these resources are more negative than positive, in the sense that those in leadership positions are better able to block action, delay scheduling, and prevent congressmen from doing certain things, than they are to promote action and induce congressmen to follow their wishes. We have especially been led to emphasize the constraints on committee and party leaders set by the parent body, boundaries which they transgress only at the risk of losing on the floor. While those constraints vary considerably in their narrowness and strength from one legislative matter to another, leaders find that they must take account of attitudes in the whole House on major legislation and on broad questions of philosophical directions of governmental policies.

NOTES

1. An argument for responsible parties is to be found in Committee on Political Parties, American Political Science Association, "Toward a More Responsible Two-Party System," *American Political Science Review* (Suppl.) 44(1950). A contrary view is found in Julius Turner's "Responsible Parties: A Dissent from the Floor," *American Political Science Review* 45(1951):143–152. For a review of the controversy, see Austin Ranney, *The Doctrine of Responsible Party Government* (Urbana: University of Illinois Press, 1962).

2. David B. Truman, *The Congressional Party* (New York: Wiley, 1959), p. 283; Julius Turner, *Party and Constituency: Pressures on Congress* (Baltimore: Johns Hopkins Press, 1951), p. 23; Lewis A. Froman, *Congressmen and Their Constituencies* (Chicago: Rand McNally, 1963), p. 88. For a discussion of the subject, see Wayne Shannon, *Party, Constituency, and Congressional Voting* (Baton Rouge, La.: Louisiana State University Press, 1968), especially his findings on pp. 38–40, 82, and 129.

3. See a discussion of the functions of party leaders in Randall B. Ripley, *Party Leaders in the U.S. House of Representatives* (Washington, D.C.: Brookings, 1967), chap. 3. See also Robert Peabody, *Leadership in Congress* (Boston: Little, Brown, 1976).

4. David B. Truman, *The Congressional Party* (New York: Wiley, 1959), pp. 237–244; and Donald R. Matthews, *U.S. Senators and their World* (Chapel Hill: University of North Carolina Press, 1960; also Vintage Books), p. 126. Truman finds the tendency stronger among Democrats than Republicans, in a session during which there was a Democratic president.

5. Truman, *Ibid.,* pp. 211–221.

6. Another, less-systemic reason lies in the personal reputations of the two party leaders. Gerald Ford was quite popular among Republicans, while John McCormack was in his last session as Speaker.

7. The Index of Comparative Margins compares the margins of victory in the two previous years. If a congressman's margin of victory got smaller, he is insecure; if bigger, more secure. The percentage lost or gained is also compared with the magnitude of the original victory. See Appendix D for a detailed explanation.

8. Julius Turner, *Party and Constituency: Pressures on Congress* (Baltimore: Johns Hopkins Press, 1951; rev. ed. by Edward Schneier, 1970). See also Frank J. Sorauf, *Party and Representation* (New York: Atherton, 1963).

9. See James MacGregor Burns, *The Deadlock of Democracy* (Englewood Cliffs, N.J.: Prentice-Hall, 1963), especially pp. 257–264.

10. See John W. Kingdon, *Candidates for Office* (New York: Random House, 1968), chap. 3, on the coalitions which support the two parties. Works on party differences in district characteristics include Frank J. Sorauf, *Party and Representation* (New York: Atherton, 1963), p. 145; and Lewis A. Froman, *Congressmen and their Constituencies* (Chicago: Rand McNally, 1963), chap. 7. For a study of the interplay between party and con-

stituency, see David R. Mayhew, *Party Loyalty among Congressmen* (Cambridge, Mass: Harvard University Press, 1966), especially p. 160.

11. Because each respondent was interviewed several times, this means there were very few congressmen in the sample involved in these decisions.

12. See Clem Miller, *Member of the House,* ed. John W. Baker (New York: Scribner's, 1962), pp. 107–109, 126–129, for corroboration.

13. Many of these are considered in Randall B. Ripley, *Party Leaders in the House of Representatives* (Washington, D.C.: Brookings, 1967), chap. 3. For an excellent study of effective use of these resources, see Ralph K. Huitt, "Democratic Party Leadership in the Senate," *American Political Service Review* 55(1961):333–344. Some literature downplays the importance of these resources. See Donald R. Matthews, *U.S. Senators and Their World* (Chapel Hill: University of North Carolina Press, 1960; Vintage Books), pp. 126 and 133; and Charles O. Jones, *The Minority Party in Congress* (Boston: Little, Brown, 1970), pp. 26–27. A recent work on party leadership is Robert Peabody, *Leadership in Congress* (Boston: Little, Brown, 1976).

14. An account of this solidarity is to be found in Richard F. Fenno, Jr., *The Power of the Purse* (Boston: Little, Brown, 1966), pp. 163–166.

15. The importance of the order in which amendments are considered is reflected in the literature on the paradox of voting. See William Riker, "The Paradox of Voting and Congressional Rules for Voting on Amendments," *American Political Science Review* 52(1958):349–366. See also Richard G. Niemi and Herbert F. Weisberg, *Probability Models of Collective Decision-Making* (Columbus, Ohio: Merrill, 1972), part 3.

16. Nicholas A. Masters, "Committee Assignments in the House of Representatives," *American Political Science Review* 55(1961):345–357; reprinted in *New Perspectives on the House of Representatives,* ed. Robert L. Peabody and Nelson W. Polsby (Chicago: Rand McNally, 1969).

17. The leadership's distribution and collection of information are discussed in Randall B. Ripley, *Party Leaders in the U.S. House of Representatives* (Washington, D.C.: Brookings, 1967), pp. 65–72. See also Lewis A. Froman and Randall B. Ripley, "Conditions for Party Leadership: The Case of the House Democrats," *American Political Science Review* 59(1965):53–56.

18. On the distinction between procedural and substantive cues, see Chapter 3.

19. Such generalizations first became prominent with the appearance of Woodrow Wilson, *Congressional Government* (New York: Meridian, 1957; first published 1885).

20. Richard F. Fenno, Jr., *The Power of the Purse* (Boston: Little, Brown, 1966), chaps. 1–2. For a comparative view of committees, see Fenno's "Congressional Committees: A Comparative View." (Paper delivered at the meeting of the American Political Science Association, 1970); and Fenno's *Congressmen in Committees* (Boston: Little, Brown, 1973). Another work on the limits placed on leaders is Charles O. Jones, "Joseph G. Cannon and Howard W. Smith: An Essay on the Limits of Leadership in the House of Representatives," *Journal of Politics* 30(1968):617–646. An instance of committee adaptation to the wishes of the whole House is provided in John Ferejohn, "Congressional Influences on Water Politics," Ph.D. dissertation, Stanford University, 1972, chap. 5. See also John F. Manley, *The Politics of Finance* (Boston: Little, Brown, 1970), chaps. 4–5.

21. Manley, *Ibid.*

22. There are marked differences among the committees in terms of their re-

lationships with the whole House. See Richard F. Fenno, Jr., "Congressional Committees: A Comparative View." Paper delivered at the meeting of the American Political Science Association, 1970); and Fenno's *Congressmen in Committees* (Boston: Little, Brown, 1973).

23. On the concept of the zone of indifference, see Chester I. Barnard, *The Functions of the Executive* (Cambridge, Mass.: Harvard University Press, 1966; first published 1938), pp. 167–170; and John F. Manley, *The Politics of Finance* (Boston: Little, Brown, 1970), pp. 129–130.

5

Interest Groups

Political scientists and other observers have long been preoccupied with interest groups. A traditional concern of the discipline, "Who gets what,"[1] implies in part, "Which kinds of *groups* get what." Over the years, from Bentley to Truman,[2] this interest in groups has been formalized into a group theory of politics. In academic and lay literature alike, it has long been thought that "pressure groups" and "lobbies" were highly influential in the legislative process.

Some recent literature has emphasized different aspects of interest group activity. One theme in the study of reciprocal trade by Bauer, Pool, and Dexter, for instance, is the disadvantages and weaknesses of lobbying organizations.[3] Milbrath voices similar suspicions in his study of Washington lobbyists.[4] Olson notes that people are not likely to organize interest groups at all without receiving some concrete, personal benefit in return.[5] But when told of this branch of literature, one higher-level civil servant snorted, "They don't know what they're talking about. Lobbies are really thick with congressmen. You better believe it." How central interest groups are and how they behave in the context of congressmen's decision-making are clearly empirical questions of some significance.

OVERALL IMPORTANCE OF INTEREST GROUPS

In this study, interest groups constitute neither the most important nor the least important of the influences on a congressman's vote. Coding construed the term "interest group" very broadly, to include lobbying organizations, identifiable but unorganized sets of people, and even such social classifications as "middle-class taxpayers." Respondents spontaneously mentioned groups in 31 percent of the cases, a somewhat lower figure than that reported for fellow congressmen (40 percent) and constituency (37 percent), but with considerably more frequency than that reported for party leadership or staffs. Interest groups were coded as being of major or determinative importance in the decision about a quarter of the time (26 percent), and were not at all important in 35 percent of the cases. Again, these figures place interest groups third in a rank ordering of actor importance, behind fellow congressmen and constituency.

Interest group importance varies according to the salience of the issue. Congressmen spontaneously mention groups in fully 53 percent of the high-salience cases, compared with 25 percent for medium- and 14 percent for low-salience cases. Table 5–1 shows, furthermore, that interest group importance grows with increased salience. In fact, it seems entirely plausible that congressmen and other participants even define issue salience partly in terms of interest group activity. A "big" issue is one in which, among other things, groups are particularly active. It could be that lobbyists are quite active on many issues in committee deliberations, but on the floor, interest group activity is not very noticeable in low-salience issues. Among decisions on high-salience issues, however, groups are of major importance nearly half the time, and involved in the decision nine-tenths of the time. Interestingly enough, none of the other standard independent variables in the study—party, constituency, seniority, etc.—are significantly related to group importance.

Among congressmen taken as a whole, interest groups' importance as a predictor of the vote is lower than the subjective importance just discussed. If a group position on the issue is known, for example, the probability that a congressman will vote with that position is .62, which is only somewhat higher than chance. The overall correlation between interest groups' positions and votes, as measured by the product-moment correlation coefficient, is .21, well below that for constituency (.49) or for fellow congressmen (.78). When one controls for the effects of other influences on the

Table 5–1 Issue Salience and Group Importance

group importance	issue salience		
	low	medium	high
None	70%	25%	11%
Minor	23	55	42
Major	6	21	47
Determinative	1	0	0
Total %	100%	101%	100%
total *n*	73	73	76

vote, furthermore, this meager predictive value is eliminated altogether. In the six-variable correlation model, the partial correlation between interest group position and the vote, controlling for the other five actors, is —.05; in the four-variable model (which excludes fellow congressmen and staff), it is .05. This result for the partial correlations, which shows other variables reducing the original relationships to near zero, fairly uniformly holds true of all study subsets—party, constituency, seniority, etc.—regardless of original group-vote correlation within each subset. We shall advance a major reason for this result under the heading "Interest Groups and Constituencies."

Ideological Direction

Interest groups are not active equally in liberal and conservative directions. In fact, liberal interest groups are involved in congressmen's floor decisions far more than conservative ones are. If an interest group position is discernible on a given issue, it is in the liberal direction 76 percent of the time. Liberal interest groups are apparently more active than conservative ones for at least two reasons. Ideologically, liberals are likely to be more interested in changing the status quo than are conservatives and hence more active. Second, much liberal agitation has to do with increasing spending levels in appropriations bills, which is not balanced by conservative organized activity to decrease spending. Conservative groups may be more active at the committee stage than is in evidence here. They may also have become more active over the decade of the 1970s.

This tendency toward a liberal direction in interest group activity, naturally enough, results in conflict with conservative congressmen. In cases of a conflict between the congressman's own attitude on the issue at hand and the position of involved interest groups, the group was more liberal than the congressman three-quarters of the time in my data. Of course, such conflicts occur more often among the ranks of Republicans and Southern Democrats than among more urban Northern Democrats. Indeed, Northern Democrats find themselves in conflict with interest groups only 15 percent of the time, compared with 39 percent for Southern Democrats and 37 percent for Republicans. This conflict for the latter two, furthermore, is overwhelmingly from liberal groups: Out of 20 cases of conflict between interest groups and Southern Democrats, 17 show the groups to be more liberal than the congressman; for Republicans, it is 28 times out of 34.

This clash between the policy attitudes of conservative congressmen and liberal interest groups is reflected in agreements between the interest group's position and the vote. Given an interest group position, the probability that a Southern Democrat will vote with that position is .49, and for a Republican, .51, neither showing better than a chance agreement. But the comparable figure for Northern Democrats is .85. The same pattern obtains for a more direct measure of ideology, the congressman's Americans for Democratic Action score: the figures are conservatives, .49; middle-score, .52; and ADA liberals, .86. So despite the lack of party and ideological differences in the spontaneous mention and subjective importance of interest groups, the groups' positions objectively agree with the votes of the liberal, Northern Democrats far more often than they do for other congressmen. This is probably due in part to simple ideological agreement with the groups, and in part to the fact that such groups are more likely to be members of the Northern Democrats' supporting electoral coalitions.

Character of Mentioned Groups

One rarely finds a head-to-head clash between opposing groups. To begin with, there are no groups involved in 30 percent of the decisions, and only one group is involved in an additional 35 percent. In this 65 percent of cases, then, either no interest group was active enough to be noticed, or the field of battle was left to only one.[6] Actually, groups on different sides of the issue were reported only 12 percent of the time. So the generation of conflict or cross-pressure in voting decisions rarely comes from the clash of opposing interest groups. To the extent that it occurs, it is instead groups versus administration, constituency versus party, or some other sort of division.

It is possible for a congressman to take account of a societal group even though that group is unorganized. When discussing the effects of taxes, for example, some spoke of "middle-income taxpayers" as an identifiable group, even though they weren't organized into a lobby. Such mentions are akin to Truman's "potential groups,"[7] in the sense that they may have an impact while still not being formally organized. Given that theoretical possibility, however, the fact is that groups in the congressman's cognitive makeup appear to be organized in some fashion most of the time. In this study, interviews were combed for any reference to groups. In the cases in which groups were involved, these groups

Table 5–2 Nature of Group Contact and Importance of Group in Decision

importance	nature of contact[a]		
	none	letters	personal visits
None	85%	2%	0%
Minor	10	79	25
Major or determinative	5	19	75
Total %	100%	100%	100%
Total n	88	86	48

[a] There are no cases of mixed forms of contact, since coding was according to the highest category possible. Some cases of personal visits, for example, include letters as well.

were unorganized 13 percent of the time. They were only organized groups 49 percent of the time, with the remaining 38 percent being a mixture of organized and unorganized. It appears, in short, that in order to be heard, one must organize and lobby. Otherwise, congressmen who are pressed for time and subjected to many stimuli from those who are effectively communicating with them will tend not to notice a less visible group. Some quantitative evidence is presented in Table 5–2, which suggests that the more visible and intense the lobbying, the more it will be noticed. As one congressman replied, when asked if a vote for water pollution abatement funds would be popular, "Not in my area. I get a lot more mail about high spending. I don't have any active conservation groups or anything." Of course organizing is no guarantee that one will succeed, but it appears to be a necessary condition to success.

INTEREST GROUPS AND CONSTITUENCIES

Congressmen repeatedly said during the course of the interviews that, unless an interest group had some connection with their constituencies, the group would have little or no influence on their decisions. Said one, "It doesn't make any difference to me unless it is from the district." Another said, "We get stuff in here all the time from the Washington offices of organizations and I often don't even read it." Another said that his mail from the national organizations "went right in the wastebasket." One congressman actually fished such a telegram out of the wastebasket to show me, but became very interested in it when I pointed out who had signed. He admitted it would have affected him, and thanked me for bringing it to his attention. A tempered view was presented by the following congressman, when asked if national education groups made any difference: "Not in the slightest. Well, let me amend that. I know they'll circulate their members just like they circulate me and to that extent the information will get back home. But it's much more important to me when the local people come in and say that the schools will go broke and they'll have a teacher strike if they don't get their money."

Without this constituency base, therefore, interest groups find it difficult to get through to congressmen. One lobbyist told me that he had written a letter stating his position to every congressman, but not a single respondent mentioned the letter. Several congressmen, to cite another example, said that foreign aid was always in trouble because of a lack of a domestic clientele. As one Great Plains Republican put it, "There's just nobody who has ever approached me personally to argue in favor of foreign aid. I've heard plenty against it, but I don't think anybody has ever asked me to vote for it."

There are a number of reasons why congressmen tend to dismiss the efforts of Washington-based lobbyists. One is that, in the absence of a constituency connection, the interest group has no negative sanction to use against a congressman who resists its petitions. As one congressman said, "If it doesn't come from my district, why should I care?" Of course, even a group with excellent constituency ties may not be highly powerful either, but it at least has some political potential not possessed by the national group alone. Another reason is that congressmen see the lobbying activities of the Washington organizations as being not quite legitimate. Constituents coming to them with petitions for redress of grievances are regarded as entirely legitimate, but national lobbyists are regarded as merely "pressuring." One congressman exhibited quite a testy reaction when a labor lobbyist asked for a commitment to vote against the surtax extension: "I told him I was probably against it, but he said he needed a more definite word. I said, 'Who do you think you are? By what authority are you telling me what I have to say to you?' He was kind of miffed. But I have to maintain my independence. Without that, without my independence, you can have this job. (Kingdon: I don't want it.) That's a measure of your sanity."

There is some quantitative evidence which supports the proposition that interest groups have little effect on congressmen aside from their constituency effects. First, in those cases in which interest groups are to some degree involved in the congressman's decision, he makes some connection between the interest group and his constituency or state, 80 percent of the time, with the remainder being a discussion of a Washington lobby only. Of those constituency-connected group mentions, half involve no Washington organization at all. Some of the literature on interest groups and lobbies is prone to emphasize the activities of the Washington lobby. But it is clear that congressmen do not tend to think in these terms. If an interest group is involved in their decision, it is highly likely to be connected with their constituency.

Furthermore, interest groups with no constituency connection are less important in the congressman's decision, even if somewhat involved. Of the mentions of Washington-based lobbies, 23 percent are spontaneous compared with 55 percent for constituency-based interest groups and 47 percent for groups with both constituency and Washington connections. Of the decisions involving Washington-based groups only, furthermore, groups are of major importance in 20 percent, compared with 42 percent for groups with some constituency base.

A further indication of the importance of a constituency connection for an interest group is found in the correlation figures. The bivariate relationship between interest group position and a congressman's vote, expressed as a product–moment correlation coefficient, is .21. When one controls for the constituency position, the partial correlation between group and vote given constituency becomes .01, which indicates that interest group positions make no unique contribution to explaining votes independent of constituency effects. Because constituency and interest group positions are themselves related, this substantial drop in the correlation when controlling for constituency position is not definitive by itself (see Appendix E). But when we add this result to the other evidence presented above, it seems that interest groups have little effect on congressmen's floor votes independent of constituency effects.

One key consequence of this evident need for a constituency link is that geographical dispersion is highly important to an interest group. If one wants to get something from the whole House membership, it is important to have group members in a large number of congressional districts. The interest group that is widely dispersed is in a position to appeal directly to a large share of the

House membership from their constituencies. The group that is more concentrated geographically must search for other ways to achieve their goals. This is one crucial advantage for school people, for instance. Said one congressman, "Schools affect everybody. All congressmen have schools in abundance, and parents are affected, which means everybody." This sort of advantage led opponents of the education lobby to speak in terms of what one called their "political muscle." One said, "Education is always a tough lobby, and since their victory on the Joelson amendment, they'll be even tougher." Another example of the advantages of dispersion was furnished by a higher-level civil servant:

Take the highway lobby. It is really pervasive. It includes truckers and those you'd think of. But it also includes construction people, gravel pit operators, state and local officials, the AAA. A lot of jobs and money are involved in highways. And they really turn it on. They plant newspaper articles, they can generate terrific volumes of letters and telegrams.

Still another example of a widely dispersed, well-placed group is postal workers. One congressman explained:

There aren't too many of them, but they do go to every door in the district every day of the week. That's why members are concerned about them. They think they'd be in a good position to spread the word around. This is one organization that unabashedly and openly threatens members. Just before I was elected, they had a pay raise bill up, and they massed in the galleries in uniform—packed them and just stayed there staring down on the floor proceedings. Guys were still talking about that years later.

STRATEGIES OF INFLUENCE

In the light of what we have already learned about congressmen's decisions, we turn now to interest group strategies. It is probably a general strategic principle that those who want something from a decision-maker must adapt their strategies to the decision rules that are being used.[8] The core of this study which concentrates on congressmen's voting decisions, therefore, should be useful in understanding the types of strategies that evolve.

Strategic considerations covered in this section apply not only to interest groups but also to anybody who would want to influence outcomes on the floor of the House, including the administration, the party leadership, and a congressman's own colleagues within the House. All of those who wish to win a floor fight are in roughly the same strategic boat, and tend to use similar strategies, with some modifications. In fact, the line between interest group and fellow congressmen, for instance, becomes blurred, in that the lobbies work quite closely with their friends in the House as part of an overall design.

Using Congressmen and Constituencies

In earlier chapters, we discussed the predominant place which fellow congressmen and constituencies have in the decision-making of House members as they vote on the floor. Those who desire to influence outcomes in the House appreciate their importance as well. Given the weakness of Washington-based interest groups, then, one general lobbying strategy is to work through congressmen and constituencies.

It has already been amply documented in the literature on interest groups that lobbies spend a good deal of time and energy working with and through their friends among congressmen. Bauer, Pool, and Dexter speak of lobbies as being primarily service organizations for their friends.[9] A few Washington lobbyists are so skilled both in the substance of their legislation and in the strategies for obtaining congressional acceptance that they participate actively in drafting and strategy sessions as a part of a general effort to pass or block a given proposal. Representatives of groups interested in increased education funding, for instance, had a long and close working relationship with receptive congressmen on the Education and Labor Committee, and helped draft the package amendment to the HEW appropriation bill and coordinate strategy with the congressional leaders of the fight. Or, as another example, anti-ABM congressmen were very active in stirring scientists of like persuasion to publicize their views, in an attempt to persuade other congressmen. Or, interested Washington tax experts and lobbyists repeatedly met with their friends on the Hill to draft amendments and proposals on both the tax surcharge and the tax reform bills. One lobbyist described his activities thus:

Everybody knows that a member is much too busy to do his own research, and he doesn't use his staff that way either. So we did a lot of providing them with information, pointing out the soft spots in the opposition case, telling them where they might probe. That's our job, and there's nothing wrong with providing this sort of information to your friends.

The importance of this lobbying through your friends was emphasized by an aide to a party leader:

My boss will see the poll and he knows who's undecided. He'll see John Doe on the floor, and he'll say to Smith, who's from Doe's state, "Say, I notice Doe is on the floor, and he's still undecided. Can you go over and talk to him and see if you can't get him to come around?" Then his colleague talks to him. That's entirely different from lobbying. That's one congressman talking to another. Then they're equals. But an administration lobbyist, or even worse, just an organization lobbyist, is in a much more tenuous position.

The other major actor in the legislative system through which lobbyists may work is the home constituency of the congressman. Interest groups' Washington offices alert their local memberships to legislative developments and, on unusual occasions, may bring them into town to talk to congressmen in person. Those interested in influencing congressmen, including party and administration officials as well as interest groups, may also contact key people in a congressman's constituency outside of group memberships. One increasingly dovish congressman who balked at sponsoring the Wright (D.–Tex.) resolution supporting President Nixon in his search for a "just peace" in Vietnam, for example, immediately received a call from a hometown newspaper inquiring about his intentions, which persuaded him to sign. Other congressmen reported a good deal of mail from poverty workers and clients in defense of the currently operating Office of Economic Opportunity programs. Home groups wanting to protect tax preferences like tax-free municipal bond interest or charitable contributions were urged to write about the tax reform bill. Labor union locals were similarly urged to contact their congressmen against extension of the surtax, after a period in which labor leaders engaged in extensive efforts to inform and prime their locals. Higher education organizations saw to it that Education and Labor Committee members who were wavering on campus unrest legislation were contacted by university administrators in their home districts or states, whom the Washington office had kept informed about the proposals and the legislative mood.

Perhaps the most vigorous of such efforts to mobilize pressure from the districts, however, was connected with the Emergency Committee for Full Funding, the coalition of education groups which played an important part in securing passage of the Joelson amendment to raise funding levels in the HEW appropriation bill. As one opponent of the education lobby said, "This Emergency Committee descended on this fair city like a plague of locusts." Descend they did. The coalition of education groups had been informing their constituent members for months about the effort, the funding levels, and what specifically they might do. Congressmen reported receiving mail about education funding four and five months prior to the time the bill came to the floor. Then at the time of floor consideration, school superintendents and other education professionals were called into Washington to visit their congressmen personally. These visitors were given repeated and highly detailed briefings about the legislation, about the parliamentary situation, and about tactics to use in dealing with congressmen. They were instructed to tie the amendment to local funding of specific projects of constituency interest, and to obtain concrete commitments to vote for the amendment. Virtually every respondent in my sample had been visited by informed, effective school people. The resulting passage of the amendment, in the words of one congressman, "was quite a tribute to the lobbying effort."

As a proportion of lobbying campaigns, of course, the one just described must be taken as atypical. Still, respondents in this study reported personal visits from people stimulated by interest groups 22 percent of the time. In another 39 percent of the cases, they reported that they had received interest group mail. The number of personal visits was greater with high- than with low-salience issues. So while a lobbying campaign such as the educators' effort on the HEW appropriation or labor activity on the surtax can be considered unusual, there still was more than perfunctory interest group activity of some intensity a substantial portion of the time. Even if unusual, furthermore, such lobbying campaigns are instructive for what they can tell us about the potential for lobbying, given initial advantages and a high degree of organization.

One development during the decade of the 1970s, the increasing number and vigor of single-issue interest groups, adds emphasis to the need for and the uses of a strong connection to members' constituencies. These groups have been employing more sophisticated direct mail and computer technologies to achieve their goals. One lobbyist told me in 1976, for example, that his organization had fed membership lists and election commission lists of campaign contributions into a computer data bank, so that he was in a position to press a button and obtain the names of four or five important contributors to a given congressman's last campaign who were sympathetic to his organization's goals and who could be called upon instantaneously to contact that congressman if it seemed desirable. The stock in trade of many single-issue groups is their ability to mobilize congressmen's constituents, either at the time of a crucial legislative vote or at the time of the next election, in favor of the incumbent or for his opponent. What has been happening, however, is not a wholesale change in politics, since the field work for this study done back in 1969 turned up similar processes at work. The 1970s have accentuated tendencies that were already present many years earlier.

In sum, Washington-based interest groups suffer from a number of disadvantages, including their relative lack of negative sanctions and congressmen's feeling that they are not entirely legitimate unless connected with their constituencies. The result is that the lobbyists tend to work through actors in the system who are in a better position, notably fellow congressmen and constituencies. They develop close working relationships with their friends in Congress, including sympathetic congressmen and staff people, particularly aides to committee members who are active in areas of interest.[10] These flows of influence are presented diagrammatically in Figure 5–1.

Scholars have attempted for years to determine how important constituency is in the legislative process. It is instructive in understanding its importance to observe the actions of participants in the process other than the legislators themselves. When they desire something intensely, and when efforts at simple persuasion fail, they go to work through congressmen's constituencies. They stimulate their members, they inform key campaign contributors or district opinion leaders, an administration will subtly threaten loss or delay of district projects and grants, and so forth. Admit-

Figure 5–1 Flows of Interest Group Influence

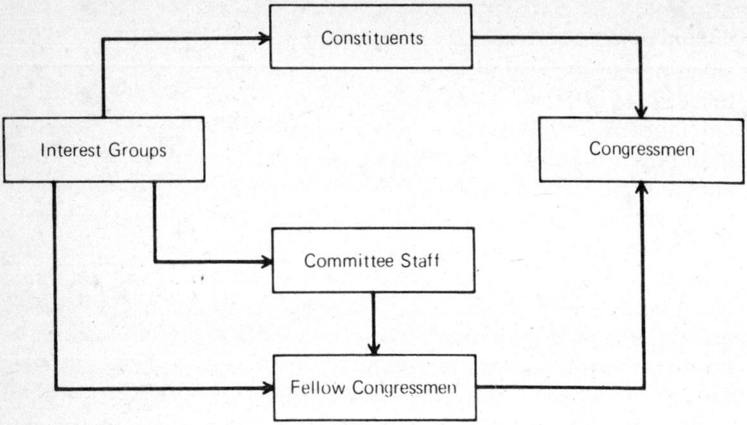

tedly, working through the constituency may not succeed, since the strategy would depend on a number of variables discussed in Chapter 2. But it succeeds often enough to make it worth the attempt. At any rate, the behavior of participants in the process, as they attempt to influence congressmen's votes, appears to indicate that congressmen do place weight on communications from their constituencies.

It is also worth noting that a concentration on congressmen's decision-making leads both an analyst and a strategist in a search for intermediaries by which communications can be effectively transmitted to congressmen. In this case, it appears that congressmen are most directly influenced by fellow congressmen and by their constituencies. Thus, those who would want to influence them tend to work through these other actors. The decision rules of the influencee determine the strategies to be used by the influencer. Attention to these decision rules and use of a decision-making approach contributes to an understanding of influence strategies in the broader legislative environment.

Timing

To mount a massive lobbying campaign such as the one the education lobby put together requires a tremendous amount of advanced planning. Constituent elements of the lobbying organization or coalition must be primed to move into action at the appropriate time, which involves a considerable period of disseminating information about the legislation and the parliamentary situation, in addition to arranging for a sequence of activities. It takes a lot of time and energy to "crank up the machinery," as one lobbyist put it. That is why an essential ingredient of most of the effective lobbying campaigns discussed in the previous section was the groundwork that had been laid months in advance. Furthermore, the machinery once evolved is very cumbersome. If a lobby has gone through the effort of priming its members for months to deal with one parliamentary situation and then an amendment's form is suddenly changed or a new amendment is offered, it is difficult to shift the gears and deal with the new situation. Massive lobbying machinery, in other words, is slow to evolve and hard to maneuver or adapt once it is in place.

The cumbersome nature of lobbying is one reason why House leadership decisions on timing can become so crucial. Timing decisions can be used to help or hinder lobbying efforts, and even when not intentionally used, have the same effects. Education and Labor Committee Republicans, for instance, have "learned through bitter experience," as one put it, that a well-timed delay in House consideration can be used to mount a lobbying campaign against their proposals. In both the education and poverty areas, the interim between announcement of their amendments and floor consideration has been used to notify constituents of the programs and to bring communication to House members from their districts, often to the effect that their proposals have been defeated. In the session under study, therefore, they adopted the tack of keeping their amendments secret until the literal eve of floor action. In the case of the Elementary and Secondary Education Act extension, the strategy worked. But in the case of their poverty bill amendment, when in the words of one committee Republican, "we sprung it at the last minute," the committee Democrats marched to the Speaker's office and refused to call up the bill. The resulting delay gave the constituents of the poverty program time to mount their campaign against the amendment which, in turn, contributed to its eventual defeat. Timing by the leadership can also be used to hinder lobbying efforts, as was the decision to take up the surtax bill before a recess which would have allowed anti-extension interest groups time to stimulate contact with congressmen while they were home. As one administration supporter admitted, "We could only lose by waiting."

One oft-repeated proposition about the timing of interest group lobbying is that it "comes too late."[11] By the time the machinery is swung into operation, the argument runs, most congressmen have made up their minds and committed themselves or a fast-moving parliamentary situation has changed. The result is wasted lobbying effort. Many of my respondents agreed. Two said that lobbying efforts on tax reform came "too late to do any good." Another said of telegrams favoring the bill to prevent the Federal Communications Commission from banning cigarette advertising, "Of course I had already made up my mind against them." Another said he had already decided in favor of poverty workers before he got their letters. In his own colorful way, one lobbyist predicted that a commission recommendation coming too late for congressional action would not "amount to a fart in a whirlwind."

The emphasis on decision-making in this study leads to a different, albeit speculative, conclusion. Many lobbying campaigns, to be sure, fail for lack of organization and membership commitment, to say nothing of the fact that they may simply be unpopular among congressmen. But I am not convinced that lobbying is generally timed poorly, for several reasons. First, many congressmen truly do not decide until a couple of days ahead, or even the moment of the vote, when they must. Until the committee reports a bill and they know the general shape of the major amendments that will be offered, many are hardly aware of the issues involved. Lobbying too early, then, would be pointless. Second, lobbies characteristically concentrate on the committees first, where they generally have as good or probably a better chance of achieving their goals than they would on the floor. Only when the committee acts unfavorably will they take the fight to the floor. But again, adverse action is not certain until late in the game, and even if it were anticipated, a lobbying campaign would be viewed as prejudging the committee's action. As one lobbyist explained his group's failure to act until the last minute: "We were committed on this thing for months. But we had the hope, right up to the day of the vote, that the committee might do it the right way. Right up to the minute they reported the bill, we thought there was some hope." Third, congressmen whom a lobbying effort cannot persuade have probably made their decisions far in advance of the vote, or have such a rigid position on the issue that they might just as well have done so. Those who are susceptible to the campaign are the very ones who decide late. Hence, late lobbying, while perhaps missing the bulk of congressmen, is timed to reach exactly those who are most reachable. Finally, even those already committed in favor of the influencer are often in need of some reinforcement. For them, the last-minute campaign keeps them properly committed and activates them, so that they talk to others and stay on the floor for votes themselves.

Strategic timing is obviously a rather delicate art. Another problem is that striking the bargains necessary to winning a legislative battle should also be timed properly. There is not always time to bargain, since congressmen become locked into positions from which they cannot gracefully escape. One major lobbying tack, in fact, is to try to obtain hard-and-fast commitments in advance of a vote, so that the bargaining which takes place closer to the vote will not affect those votes that already have been pinned down. Education lobbyists, for instance, placed great stress on obtaining concrete commitments to vote for the amendment raising spending levels. One Appropriations Committee member complained, "They hit all these guys and got commitments for the Joelson amendment before something else was worked into shape." These same Appropriations Committee members, far in advance of floor consideration of the water pollution abatement funding, were circulating among their friends asking them to remain uncommitted until they saw what the bill reported from committee would contain. Indeed, one Republican told me that he would have stayed with the committee on the pollution abatement funding if he had not been publicly committed in advance of the time he was approached. In another instance, one staffer said that the Education and Labor Committee majority "compromised too late" on the ESEA extension. "They wanted five years and committed the leadership, and then they realized that they didn't have the votes. By that time, Mrs. Green had talked to quite a few people and they were locked in with her on it." These timing constraints on bargaining affect the leadership as well as the followers. One leader in a given battle explained: "The word had gone out that we were going to resist all amendments. If we'd turned around and supported one of them, we'd have confused the troops. You have to avoid that. They start to question your leadership, and they lose interest if they're confused." Indeed, bargaining flexibility runs counter to the widely shared norm in legislative bodies that once a commitment is given, it will be honored. As one congressman said, "It's an inviolable rule that once you give your word, you don't back down on it. The whole system depends on it."[12]

The Head Count
Central to any mass lobbying effort in anticipation of a floor vote is a head count of congressmen's voting intentions; for, against, or undecided. This head count is used to decide whether to mount a fight in the first instance, and if so, gives some guidance about where persuasive efforts must be directed, and about the extent of compromise needed. One informal measure of a lobbyist's reputation is his perceived prowess at obtaining accurate counts —it appears to be the supreme compliment to his strategic ability to say that he "knows how to count heads." A terrific amount of lobbying energy is expended in establishing a reliable head count. The major lobbying campaigns mounted in this session—HEW funding, surtax, ABM, and others—all stressed to their amateur participants the importance of obtaining a good count, to the point where congressmen were occasionally much irritated at the efforts to pin them down to a definite commitment.

The mechanisms of head-counting involve, as one party aide put it, "coordinating the counts that various people are taking." One congressman is best approached by one organization or individual; another congressman by another. The lobbying campaign becomes a central clearing house where the various lobbyists and amateurs trade information and develop their tactics. Several lobbyists told me in some detail about how they went about head-counting. The one following quotation will suffice to give a rather complete picture:

If you're interested in the machinery, we have meetings of all the lobbyists and compare notes. On something major like this, we coordinate very closely. We went down the list of congressmen, and each guy took his assignment. Each guy took members that he had worked with. Maybe he's been dealing with him through his work with his committee, or maybe he has a political association. Then we'd call back in, when we had a good reading on what the guy was going to do. We'd start filling in the list—definitely for, definitely against—and the list of undecideds narrows. Then we start to go to work on them. All this time, we've been getting people back in their districts to write—telegrams, phone calls, delegations, everything. We particularly put it to the undecideds. Then we get down to a couple of days before the vote and we had only 20 or 30 still to work on. We crank it up on these guys.

As this lobbyist illustrates, the head count is at the center of the effort in several respects. First, it may determine whether an effort will be undertaken at all. One lobbyist who never even started a campaign said, "I knew we were going to get beat on this anyway. I can count." Another said he had not concentrated on floor action at all, because he was confident that he would win by a comfortable margin. Under those fortunate circumstances, said one lobbyist, "You leave it to the committee to carry the ball." In both winning and losing cases, the outcome is perceived as certain, and a lobbying campaign is thus thought to be hardly worth the effort, time, and good will expended. An inaccurate head count, secondly, can throw off some major decisions. One lobbyist said that several non-Washington amateurs who were counting for him fell victim to what he described as a congressman's "con game," or his assurance that he was all for them in general terms without committing himself on the specific proposal at hand.

Third, once the campaign is launched, the head count determines where it will be concentrated. Those who are with the lobbying campaign are simply counted and then left alone until the day of the vote. One congressman said that he had told education people he was with them, and they replied that they knew that but were just checking. On the other side, many congressmen are written off. It was quite common for respondents to tell me that they had not heard anything from lobbies because they were "too independent" or "hopeless" or something of the sort. Bauer, Pool, and Dexter argue that, in fact, lobbies write people off much too readily.[13] In my observations, congressmen who are on the fence receive the most attention.

Finally, once the heads are counted and the persuasive efforts completed, it remains for the lobby to make good its campaign by seeing that its people get to the floor and stay there for the crucial votes. Education people, for instance, told congressmen they would be sitting in the gallery during the votes on the HEW appropriation bill, and did so in force, both to see that their supporters were there and to check on how they voted on non-record votes. For those congressmen who were not on the floor, they went to their offices to urge them to attend, repeatedly if necessary. Massing in the gallery did swing some votes. One congressman said that he would have voted against the Joelson amendment but for the fact that his bishop was staring at him. To cite a different example, those favoring increases in funding for water pollution abatement did not engage in this sort of lobbying, which undoubtedly would have picked up the two votes necessary to reverse the negative outcome.

It must be stressed, however, that interest groups do not usually crank up the kind of campaign which we have been discussing. In part, this is because they may not feel intensely enough about an issue to go to the great trouble that such an effort obviously takes. Most of the time, they may also want to take their chances wtih the committees, to avoid using what little stock of credit they have. If the outcome appears to be certain, furthermore, either for or against the interest group, they are not likely to engage in this kind of vigorous activity. So in the normal course of events, these mass lobbying campaigns are likely to commence only when the group or coalition of groups cares enough and when the outcome is in doubt. These kinds of issues, of course, may be precisely those that are most interesting to study from the point of view of obtaining a picture of interest groups at work. Study of them at least illuminates what a lobby *can* do, given the proper initial advantages and the appropriate circumstances.

Concentration of lobbying effort on only a few congressmen illustrates a general problem with some literature on lobbying: It tends to consider the activities of lobbies concerned with congressmen across the board, when actually the lobbying is directed intensively at only a few people. It may well be true that the average congressman neither is approached by, nor pays much attention to, interest group representatives. But the average congressman is unimportant in a strategic sense. The crucial one is undecided, on the committee, or otherwise in a pivotal position. Such congressmen do receive a good deal of attention. In fact, one lobbyist claimed that some of them even seem to seek it, in that they appear to hang on the fence waiting for persuasive efforts and expenditure of credit on them.

This concern with the strategic focus of activity has some interesting implications for the way in which participants in the legislative system perceive the process, especially by comparison with the academic's perception. Most political science work concentrates on explaining the total vote in the House on a series of roll calls. Actually, participants are interested in quite a narrow subset of the total vote, particularly those votes which are in doubt. They would regard explaining total variance as a useless enterprise, partly because they cannot affect the votes of a substantial number of congressmen, but also because they believe that they can account for the nonswinging part of the vote intuitively and very easily, without resorting to very sophisticated techniques of analysis. It is the swing votes that are hard to explain conceptually. Said one surtax fight leader, "When you're talking about three or four votes, just about anything is important." This is one reason why practitioners will often tell academics that "you can't predict it," or "it's too complex to systematize." So accustomed to ignoring the predictable and concentrating on the unpredictable, they have a much more volatile and complex view of behavior than one who deliberately concentrates on the total picture.

One illustration of this point was the Sikes amendment to add planes for Nationalist China to the foreign aid bill. I heard from several sources that the sponsors of that amendment were, as one congressman put it, "twisting arms all over the floor," and that its passage was due to such pressure. In a sense, the final result was indeed determined by such activity, since there was a narrow group of waverers who could have gone either way. But that group made up a very small percentage of the total House. In such a case, the final result actually is determined both by the waverers and by the original distribution of attitudes within the House which made the vote close in the first place. Journalists and participants would tend to concentrate on the waverers, while political scientists would tend to concentrate on the general distribution. A complete accounting of the events would include both.

Appeal to Congressional Values

A lobbying campaign is most likely to be successful when it is aimed at preexisting values that congressmen hold. One close sympathetic observer used as an example the campaign for the bill which was aimed at preventing the FCC from banning cigarette advertising:

What you do is try to figure out first what the congressmen's interests and problems are. Then you make an appeal to those interests. In this case, they could start with a group of tobacco-district congressmen. For them tobacco is important, since actual jobs are at stake. They started with that core. Then there was a group who were worried about the usurpation of powers by the regulatory agencies. They could appeal to them on that basis. You gradually build your support by making these appeals according to what the congressman is interested in.

To cite another example, one initial advantage that education lobbyists have is that the general idea of supporting education is sympathetically viewed by many congressmen. One congressman said that the education lobby's geographical dispersion and discipline were "piled on top of being for education, for the kids. Everybody's for the kids. Labor seems self-interested by comparison, but when teachers want something, they can always say it's for the kids." Or finally, labor's opposition to the surtax extension was viewed by one source as capitalizing on several attitudes already held by Northern Democrats:

I think the main thing labor provided was some glue. When they took their stand, they provided a way for members to come around to being against it. After all, for many of them, it was a pretty easy vote. What the hell, the taxpayers are mad, it's a chance to get in a pretty healthy kick at Nixon, and you can embarrass the leadership in the bargain. There were a lot of reasons for voting against it. All it needed was some glue. Then members could add the justification that labor was against it, and that's handy for some of them.

Groups sometimes fail to achieve their objectives in part because they miss the things that interest congressmen about a piece of legislation under consideration. Many congressmen, for example, said that some issues raised by the education people in the Elementary and Secondary Education Act battle simply were not the major bones of contention as congressmen saw them. One showed me several letters written by district education professionals, which were highly general pleas for education programs nearly devoid of specific advice on the issues at hand, the length and form of the extension. He commented, "It's often like that." Lobbyists, however, present a different side of the picture, which emphasizes their difficulties in constructing arguments that appeal to congressional interests. One admitted that his organization shied away from mass campaigns, because they couldn't control the communications that would result: "The problem is that if you send out a general appeal to your membership to contact their congressman, you'll get Sister Penguin from Nothing, Illinois, calling her congressman and saying exactly the wrong thing. We try to be more selective." Another spoke of difficulties even in his own personal contacts on a matter in which his organization was heavily involved:

One basic problem was that congressmen and the press didn't understand the legislation and it was hard to get them to understand it. You'd go up to them and start talking about it: "Congressman, these programs are involved; a,b,c,d, and the amendment would do so-and-so to them." You'd start to go through this whole complicated thing with them, and after a few steps they'd say, "Say, what are you doing on Interior, Charlie? Heard of any good irrigation projects lately?" I don't blame them, or the press for that matter. It's awfully hard to be informed about things like this. Even the most conscientious ones can't.

We noted in Chapter 3 that congressmen often use fellow congressmen in a reality-checking sense. They have a general position, and simply check their position with colleagues of like persuasion to be sure that their perception of the situation and their decision is similar. If it is not, they search further in their decision process. Congressmen sometimes use interest groups the same way. They know which organizations are generally in agreement with them and which ones are generally opposed, and they use this bit of past history to help determine which side to be on in the current instance. One liberal Democrat said of the surtax extension, "It appeared that labor was against it, the NAM [National Association of Manufacturers] was against it, the bankers and finance people were for it, and big oil was probably for it too. That sort of lineup adds another reason why I'd be against." Another said that labor's lobbying against the surtax "solidified a lot of congressmen in what they were thinking of doing anyway." Even if lobbying only reinforces, that effect is highly important.

One implication of this importance of preexisting agreement between congressman and interest group, or at least a willingness on the part of the congressman to listen, is that some groups find themselves at a severe disadvantage which no amount of clever strategic planning can overcome. Supporters and opponents of the Joelson amendment to the HEW appropriation bill alike described the package as "an attempt to tie the unpopular programs to impacted aid," as one put it. "A lot of these programs have no constituency." If such programs were not in the same package with the popular impacted aid, many amendments designed to fund them at higher levels would have gone down to defeat. Another incident was consistent with the proposition that lobbyists are at a severe disadvantage without previous agreement. During debate and voting on another bill, I saw several lobbyists in the hall attempting to persuade congressmen who agreed with them to stay on the floor and vote for amendments to the committee bill. Repeatedly, congressmen rushed out after the quorum call and despite entreaties to "help us on this," headed for their offices. It was clear that many congressmen did not place this bill ahead of many other claims on their time, and there was little, if anything, the lobbyists could do to change that fundamental fact.

In fact, there are occasions on which Washington-based lobbyists judge that their involvement would be counterproductive. Liberal groups consciously decided not to be active in both the Powell seating and the Un-American Activities Committee matters on the theory that, as one lobbyist said, "Outside pressure wouldn't help that much. In fact, it might hurt." Their judgment is often correct. One congressman, smarting over the opposition of the postal workers to postal reform proposals, fumed, "They've been absolutely arrogant. I got so pissed off at them that I voted against their pay raise." The lobbyist faced with a decision concerning his organization's involvement in a given campaign, of course, finds the judgment about whether involvement would be counterproductive a rather difficult one to make. Bauer, Pool, and Dexter argue that they too often opt for noninvolvement.[14] Their problem is that they often have no reliable way of predicting the outcomes of their actions.

Strategic Limitations

It is appropriate to end a section on interest group strategies with some commentary on the limitations of groups. Actually, we have already considered several conceivable limitations. A group with some connection in the congressman's constituency, for example, is in a better position to influence him than one without such a connection. Groups that are not dispersed geographically, therefore, find themselves at a comparative disadvantage. Another limit, just considered, revolves around the ability of a group to play on some preexisting attitude that congressmen hold. Many groups simply find that congressmen either do not agree with them or do not care about their interests, and this initial disadvantage is very difficult to overcome.

We should add to these possible limits on group strategies one not yet considered: possible problems of internal organization. As Bauer, Pool, and Dexter argue, a premise of interest group action is quasi-unanimity.[15] Without at least a modicum of unanimity, a group finds itself unable to take a position and base legislative action on it. Congressmen and lobbyists alike, for example, appeared to agree that one reason for the inaction of agriculture groups in the battle over the $20,000 limitation on payments was that each group was faced with some internal dissension, especially between large and small farmers, which prevented them from taking a forceful position. As one congressman said, "If they can't get their own members together, they aren't going to start lobbying."

Once in action, furthermore, interest group leaders do not have all the flexibility they would like in making tactical shifts and other decisions. This constraint is partly due simply to the sheer mechanical problem of manipulating a scattered and undisciplined membership. Once having embarked upon a course, and having started the lobbying process along that course, it is extremely difficult to shift in midstream. But more than that, feelings within the organization headed by the lobbyist may prevent him from making compromises or otherwise adjusting himself to a developing strategic situation. One education lobbyist, for instance, said that they were obliged to support one change in their own HEW appropriation bill amendment "for internal coalition reasons." Their leaders among congressmen, however, overruled them, because it was "their strategic judgment that it would just confuse people and they wanted to go for opposing all amendments."

These strategic constraints on the leadership of interest groups highlight the possibility that in more general terms, there may be some tension between leaders and followers within interest groups.[16] As one Hill staffer said, "The Washington office develops its own interest, and it doesn't necessarily correspond to the people back home." Under such circumstances, a lobbyist may adopt the stance that he should go along with his membership. Said one, "The fact is that I've got this job and I like it here. So I'd better look after my members." Other groups believe they should attempt to "educate" their members and lead them in new directions. Labor union leaders, for instance, take on many legislative fights that their members at least do not demand, and perhaps may even oppose. One labor lobbyist said of the surtax:

This is a pocketbook thing. Laboring men are interested in it. It's not like a lot of the other stuff we get involved in. Somebody has to carry the ball for these social programs, so we do it. But you go in to a congressman and say the laboring men are really hot for some welfare program, and he'll say, "Hell, man, I've been in these union halls in my district and they don't give two hoots about this."

Despite the limitations under which the lobbyist is forced to work, too much concentration on his limitations would be immobilizing. In a sense, it is well to be active even if one loses some legislative battles in the short run. Education people, for instance, lost the early battle to have the Elementary and Secondary Act extended for five years. But in a longer-run view, they had served notice on congressmen that they were vigorous and would be a force to be reckoned with when something more major was on the agenda. This notice turned out to be quite useful in the later battle over education funding in the HEW appropriation bill. Early lobbying action, though a failure in the short-run sense, trained amateurs in lobbying techniques and helped structure congressional perceptions of the education lobby, which rebounded to a long-run benefit.

COMMITTEES AND AGENDA

This book is directed at congressmen's voting decisions on the floor of the House. In adopting this focus, we perforce must slight other arenas of the legislative process which might be quite different from the floor arena. It is well to consider two such arenas of interest group influence briefly: the standing committees and the legislative agenda.

Committees

For a number of reasons, interest groups probably concentrate a greater share of their efforts on the committees that are shaping legislation of interest to them than they do on the floor.[17] First, many decisions affecting their vital interests are made in committee, even though the bulk of congressmen would consider them as minor decisions. Firms or associations interested in maintaining tax preferences, for instance, sent many letters, telegrams, and even personal delegations to members of the Ways and Means Committee, even though non-Committee congressmen reported rather little contact. The members of the Appropriations subcommittee dealing with education funding similarly received very high volumes of mail from education people protesting the low funding levels in the administration budget. Observers often overlook highly important lobbying, just because it is highly concentrated, perhaps only on two or three important individuals.

Another reason that lobbyists concentrate on the committee is that mounting a mass campaign to influence events on the floor is often logistically out of the question. Given the possibilities for failure, given the fact that cranking up the machinery is terrifically time- and energy-consuming, and given the unwieldy character of the machinery once in action, the lobbyist often concludes that he had better use less costly means on the committee and rest content with what he obtains in that arena.

Third, committee members are likely to be more sympathetic with the interest group goals than is the common member of Congress. As Masters points out, committee assignment procedures emphasize the congressman's own preferences and the help the assignment would give him in reelection.[18] The result is that profarm congressmen serve on the Agriculture Committee, proeducation on Education and Labor, prodefense on Armed Services, and so forth. Once congressmen who are sympathetic to the clientele of the committee are assigned to the committee, lobbyists then develop rather close working relationships with their friends on the committee. Education and Labor Committee leaders, for instance, had a long working relationship with the major education lobbyists, and were in constant touch with them on both campus unrest legislation and the HEW appropriations battle. In another case, one agriculture commodity lobbyist told me that he had talked personally to about half the committee members concerning a bill which interested his organization, a fraction which he could never approach on the floor either in terms of numbers or in sympathetic hearing. Or disproportionate numbers of tax-writing committee members come from oil-rich states, giving tax preferences for the oil industry a greater chance in committee than they have on the floor.

The major consequence of these patterns of access and communication is that interest groups concentrate on the committees and the committees tend to protect their clientele. This committee sympathy may not extend to the whole House. Farm payment limitations are defeated in committee and added on the floor. The voting rights bill remains intact in the Judiciary Committee and is seriously amended on the floor. Perhaps the best example of the session is college unrest legislation, which was bottled up in the committee by prouniversity congressmen when reporting a bill was seen by higher-education people to be potentially disasterous in the emotional climate of the time. Another way to state this consequence is that the committees tend to protect the minorities which constitute their clientele against injury from majorities.

The Agenda
Decision-making does not involve simply a choice among specified alternatives, but includes also the processes by which the alternatives are generated, and even a step before that, by which the agenda of subjects for consideration is determined. It may be that interest groups have as great an influence on the agenda as on the choices which congressmen make among specified alternatives on the floor.[19]

Interest groups, first of all, sometimes serve as attention-focusing mechanisms or filters for information. They bring matters to the attention of sympathetic congressmen who would not otherwise have taken any action. Many congressmen, for instance, told me that they learned about provisions of the tax reform bill from lobbyists whose organization members would be hurt by a particular reform. Lobbyists also attempt to withhold other information that would be damaging. One, when asked if his organization could live with a given amendment, replied, "Well, I don't want that word getting around, but that's what it amounts to." But several congressmen who were responsive to that group's point of view expressed their conviction that the amendment would be very damaging.

Much of lobbying, futhermore, is aimed not at obtaining a specific output, but rather at simply keeping a subject on the decisional agenda. The Poor People's Campaign sponsored by the Southern Christian Leadership Conference, for example, was probably a "failure" in terms of concrete accomplishments, but it did serve to keep the subject of poverty in official Washington's consciousness at least for a time. Unless a matter is up for consideration, the interest group is hardly in a position even to begin to achieve more concrete goals. Simply keeping a subject on the agenda is no mean accomplishment. With so many routine and nonroutine matters vying for congressmen's attention, simply penetrating their perceptual field is extremely important, whether or not one wins in the short run. Education lobbyists, for instance, "lost" the fight on the Elementary and Secondary Act extension, but in the process kept their interests in the forefront of congressional attention, which was useful in the subsequent fight over the HEW appropriation. The obverse was true as well: One congressman, who voted for both increased education funding and increased pollution abatement funding, attributed the defeat of the latter to a lack of a vigorous, identifiable group such as educators, saying, "Who speaks for pollution abatement?"

One consequence of lobbyists' concentration on attention-getting mechanisms and agenda is that they have a rather distinctive view of congressmen's decisional processes. Partly because those who would want to influence congressmen concentrate on the rather narrow segment of congressmen who are undecided, and partly because they are preoccupied with tactics of influence, they come to conclude that congressmen respond to "pressure." Congressmen themselves, naturally enough, maintain that they do not. One lobbyist told me, for instance, that a given congressman had stayed away from a crucial vote because his organization's people in his district had requested him to do so, while the congressman assured me that his absence was due to nothing of the kind, that a fortuitous set of circumstances and previous commitments had forced him to be out of town. Another congressman said that he had prodded an organization to do something, whereas the personnel in that organization told me that they were planning it all along and they simply structured it so that the congressman got the publicity. A committee aide maintained that clever timing of a given bill was designed to catch Republicans off balance and result in the liberal Republicans voting with Democrats, while one of these target liberal Republicans assured me that he had been against the Democrats on the matter right from the start and that the timing couldn't possibly make any difference.

Neither congressmen's nor lobbyists' views of the decisional process are necessarily more accurate. They simply convey their perceptions of different phases of it. The congressman concentrates on choices among prescribed alternatives, since that is what confronts him on the floor. Interest groups may very well not have much direct influence on these choices. But influencers concentrate on information manipulation, agenda-setting, specification of alternatives, and like matters, which lead them to a rather different view of the process. To use an example that is closer to the experience of many readers of this book, consider a professor who has chosen the textbook for the large introductory course he teaches. He would tell an interviewer how he chose among the various books available, what his criteria were, and how the winning book seemed to meet these criteria better than the others. The salesman of the winning book, on the other hand, would tell how he cleverly got his textbook into the hands of the professor, how he called on him just at the right time and made the effective appeal, and so forth. Each does accurately describe a part of the process. The book salesman did put his book into the professor's decisional field, but the professor did freely choose it from among the alternatives.

I have argued elsewhere that winning candidates for office congratulate themselves on a clever campaign, while losers rationalize their defeats by blaming them on factors beyond their control.[20] This "congratulation-rationalization effect" appears to be in operation here as well. Successful influencers like to think that their activities made the difference in a given outcome. As one congressman who tried to push his committee in a given direction confided: "There were some things in the committee bill that we proposed. Now, I don't know why they were put in there. It could be that the Chairman just decided on his own to put them in. But it's always tempting when you have initiated these things in the first place to look to the final product and assume that you had some influence on it." As in the electoral case, it is also convenient to attribute one's defeats to factors beyond one's control.

CONCLUSIONS

As compared with other possible influences on congressmen's votes, interest groups are among neither the most important nor the least. Congressmen appear to consider them quite important, but they do not necessarily vote according to their wishes. This rather mixed picture leads away from global statements about group importance toward an emphasis on the conditions of group influence. In particular, interest groups appear to have slight influence on congressmen's voting decisions unless the groups are connected with their constituencies in some fashion. Another circumstance in which they seem to be more important is with issues of high salience. It also appears that, because interest groups in floor fights are more active from the left than from the right, they turn out to be closer to the positions of liberal Northern Democrats than to those of Republicans or Southern Democrats. In addition, we have speculated that they may exercise greater influence in committee decisions and on the legislative agenda than in floor choices themselves.

Congressmen's decision rules have important effects on strategies of influence in the legislative process. Working through constituents and fellow congressmen, for instance, is a systematic adaptation of strategy to congressmen's modes of decision, as are the adaptation of lobbying timing to a congressional decision rhythm and the central importance of head-counting. The importance of understanding congressmen's voting decisions extends beyond the bounds of those decisions themselves, toward an understanding of the legislative environment and the legislative system in general.

NOTES

1. Harold Lasswell, *Politics: Who Gets What, When, How* (Cleveland: Meridian Books, 1958; originally published 1936).
2. Arthur F. Bentley, *The Process of Government* (Chicago: University of Chicago Press, 1908); and David B. Truman, *The Governmental Process* (New York: Knopf, 1951).
3. Raymond A. Bauer, Ithiel de Sola Pool, and Lewis Anthony Dexter, *American Business and Public Policy* (New York: Atherton, 1964), chaps. 22–23.
4. Lester W. Milbrath, *The Washington Lobbyists* (Chicago: Rand McNally, 1963), chap. 17.
5. Mancur Olson, Jr., *The Logic of Collective Action* (Cambridge, Mass.: Harvard University Press, 1965), chap. 1.
6. "One" group may actually be a coalition of several who are working toward the same end in a coordinated fashion, such as the "education lobby."
7. David B. Truman, *The Governmental Process* (New York: Knopf, 1951), pp. 34–35.
8. For an argument about this adaptation in the context of the budgetary process, see John W. Kingdon, "A House Appropriations Subcommittee: Influences on Budgetary Decisions," *Southwestern Social Science Quarterly* 47(1966):68–78.
9. Raymond A. Bauer, Ithiel de Sola Pool, and Lewis Anthony Dexter, *American Business and Public Policy* (New York: Atherton, 1964), chap. 24. See also Donald R. Matthews, *U.S. Senators and Their World* (Chapel Hill: University of North Carolina Press, 1960; also Vintage Books), pp. 182 and 191. Bauer, Pool, and Dexter also discuss the technique of a lobby working through other political actors in chap. 25.
10. In this context, I am not referring to the personal staffs of congressmen across the board. In fact, in Chapter 7 we will discover that they are not very influential in congressmen's voting decisions. The staffs which are part of this communication pattern are those who serve congressmen who are particularly active in the legislation and who are likely to be informants for other congressmen. These may be committee staffs, or may be personal aides of active congressmen who are assigned work on the legislation under consideration.

11. For an example in the literature on interest groups, see Raymond A. Bauer, Ithiel de Sola Pool, and Lewis Anthony Dexter, *American Business and Public Policy* (New York: Atherton, 1964), p. 431.

12. For a discussion of the congressional norm of reciprocity, see Donald R. Matthews, *U.S. Senators and Their World* (Chapel Hill: University of North Carolina Press, 1960; also Vintage Books), pp. 99–101.

13. Raymond A. Bauer, Ithiel de Sola Pool, and Lewis Anthony Dexter, *American Business and Public Policy* (New York: Atherton, 1964), pp. 350–351.

14. *Ibid.*

15. *Ibid.*, chap. 22. A further discussion of group cohesion is found in David B. Truman, *The Governmental Process* (New York: Knopf, 1951), chap. 6.

16. Truman, *ibid.*, chap. 7. Lipsky finds some of this tension in protest groups. See Michael Lipsky, "Protest as a Political Resource," *American Political Science Review* 62(1968):1148–1151.

17. The importance of interest groups in the Ways and Means Committee arena is discussed in John F. Manley, *The Politics of Finance* (Boston: Little, Brown, 1970), pp. 233, 319, 356, and 381.

18. Nicholas A. Masters, "Committee Assignments in the House of Representatives," *American Political Science Review* 55(1961):345–357. A more recent work on committee assignments is David Rohde and Kenneth Shepsle, "Democratic Committee Assignments in the House of Representatives," *American Political Science Review* 67(1973):889–905.

19. Edward Schneier, "The Intelligence of Congress: Information and Public Policy Patterns," The *Annals* of the American Academy of Political and Social Science, 388(1960):16. See also Donald R. Matthews, *U.S. Senators and Their World* (Chapel Hill: University of North Carolina Press, 1960; also Vintage Books), pp. 181, 192–193; and Raymond A. Bauer, Ithiel de Sola Pool, and Lewis Anthony Dexter, *American Business and Public Policy* (New York: Atherton, 1964), p. 413.

20. John W. Kingdon, *Candidates for Office* (New York: Random House, 1968), chap. 2.

6

Administration and Executive Branch

It must by now be a commonplace generalization in nearly all introductory American government textbooks that national government policy-making is centered on the executive branch. Congress has lost to the executive at least its ability to initiate legislation, the argument runs, if indeed it ever had such ability. Congress may also have lost a good deal more, particularly in its inability to affect program execution, and even to alter substantially the proposals which come before it for action. This abundantly familiar argument is firmly entrenched in the lore on American politics.

The executive branch, of course, is a rather far-flung and disjointed entity. It is an admittedly frightful simplification to treat it as some kind of unit. While we do examine disagreements within the executive branch in this chapter, however, for the most part we will treat the administration and executive branch together as a single cue or source of influence. While such a conceptual tack would make no sense in a study of the federal bureaucracy, it does in this study. As an object in the environment, the administration together with the executive branch is in fact treated by most congressmen on any given floor issue as a single entity most of the time. By the time a measure reaches the floor of the House, there is generally one voice which is speaking for the administration, if any voice at all is speaking.[1]

OVERALL IMPORTANCE OF ADMINISTRATION

For all the leadership which the executive branch and administration supposedly give to Congress, individual congressmen pay them remarkably little heed in their voting decisions. Administration officials are mentioned spontaneously in the interviews one-quarter of the time. In fully 61 percent of the decisions, the administration is of no importance whatever, and is of minor importance in 21 percent, of major importance in 14 percent, and is determinative in 4 percent of the cases. As compared to other actors in the system, the administration thus seems to exercise rather little influence on congressmen's decisions.

As a predictor of congressmen's votes, furthermore, the administration position fares even more poorly. As in the case of the party leadership, we use the objective position of the administration, rather than the congressman's perception of that position, as the predictor of the vote. Given an administration position, the probability that the congressman will vote with that position is only .56, which is little better than chance occurrence. The product-moment correlation between the administration position and the congressman's vote is only .12; again a low figure. But the partial correlations do not affect this relationship, indicating that the meager administration influence persists in the face of controls for other variables. The partial correlation in the six-variable model is .12, and in the four-variable model, .19.

It must be remembered that the field work for this study was conducted during the first congressional session of the Nixon administration. Given the time that it takes for a new administration to become legislatively operational, it could be that as time went on, administration importance would increase. Actually, however, this did not occur to a great extent, at least during the whole of the first session. The administration is regarded by congressmen as somewhat less important at the very beginning of the session than it is in the middle or toward the end, but this is simply because a couple of the votes at the beginning were internal House procedural votes, on which the administration could not be expected to intervene. In terms of the correlation figures, the administration position as a vote predictor actually declines as the session progresses. For early, middle, and late in the session, the product-moment correlations are .26, .16, and —.05, respectively. It may of course take more than a single session for a new administration to begin pushing through a legislative program. But there were many measures, even in the session under study, in which the administration took an acute interest, and at least within that session, administration importance did not rise as the session progressed.

There are a number of reasons why the administration and executive branch do not appear to be highly important in the voting of congressmen. One of the most obvious is partisan: In view of the fact that this was a period with a Democratic Congress and a Republican president, one could hardly expect the agreement to be high or the administration to be highly regarded. This possibility is considered explicitly in the section entitled "Party Differences," where party differences in administration importance are discussed. Aside from that, however, there are a number of more institutional explanations for the findings.

First, there is a certain antipathy between the branches of government.[2] Administrators view congressmen as rearranging and even ruining good programs for "political" reasons, while congressmen view the "bureaucrats" as not being sympathetic to their problems and too rigid in adjusting to political realities. One civil servant, after going through his own sordid pressure group theory of politics, said, "I have a very dim view of Congress. I wouldn't trust a single man up there." And for his part, an aide to a liberal congressman said: "The administration is sort of suspect. They've got their axe to grind, and you can't always trust what you get from them. The White House is even worse. There's a lot of suspicion between Congress and the executive branch." This suspicion was evident in the feeling of one Southern Democrat as he defended impacted aid to school districts: "The people who don't believe in it are the do-gooders down in HEW. The reason they don't is that they can't get their hands on the money. It goes right to the child, and no bureaucrat can siphon off some of it for a study or something."

Part of the distrust of bureaucrats is congressmen's realization that administrators have their own political problems, and that solutions to these problems are not necessarily compatible with congressmen's interests. Administrators are in the position of having to defend their agency, lest organizational morale slip dangerously, and of having to protect the agency's clientele. Congressmen realize this problem, and tend to discount the administrator who appears to be behaving in such a fashion, particularly if the congressman would be inclined to be against him in the first place. One congressman said of Agriculture Secretary Hardin's opposition to the farm payment limitation, "He's got his constituency to protect, and he was doing it." Another said in the same instance, "He's got his own problems over there, and they aren't mine." Another congressman explained away Office of Economic Opportunity Director Rumsfeld's defense of a simple extension of the poverty act by saying, "Rumsfeld has his own problems too. He has to do what he's doing in order to avoid a complete rebellion in his own agency."

PARTY DIFFERENCES

Thus far we have been considering the subject of administration influence in the legislative process in something of a political vacuum. But of course even the most casual observer of Congress would say that the administration wields more influence on members of the president's political party than on the other party's members. This is one advantage that does set the administration off from others who would wish to influence congressmen. In the session under study here, Republican congressmen often referred to their stake in the administration's success, their unwillingness to embarrass the administration, and their personal loyalty to the president. Part of this attachment to the administration was grounded in the fact that they had personally campaigned long and hard for this administration and thus had quite an emotional commitment to a Republican president once elected, especially after a long, frustrating period of Democratic control of the presidency. The following quotations, dealing with several different votes, will suffice to present the flavor of this commitment:

This was something the Nixon administration wanted, and I'm a Republican. I support this administration, and I'll go along with them when I can.

I really believe that Nixon is a good president. I'll support him unless it's just something that I utterly can't take.

I'm a party man. I worked hard for Nixon, and I want to see him succeed.

The Nixon administration wanted this, and I wouldn't want to do anything to embarrass them.

As a party matter, this means a great deal to the administration, and it's *my* administration. If there would be something that I was sure they were wrong on, I'd go against them. But when in doubt, I don't want to see the administration embarrassed.

Reinforcing this loyalty to the administration on the part of congressmen in the president's party is an active distrust of the actions and motives of the opposition. The opposition is seen as being fully prepared to undercut the administration, and by extension, the president's followers, including congressmen. Several Republicans, for instance, charged that the Education and Labor Committee voted out a five-year extension of the Elementary and Secondary Education Act simply to "box in" the administration and prevent it from making changes. Several others pointed with some bitterness at Democratic opposition to the surtax, after having supported their own president on it only a year earlier. Finally, one Republican said of his vote against increases for water pollution abatement:

It would have been good politics for me to vote for it. But the administration is trying to resist this budget-busting. So it would be bad politics for the administration. I ended up going along with the administration. It has become clear that the crowd on the other side of the aisle is doing this over and over again. They want to bust the budget and embarrass the administration, and I won't be sucked in by that.

This partisan distrust, of course, was reciprocated in kind on the Democratic side. One Democrat accused the administration of adjusting the bookkeeping on the national debt "just to get credit for lowering the debt." Another said of administration pressure for a surtax extension, "The fact of the matter is that they want to have some extra revenue to finance ABM." Another replied to the charge of "budget-busting" in these words: "Oh, these are the same people that will vote a billion extra for the navy and millions for a C-5A with a cracked wing." A Democrat summarized the distrust: "When my guys are in the White House, the vote is close, and they need my vote, then I'll go along. But when theirs are there, and they've always voted against my guys out of political motives, then why should I go along with them?"

Administration Change and Divided Government
One test of the proposition that the president has a special claim on the members of his own party is to observe differences in the behavior of those party members under administrations controlled by presidents of different parties. It happened that the session under study presented us with just such an instance, since President Nixon took office at the beginning of the session. There were, in fact, several votes in which substantial numbers of Republicans voted with the administration, after having cast their votes in the opposite direction previously. One of the first was the vote to increase the debt limit. Traditionally Republicans vote very heavily against such increases. Yet a heavy majority of

the Republicans voted for it when their own president requested them to do so. The process by which they rationalized this change was highly interesting, and is examined in Chapter 11. But one Republican congressman, with his tongue firmly implanted in his cheek, remarked: "See, before, I could vote against the debt limit in good conscience, I categorically disagreed with Johnson's approach, so I could be utterly irresponsible. Now I find myself in the embarrassing position of having to be responsible, and it's not easy."

Many other such examples occurred during the session. One Republican changed from support to opposition on the farm payment limitation, as a result of "some new information that came along," namely the arguments of a trusted source, Secretary Hardin. As he said, "The more I thought about it, the more I figured that these arguments were persuasive and that I had made a mistake last year." Many Republicans voted for foreign aid programs for the first time. Several observers agreed that one reason for the surprise victory of the poverty program officials in defeating the package amendment to the authorization was the personal loyalty of many Republicans to a former House colleague, OEO Director Donald Rumsfeld. One Republican summarized the change that had come over his voting behavior:

I've been less negative in my voting this year than I have been in the past, for two reasons. For one thing, it's my administration. For another, I think I can influence events, because of a changed administration and a changed atmosphere in the House. Even though I lose a lot of battles, I'll go along more than I did before, because then there was nothing to make me anything but negative. Now there is.

Similar changes took place among Democrats, in the other direction. The dramatic shift from support to opposition in the case of the surtax is one example. Another, the foreign aid bill, was discussed by one Democrat on the committee: "It makes a difference which administration it is. During the years of Democratic presidents, we tried to keep the authorization just as high as we could. We took a licking on the floor sometimes by keeping that bill high. Now when Nixon's in, we don't have to be worried about making him look good. So we can avoid taking this licking by cutting the bill more."

In addition to being a session in which there was a change in party control of the presidency, this was also a session of divided government, with the presidency controlled by Republicans and the Congress by Democrats. Observers of American government have long concluded that such instances of divided government lead to stagnation and inability for either party to accomplish its goals. This study provides a number of examples of such problems due to interparty conflict, several of which were just discussed. But it also provides some basis for speculation on the conditions under which divided government may lead instead to actual expediting of governmental action. One such condition is the case in which the program under consideration is perceived to be popular in the country at large. In such a case, far from producing stagnation, divided government encourages each party to beat the other to the punch and take the credit for the resulting legislative passage. The tax reform bill was the leading case in point in the session under study. One Republican remarked that "the Democrats took the ball away" from the administration. As Republicans and Democrats vied for leadership of the tax reform legislation, action was accelerated. Another condition of legislative action under divided government is the case in which the president's party furnishes a core of votes for his program due to party loyalty, and enough members of the other party join this core on ideological grounds to furnish a winning margin. The administration's voting rights bill, for instance, prevailed with a coalition of Republicans and Southern Democrats. Or the president's welfare reform legislation passed with a coalition of Republicans and liberal Democrats. Some of these measures might actually have been stalled, but for the core of Republican votes that a Democratic president could not have delivered. As discussed in Chapter 4, furthermore, the president's party also often has a small group of congressmen ready to change their votes in his favor if the outcome is extremely close.

Some Quantitative Evidence

There is good evidence for the proposition that the wishes of the administration are much more involved in the voting decisions of the president's party members than in those of the opposition party. In my data, while Northern Democrats spontaneously mention the administration in their accounts of their decision only 14 percent of the time, and Southern Democrats do so in only 12 percent of the cases, Republicans, without prompting from a question, bring up the administration position and activity fully 42 percent of the time. For spontaneous mentions, this is a very high figure and suggests strongly that the administration is much on the minds of congressmen from the president's party. It is also a considerably higher figure than the comparable measure for the party leadership (20 percent among Republicans), indicating that party voting is more a function of the administration than of the party leadership position.

In addition to the spontaneous mentions, there are striking differences between the parties in the evident importance of the administration in the congressman's vote. As Table 6–1 shows, the administration is more likely to be involved in the thinking of Republicans, and the only substantial number of cases in which the administration is of major or determinative importance is among Republicans. In sharp contrast, Northern Democrats exhibit virtually no regard for the administration position, and Southern Democrats little more. This substantial party difference holds true within all subsets of other variables—within seniority, district, delegation, and other categories.

It is interesting, however, that the sharpest party differences in administration importance are found among the congressmen with the least seniority. Junior Democrats are particularly prone to ignore the administration, and junior Republicans are particularly prone to pay attention to administration requests. While the party difference is still evident at the most senior levels, it is more muted.[3] Apparently, senior Democrats, more than their junior colleagues, have become accustomed with years of experience to turning to Democratic presidents for leadership, while senior Republicans are accustomed to avoiding presidential leadership. When the administration changes, patterns of party response change as well, but more slowly for senior congressmen of both parties than for legislators of lower seniority. Several junior Republicans, furthermore, had just been elected on President Nixon's coattails, and saw their own future as being particularly dependent upon his success.

Table 6–1   Party and Administration Importance

Importance	Northern Democrat	Southern Democrat	Republican
None	84%	71%	39%
Minor	10	23	29
Major	7	4	25
Determinative	0	2	7
Total %	101%	100%	100%
Total *n*	74	52	96

Turning now to the objective agreement between administration position and congressman's vote, various measures of the predictive value of administration position are presented in Table 6–2. In general terms, similar party differences emerge in the actual voting behavior of the congressmen. Northern Democrats display the same disdain for the administration position: There is actually a slight negative relationship between the administration and the vote, and the probability that a Northern Democrat will vote with an administration position is considerably lower than chance.

Quite obviously, Republicans agree with their administration more than do Northern Democrats. Two features of the Republicans' behavior, however, should be noted. First, the correlation is not particularly high, even for Republicans. While the administration apparently exercises more influence on Republicans than it does on Northern Democrats, its influence still is not nearly comparable to that of fellow congressmen or constituency. Actually, this is the same result that can be found in Table 6–1, where, in spite of the important party differences, Republicans consider the administration of major importance one-third of the time, and claim no administration influence on their vote in 39 percent of the cases.

Second, the influence of the administration on the Republicans is evidently greater than is that of their own party leadership. In the partial correlation presented in Table 6–2, the bivariate relationship between administration and vote for Republicans persists when other variables are controlled. But a relationship of similar magnitude in the case of party leadership is actually reduced to a negative value. The Republican party leadership as a vote predictor, therefore, does not display the same resilience as the administration.

Finally, in spite of the fact that Southern Democrats showed far less tendency than Republicans to consider the administration important in their decision (see Table 6–1), their objective

Table 6–2   Party and Agreement Between Administration and Vote

	conditional probability	product-moment correlation	partial correlation[a]
Northern Democrat	.34	—.02	—.11
Southern Democrat	.66	.18	.26
Republican	.68	.28	.23

[a] Correlation controlling for the other five variables in the model.

agreement with the administration position is similar (see Table 6–2). The juxtaposition of the two tables indicates that Southern Democrats, in contrast to Republicans, vote with the administration position, not out of party loyalty or overt influence by the administration, but rather out of simple attitudinal agreement. In other words, Southern Democrats do not consciously take account of the administration position, but rather simply agree with it more often than do their Northern colleagues. Republicans, on the other hand, agree with their administration more often than Northern Democrats and also take account of it in a highly self-conscious fashion. When they vote against their administration, they are more likely to evidence some discomfort over it. One Republican, voting against his administration on the surtax, exclaimed: "Politically, I'll do everything I can to support this administration. I like what they're doing. It pains me to be against them."

Regardless of the overall agreement between Republicans and their administration, it is probably true that a president enjoys a store of credit with his own party members which he can tap in case of emergency. When a measure is of central importance to the administration and the vote is close, enough votes will be found within the president's party to carry the day. These few votes are insignificant in such overall figures as are presented in the tables, but are highly crucial in certain salient political outcomes. It is also evident that the administration intensity is balanced against the congressman's own intensity, much as congressmen balance constituency intensity.[4] Republicans repeatedly said that they would go along with their administration "when I can," or "when in doubt." It is clear that the administration has a greater claim on its party members when their own intensity is weak.

The magnitude of the president's store of credit with members of his own party probably depends to a degree on the standing of the president in the country at large and, in particular, that standing in the legislator's constituency. If the president is highly popular, especially with party regulars back in the congressman's district, that popularity represents a resource upon which the president can call. If the president is quite unpopular, then one observes members of Congress trying to put as much distance between themselves and the president as possible. This tendency may even reach the point where identification with the president becomes a political liability. Republicans found that true during the Watergate era, for instance, and many of them paid the price in 1974 with significant loss of votes and even with loss of their seats. Support for President Carter's proposals among Democrats also may be affected by his standing in the public, particularly in relatively active or attentive parts of the public that have a special impact on representatives' thinking. Of course, there have been multiple sources of Carter's apparent troubles in dealing with Congress, but the vicissitudes of public support may have something to do with his ability to call forth the loyalty of his fellow partisans.

INTRAADMINISTRATION COMPLEXITY

Even as the constituency is an object of considerable complexity, so is the administration characterized by substantial differences among its various components. Normally, intraadministration conflict does not surface in a setting of legislative voting, because of a well-developed set of norms and clearance procedures which attempt to insure at least public unanimity. On occasion during the session under study, however, conflict did become evident, particularly conflict between the White House and the agency most concerned with the legislation. Aside from actual conflict, furthermore, it is of some interest to observe which agency of the administration is involved in the congressman's decision and how often the White House itself becomes involved.

Speaking of objective disagreement within the administration on issues on which the administration had any position, there was conflict between the White House (including the Bureau of the Budget) and the agency concerned with the legislation in 21 percent of the decision cases under study. These included the Sikes amendment to the foreign aid bill to add planes for Nationalist China, on which several Republicans both pro and con told me that Secretary of Defense Laird had spread the word among Republicans that he favored the amendment, even though it developed that the White House opposed it. Another case cited by several respondents was OEO Director Rumsfeld's battle against the Quie-Green-Ayres amendment to the poverty bill, in which the White House formally supported the director, but informally let their reservations about his position be known. A few respondents, finally, said that the Office of Education privately disagreed with the official opposition to increased funding for education programs. In such cases, agencies will often not only privately communicate their discomfort with administration positions, but will also leak information to their friends on the Hill that will be useful in waging the battle.

Given this sort of conflict between agency and White House, congressmen voted with the agency position 61 percent of the time and with the White House in the remainder of cases. Contrary to expectation, in terms of which actor they choose—agency or White House—the party differences are too slight to be mentioned. Apparently, when there is such a conflict, the congressman concludes that he may choose between administration actors with little constraint, and most of them make the choice according to their policy attitude or constituency position.

Finally, in cases in which there is no conflict between agency and White House, how often does the White House become involved, and how often do they leave the legislative work to the agency? Of the cases in which the administration took a position without intraadministration conflict, only the agency was involved in the administration activity 44 percent of the time, while the White House became involved in addition to the agency in the remaining 56 percent. It is quite likely that in issues of lower salience than those considered in this core sample, the White House would be involved much less frequently. But many of these were of major administration interest, and counting instances of conflict with the agencies as well as no conflict, the White House was involved in nearly two-thirds of the cases on which there was an administration position.

ADMINISTRATION STRATEGIES

In many ways, the administration can be conceived as being similar to any other interest group seeking to influence the legislative process. Most of the consideration of administration strategies, therefore, would repeat the discussion of interest group strategies in Chapter 5. The administration just like any lobbyist, for instance, works in part through congressmen's constituencies and makes very similar calculations about the timing of a lobbying campaign. In fact, as we considered strategies of interest groups in Chapter 5, we specified that they could apply just as easily to any actor seeking to influence congressmen including groups, administration, fellow congressmen, and others.

There are other respects, however, in which the administration as a lobbyist differs from interest groups. The administration has an emotional hold in party loyalty over a numerically significant set of congressmen, which is probably unlike the hold of any interest group. It also has both more efficient means for communicating to congressmen and a few sanctions not available to most groups. Instead of reviewing the entire range of administration strategies, therefore, we will concentrate on those respects in which the administration is different from other actors that would seek to influence congressmen.

Loyalty and Prestige

In Chapter 5, we emphasized that lobbies tend to write off as hopeless certain congressmen who disagree with their positions, and to concentrate instead on their supporters and those who are wavering. The administration does the same. Many congressmen cited instances in which they received no communication from the executive branch because they were known to disagree with administration positions, or cases in which they were repeatedly contacted when they were undecided.

One major implication of this strategic reasoning is that congressmen from the president's party are contacted more than those from the opposition. Their party loyalty, which they evidence in their account of the importance of the administration in their decision, would indicate that they would be fertile ground for administration persuasive efforts. The president and his administration have no such claim on the members of the opposition party. So, as one old-time Democrat put it, "They'll twist the Republicans' arms, just like Johnson twisted ours." The president has an added advantage in the simple prestige of the office. For members of his own party, it must be more difficult to resist an appeal from the occupant of the highest office in the land than it is to resist one from practically any other potential influencer.

Communication Patterns

Some of the time, administration officials communicate directly with congressmen voting on the floor, without intermediaries. Donald Rumsfeld, as did his predecessor as Director of OEO, personally spoke to a substantial percentage of the House in his successful attempt to preserve the poverty program intact. Secretary Hardin also came to the Hill to talk to congressmen about the agriculture payment limitation. On the days of several votes that were of interest to the administration, liaison personnel would populate the hallways outside the chamber, talking to congressmen as they arrived or calling them off the floor. One sponsor of a major amendment to an administration measure told me that, as the afternoon wore on, congressmen who had been committed to him drifted away in response to the urgings of administration people outside. The ultimate in direct communication is a call or meeting with the president himself, such as the breakfast meeting which he held with a number of conservative Republicans to persuade them to vote for extension of the surtax.

This ability to communicate directly with congressmen, in part because of party loyalty and the prestige of the offices held, sets the administration somewhat apart from other interest groups seeking the influence congressmen. But as a number of respondents pointed out, such a political resource is expendable and thus must be preserved. One staffer said of possible calls from the president, "You want to do that as an absolute last resort. If he does it too often, he'll use up that technique in a hurry." Administration strategists, therefore, often work through others in the system, attempting to obtain the same results without expending their stores of direct contact. Congressmen, particularly Republicans, often told me that the administration's wishes did have a substantial impact on their thinking, even though they had received absolutely no direct communication from them. Indeed, of the Republican decisions in which the administration was of major or determinative importance, there was no direct administration communication in 55 percent.

One of the intermediaries used, as in the case of interest groups, is fellow congressmen. But more often with the administration than with interest groups, the set of fellow congressmen through which administration wishes are communicated is the party leadership of the president's party. The Republican leadership would meet regularly with the president and other highly placed administration officials, and transmit their views to other congressmen. Republicans would often mention the party leadership and the administration in one breath, as if they hardly disassociated the two. One said in response to a question about administration contact, "We did have a whip check." Another said in response to a question about the party leadership, "I don't think the administration really cares about this." Without explicit evidence to the contrary, congressmen assume that the party leadership of the president's party is speaking for the administration, or at least speaking in a way consistent with administration policy.

While the Republican party leadership is the major Hill informant used by a Republican administration, on occasion other congressmen were used to transmit information. In the case of the poverty program, for instance, OEO officials apparently felt unable to trust the party leadership and instead worked directly and partly through an informal, nonparty whip system on the Republican side. At other times, other congressmen are simply used as a supplement to the party leadership. The word goes around communicating the administration position. Secretary of Defense Laird's private support of the Sikes amendment adding planes for Nationalist China, for instance, was communicated through his friends on the Republican side. Or one Southern Democrat said of the administration position on the Joelson amendment raising funding in HEW, "I heard they were against it. But I didn't hear from them myself. It was just the word that was going around." Congressmen receive such information, not only about the administration's position, but also about the intensity of that position, partly through the number of contacts made. A Republican congressman on the receiving end of pressure for the surtax said, "They were repeatedly after me. I've never seen such pressure."

Aside from fellow congressmen, another intermediary in the communication process, which is available to the administration far more than to ordinary interest groups, is the mass media. A statement made by the president at a press conference, for instance, is immediately picked up and much discussed on the Hill. The interpretation of such statements is a rather delicate art, learned through long experience. When President Nixon announced his support of OEO Director Rumsfeld, for instance, many Republicans interpreted it, not as active support, but as a lukewarm endorsement intended for public consumption and not to be taken seriously. Said one, "That was a very mild statement. He said what he had to say. Of course he has to support his director when asked."

Figure 6–1 summarizes the various indirect communication paths from the administration to congressmen. These patterns are similar to those for interest groups, since the administration also works through fellow congressmen, committee staffs, and constituencies. But in this case, fellow congressmen are augmented by the president's party leadership. Another new path, through the mass media, is also added here. Congressmen follow the media themselves, and the media also transmit information to

Figure 6–1   Indirect Administration Communication to Congressmen

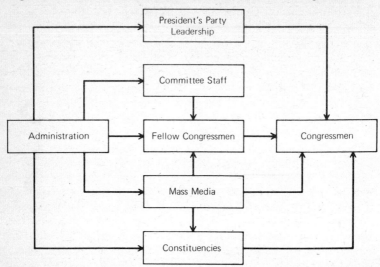

fellow congressmen and key constituents, who then contact the congressman. In the administration case, furthermore, in contrast to most Washington-based lobbyists, there is more direct communication with congressmen which is not pictured in this diagram.

It is possible quantitatively to give some indication of the frequency of each of these various types of communication channels. First, there was no administration position communicated to the congressmen in this sample 41 percent of the time, either because the administration took no position or because its position was not passed along. (In 19 percent, the administration took no position; in the remaining 22 percent, there was a discernible position which was not communicated.) Having no position communicated for either reason took place more often among Northern Democrats than among Republicans: In 55 percent of the cases, Northern Democrats discerned no administration position, compared with 40 percent for Southern Democrats, and 31 percent for Republicans. As we might expect, therefore, the communication is better developed for the members of the president's party. Of the occasions in which an administration position was perceived, Table 6–3 shows that Democrats, more than Republicans, are prone to rely on informal channels such as the word going around among colleagues or statements read in the press, while Republicans look more to their party leadership than Democrats do. Letters and visits from administration officials appear to be spread fairly evenly among the party groupings.

Finally, it was fairly common, especially early in the session, for members of both parties to complain of the poor liaison between administration and Congress under the Nixon regime; Democrats by way of chastizing the administration and Republicans by way of pointing out how long it takes for a new administration to develop effective standard operating procedures. Said one Democrat, "I haven't heard anything from them all year. I've never even met [Liaison Chief] Bryce Harlow. And that's strange, because they need crossover votes and I'm one guy they could work on." Or consider the following Republican:

I'm told by guys downtown that it takes something like 18 months to get a new administration really geared up. Take the water pollution thing. We were after them for months and months to take a position on it. We waited and waited and heard nothing. Then the very last day, they come in saying that they're settling for $600 million and hope that we'll stick with them. It's too late then. We'd committed ourselves to the full amount.

Many congressmen contrasted this sort of liaison performance with the kind of operation that President Johnson maintained on the Hill. One aide described how it worked:

Table 6–3 Party and Communication

channel	Northern Democrat	Southern Democrat	Republican
Media or talk	64%	68%	39%
Republican party leadership	3	7	30
Letter from administration official	9	13	6
Visit from administration official	24	13	21
Personal contact from president	0	0	3
Total %	100%	101%	99%
Total *n*	33	31	66

Johnson had a terrific operation up here. They split up the Congress and each took a group. They were politically savvy, most of them from the home states, and yet informed and committed to the president's program. They would see these congressmen all the time. Maybe they'd blow a man's project loose from the bureaucracy one week, and the next week be talking to them about beautification. It was a continuing operation.

The importance of this continuing relationship was emphasized by one Southern Democrat, who was amused at the Nixon administration's sudden concern over the surtax extension: "I can hardly get them to answer their phone over there, and here was the number two man in the Treasury right in my office."

Using Administration Resources and Sanctions

A final feature of the administration which distinguishes it from other interest groups is that it presumably has several resources which it can use in influencing congressmen. One of these supposed advantages is sheer information. It is a commonplace in political science literature to argue that the executive branch possesses an overwhelming advantage in expertise and substantive information. As one congressman, who voted against the bill preventing the Federal Communications Commission from banning cigarette advertising, said, "How could I improve on the Surgeon General's report? I'd need a gargantuan staff."

Despite this presumed information advantage, however, congressmen do have ready access to independent sources of information that provide them with alternatives from which to choose. Even in the case of the Surgeon General's report, for example, tobacco lobbyists presented their friends on the Hill with a flurry of information and arguments designed to discredit the report. If there is disagreement about a given administration initiative, information on the side opposite from the administration position is brought by organized interest groups, independent experts, or even from leaks within the executive branch. Similarly, as pointed out in Chapter 2, the congressmen's own constituencies provide independent information on the operation of federal programs. So while recognizing the obvious executive branch informational advantage, the possible pluralism and diversity of congressional information sources must also be emphasized.

Beyond simple informational advantages, the administration is also in a position to grant or withhold favors from congressmen, partly in accordance with the congressmen's willingness to go along when needed. Several congressmen, in discussing the Johnson administration's lobbying operation, referred to the constant service to congressmen and the granting of various favors such as speeding district projects. Then, as one staffer put it, "When the time came, they could call in the chits." During the Nixon administration's battle for the surtax extension, there was a veritable flurry of accounts of administration reminders of projects pending and the like. Such tactics, of course, are used more on members of the president's own party than on the opposition. Opposition congressmen conclude that they are not likely to be favored by the administration in any event, and the threat of withholding favors is thus not highly powerful.

Even with the members of the president's party, furthermore, there must at least be considerable discretion in the use of negative sanctions. One Republican staffer said:

If they go in there and start talking about an irrigation project or a new post office or something, and then ease into the surcharge extension, that's one thing. But if they barge in there and say the president wants your vote, they'll get a hostile reception. It would do more harm than good. You know, when congressmen get up here, they become prima donnas. They're Caesars in a toga. You aren't just going to send some lower-echelon liaison man in to them and pressure them.

The president himself treads softly. Just before the surtax vote, he invited several Republican congressmen who were wavering to the White House for a breakfast meeting. The importance of the resulting soft sell was graphically illustrated by one of these congressmen, who finally did vote with the president:

It was interesting. He's very skillful. He started by asking us what we thought, and we all told him. Then he said, "I don't want you to vote against your conscience, but here's the way I see it from where I sit. I'd appreciate it if you could go along." If he'd said, "You'll lose a dam in your district," you'd say, "Hell with you, you dirty politician." But it's awful hard, the way that he did do it.

Negative sanctions, of course, are negative only if perceived that way by the congressman. But Republicans often claimed that they would not be swayed, even by an administration threat to withhold favors, because the supposed favor was not of great importance. One who voted for increased funding for education, for instance, when asked if the vote would hurt his chances of getting something he might want from the administration, replied, "Oh yes, but I'll pay that price." Another, discussing a delegation colleague, said, "He's concerned about patronage and things like that. I'm not oriented that way, so it wouldn't make any difference to me." Once again, however, it is a matter of weighing his own intensity against that of the administration. On the ABM vote, for instance, one dissident Republican told me, "They had votes to burn on this, so I don't think it'll go against me too much. On a closer vote, it would be different."

ADMINISTRATION INITIATIVE

Finally, it is possible that concentration on floor voting fails to capture the full extent of administration influence in the legislative process. The old saw goes, "The President proposes, Congress disposes." In the process of proposing, the administration might influence the agenda and alternatives that congressmen consider.

Several examples of the generation of information and proposals from the executive branch occurred in this session. One member of the Appropriations Committee, for example, told me of the manner in which the amount of $600 million for water pollution abatement was arrived at:

Very quickly, in our full committee meeting, nearly everybody decided that 450 was too low. There were several figures mentioned—750, the full billion. Finally, someone decided to call the department and ask what they thought. After a little while, they called back and told us that they couldn't spend any more than 600. This was because of the way the formula is set up. Now we had some reason, some argument for setting it at 600. We thought we could go to the floor and defend that figure.

In another example, the administration wrote sweeping amendments to the voting rights act, attempted unsuccessfully to get Republicans on the Judiciary Committee to introduce it, finally persuaded Minority Leader Ford to introduce it as a substitute on the floor, and obtained its passage in the House.

One limitation on the importance of administration initiative is the tendency for executive branch officials to anticipate Hill reaction to their proposals and to structure their proposals so as to minimize changes. To the extent that such anticipation occurs, it can be said that congressional attitudes have affected the product, since they affected the ways in which the proposals were framed. Wildavsky writes that in the budgetary process, for instance, agencies and the Bureau of the Budget anticipate what will go on the Hill, scaling down their requests so as to avoid having them cut too badly.[5] During the session under study, after it appeared that there would be substantial congressional cuts forthcoming in the defense area, Secretary Laird cut his own budget first, in what one major magazine called a "preemptive strike."[6] Or when the administration's proposal for a proportional plan for the election of the president was given short shrift by the Judiciary Committee, they quietly dropped it.

There is some doubt, furthermore, how much the administration initiates in general. In an interesting essay on the place of Congress in policy-making, Polsby argues that Congress, particularly the Senate, plays an important part in the process of incubating new ideas and initiating policy changes. Other scholars have also noted the importance of Congress in policy initiation.[7] In the session under study here, as Figure 6–2 indicates, there is a question about administration initiative in 11 of the 15 legislative measures

Figure 6–2   Categories of Initiative

True administration initiative: four cases (debt limit increase, surtax extension, ABM, and supplemental appropriation*)

Nonadministration initiative that prevails on floor: five cases (farm payment limitation, Joelson amendment for education funding, tax reform, cigarette advertising bill,** direct election of president)

Nonadministration initiative defeated on the floor in part by administration reaction: two cases (water pollution abatement funding, five-year ESEA extension)

Administration divided: two cases (OEO authorization, Sikes amendment to foreign aid bill)

No administration involvement: two cases (Powell seating, HUAC name change)

   *One key feature of the supplemental, the ceiling on expenditures, was not an administration initiative.
   **Strictly speaking, the cigarette bill was a response to regulatory agency threat of restrictions.

that form the core sample of this study. In some cases, initiative came from Congress or from nongovernmental actors. In others, the administration was not involved at all. In still others, the administration was split. But in only 4 of the 15 can it be said unambiguously that the initiative came from the executive branch. We are working with small numbers in this case, of course, and sources of initiative are admittedly difficult to establish, but this sort of finding is not consistent with the textbook maxims about the origins of proposals in the American national government.

There are at least two reasons why this result might have occurred. The simplest is that this was the first congressional session of a new administration, and that one could not expect a great deal of initiative so early. Perhaps a period later in the administration's tenure would produce a different picture. But second, it could be that Democratic presidents would be expected to initiate legislative proposals more so than Republican ones. Sundquist's study of postwar social legislation, for example, would certainly point in that direction.[8] This picture should not be overdrawn. The Nixon administration, even this early in its tenure, did make substantial proposals in the field of crime, welfare reform, and many other areas. And some of the cases of non-administration initiative (e.g., farm payment limits, tax reform) were started under Democratic presidents. But it could be that one reason why our conventional wisdom has found high degrees of presidential initiative is simply that the presidents studied happened to be Democrats.

One can speculate, therefore, that the proposition that the executive branch initiates legislative proposals is at least in need of further study, and may also be due not to advantages inherent in the executive branch, but rather to partisan control of administrations. Similarly, the textbook adage that Congress is a mere rubber stamp for administration proposals may be overdrawn. It has often appeared that way because the administration and the Congress were both controlled by the same party. But in a period of divided government such as the one under study, the adage comes up wanting. If committee chairmen in this session had been Republicans, they would undoubtedly have often appeared to be rubber stamps. Many of the patterns which we have traditionally attributed to institutional factors, therefore, may instead be functions of partisan and ideological conflict or consensus.

CONCLUSIONS

By any measure, the administration and executive branch do not appear to be particularly important in congressmen's voting decisions. Congressmen of the president's party pay greater attention to the administration than do those of the opposition party. This party difference is particularly strong among congressmen with low seniority of both parties, while differences between Republicans and Democrats at the senior levels are more muted. Even among Republicans, however, the correlations between administration position and congressman's vote are not very high, which indicates that congressmen of the president's party may think of the administration more, but that this advantage is not always translated into votes.

The strategic position of administration is much the same as that of interest groups, except that the administration has some political resources that most interest groups do not have. The president is capable of commanding awesome public attention, and enjoys a place in the thinking of members of his own party which most interest groups are unlikely to match.

These results may be affected to some degree by the fact that the study was conducted during the first session of the new Nixon administration. Executive branch importance might increase as an administration gears up a legislative program, although such a line of argument is not consistent with the fact that the administration's importance declined, rather than increased, as the session progressed. It is a plausible conjecture, however, that one might find greater administration activity and importance in voting decisions if the president were a Democrat. Congress might also appear much more the rubber stamp for the executive branch in the absence of the party rivalries which mark a period of divided government.

NOTES

1. A sampling of the literature on the relationships between Congress and the executive branch would include Wilfred E. Binkley, *President and Congress* (New York: Vintage, 1962); Joseph P. Harris, *Congressional Control of Administration* (Washington, D.C.: Brookings, 1964); R. Douglas Arnold, *Congress and the Bureaucracy* (New Haven: Yale University Press, 1979); Richard E. Neustadt, "Presidency and Legislation: The Growth of Central Clearance," *American Political Science Review* 48(1955):641–671; Neustadt, "Presidency and Legislation: Planning the President's Program," *American*

Political Science Review 49(1955):980–1021; a key study of the budgetary process, Aaron Wildavsky, *The Politics of the Budgetary Process* (Boston: Little, Brown, 1964); and a recent work on oversight, Morris Ogul, *Congress Oversees the Bureaucracy* (Pittsburgh: University of Pittsburgh Press, 1976).

2. Several scholars centered at the University of Michigan are currently engaged in a cross-national study of the relationships between parliamentarians and bureaucrats which considers areas of antipathy and cooperation. For a description of this project, see Robert D. Putnam, "The Political Attitudes of Senior Civil Servants in Western Europe: A Preliminary Report." Paper prepared for the Annual Meeting of the American Political Science Association, 1972. For this project in the United States, see Joel Aberbach and Bert Rockman, "Clashing Beliefs within the Executive Branch," *American Political Science Review* 70(1976):456–468; and Aberbach and Rockman, "The Overlapping Worlds of American Federal Executives and Congressmen," *British Journal of Political Science* 7(1977):23–48.

3. Of junior Northern Democrat decisions, 95 percent had no administration involvement at all, compared with only 27 percent for junior Republicans. Comparable figures for senior congressmen are: Northern Democrats, 72 percent; Republicans, 50 percent.

4. A discussion of the balancing of constituency intensity against the congressman's own intensity is found in Chapter 2.

5. Aaron Wildavsky, *The Politics of the Budgetary Process* (Boston: Little, Brown, 1964), pp. 21–31, and 41. John F. Manley discusses the same phenomenon in *The Politics of Finance* (Boston: Little, Brown, 1970), pp. 327–328.

6. *Newsweek,* September 1, 1969, p. 22B.

7. Nelson W. Polsby, "Strengthening Congress in National Policy-making," in *Congressional Behavior,* ed. Nelson W. Polsby, (New York: Random House, 1971), pp. 3–11; originally appeared in *Yale Review* (1970):481–497. John S. Saloma also discusses a concept of "secondary initiative," in *Congress and the New Politics* (Boston: Little, Brown, 1969), pp. 94–97. An example of the importance of Congress in initiative and other phases of policy-making is in Harold Wolman, *Politics of Federal Housing* (New York: Dodd, Mead, 1971), chaps. 1, 4, and 7. For a general statement, see Lawrence Chamberlain, *The President, Congress, and Legislation* (New York: Columbia University Press, 1946); and Ronald Moe and Steven Teel, "Congress as Policy-maker," *Political Science Quarterly* 85(1970):443–470.

8. James L. Sundquist, *Politics and Policy* (Washington, D.C.: Brookings, 1968). For a study of presidential activity and success over the entire sweep of U.S. history, see Jeffrey Cohen, "Passing the President's Program," Ph.D. dissertation, University of Michigan, 1979.

7

The Staff

Congressmen and observers have often felt that proper legislating imposes impossible burdens in terms of the amount of information one must digest. Much legislation is too complex, too involved, and in too great a volume for normal human beings to handle. A long-recommended means of dealing with this problem has been professional staff help. Adequate staff, the argument runs, could considerably ease the information burdens and the claims on the congressman's time. In the process, the staff could be expected to be an influence on congressmen's decisions of considerable importance, since they work with the legislators day in and day out, presumably have their confidence, and supposedly are in a position to furnish and withhold information, suggestions, and advice.

Staffs on the Hill, for all their potential importance, have been little studied. We know something about the recruitment and activities of professional staff, and are learning something about their place in the information systems of Congress.[1] But we know little directly about the influence of the staffs on important legislative decisions. This chapter, therefore, provides an opportunity to present some new information on the importance and activities of staff at least in a voting context. We will also examine possible changes during the 1970s.

OVERALL IMPORTANCE OF STAFF

In terms of the importance in voting decisions that congressmen themselves report, the staff is not at all prominent. Congressmen spontaneously mention staff as being involved in their decision only 5 percent of the time, the lowest figure for any actor in the system. In terms of our standard importance coding, the staff is of major or determinative importance only 9 percent of the time, and of no importance at all a full 66 percent, the highest percentage of all the actors.[2] In short, if staff members are important in voting decisions, their influence is either extremely subtle, or is restricted to those issues in which the congressman has a particular interest and asks his staff to do more extensive work.

Despite this overall picture, however, staffs apparently are noticeably more important for congressmen who are low in seniority or who come from competitive districts, as is seen in Table 7–1. The junior members of the House use their staffs more than do senior members or those of medium seniority. The importance of staff is still minor at the junior level, but they are involved more frequently there. Apparently, it takes some period of time for congressmen to develop either habitual patterns of voting or comprehensive sets of fellow congressmen to whom to turn for cues; in that period of feeling one's way, the congressman uses his staff more than he does after a few years in the House. While the consultation is again still of minor importance, congressmen from competitive districts also use their staffs more than others. Apparently, here because of political uncertainty back home, the congressman will consult with his staff more frequently, in order to check the possible political ramifications of his vote. Congressmen from safer districts, on the other hand, appear to have less of this sort of problem.

When one controls the impact of seniority for competitiveness and vice versa (as is presented in Table 7–1), one finds that each variable is related to staff importance independent of the other. The most junior congressmen pay about equal attention to their staffs regardless of district competitiveness, and the congressmen from the most competitive districts pay about equal attention to their staffs regardless of their seniority. But the differences among seniority levels are found in safer districts, and the differ-

Table 7–1 Seniority and Competitiveness, Related to Staff Importance

staff import- ance	competitive			medium			safe		
	jr.	med.	sr.	jr.	med.	sr.	jr.	med.	sr.
None	50%	47%	50%	67%	73%	81%	50%	85%	79%
Minor	35	53	36	22	24	19	33	9	11
Major	12	0	14	11	3	0	17	6	11
Determin- ative	4	0	0	0	0	0	0	0	0
Total %	101%	100%	100%	100%	100%	100%	100%	100%	101%
Total *n*	26	15	22	18	37	21	30	33	19

Abbreviations used: jr., junior; med., medium; sr., senior.

ences among competitiveness are found with greater seniority. The presence of either low seniority or high competitiveness, in short, tends to accentuate staff importance.

Despite the apparent neglect of staff in voting decisions, the objective agreement between the staff and the congressman's vote is quite high. Given that the staff is involved, for instance, the probability that the congressman will vote with the staff position is .88. The correlation between staff position and vote, furthermore, is .44. If taken at face value, these sorts of figures would place the staff as a good predictor of the vote and as of substantial importance in congressmen's decisions, at least as important as their constituencies. For a number of reasons, however, the general agreement scores must be interpreted differently. First, when one controls for the influence of other actors in the system, the partial correlation between staff and the vote drops to .19. This is a very precipitous drop, a greater difference between the correlation and the partial than for any other actor. Even though the original figure seems high, it appears that staff position does not have much predictive value independent of other influences on the vote. Second, when one juxtaposes the agreement scores with the congressmen's estimate of the staff's importance, the agreement being much higher than the perceived importance, it appears that agreement between the vote and the staff position is not the result of the staff's influence on the congressman.

As is true with subjective importance, there are differences in agreement scores among levels of district competitiveness. The staff is most important to those who come from the most competitive districts, as Table 7–2 shows. But in contrast to the subjective importance case, there are no regular differences among seniority levels.

Why does one find the rather high agreement between the congressman's vote and the staff's position, especially in view of the low importance which congressmen attach to staff participation? One major reason is that staff members are recruited partly

Table 7–2 Competitiveness and Agreement with Staff

competitiveness	correlation	partial correlation
Competitive	.59	.31
Medium	.41	.25
Safe	.33	.10

because of their general agreement with the congressman. Staff people themselves prefer not to work for someone with whom they fundamentally disagree, and congressmen reciprocate that feeling. Either they generally agree, or they find another job. One congressman said of his conversations with his staff about the surtax extension, "We talked it over. We always do. We're pretty much of like mind, though, so it wouldn't change me." In addition to the staff recruitment process which keeps dissident staff members away and weeds out those who have perchance been hired, staff people hesitate somewhat to challenge congressmen. Finally, as a technical matter in this analysis, aides are often coded as agreeing with the congressman when they did some strictly routine work such as keeping him informed and checking certain details. Such activity can probably not be usefully conceptualized as "influence," though for the purposes of the correlation model, it appears important.

As a result of the recruitment and the staff's self-effacement, congressmen often find their staffs reinforcing their original opinions. Said one, "I talked to Tom about it, told him what I was going to do, and he didn't disagree, so I guess it was all right with him." Said another, "I talked it over with them, and they supported me in what I already had decided to do."

On the rare occasions in which there is some disagreement between the congressman's vote and the staff position, the staff is always more liberal than the congressman, never more conservative. One congressman said his staff was against ABM but that he voted for it. Another said that he had "a pretty liberal bunch here, and I have to disappoint them from time to time," since he could not be as liberal as they would like and survive politically. I would speculate that this ideological direction is due partly to the greater liberal slant in the Washington professional community than exists in the home district circles in which the congressman is accustomed to moving. Congressmen and staff, in other words, circulate in somewhat different settings; the rare disagreements between them are due to the different socialization that results.

STAFF ACTIVITIES

By far the most common comment concerning staff activities related to voting was to the effect that the staff was not involved at all in the congressman's decision. The following quotations illustrate the prevailing view:

I don't have a staff like that. I'm the only expert in this office.

I never listen to them. They don't know me well enough. They read the mail, they watch how I vote, but that's all.

Maybe I should have the kind of staff that I bat ideas around with, but most of the time we don't.

I do the legislating here.

If staff members are involved in the congressman's decision, the types of activities in which they engage range widely, from the strictly routine and peripheral to, in a few cases, some truly substantial involvement. The minor activities include such things as devising a form letter to constituents about an issue before the House; checking with them to get the direction and volume of the mail or, as one put it, "to make sure I hadn't received a letter from an important constituent or something;" casual conversation around the office; and the like. Moving a step up in the importance of staff activities, some congressmen use an assistant to review the available information; do some clipping and underlining; and perhaps to prepare a kind of summary of the legislation, the major anticipated amendments, the major considerations which the congressman might weigh, and the like. One said, "This sort of thing is invaluable and I rely heavily on it." Another said, "It's bound to influence your judgment." Finally, and more rarely, one finds a case in which the congressman reports heavy staff involvement, generally in terms of the staff preparing an amendment to the legislation or something of the sort. One even went so far as to say of his legislative assistant, "I go by what he says."

It is possible to give some quantitative picture of the frequency with which these various staff activity patterns are in evidence. First, the staff was not involved in the congressman's decision 65 percent of the time. An additional 12 percent of decisions showed the staff was involved, but only to the extent of some conversation around the office, and not in any sort of formal work activity. In 6 percent of the decisions under study, the staff did some routine work, such as checking details and answering mail. The type of systematic screening assignment described above, involving reading reports and preparing a summary, was evident 11 percent of the time. In the remaining 5 percent, there was really heavy staff work and consultation. Most of the time, this heavy staff work involved committee as well as personal staffs. So in terms of these frequencies, in an overwhelming majority of the cases, the staff is either not involved in the congressman's decision or only peripherally involved.

STAFF IMPORTANCE: A RECONSIDERATION

There may have been a change in the importance of staff from the time the field work for the first edition of this book was completed. The decade of the 1970s certainly saw a very substantial rise in the number of congressional staff positions. Between 1967 and 1976, for instance, the number of staff members working for the committees of the House of Representatives grew from 589 to 1548. In the same period, the number of House personal staff members increased from 4055 to 6939.[3] The decade of the 1970s also saw the establishment of two new major staff agencies, the Congressional Budget Office and the Office of Technology Assessment; and the considerable growth and invigoration of two others, the Congressional Research Service and the General Accounting Office. All of these changes raise the real possibility that staff influence on legislative voting decisions is greater now than this chapter's portrayal would indicate.

Another argument for considerably increased staff importance since the late 1960s is the dramatic rise in the sheer number of votes to be cast in a session, which we discuss in Chapter 9. As the number of decisions has increased to unmanageable proportions, congressmen are obliged to rely more on their staffs simply as a way of keeping abreast of developments. The proportion of offices with aides labeled as legislative assistants, for instance, has increased. Some observers have also noticed that many legislators have resorted to short briefings by staff members as they are walking to the chamber to vote. Of course, any decisional shortcuts, such as taking cues from fellow congressmen, also come to assume greater importance under such circumstances. The desire of many new legislators to style their decision-making to be independent of party, presidential, or even colleague influence, furthermore, would lead them to rely on their own staff. The fact that a high proportion of the House was of relatively low seniority in the late 1970s, coupled with the observation presented earlier in this chapter that low-seniority congressmen are particularly prone to rely on staff, would also argue for greater staff importance than I found in 1969.

I would not want to overstate the magnitude of the change,

however. First, it could be that larger personal staffs are being used partly for various activities not directly related to floor voting, such as constituency relations, casework, and handling mail. If the volume of mail, requests, and other demands on a member's office has increased dramatically, and if members are interested in reelection, both of which seem likely, then some share of added personal staff is probably devoted to handling that workload, not to advising members about floor votes. To the extent that increased staffing may have impacted on public policy decisions, furthermore, it could be that the effects are to be found in arenas other than House floor voting. Increasing numbers of committee and support staff, for instance, might very well affect committee deliberations without changing the game on the floor a great deal. Even the use of personal staff for legislative purposes might be concentrated particularly on the member's committee work or on other causes which the member is pursuing, rather than on floor votes on subjects in which the member is not specializing. Fox and Hammond's summary of staff impacts,[4] for instance, concentrates on the priority areas of constituency service and subjects of specialization, rather than floor decisions. Finally, it is possible that staff is more important in the Senate than in the House, where the staffs are larger, the members are less specialized in their own right, and some of the Senators are more policy- and publicity-oriented than the average House member.

Without repeating an entire set of observations similar to the ones which I made in 1969, it would be impossible to be sure of the dimensions of the changes. On the one hand, it does not seem likely that staff has been propelled during one decade into a position of importance similar to such central influences as constituency or the congressman's own policy attitudes. On the other hand, the increased size of staffs, the increased number of floor votes to be cast, and the relatively low seniority of the House in the late 1970s all argue that staff importance has increased. I would conclude that staff probably constitutes a noticeably greater influence on voting decisions than my original observations indicated, although not so dramatically more important as to place them among influences of the first rank.

Finally, we have been conceiving of staff as an influence on members' voting decisions. It could be that we should arrive at an alternative conception of the staff role. It might be more fruitful to conceive of staff not as an influence *on* a member, but rather as an extension *of* a member. Because of the highly personalized hiring and firing practices, the strong tendency of staff and member to hold similar orientations and ideologies and even to have been closely associated prior to the aide's employment, and the close working relationship between staffer and boss, it may be more appropriate to think of staff and member as parts of a single decision-making unit than as separate entities. If that is a useful conception, then the issue of staff influence on votes becomes less important than it would be under an assumption of staff as one among several influences on decisions.

CONCLUSIONS

If we confine our attention to staff as an influence on decisions, treating that actor in the same way in which we treated others earlier, the degree to which the staff influences congressmen's voting decisions seems lower than the high agreement between the staff's and the congressmen's position would indicate. Low seniority and high competitiveness produce a greater reliance on staff, although the staff is not often of major importance even for those congressmen who turn to them the most.

These findings do not imply that staff is unimportant in the larger legislative process. For one thing, one would probably find greater staff involvement in voting decisions in the Senate than in the House of Representatives,[5] where offices are more amply staffed and organized for legislative work. Furthermore, if one were studying activities other than voting on the floor, staffs, even on the House side, would take on a greater importance. As my charts of indirect information flows from interest groups and administration to congressmen acknowledge, committee staffs and personal aides to congressmen who are actively involved in particular pieces of legislation are quite important in shaping legislative outcomes. It is also possible that staff importance increased during the 1970s. Still, staff is not among the most prominent influences on floor voting decisions.

NOTES

1. See Kenneth Kofmehl, *Professional Staffs of Congress* (Lafayette, Ind.: Purdue University Studies, 1962); and Samuel C. Patterson, "The Professional Staffs of Congressional Committees," *Administrative Science Quarterly* 15(1970): 22–39. A study of the place of staffs in congressional information systems is found in Norman Ornstein, "Information, Resources, and Legislative Decision-

making," Ph.D. dissertation, University of Michigan, 1972). See also Harrison Fox and Susan Webb Hammond, *Congressional Staffs: The Invisible Force in American Lawmaking* (New York: The Free Press, Division of Macmillan, 1977).

2. The one case of determinative importance involved a congressman who was tempted to change his mind on the floor, but stuck with his original decision because his staff man had worked so hard on his statement that he did not want to disappoint him.

3. Fox and Hammond, *op. cit.*, p. 171.

4. *Ibid.*, pp. 143–145.

5. A major theme emerging from Ornstein's work is that the staff is far more important in legislative decisions in the Senate than it is in the House. See Norman Ornstein, "Information, Resources, and Legislative Decision-making," Ph.D. dissertation, University of Michigan, 1972, chaps. 5–6.

8

The Media and Other Reading

Like most attentive citizens, congressmen follow the printed and broadcast media, and also may do some other reading, both of internal congressional documents and of other sources. There is some literature on the place of the mass media in political systems.[1] But as is true in the case of staff, we know little about the influence that written and broadcast media and other reading sources have on the behavior of congressmen.

OVERALL IMPORTANCE

We have no agreement figures for reading and media which are comparable to the correlations that are presented for other actors, for two reasons. As explained at the end of Chapter 1, congressmen's reading often is not fruitfully conceived as an independent influence on his decision, but rather as a channel of communication by which he receives information from other actors in the system. When he reads the committee report, for instance, fellow congressmen are communicating to him through the printed page. Or he may read of a presidential statement in the newspaper. Second, much of his reading does not explicitly take a position on the issue at hand, which makes it less useful as an aid to decision than it might otherwise be.

We are able, however, to code the apparent importance of reading in the congressman's decision. Congressmen spontaneously mention some reading they did 9 percent of the time, a figure comparable to that for the staff and party leadership, but considerably below that for other actors. They do not report reading anything having to do with the legislation 52 percent of the time. Reading is never determinative, and is of major importance only 17 percent of the time. Again, these figures suggest that reading is less important than constituency, fellow congressmen, and interest groups, but is on a par with the other system actors.

Part of the lack of really serious reading has to do with general search procedures, which we will consider in Chapter 9. Cyert and March maintain the decision-makers engage in "problemistic search," that they do not look for information unless presented with a problem which must be solved.[2] Congressmen evidence the same behavior. In the absence of a decisional problem such as uncertainty or incomplete information, they will not search, particularly through the printed word. One respondent, when asked if he had read anything on the farm payment limitation, replied, "No. This was an easy one for me." Another said about the ABM issue, "Actually, I didn't go out and read and study this too much, because my mind was closed." So congressmen save their reading, if they do any at all, for matters that are more important to them. One said about the Elementary and Secondary Education Act extension: "I've got too much reading to do as it is. I save my time for more complex matters, and this was really simple. And for my committee work. I don't read unless I'm going to make a speech on the floor or something. Besides, I've learned that congressmen don't like a guy who knows about everything."

There are no major differences among congressmen in their level of reading according to most of the standard independent variables such as seniority, party, and the like. But there is a difference between the most salient issues and the others. On high-salience issues, congressmen said they read something about the issue 68 percent of the time, compared with 34 percent for low- and 42 percent for medium-salience issues. Apparently, on votes such as ABM or the surtax, the combination of greater media exposure and greater need to search for information results in greater exposure to the printed word. But on less salient issues, these considerations are less important.

Finally, much of the reading that is done simply reinforces the congressman's opinion. This is due partly to his human tendency to selectively perceive what he reads, noticing that which agrees with his point of view and discarding that which disagrees. Several congressmen from small states who were opposed to direct election of the president, for example, cited a chart in the committee report which purported to show that the small states would lose power in the reform because it bolstered their view of the realities. Congressmen not only selectively perceive the media that they do read, but they select them in the first place for attention partly on ideological grounds. Conservative congressmen when considering the surtax extension, for instance, mentioned such publications as "*Barrons,* several financial services, stuff from banks and financial circles," while a liberal is more likely to subscribe to and follow other periodicals. Finally, congressmen often very consciously use their reading to reinforce their original opinion. One opponent of the ABM, for instance, described his reading thus: "I did quite a bit, yes, just to feel that I had a lot of information and arguments at my disposal in case someone questioned me." Another said about the poverty program, "I've read the materials OEO has sent over, but that's more by way of giving me ammunition than anything."

TYPES OF READING

To the extent that congressmen read anything about an issue that is up for a floor vote, much of this reading is internal to the Congress. It consists of the committee report, the *Congressional Record,* and similar sources. The committee report is a particularly useful source of information about the bill. It not only contains the committee majority's summary of the legislation, but also contains any dissenting views within the committee. Thus, the report is a relatively concise summary of the major decisions upon which the congressman is likely to be called to vote, together with information about the positions of the relevant congressmen. Its brevity and summary nature, its ready availability on the floor, and its usefulness as a kind of communication channel for members of the committee, make the report a particularly valuable source, if the congressman is inclined to do any reading at all. Of all the types of reading available, this one probably has more direct, immediate impact on specific votes than any other. In response to my interview question about whether they had done any reading on the issue, I sometimes received an offhand but interesting response similar to, "No, except for the committee report," or, "I looked at the committee report, that's all."

If the congressman wants to do other reading internal to the Congress, the *Congressional Record* and various committee materials, including hearings, can furnish him with more. Many congressmen either skim the previous day's *Record* or have their staffs do so, as a rather efficient way of keeping track of the day's happenings as well as supplying information regarding who is taking what position and for what reasons. The *Record* thus constitutes an important internal communicating device, and it is a far more efficient way of following the proceedings than spending time on the floor. The introduction of closed circuit television of the proceedings in each congressional office has, of course, altered this use of the *Record.*

For the congressman who wants to delve even deeper, the committee hearings provide a true gold-mine of information. In addition to the publicity and advocacy functions of hearings which have been observed,[3] it is important to remember that the hearings also simply provide congressmen with a mass of information, presented in the advocacy setting which many of them, as attorneys, prefer. Congressmen themselves believe that the hearings do provide them with the bulk of information needed to legislate, and the hearings do affect their decisions. One referred to the hearings as the "technical material" on the legislation, as distinct from the mass media and so forth. Another said, "There are voluminous hearings on this. Experts come in to testify, and Congress hears them. It's an invaluable source of information." However, the hearings are more useful to members of the committee who attend them than to nonspecialist members casting floor votes, due to their unmanageable volume.

In addition to this internal information, many congressmen, of course, pay some attention to the mass media. They may scan a number of newspapers and magazines on a regular basis, and the interviews often contained passing comments on this sort of activity:

I didn't do any special study of it. I read what I always read—*U.S. News, Time,* newspapers, you know.

I always read the *Post* and *Star,* of course.

I've read a lot of newspaper and magazine articles about cigarettes, just like you have. I couldn't give you a bibliography or anything.

One congressman summed up this sort of reading very well, referring to the ABM issue, which might be thought to be highly complicated in both technical and policy senses: "As far as information is concerned, we may get a few more pamphlets and things across our desk than the general public, but basically, it's the same information that's available to anybody. I read what any well-informed person would have read."

Some congressmen supplement this general media reading with somewhat more specialized articles in areas in which they have a particular interest. They may also instruct their staffs to keep a file of clippings from various papers, magazines, and more specialized journals, for reference when the time of the vote approaches.

Figure 8-1   Flows of Media Communication

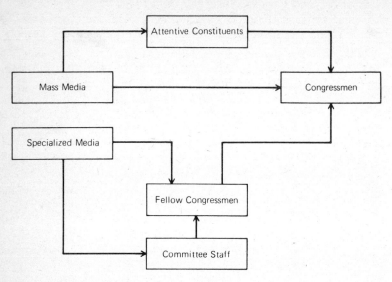

Thus far, we have referred to the media as if there were only a direct communications path to the congressman, as if he read the media himself. Actually, communications patterns involving media external to Congress are somewhat more complex. Figure 8-1 sets forth a plausible account of these paths. The mass media, of course, are followed by congressmen themselves. But they are also followed by attentive constituents, which results in an indirect path of their influence. Constituents pick up information from the media, which, in turn, forms one informational base upon which they base their actions with respect to the congressman. In fact, it is likely that the congressman himself follows the mass media in part *because* various attentive publics whom he regards as important do the same, and he must be able to explain his own positions and to discuss issues with them on the basis of their information.

In addition to the general mass media, there are more specialized publications, some of which the congressman also may read, but which much more likely are fed into the system via the congressional specialists, particularly committee staffs and committee members. These media would include trade publica-

tions, financial services, professional journals in various specialized areas, and the like. This "two-step flow"[4] even applies on
occasion to mass media. One very widely cited chart in a committee report, for instance, had been lifted from a weekly news
magazine.

One consequence of these media attention patterns is the
effect they have on those who desire to influence congressional
outcomes. As we observed in Chapter 5, it is difficult to get the
attention of congressmen long enough to have some sort of impact. Lobbies must therefore operate indirectly, through constituencies and through fellow congressmen. Another way of
operating indirectly is through the media, by getting publicity for
their positions. Interest groups attempt to do this, and the administration and president are in a particularly good position in
this regard. Congressmen do read the papers, and do pay some
degree of attention to the media that are likely to be important
to attentive constituents. The emphasis in many interest group
and administration campaigns on media publicity, therefore, is
occasioned in part by these sorts of congressional information
channels.

Finally, we can obtain some quantitative picture of the extent
and type of reading done by congressmen on issues that come
before them for floor votes. First, congressmen report no reading
that affected the way they thought about the issue slightly over
half of the time (51 percent). This figure probably somewhat
underestimates the importance of reading, simply because there
may have been reading which the congressman did, but which
he didn't think was important enough to mention. Particularly his
scanning of printed and broadcast media and his quick look at
the committee report probably failed to make their way into these
statistics with some frequency. At any rate, of the remaining
cases in which the congressman did report some reading, 32
percent involved reading only in the media, possibly supplemented by a few vague references to something else, but
basically their reading was restricted to the media. Forty-seven
percent of the cases in which reading was reported involved
some sort of internal congressional source like the committee
report or the *Congressional Record*. And in 21 percent of the
cases in which reading was reported, the congressman described
a truly extensive search, including books, reports, and the like.
These extensive searches were often made by those on the committee that considered the legislation.

INDIRECT MEDIA IMPACT

In addition to the actual act of voting itself, there are a number of ways in which the mass media have an impact on congressional policy outcomes. Two of them seem to be particularly important: interpretation and agenda-setting.

Interpretation

In Chapter 2 on constituencies, we noticed that congressmen are quite concerned about "explaining" their votes. They feel that they must at least devise a graceful way of explaining their votes, and in the absence of such a convincing explanation, they may even vote in a certain way because it would be too difficult to explain a vote to the contrary.

Much of the problem of explaining one's vote is directly tied to the media coverage which reaches the district. The media are capable of interpreting a given issue in such a way as to make it extremely difficult for the congressmen to vote in a way that appears contrary to their interpretations and still have a graceful explanation for the vote. House doves, for instance, found the Wright (D.–Tex.) resolution commending President Nixon for his search for a "just peace" in Vietnam particularly painful in this regard, because they knew that broadcast and printed media would interpret a vote for it as a vote for the president's policies, despite assurances from its sponsors that they did not intend it thus. In accordance with their expectations, even as liberal a paper as *The Washington Post* carried a headline the next day on the first page reading, "President Upheld on Vietnam," with the first paragraph reading, "The House . . . affirmed its support of President Nixon's peace efforts in Vietnam."[5] In the face of the resolution's wording, however, how was one to explain his vote against a "just peace"? Just such a consideration prompted several reluctant votes for it.

Media interpretations, therefore, are seen as structuring the sorts of explanations which can be devised for votes. Attentive publics, because they do pay attention to the media, are likely to resist explanations which do not square with the prevailing media view. Many congressmen, for instance, would find a vote against the limitation on agriculture payments rather difficult after the coverage that had been given the large payments all over the country. In another example, a member of the Ways and Means Committee told me that he would find it difficult to vote for a tax reform bill which did not include a reduction in oil depletion allowances, because of the tremendous symbolic importance that was attached to it as a result of continuous media exposure. Or as another congressman said of a nearby colleague who had received a good deal of local coverage on his position against the surtax extension, "When there's a member whose district overlaps with yours in media coverage, and he's aggressive in getting headlines, that's bound to affect the way you do things." Another congressman accounted for his last-minute switch from support of the surtax to opposition by saying:

I saw the way the vote was being interpreted in the press and by the people. A vote for the bill was being interpreted as a vote against reform. I'm strongly for reform, so I decided to vote against the surtax as my expression of this feeling about reform. I just saw that it was being interpreted that way. I hadn't seen it in that light before, so I voted against it.

The problems presented by interpretations in the media are further complicated by the perception advanced by many congressmen that the media are shallow in coverage and superficial in understanding.[6] Given inevitable time and space pressures to select a few things to report and to pare these down to manageable stories, it is little wonder that the media often present interpretations of congressional events that do not entirely please the participants. Many congressmen simply accept felt distortions as inevitable, while others will go to some lengths to try to "educate" the press. After having spent the better part of the morning with a writer for a nationally respected newspaper, one congressman told me: "You have to explain these things in great detail to these reporters. I have to spend a lot of time with them. This guy doesn't know anything about ———, and I just have to lead him by the hand." Another said, "The press and the people back home only present things with the broadest of brushes. They don't understand subtleties in legislation. If you are considering how it will be interpreted back home, you have to keep that in mind."

There is one major thing which congressmen can do in order to see that they are interpreted as they wish to be, and they do appear to consider it carefully. Interpretation depends in large part on which bloc one is associated with or, in the terms of Chapter 3, in being with the "right crowd." For instance, the vote against the surtax extension could be interpreted in a variety of ways—simply against the surtax, for tax reform, for fiscal irresponsibility, and so forth. The press will interpret it largely according to who is on which side. Thus in the surtax case, as the congressman above recited, it came to be interpreted as a vote for reform in some segments of the press, because a good many liberal, reform-minded Democrats were leading the fight against extension. To give another example, one congressman told me in advance of the vote on the supplemental bill that he was considering voting "present" as a protest against Vietnam spending, but that he wanted to consult with several other members of like mind. As he put it: "I don't mind being alone. But I want it interpreted right, by the press and others. If I do it myself, they'll just put it off to a kook. But if I do it with twenty others, then they'll interpret it correctly." He finally voted "no," and when I asked him about it, he said that he had indeed consulted his colleagues, and they had all agreed that they would vote "no" instead, since it was the "consensus" that it would be a clearer position to take. Another liberal congressman, confronted with the victory for the administration's voting rights bill as a substitute amendment on the floor, and having to decide whether to vote for it, expressed similar sentiments about popular interpretations attached to his and others' votes: "We wanted to show the Senate that we were against this bill. If we just caved in, then they wouldn't necessarily get that message. It was important to demonstrate our opposition. I'll admit that I was undecided on what to do at that point, but this position evolved on the floor."

Agenda-setting

Decisions on questions of public policy do not simply involve the final decision on the floor of the legislature. There are a number of steps both antecedent and subsequent to the floor vote. One of the most important of these other steps is the determination of the public agenda, or the list of subjects which will come up for decision in the public arena and those that will not. There are a number of ways in which the mass media may play a role in the structuring of this agenda.[7]

First, congressmen often initially hear of a given item for decision from the mass media. Given the severe constraints on time and attention span under which they operate, anything which simply catches their eye is of great importance. Congressmen are fond of using the phrase "brought to my attention," to describe this process—a problem, fact, or interest group viewpoint is "brought to my attention." Often, the agent which accomplishes this attention-getting is the media. One congressman, when asked how he first became aware of the ABM issue, replied in the following semibewildered fashion: "I first became aware of it when it appeared in the papers and on television, and people in the street started to discuss it. Is there some other way I should have become aware of it? Anything I missed? That's always the way it is." Another acknowledged the importance of newspaper reports on financing of slum real estate in Washington in precipitating a congressional inquiry: "We have been told that the information in these articles was old stuff. But it was the first most of us who write housing laws knew of these situations."[8]

Another congressman furnished a kind of case study in this attention-getting process. He laid out in great detail for me his experience in trying to get committee hearings on a certain subject, which he regarded as highly important. He had been making speeches on the floor and writing the committee chairman for months, to no avail. Then an editor for a minor magazine noticed it and asked him to write an article. When the article, drawn from his speeches, appeared, the editor of an important newspaper in the district of a senior committee member picked it up and wrote a prominent editorial. That committee member, in turn, inquired of this congressman and became a leading advocate of hearings. Then the editor of another newspaper, this time in the district of another committee member, also picked it up and wrote a prominent story. That committee member called the congressman, asking for a copy of his bill, and eventually introduced it. Finally, after the chairman's initial reluctance, hearings were scheduled. As is so often the case, nothing happened until well-placed media decided to play up the story, which in turn forced congressmen to respond in some fashion.

A second way in which media play a part in the agenda-setting process is by stimulating constituency interest and resultant mail. We noted in Chapter 2 that congressmen, while expressing disdain for "stimulated" mail, do pay attention to what appears to be a spontaneous outpouring of mail from their constituents. One agent in the system, perhaps the only one, that is capable of stimulating such a "spontaneous" outpouring is the mass media. Continuous or prominent coverage of a given story ensures that congressmen will have it constantly before them, partly because they read it themselves and partly because it stimulates constituents' interest and even their action. Because of this sort of coverage, there are some issues which congressmen find it virtually impossible to ignore.

Examples of mail outpourings related to the media coverage are not hard to uncover. Many congressmen noted the dramatic difference between the votes on the seating of Adam Clayton Powell during the session under study as compared to two years previous. This time, there was hardly a ripple in the public, and the House voted to seat him. But earlier, it had been an entirely different story, because of the repeated stories about various Powell activities which had appeared in the press over several months, resulting in a public outcry. One congressman, describing the difference, said, "Last time, there had been a long period when the disclosures were in the papers every day, and people got stirred up." The fierce mail which congressmen received on the pay raise bill is another example of prominent media coverage resulting in a public outcry.

Perhaps the most pronounced instance of such mail during the session under study, however, was the mail regarding taxes. When asked why tax reform had come up this year rather than at some other time, congressman after congressman referred to the importance of the heavy volume of "spontaneous" mail which had poured in from the constituencies. Many attributed this outpouring in the first instance to several recent tax raises at all governmental levels experienced by their constituents, including very prominently the federal surcharge. This general dissatisfaction, however, would probably not be enough in and of itself to start a strong public reaction. However, the fact that a number of wealthy people were escaping taxation altogether was prominently displayed in media all over the country. This relative deprivation apparently offended many people's sense of fairness, and they wrote and talked to their congressmen in great volume and with great heat. One congressman exclaimed, "They read in the papers about some millionaires, and they hit the ceiling." Said another: "I got volumes of letters, as did everybody else, and then you'd go back to the district and all they'd talk about was taxes, taxes, taxes, and cost of living too. The pressure from the public was really on and Congress had to respond." Finally, congressmen who had always been aware of the inequities in the tax system now had to respond in some way. It became impossible to explain inaction in view of the public pressure. This need to do something was translated into a tax reform bill, although it could have taken another form. One congressman summarized the process in this fashion:

These people got a surtax on top of high taxes. Local and state taxes were raised, so they got it socked to them again. Then Drew Pearson starts hammering away at oil depletion and a lot of people read him. On top of it, Barr testifies to a "taxpayer revolt" and talks about millionaires who aren't paying. Well, the public rose up in outrage and letters started pouring in. It was just like the flood of letters over Adam Clayton Powell. And Congress responded to the public outcry.

A third way in which the media are important in agenda-setting is that they tend to structure the public discussion. The ways in which issues are reported, and the terms in which stories are phrased tend to establish the dimensions along which congressmen and others think about the policy questions involved. One unusually introspective congressman said of his thinking on the ABM:

I'm reading everything I can get my hands on. The president's message, newspaper articles, magazines, mail, everything. Look at this ad. "It won't work." Well, will or won't it? "Takes money away from domestic programs." See, this sort of thing gives me the outlines of the argument. Then it's a question of tracking down the technical details. The public arguments sort of set the parameters. Now I have to fill in the details and answer the specific questions.

Perhaps the best instance of the media's power in structuring discussion was their coverage of campus unrest early in 1969 and the resultant dimensions along which congressmen and others tended to think about campus problems. Many newspapers took to publicizing the most major campus disruptions, such as the guns on the Cornell campus, and then printing a virtual box score of other campus disruptions, that is, a short paragraph on each of five or six problem campuses describing the latest act of disruption or riot. These reports were characteristically very shallow, concentrating on the "riot" itself and saying little else. This sort of reporting left the unmistakable impression, day after day, that most of the campuses of the country were beset by rebellion from all sides. Many congressmen, like everyone else, flew into a rage. One said, "We have to get tough with these militants. Here I read about them taking over a building with bullets and guns. We can't have that. I'm a real hardliner on this, and this is a common sentiment." It is important to note that for most congressmen, this box score approach in media coverage was the only information about the campuses that they had, and the only information on which they and their constituents were relying. It undoubtedly affected the ways in which they thought about the campus unrest, blinding them to complexities, concentrating their attention on the violent acts themselves, and, in more general terms, structuring the discussion of the issue.

Finally, in addition to noting how important the media are in bringing subjects, facts, and interpretations to congressmen, it is also important to mention that the media also play some part in determining which pieces of information will *not* be brought to congressmen. It is already customary to think of the media's effects on the general public in these terms. But the same applies to some degree with congressmen as well. Congressmen follow the mass media, and for many issues, especially on the floor, their sources of information are not necessarily much broader than that. In structuring what congressmen will not hear, therefore, the media play a central role. This is true in part because the media themselves do not bring some things to the congressmen's attention, and in part because media tend to divert their attention from other sources of information. Furthermore, because of media effects on attentive publics, the congressman will not tend to hear from his constituency in any volume unless the subject is reported prominently in the mass media. Probably one reason that congressmen follow home district newspapers is that they can implicitly assume that if the local media are not covering a story, the chances are that district attentive publics have not heard of it. This assumption rules out a good deal of territory as a subject for political concern, and gives them some clue as to the subjects on which the public is likely to be concentrating its attention.

CONCLUSIONS

Something that a congressman reads or hears in the mass media or elsewhere rarely appears to be of major importance in his voting decisions. Reading is more important on the issues of highest salience than on others, but even on these issues, the amount and influence of reading appears to be low. Despite this picture regarding voting choices on the floor, the more indirect impacts of the media may be very substantial. Some media may be fed into congressmen's decisions through indirect channels.

Mass media interpretations of votes may structure whole dimensions of issues facing congressmen. Finally, the mass media may be powerful agenda-setters. Media choices about which stories to emphasize and how to treat them may have a substantial impact on the determination of which issues will be seriously considered and which will not.

NOTES

1. See Delmer D. Dunn, *Public Officials and the Press* (Reading, Mass.: Addison-Wesley, 1969); Bernard C. Cohen, *The Press and Foreign Policy* (Princeton, N.J.: Princeton University Press, 1963); Dan D. Nimmo, *Newsgathering in Washington* (New York: Atherton, 1964); Douglas Cater, *The Fourth Branch of Government* (Boston: Houghton Mifflin, 1959); Michael Robinson, "Public Affairs Television and the Growth of Political Malaise." Ph.D. dissertation, University of Michigan, 1972; and Arthur Miller, Edie Goldenberg, and Lutz Erbring, "Type-Set Politics," *American Political Science Review* 73(1979): 67–84.

2. Richard M. Cyert and James G. March, *A Behavioral Theory of the Firm* (Englewood Cliffs, N.J.: Prentice-Hall, 1963), pp. 120–122.

3. Ralph K. Huitt, "The Congressional Committee: A Case Study," *American Political Science Review* 48 (1954):340–365, reprinted in Huitt and Robert L. Peabody, *Congress: Two Decades of Analysis* (New York: Harper & Row, 1969).

4. The concept of the two-step flow of communication was developed in studies of the electorate, particularly in the work of Bernard Berelson and Paul Lazarsfeld and their associates. See Elihu Katz, "The Two-Step Flow of Communications: An Up-to-Date Report on an Hypothesis," *Public Opinion Quarterly* 21 (1957):61–78. Other uses of the concept include David Kovenock, "Influence in the U.S. House of Representatives," *American Politics Quarterly* 1(1973):407–464; Donald R. Matthews and James A. Stimson, "Decision-making by U.S. Representatives," in *Political Decision-Making*, ed. S. Sidney Ulmer (New York: Van Nostrand, 1970), p. 23; and H. Owen Porter, "Legislative Expertise in Michigan." Ph.D. dissertation, University of Michigan, 1971, chap. 4.

5. *The Washington Post,* December 3, 1969, p. A-1.

6. For one such view, see Clem Miller, *Member of the House,* ed. John W. Baker (New York: Scribner's, 1962), pp. 57–62.

7. A discussion of the political role of the reporter which is relevant is Donald R. Matthews, *U.S. Senators and Their World* (Chapel Hill: University of North Carolina Press, 1960; also Vintage Books), pp. 203–205.

8. *The Washington Post,* June 10, 1969, p. A-8.

PART III

Decision-making

9

Decision Problems and Information

Thus far in this book, we have considered the impact of several actors on the decision-making of congressmen, taking each actor in turn. Such an approach, of course, tends to segment the decision process somewhat unrealistically, and fails to treat it as a whole. This final part of the book, therefore, considers some decision-making topics of a more general variety. The current chapter discusses information flows and information processing.

In many theories of decision-making, information processing and communication are seen as crucial components. The pattern of information inputs into a decision both affects that decision and determines what kinds of information will *not* be considered. Once information is fed into a decision system, the ways in which it is processed loom large in the outcome that will result. Not only is information important, but some theories argue that it is all-important, that humans and social systems can be seen essentially as information-processing mechanisms and understood in terms of the communications patterns one finds within such systems.[1]

Throughout this book, we have considered many findings about information flows and processing. We already know something about the sources of information which appear to influence congressmen most, as well as those sources which are of lesser importance. We also know something about information flows in the legislative system. Actors who do not have good legislative access tend to work through those that do, such as the instance of lobbies working through constituencies. This chapter considers a few topics of general interest about information which have not been completely covered in the actor-by-actor consideration. We shall begin with comments about legislative search procedures: problemistic search, the conditions under which it takes place, the kinds of information sought, and search through unorthodox communication channels. We will then proceed to consider information flows in the system apart from congressmen's own search procedures.

SEARCH PROCEDURES

Human beings are continually faced with greater demands on their time than they have time to allocate. So many decisions face them during the course of the day that there is insufficient time to consider each one thoroughly, and many more bits of information reach them than can be thoroughly evaluated and used. One result is a resort to what Cyert and March call problemistic search.[2] Individually or collectively, people dramatically reduce the necessity to search out and examine information by limiting their searches only to those decisions which they have some kind of problem or difficulty in making. For the rest of their decisions, their search for information is rudimentary at best, and perhaps absent altogether. This kind of tack both drastically simplifies the decision itself and frees up substantial blocks of personal and staff time.

To an exaggerated degree, congressmen face this problem of too many decisions and too little time in which to make them.[3] Such demands on their time as committee work, constituent service, travels, and meeting with various categories of important people, all conspire to prevent them from studying carefully the votes which they are called upon to cast on the floor of the House. In addition to the inevitable demands on their time, many congressmen quite deliberately choose to allocate their time to activities other than floor voting. Even if they were to devote extraordinary amounts of time to floor votes, furthermore, the sheer volume of the bills and amendments and the incredible diversity of the subjects involved would necessitate some kinds of decisional shortcuts. Thus congressmen, fully as much as other decision-makers, and perhaps much more than many of them, avoid time-consuming information searches unless they feel that they need the information because of a decisional problem that is presented to them. On the farm payment limitation, for instance, one congressman said: "On something that I would be unsure about, I'd talk to ———. He's on the committee, and he knows the problems and knows my state too. (Question: Did you on this vote?) No, I knew what I thought on it." Said one liberal Northern Democrat about the ABM controversy, "Actually, I didn't go out and read and study this too much, because my mind was closed." As another congressman expressed it, "I didn't need any coaching on this one."

In addition to the general human need for problemistic search, there is another reason for it which is peculiar to the legislative voting context. Congressmen find through some experience that an extensive search for information on a given issue is not only impractical in the general sense, but often wasted if undertaken. One recounted such an incident: "Once I studied something for hours, went over to the floor, and it went through on a voice vote." Or the congressman may spend a good deal of time developing an elaborate rationale for a politically difficult vote, only to find that he is never called upon to deliver himself of it. In order to consider a given vote thoroughly, the congressman would need to begin his search some time ahead. But at that point, he does not know the dimensions of the issue that will finally be presented to him for decision, or even whether it will come up at all. Thus, seeing that his valuable time might very well be wasted, he does not begin considering a search until it is too late to do it at all extensively or thoroughly. In fact, in cases in which the congressmen did report some uncertainty about how to cast a vote, they decided how to vote during the debate 23 percent of the time, and only days before the vote an additional 41 percent of the time.

Events that have transpired since the field research for this study was completed in 1969 serve only to reinforce the image of a legislator overwhelmed with the sheer number of decisions to make on the floor. In plain quantitative terms, the number of votes has increased dramatically. In 1970, for example, there were 266 record votes in the House of Representatives. The comparable figure for 1977 was 706.[4] Several factors contributed to that increase. Recorded teller voting was introduced in 1971, which transformed many votes that would have been nonrecord votes into votes cast on the record, from which legislators could not absent themselves without suffering embarrassing drops in their attendance records. Electronic voting was also introduced in 1973, which made it somewhat easier to record votes and may have contributed to the larger number of votes. That device also resulted in the time for decision being cut approximately in half, which lent even further urgency to the need for simple decision rules. Finally, various political forces—the drive for openness in government, the increase in single-issue interest groups, and the emergence of issues of considerable controversy—may have contributed to the larger number of votes. Whatever the reasons, a fundamental argument about voting decisions presented in this book has been that members of Congress are forced to avoid extended searches for information and to rely on extremely simple rules of thumb as decision-making procedures. The substantial increase in the numbers of decisions during the 1970s makes that argument all the more compelling.

Maintaining that congressmen engage primarily in problemistic search with regard to their voting decisions, of course, necessitates some definition of what constitutes a problem for a congressman. When a congressman says that he did not engage in an extensive search for information, he generally means one of three things by that statement, or a combination of any of the three. First, the issue may present him with no conflict in his immediate environment, in the field of forces that affects his decisions. If the congressman finds minimal conflict in that field, he is presented with no decisional problem and thus tends not to engage in any extensive information search. This no-conflict situation includes those cases in which he sees no political problem with his vote back in his district. Second, he may have an intense, fixed opinion on the issue, and thus sees no point in pursuing the matter further. He reasons that he is so unlikely to change that more information would have no practical effect on his decision and that to search for it would be wasted motion. Third, the congressman may have an established voting history on the issue. According to an incremental approach to his decision-making, if he has been through the process of decision before and has reached a satisfactory decision then, there is little point to repeating the process anew. In such a case, he relies on his previous voting history without a new search. On the basis of such factors as these, congressmen often cast their votes without reflecting on the matter much or searching for new information. They find themselves voting according to what they variously describe as a "gut reaction," "snap judgment," "more instinctive than substantive" voting, or "flying by the seat of your pants." As one congressman very elegantly summarized the normal case, "This decision was not really complicated enough for you to analyze. I just did it."

A rough quantitative indication of the frequency with which congressmen engage in an extended search can be obtained by referring again to the use of reading and staff.[5] As the discussions in earlier chapters indicate, congressmen simply engage in a routine search procedure most of the time. They do not search for information at all, simply notice things that come their way, rely on a few fellow congressmen, or do something of the sort. They engage in a more extended search, involving staff work, extra reading, or a somewhat more thorough process of consultation, only infrequently. The infrequent use of reading or staff work, especially, would lead one to the conclusion that congressmen's information search is usually quite perfunctory. A high-salience issue is capable of generating somewhat more extended search behavior, apparently because congressmen are impressed in such cases both with the greater importance of the issue and with the greater probability that they may be called upon to explain their vote or otherwise to discuss the issue publicly.

The results of a limited search for information or limited thought about the issue at hand are repeatedly evident in the interviews. When asked if he was satisfied with the tax reform package, for instance, one congressman replied, "I told you, I don't know what's in the bill." Another, when asked about the supplemental appropriations bill, replied, "I voted for it, didn't I? Frankly, I don't remember much about it." Another admitted with regard to as high-visibility a vote as the surtax extension bill, "I didn't know what was in the bill. It was as simple as that." I encountered another congressman, a member of the committee that reported the bill, who had not the foggiest notion of what he had voted on the day before, and was reading the previous day's *Congressional Record* to find out what had happened. He even confused William Scherle (R.–Iowa) with Shirley Chisholm (D.–N.Y.) when asked about the "Scherle amendment," because their names are pronounced similarly. As one congressman summarized the situation, "Members don't study things much. They often go in there and vote without knowing anything about the measure."

Importance of Usable Information

As has already been argued, the congressmen's time and their abilities to process information are severely constrained. Not every piece of information, indeed, not every source of information, is equally useful. In fact, for information to be useful, it must meet a number of rather stringent requirements.

First, the information must be digested. In terms of its sheer volume, it must be compressed to the point that it can be managed within the time and cognitive capabilities of the congressman. This one criterion alone eliminates a fair amount of potentially useful information from congressional view, simply because there is too much of it to handle. One congressman complained of the Armed Services Committee hearings on the ABM: "They did send over the hearings. But here it is, 8000 pages long or something like that. How can you go through all that? It's useless to me."

Second, their information should be politically relevant. A congressman needs to know not only what the policy consequences of given votes will be, but also what the political consequences will be, either in terms of effects in his constituency or in terms of the reward structure within the House. Useful information, therefore, takes account of the political consequences, modifies the information in the light of these consequences, and becomes politically realistic. One congressman knew that in order to avoid arousing the ire of farmers in his district, he would be obliged to vote for the agriculture payment limitation, contrary to his judgment concerning the correct course for public policy to take. When asked what he thought of Secretary Hardin's plea that the limitation be defeated, he replied, "I thought it was very well stated, and much to the point. But that didn't help me."

Third, the useful information is explicitly evaluative. Observers often note the need for congressmen to have "neutral" information that is not tainted with vested interest or other bias. Actually, such neutral information is much less useful than information which takes a position and buttresses the argument with selected facts.[6] This is true because evaluative information is of necessity directly focused on the issue at hand, and is thus largely devoid of irrelevant arguments and facts. If the congressman were presented with neutral information, furthermore, he would be obliged to sift through it himself for clues as to which position he should take, and he would also never know whether the selection of facts was neutral in the first place. It is more useful, therefore, to have "biased" information which does take an identifiable position. Then the congressman can simply select the information with which he agrees, or, if he desires to dig deeper, he can get information from the opposition side and confront the two in a kind of adversary process. As attorneys, many congressmen are comfortable with this sort of reasoning.

These kinds of requirements for useful information help to explain why certain sources are relied upon as extensively as they are. In particular, fellow congressmen tend to meet these criteria admirably. Sensitive to their colleagues' information needs, they do digest information well, take political consequences into account, and explicitly evaluate or urge their positions on others. And of the kinds of reading matter available, the committee report again meets the requirements more completely than other materials. Paying attention to constituency is also important in terms of political implications.

Congressmen often complain that they have insufficient information on which to base an intelligent judgment. Actually, the information is rarely insufficient; rather, it is overwhelming. It simply often does not come to them in a usable form.[7] What they need is not more information, but information which has the characteristics of brevity, evaluation, and political calculus.

Unorthodox Search

Like the rest of us, congressmen are creatures of habit. They rather rarely seek out new information sources. They tend instead to rely on conventional sources such as the media, the mail, and their colleagues, and within those sources, on those with whom they agree. If they semisystematically sought out unaccustomed sources of information, their perspective would be considerably widened, and their decisions might be somewhat different in content. Those congressmen who do develop new information, furthermore, have a disproportionate influence on congressional outcomes.[8]

It is instructive, therefore, to examine some less orthodox information-gathering devices. One is a conscious broadening of personal experience. For instance, most congressmen obtained their information about the disturbances on the campuses in the early part of 1969 from the mass media. This information was shallow, and adopted what I have referred to as the "box score" approach to campus unrest, with a front-page article containing a paragraph on each latest riot, devoid of explanation or context. A group of younger Republican congressmen, some of them of rather conservative bent, undertook to augment their usual sources of information in a rather innovative way. They arranged to visit several campuses across the country, without fanfare or publicity, observing people and talking to faculty, administration, and student leaders on an off-the-record basis. Even the most conservative of them returned with a very different impression from that of their colleagues who had not been exposed to this unorthodox type of information. They were much more aware of the complexities of the problem and of the need to avoid simple and repressive solutions than they had been when they began their travels.

Another unorthodox source of information is the imaginative use of polling or other sampling studies. By now most congressmen are used to polling of some sort in a campaign context. But a survey that can be used in legislative decision-making rarely finds its way into their consideration. Few would seriously argue for opinion polls as a kind of plebiscite. But to illustrate their occasional uses, one instance in the session under study in which polling did have noticeable effects was on the subject of electoral college reform. For years, an argument which had always been used against various plans for electoral college reform was that reform was impractical, since it lacked both popular support and, more important, sufficient support in the state legislatures to see it ratified. Because the condition of public and legislative opinion was obviously such a crucial part of congressmen's calculations, some sort of polling information became relevant. It did happen that congressman after congressman told me that the public opinion polls, both the ones published in the media and their own unpublished soundings, showed heavy support for direct election. This was something of an impressive fact to many of them. Furthermore, at least one poll of state legislators was widely circulated which showed that there was considerably less resistance to direct election in the legislatures than would have been previously supposed, even in the small states. These bits of new information, whether from a high-quality survey or not, led many congressmen to believe that ratification was a live possibility, which they had not believed in the absence of such polls. In turn, the polls tended to structure subsequent discussions about the practicality of various reform plans, particularly that of direct election.

A final source of information which is not used a great deal by congressmen, at least not in their floor voting decisions, is the expert outside of the Congress. These experts are not readily identifiable, are not nearly as available as information sources closer to hand, do not tend to present digested information, and are not as willing or able to offer political or evaluative information. They do form a potential for information which, if properly used, could be quite influential; however, congressmen tend not to seek them out. They probably do so much more in connection with committee business, and committee staffs certainly do.

There were a few occasions in the votes under study in which outside "experts" of one kind or another took positions that were prominently displayed for public and congressional view. Economists united in support of the surtax extension and the debt limit increase; unified medical opinion concerning the hazards of cigarette smoking had been well known for years; and highly publicized disagreements within the scientific community over ABM were much in evidence during consideration of that issue. Interestingly enough, in those instances in which the outside experts were united, congressmen voted against them nearly as often as they voted with them (25 cases with, 21 against). On the surtax extension, for instance, many northern Democrats voted against the extension and thus against the unified opinion of most economists. Many Republicans cited this unified opinion as one reason for their support. As one said, "Who am I to say that they're wrong?" Democrats who voted against their advice, by contrast, tended to question the assumptions on which the economists based their recommendations. Said one, "As a congressman, I have to consider what burdens we're imposing on people and how they're reacting to it. The economists all said to vote for it. But they don't have the same perspective that I do." Another generalized from this experience:

This is one thing that a congressman has to learn, and many never do: how to assess expert advice. An expert always speaks from his own frame of reference. In this case, the economist is concerned only about the economy—inflation, the dollar, and so forth. But a congressman has to have a broader frame of reference than that. Many congressmen don't appreciate this.

Given these kinds of comments, it should come as no surprise that on these few votes Northern Democrats tended (by a two-thirds margin) to vote against unified experts, and Republicans tended by an equal margin to vote with them.

On the occasions which find the experts divided, such as the ABM vote, congressmen tended heavily to set aside the experts and use other criteria, rather than attempting to wade through the various claims and counterclaims. One would find references on ABM like, "I'll err on the side of peace," or "I'll gamble on the side of security." Another said, "There were a lot of arguments for and against, so the information didn't help too much. We had to fall back on our own experience and judgment." Said another, "I didn't pay much attention to the scientists. You could pretty much pick your expert to suit your tastes. I was more moved by the international implications." Finally, when asked in good neutral interviewing fashion how he sorted out the conflicting scientific claims, one congressman snorted: "We don't. That's ridiculous. You have a general position. Once you assume that posture, you use the scientists' testimony as ammunition. The idea that a guy starts with a clean slate and weighs the evidence is absurd."

INFORMATION FLOWS

Aside from congressmen's search procedures, there are a number of information flows in the legislative system. There are sources of information which congressmen may or may not seek out; extra-search information does flow through identifiable channels, and this information is fed into decisions at certain points and has an impact. It is well to consider, therefore, information flows in a broader context than in the context of search procedures.

Gatekeeper Sources[9]

Through the course of this book, we have discovered that certain actors in the legislative system are much more prominent in the decision-making of congressmen than are other actors. In particular, on both subjective and objective measures, two actors —the fellow congressmen to whom he turns for advice on the legislation at hand, and his own constituency—appear to be more important than the others. Congressmen trust information from these sources, or they are politically important to the congressmen, or both. In any event, these sources can be seen as gatekeepers in the information flows in the legislative system.

Actors in the system that do not have the kind of favorable access that the constituency and trusted fellow congressmen do, find that, in order to get information into decision-making, they must work through the gatekeepers, by and large. We have found, therefore, that interest groups work through congressmen's constituencies or through their friends in the Congress, in the hope that their positions and information will be passed on. Staffs, particularly committee staffs, work through their bosses on the committees, and also provide another conduit for interest group information.

The administration is in a rather peculiar position. In most respects, the administration resembles interest groups in terms of the information flows. But with congressmen of the president's party, the administration takes on a greater importance. With some of those members, the administration may be of some direct influence on them, or may work through the party leadership of the

Figure 9–1 Overview of Information Flows

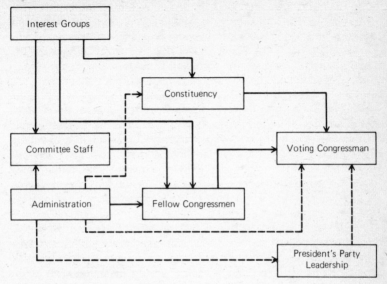

president's party. So while in most respects the administration assumes the rather weak position of interest groups, with congressmen of the president's party it may be of somewhat greater importance.

These various paths of information flow are graphically represented in Figure 9–1. The constituency and fellow congressmen form the gatekeeper roles, through which other information is channeled to the voting congressman. The dotted lines connecting administration, party leadership, and voting congressmen symbolize the channels through which administration information may be communicated in the cases of congressmen from the president's party. Tracing out these paths does not imply that information always follows these channels, of course, but rather that these are the normal flows.

It is important to emphasize that the information flows in the system are structured by the congressmen's own decision rules. Given that congressmen tend to weigh constituency and fellow congressmen most heavily in their decisions, other actors in the system come to discover congressmen's decision-making procedures and adapt their own behavior to them. Naturally enough, they attempt to make use of the sources of information upon which congressmen themselves rely. These information flows, in other words, have not simply evolved in a haphazard fashion. They are systematic adaptations to congressional decision-making. Once again, an examination of the rules by which congressmen make decisions appears to be useful in understanding the structure of interrelationships in the larger legislative system.

Although they are not pictured in Figure 9–1, one could also build in a series of feedback loops in the information flows. It is clear that not only does information flow toward the congressman, but that he also affects the information sources. Those who would try to influence him adapt to his values and his modes of decision. In addition, congressmen explicitly communicate to the various actors. They are not only influenced by constituents, for example, but they also attempt to educate them and lead them to an extent. They do not simply respond to the administration, but they also try to influence administration officials. It should also be noted that the gatekeeper sources, of course, are not simple transmitters of information, but that they shape information and act independently as well.

Source versus Content

Thus far, we have emphasized the importance of the source of information. Congressmen come to trust some sources and to mistrust others. An important part of influencing a congressman, therefore, is communicating information to him through the trusted sources. The following exchange with a Northern Democrat about the administration's voting rights bill illustrates the importance of sources nicely:

I'm not opposed to the extension nationwide on principle, but I don't trust [Attorney General] Mitchell. When it comes from him, I'm suspicious. (Question: What if the proposal had come from the NAACP?) Then I'd have to look at it more carefully. (Question: How much difference does the source make?) It's all-important. That's one thing you learn around here very quickly. That doesn't mean I don't support sources I don't trust sometimes. I'm supporting Nixon's welfare program, for instance. But you do develop trusts and suspicions easily.

Another Northern Democrat expressed the same feeling about military advice on the ABM: "We have had such wrong advice from the military. I tend not to trust their judgment. When it's the same crowd coming in asking for this, I'll take a second look." Congressmen, in short, often make their judgments on the basis of the source of the argument, information, or position, rather than according to the content of the communication.

Despite this common pattern, one often comes across a contrary type of behavior. Congressmen also discuss the content of an issue without being particularly aware of the source from which their information came. One congressman, for instance, mentioned his support for a proportional plan for electing the president, but the following exchange demonstrated that he was not aware of the origins of his position: "I've read a good deal, but I can't say just what. (Kingdon: Well, the proportional plan must have drifted across your vision at some point.) Yes, it must have, but I don't know exactly where. There has been so much written, both here in Congress and in the press." Another respondent talked of the information he had received about ABM: "I've been reading about this over the space of several months. I couldn't say if something struck me during that time. It's been current for so long." Said another, with regard to letters from national organizations on Health, Education, and Welfare funding, "Well, everything perhaps has *some* impact."

The fact that congressmen often pick up information and arguments from "somewhere," without being particularly attentive to the source, leads one in a somewhat different direction, in terms of considering the importance of the source itself. Of course a source must be credible to have much impact. But credible sources may also be shunted aside, depending on what is said by them and by others. As one conservative Republican replied, when asked if he would support an amendment to the poverty bill offered by Quie, Ayers, and Green, "Probably. I have to wait to see what they come up with, of course." The source must not only be a credible, trusted source, but it must also be persuasive concerning the issue at hand. Very few congressmen would admit even to themselves that they blindly followed anybody, inside or outside the Congress. This is one reason why interest groups spend so many organizational resources in developing "positions"; they cannot simply tell a congressman how to vote, but must persuade him, in addition to being a credible source in the first instance.

This sort of reasoning leads one to the conclusion that both the source of the communication and the content of the communication are necessary ingredients of successful influence attempts. A beautifully researched and well-presented position coming from the wrong source will be ignored. But a poorly developed and poorly presented position coming from a normally trusted source, or a position with which the congressman simply does not agree, may also be set aside. Both the source and its content are important, and simple persuasion is an important part of the influence process.[10]

CONCLUSIONS

Like most busy people, congressmen have limited time to devote to any one activity, and are faced with much more information than they can systematically sift and consider. Most of them, therefore, engage in an extended search for information only rarely, and then only when confronted with some unusual problem, such as an intense conflict among the factors they generally weigh, a new situation not governed by their past voting pattern, or an issue on which it is difficult to use their ideology. Otherwise, congressmen confine their searches for information only to the most routine and easily available sources. There is more reading, talking, and seeking out of information during consideration of the highest-salience issues than with other issues.

Congressmen need not just information, but information that is usable. It must be predigested, explicitly evaluative information, which takes into account the political as well as the policy implications of voting decisions. Trusted colleagues within the House, sensitive to their fellow congressman's information needs, generally meet these requirements quite nicely. Constituency information is also very valuable in terms of political impact.

Because congressmen rely most heavily on colleagues within the House and on constituents for guidance as they vote, other actors in the system such as lobbyists and administration policymakers tend to work through these two gatekeeper sources. Much of the behavior of those who would wish to influence legislative outcomes can be understood as being a systematic adaptation to congressmen's decision rules. Once again, an understanding of congressmen's decisions is useful in terms of understanding a wider set of phenomena.

NOTES

1. Literature on the importance of information-processing and communication

in decision-making includes James G. March and Herbert A. Simon, *Organizations* (New York: Wiley, 1958), pp. 161–169; Richard M. Cyert and James G. March, *A Behavioral Theory of the Firm* (Englewood Cliffs, N.J.: Prentice-Hall, 1963), pp. 67–82; and Raymond A. Bauer, Ithiel de Sola Pool, and Lewis Anthony Dexter, *American Business and Public Policy* (New York: Atherton, 1964), chaps. 12 and 32, and pp. 466–472. A cybernetics theory uses information and communications as its central construct. For one political use of such a theory, see Karl W. Deutsch, *The Nerves of Government* (New York: The Free Press of Glencoe, 1963).

2. Cyert and March, *ibid.,* pp. 120–122.

3. Such an argument is made in Raymond A. Bauer, Ithiel de Sola Pool, and Lewis Anthony Dexter, *American Business and Public Policy* (New York: Atherton, 1964), chap. 29; and in Donald R. Matthews and James A. Stimson, "Decision-making by U.S. Representatives," in *Political Decision-Making,* ed. S. Sidney Ulmer (New York: Van Nostrand, 1970).

4. Walter Oleszek, *Congressional Procedures and the Policy Process* (Washington: Congressional Quarterly Press, 1978), p. 124.

5. A more summary coding of search was also used, but it was so closely related to reading usage, and was sufficiently unreliable so that reading and staff seemed to be a better measure.

6. On this point, see Edward Schneier, "The Intelligence of Congress: Information and Public Policy Patterns," The *Annals* of the American Academy of Political and Social Science, 388(1970):20.

7. See Heinz Eulau, "The Committees in the Revitalized Congress," in Alfred de Grazia (ed.), *Congress: The First Branch of Government* (Garden City: Doubleday Anchor, 1967), p. 240.

8. One account of these innovative congressmen's uses of information is found in Norman Ornstein, "Information, Resources, and Legislative Decision-Making: Some Comparative Perspectives on the U.S. Congress." Ph.D. dissertation, University of Michigan, 1972, chap. 3.

9. On the notion of gatekeeper sources, see Edward Schneier, "The Intelligence of Congress: Information and Public Policy Patterns," The *Annals* of the American Academy of Political and Social Science, 388(1970):17–18, 20–21.

10. See the importance of congressmen's own policy attitudes, discussed in Chapter 11, for further discussion of this point. See also Raymond A. Bauer, Ithiel de Sola Pool, and Lewis Anthony Dexter, *American Business and Public Policy* (New York: Atherton, 1964), p. 468.

10

The Consensus Mode of Decision

We have been concerned with the degree to which a set of actors —the congressman's constituency, House colleagues, interest groups, his party leadership, the administration, and his staff— influence his voting decisions. We have found that no one actor in this set is preeminent in congressmen's decision-making. There are differences among them, of course, and some appear to be singularly *un*important. But none is important enough that one could conclude that congressmen vote as they do because of the influence of that one actor.

This result leads us away from an actor-by-actor consideration in the direction of examining a decision *process* which might account for congressmen's behavior. An adequate model of this decision-making process not only would be able to account for congressmen's votes statistically, but would also be plausible, in the sense that it would be both an accurate reflection of congressmen's actual decision-making as represented in the interviews and a picture of their decision-making which intuitively seems to be realistic. Such a model, for instance, cannot be so complex and so elaborate that congressmen could never be conceived as using it. Given the sharp constraints on their time, the competition of many legislative and nonlegislative matters for their attention, and the inclination of many to be not very concerned with many of the subjects before them, congressmen must perforce be portrayed as avoiding extensive search for information, as incompletely considering legislative provisions, and as following fairly simple decision rules when they vote.[1] Such a model not only should be a plausible account of a decision-maker at work, but should also be politically sensible, allowing for the full play of such important forces as avoidance of constituency trouble and interaction with close friends within the House.

The basic model of decision that emerges from this study, the consensus mode, possesses these qualities rather completely. This chapter and Chapter 11 are devoted to an exposition of this model and of its antecedents. Throughout, the consensus mode should be seen as congressmen's response to the various decisional problems we have been discussing, including the overload of voting decisions facing them, constraints on their time and cognitive capacities, and assessment of the political consequences of their decisions.

A DESCRIPTION OF THE CONSENSUS MODE

Congressmen begin their consideration of a given bill or amendment with one overriding question: Is it controversial? For virtually every participant, legislative matters are immediately divided into two categories as a first step in the decisional process: controversial and noncontroversial. When I called the whip's staff to inquire about the legislative program for the coming week, for example, I would receive a reply which clearly used this basic distinction. They would say that A, B, C, and D would be up, but "there's nothing controversial there." On the other hand, X and Y are also up, and these are "hot ones."

When there is no controversy in the congressman's environment at all, his decision rule is very simple: Vote with the environment. As one congressman described it, "The first thing I do is look to see if there's any opposition from any source. If there's not, then there's no problem with it." Another said, "The herd instinct is pretty common." Many, many legislative measures fall into this sort of category. For instance, a unified committee reports a bill and nobody opposes it in any particular. Or on final passage of numerous bills, and on some amendments, the congressman simply sees no conflict in his environment at all; he often does not even bother to look further into the matter. When asked about the Interior and State Department appropriations bills, for instance, one congressman replied, "There was no controversy over those, so I'm not acquainted with the details." Given the terrific press for time and the competition among various matters for his attention, there is little point to studying those over which there is no controversy. The first decisional step, therefore, is to ask whether there is any controversy, and if the answer is no, to vote with everybody else. This question and answer are portrayed as the first step in the decisional flow chart in Figure 10–1.

If the congressman does see some conflict in his total environment, no matter from what source, he proceeds implicitly to the next step in that decisional flow chart. The environmental con-

Figure 10–1 A Model of Legislative Voting Decisions

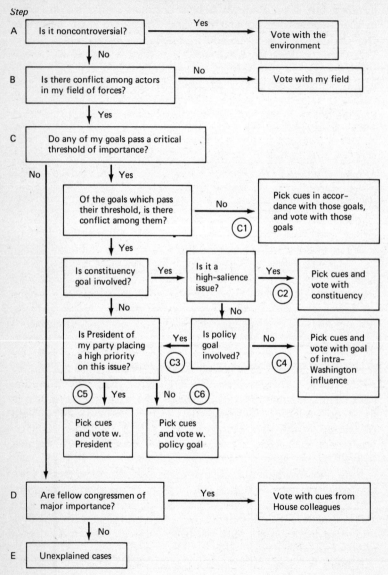

flict may be coming from sources to which he would pay no heed in any event. Many Republicans, for instance, would see no need to pay attention to organized labor, nor would many Northern Democrats see the Nixon administration as an important factor. Thus the congressman asks himself at Step B not about conflict in the entire environment, but rather about conflict in the "field of forces" that would affect his own decision. One congressman called this field "my circle of relevant factors." It includes the various actors in the legislative system which are most critical to the congressman on the given vote, such as his own constituency, trusted associates in the House to whom he pays attention, and interest groups that press their demands on him. As I use the phrase, the field of forces also includes his own public policy attitudes on the issue. Thus a conflict in this field might find his constituency arrayed against friends among fellow congressmen, interest groups against his own attitude on that particular matter of policy, and other such conflicts.

Much of the time—even though there may be some conflict in the environment as a whole—the congressman finds this more immediate field of forces that bears on his decision in agreement. His constituents, fellow congressmen, and other reference groups all agree with his attitude on the matter before him or, at least, are neutral. As one Republican hawk said of the Sikes amendment to add planes for Nationalist China to the foreign aid bill, "———— is the dean of our delegation, and an authority on this. He was for it, Ford was strongly for it, and that was good enough for me." Another congressman, considering the poverty program, said, "I'm sympathetic to the program, and everybody I look to is for it too." Another, observing such a unity in his immediate field of forces on the amendment to add funds for water pollution abatement, exclaimed, "There was no reason in the world to think twice."

If he finds his personal field of forces free of conflict, then the congressman votes with that field. I assume, as a legislator does, that if there is no consideration which would prompt him to vote in a way different from that toward which he is impelled by every important factor in his field of vision, then his decision is completely uncomplicated.

If there is some conflict among the member's relevant actors, he then proceeds to consider his goals, or what he hopes to accomplish by voting in one direction or the other. I assume that legislators are goal-seekers. Their behavior is purposive, and is not simply reaction to external forces. But if they are goal-seekers, we need to identify the goals which seem to affect most legislators most of the time. Adapting categories used by Richard Fenno,[2] representatives can be realistically portrayed as pursuing some combination of the following three primary goals:

1. SATISFYING CONSTITUENTS

Many authors[3] argue that one critical preoccupation of congressmen is their interest in being reelected. Surely nothing in this book would contradict that view. Indeed, as we discovered in Chapter 2, constituency opinions have quite a marked effect on voting decisions. But as we also discovered in that chapter, constituency considerations extend well beyond a simple concern with reelection. Legislators take account of constituency reaction long before and much more frequently than they worry explicitly about gain or loss of votes in the next election. It is therefore accurate to use the formulation, "satisfying constituents" rather than "reelection," to describe this goal.

2. INTRA-WASHINGTON INFLUENCE

Another set of considerations in voting has to do with satisfying a set of actors within Washington who are not necessarily closely connected to the constituency. These include going along with one's party leadership, favor-trading among fellow legislators, and following the lead of the administration, particularly if the president is of the deciding legislator's party. One takes these into account, presumably, in order to build influence within the government, a set wider than the House itself. We found in Chapters 3, 4, and 6 that those considerations sometimes affect voting decisions.

3. GOOD PUBLIC POLICY

Most legislators have their conception of good public policy, and act partly to carry that conception into being. Their policy attitudes decidedly affect their behavior both directly, as we will see in Chapter 11, and indirectly, through following fellow congressmen who agree with their own philosophy, as we discovered in Chapter 3. In addition to these effects of policy positions, representatives also develop well-established voting histories on many issues. A member's current decision is sometimes simply a repetition of past decisions on similar issues,[4] or a repetition with minor adjustments. This voting history thus plays an important part in defining the legislator's policy position, and we will explore its importance in Chapter 11. Whatever the mechanism, legislative voting decisions are often affected in important ways by the members' desires to enact what they regard as good public policies.

Of course, not all of these goals are brought to bear on each decision. With any given issue, a goal may seem unimportant to the legislator. For example, a congressman's constituency may have a vague and largely unarticulated opposition to foreign aid. In that case, he would say that there was a constituency opinion on the issue, but that it was not intense enough to bother taking into account. Or in another instance, the legislator may not have a very firmly fixed idea of what would constitute good public policy. A goal must pass what I have labeled in Figure 10–1 a critical threshold of importance in order to be evoked and be relevant to the decision.

If none of the goals is important enough to the congressman in a given decision to be relevant, he proceeds to follow trusted colleagues within the House (Step D). This situation is particularly exemplified by the many low-visibility, minor issues that come to the floor about which very few people apart from a few involved colleagues care. Yet these votes must be cast, because a poor attendance record is a considerable liability with constituents in the next compaign. In such a case, the congressman's own policy attitude does not provide sufficient guidance to make a decision, since he does not care about the issue; his constituency may be utterly indifferent; and there may be no intra-Washington consideration that would prompt him to vote one way or the other. Both the literature and practical experience are replete with examples of such votes, in which a deciding congressman is bereft of other guidance and simply follows a trusted colleague, sometimes quite blindly.

If one or more goals are important, the basic logic of the consensus mode of decision applies once again. If there is no conflict among the goals that are important, the choice is clear: Vote with the evoked goal or goals (Step C1). It could be that only one of the three goals is relevant to the decision, or that two or even all three are, but they all point him in the same direction.

A prominent way for legislators to translate their goals into votes is to turn to their colleagues within the House for cues which they follow in voting.[5] If a congressman wants to vote so as to satisfy his goal of bringing about good public policy, for instance, one easy and frequently used way to accomplish this aim is to pick fellow congressmen as cue sources who agree with his own general philosophy. Or to vote in a way most likely to satisfy constituents, a deciding congressman may follow the guidance of colleagues whom he considers to have "good political judgment," particularly from his state party delegation. In fact, we repeatedly observed those dynamics at work in Chapter 3, and they are reflected in all the outcomes of Steps C and D in Figure 10-1.

Thus far, we have considered the cases in which there are consensus decisions of various definitions which are easy for the legislator to make. As I demonstrate below, those exceedingly simple decision rules govern nearly all of the voting decisions that the representative makes on the floor. There are a few cases, however, in which the congressman faces a situation in which neither the whole environment nor his own immediate field of forces presents him with consensus, and in which his goals are both important to him and in conflict. In those few cases, he proceeds implicitly to some decision rules which help him sort out the conflicts and make a satisfactory choice.

There are various ways in which the decision rules could be stated in this part of the model. As portrayed in Figure 10-1, the congressman considers the constituency interest first. He may not end up voting with the constituency, but he always considers it when it is above the minimal level of importance. Placing this goal first is in keeping with the fact that the congressman owes his tenure in office to his constituency, and as Fiorina and Mayhew argue,[6] reelection is of critical importance to him.

If the constituency is not involved, the only logically possible conflict remaining among the three goals is between policy and intra-Washington influence. In that case, I hypothesize that the congressman has a disposition to vote with his policy goals, unless he is of the same party as the president and the president places a high priority on the issue. Intra-Washington considerations other than that one, such as party leadership requests or favor-trading, would not be enough to overcome a really strong policy predisposition. But a high-priority request from a president of his party would. We have considered some evidence on these points in Chapters 4 and 6. The results in Steps C5 and C6 of the model reflect this reasoning.

If the constituency goal is involved, the congressman weighs that consideration against policy and/or intra-Washington influence in much the way that balancing is portrayed in Chapter 2.[7] The key here is that there is a filter for the salience of the issue— the general visibility of the issue in the press, in the attentive public, and among the participants in the legislative process. If the issue is of high salience, and if constituency is a relevant consideration, the model postulates that in view of the likelihood that important constituents will notice and disapprove of a vote out of keeping with their interests, the constituency consideration will dominate the others (Step C2). If the issue is of lower salience, however, the congressman has more freedom to allow his policy views or intra-Washington considerations to control the choice.

In the case of low- or medium-salience issues, if the policy goal is relevant to the issue, the congressman is disposed once again to favor it. He must check the possibility, however, that the intra-Washington goal would be involved and would center on a priority request from a president of his party that conflicts with his policy goal. He therefore (at Step C3) cycles through the presidential step described above, but in most cases ends up voting in accordance with his policy views (Step C6). If the policy goal is not relevant, the only logically possible conflict (Step C4) is between constituency and intra-Washington influence. Since it involves a low- or medium-salience issue at that point, I hypothesize that the congressman decides in favor of the intra-Washington consideration in line with the argument presented above.

An alternative way of stating the decision rules in cases of conflict among evoked goals is that the congressman prefers his own policy attitude, unless he is pulled away from it under specified circumstances. Thus a high-priority request from a president of his own party or an intense constituency preference on a high-salience issue may overrule his own attitude. Short of those rather extraordinary circumstances, the legislator's goal of promoting his conception of good public policy carries the day. In the event that this policy goal is not relevant to the decision, for example when the member does not care much about the issue, then he prefers the constituency in the high-salience case and the intra-Washington influences in the rest.

The sequence described in Figure 10–1, finally, is not necessarily a conscious process in the mind of the legislator. It may be in some instances, but on other occasions it may be more implicit in the way he decides. The attractions of the model have more to do with its other properties. For one thing, its logic is compelling.

It starts with the simple and proceeds to the complex, in much the way that legislators actually work. The process model pictures the legislator as beginning with a very simple decision rule. If that rule can be applied, he does so, and he is finished with the decision on that particular vote or bill. The first step is exceedingly simple, because the only requirement is that the congressman must notice no conflict at all in the environment. In the second step, the congressman must, in addition to noticing no conflict, notice a field of forces that is acting upon him. If the legislator cannot apply the early, most simple decision rules, he proceeds to one which is somewhat more complex and applies it if he can. That is not to say that even the final steps are particularly complex. Throughout, the congressman is never obliged to engage in an extended search for information or to survey systematically the opinions of each and every one of the possible influences on his vote. Instead, he simply uses the information that happens to be in his field of vision at the time of decision and makes his assessment. Thus the model exhibits the desirable features with which we began this chapter: simplicity, plausibility, and political realism. It also accounts for votes statistically, as we see in the next section.

THE FIT TO DATA

In my sampling of votes for this study, I deliberately excluded from the core sample those votes in which there was no controversy present in the environment and many votes in which the controversy was not at all intense. Thus in my own data, the first step in the model presented in Figure 10–1 never applies; there is always controversy present somewhere in the environment since the votes were selected in that fashion. It does not take great imagination to argue, however, that the first step alone accounts for scores of votes cast in every session of the Congress, perhaps well over half of them. Over and over, the congressman simply sees no conflict in his environment at all, and votes with the environment. Still dealing with the types of votes that are not in my sample, furthermore, it is also likely that if there is conflict somewhere in the environment, the congressman's own immediate field of forces will not evidence it. Thus, in the normal case of legislative voting (though with these data it is impossible to set a precise figure), it is highly likely that the first two steps in the model alone account for a very high proportion of the votes. The congressman sees no conflict either in the environment or in his own field of forces, and votes accordingly.[8]

This speculation is doubly plausible given the good fit which the model has to my sample of votes, which should be among the decisions which are hardest to explain. The congressman's own field of forces is defined for this purpose as having seven possible actors: his own specific policy attitude toward the issue under consideration, his constituency, fellow congressmen to whom he says he paid attention, interest groups, his staff, his party leadership, and the administration. Each of these can take one of three positions: It either tends in the liberal direction, tends in the conservative direction, or is neutral or not involved in the congressman's decision. A Republican administration position, for instance, is often not involved in the thinking of Northern Democrats; the staff is often not involved in the thinking of many congressmen across the board. This field shows no conflict if all of these seven actors are either of the same (i.e., liberal or conservative) tendencies or are neutral. If four of them are liberal and three neutral, for instance, that field is defined as showing no conflict. If four are liberal, one conservative, and two neutral, that field does have conflict, with one actor out of line from the rest. (Details of the procedures involved and several important methodological issues are discussed in Appendix F.)

In my data, this field of forces for the congressman is free of conflict 47 percent of the time, and in such instances he, of course, always votes with the field. Given the fact that these votes were selected partly in order to maximize conflict, it is highly instructive that in nearly half of the cases, the congressman's field should present him with none. If this pattern obtains in this sample of votes, that fact surely argues that in legislative votes in general, the first two steps in the consensus model must have a very high explanatory power, since the general case is surely less conflict-ridden than these votes.

Starting with Step C, a major question of measurement is the critical threshold of importance for each of the three important goals. What indicators would tell that a constituency interest, for instance, is sufficiently important that the legislator considers the goal of satisfying constituents at Step C, rather than noticing but largely neglecting the constituency position in his decision? There is such an indicator in my data—the "importance" coding for each actor which was first described in Chapter 1 and is used throughout the book. With this coding, each actor is characterized as being of no, minor, major, or determinative importance in the decision.

In building on this coding, the goal of satisfying constituents is said to pass its critical threshold of importance on a given decision if his constituency is coded as being of major or determinative importance. If it is coded as being of minor or no importance, we consider that the threshold has not been passed, and that the constituency goal is not sufficiently important to the congressman on that decision to be involved in Step C of the model. Substantively, passing this threshold could be due to one or both of two reasons: Either the constituency feeling is quite intense on the issue and any congressman would want to take account of it, or the congressman considers catering to constituency interest an important goal regardless of constituency intensity. For present purposes it is not so critical which or what combination of these two reasons is responsible for the constituency being of major importance in the decision. Whatever the reason, the congressman's goal of satisfying constituents is evoked.

The constituency position, it should be noted, may not be the whole constituency, the mass public, or even a majority of the constituency. It could be these, but it could as easily be the position of a fairly narrow subset of the constituency, such as school administrators on education funding. In this connection, interest groups do not appear as a separate force in the model, because, as I maintained in Chapter 5, they appear to have little impact on congressmen's voting decisions apart from their constituency connections. Thus interest groups are subsumed under constituency for present purposes and ignored as being important in their own right.

The intra-Washington goal is treated in a similar fashion. If either the congressman's party leadership or the administration is coded as being of major or determinative importance, the congressman is considered to have passed the threshold on this decision and the goal is evoked. In addition, fellow congressmen could define the passing of the threshold on this goal if they are coded as being of major or determinative importance, *and* if some consideration of vote-trading or intra-House power is involved. In other words, fellow congressmen do not trigger this goal, even if coded major or determinative, if the deciding legislator uses his colleagues simply to reinforce ideology, constituency, or party, or if colleagues are used in the absence of other guidance. These uses of fellow congressmen are provided for elsewhere in the model. To be relevant to the goal of intra-Washington influence, colleagues must be important for their own sake, not because they are convenient surrogates for something else or because they are the only cues left. This supplementary coding was made by a rereading of the interview protocols in the cases involved to see how colleagues were being used.

The goal of good public policy presents something of a problem in these data. Because the interviewing was done at the time of decision, respondents nearly always held some articulated policy attitude toward the bill or vote at hand, and voted consistent with it. But it would be very difficult, given these data, to determine the intensity or background of that attitude earlier in the process of decision. Therefore, some measure of the importance of the policy goal other than the intensity of the congressman's policy attitude toward the vote at hand is needed. I use here two measures of the congressman's policy position. The policy goal is considered to pass the critical threshold of importance if *either* his voting history on similar issues is coded as being of major or determinative importance in his decision (see Chapter 11), *or* his ideology as measured by Americans for Democratic Action (ADA) and Americans for Constitutional Action (ACA) scores is sufficiently extreme as to be a good guide to his decision. Some congressmen are simply considered extreme "liberals" or "conservatives" by themselves and by everyone associated with the process. If they are, I assume that their ideology is sufficiently strong to give them considerable guidance, and to cause the congressman to pass the threshold on the policy goal. Because of a well-established voting history or a relatively extreme ideological position, in other words, he has a pretty fair notion of what constitutes "good public policy" for him in the current instance. (See Appendix F for the specific uses of these measures.)

Other operationalizations of the model are fairly straightforward. (1) Salience of the issue is a trichotomy (low, medium, high), as defined by the attention the issue appears to be receiving in the press, among congressmen, and among other participants in the legislative system (see Appendix D). The model's specification of the cutting point being between high and medium salience is consistent with evidence presented in Chapter 2 that high-salience issues are distinctively constituency-oriented, whereas low- or medium-salience issues are less so. (2) The priority which the president places on the issue is determined from my knowledge of the administration's position and lobbying activities. In the first year of the Nixon administration, priority items tended to have to do with the budget, and these cases centered particularly on the debt limit and the surtax extension. (3) At Step D, fellow congressman importance is once again the importance coding, with major or determinative importance constituting the criterion of entrance into that step.

The quantitative fruits of the model generation and data analysis are presented in Table 10–1, with a subset for Steps C2 through C6 more fully elaborated in Table 10–2. Overall, the model predicts correctly 92 percent of the voting decisions. Of those, only 10 percent are accounted for by Steps C2 through C6, the most elaborate part of the model, which itself is not very elaborate. It seems clear that legislators' voting decisions can be understood as the workings of extremely simple decision rules, rules which are not generated in some arbitrary fashion, but in a way that is consistent with quite a rich body of previous literature on legislative voting. It must be remembered also that this particular sample of votes contains those decisions that should be the hardest to predict. I deliberately selected votes that were among the most conflict-ridden of the session, which makes the high degrees of consensus (at Steps B and C1) really quite striking. One would not have expected these results, given the votes selected. Thus the model should do even better for run-of-the-mill votes. If there is little conflict among actors and goals with these relatively "big," high-visibility votes, then there should be even less with more routine votes. I would expect that for those votes, the simpler Steps A, B, C1, and D (stressing no conflict and House colleagues) would account for more of the total than these data indicate, and the more elaborate Steps C2 through C6 would be resorted to even less frequently than these data indicate.

The model does specify that the congressman *pick cues and votes* in accordance with the specified goal. Thus far, we have only considered the percentage of *votes* predicted, without reference to whether or not the congressman also picked cues to reinforce those votes. I take it that "picking cues" here refers to choosing fellow congressmen on whom to rely, according to their agreement with the goal specified in the model. Thus fellow congressmen at Step C2 should not be opposed to the constituency position, if the model is right; or at Step C6, they should not be opposed to the deciding legislator's policy position. If this factor is taken into account, we lose five cases which would otherwise

Table 10–1. Quantitative Performance of the Consensus Model

Step (see Figure 10–1)		Accuracy[a]	Percentage of cases[b]	Cumulative Percentages[c]
A	Noncontroversial votes	—	0%	0%
B	No conflict in field	104/104 = 100%	47	47
C1	No conflict among goals	74/79 = 94%	33	80
C2–C6	Conflict among goals (from Table 10–2)	22/27 = 81%	10	90
D	Fellow congressmen	5/5 = 100%	2	92
E	Unexplained cases	$n = 7$		

[a] Accuracy equals the percentage of the cases in which the congressman votes as the model specifies. For example, at Step C1, there are 79 cases in which there is no conflict among the goals, and the congressman votes in accordance with the evoked goals in 74 of those cases. Thus accuracy = 74/79 = 94%. The number of "mistakes" made by the model at this step is five.

[b] Percentage of cases equals the percentage of the total ($n = 222$) accounted for by that decision step. For example, in Step C1, it is 74/222 = 33%.

[c] The cumulative percentage equals percentage of 222 accounted for by that step plus all previous steps. For example, at Step C1, it is $\underline{74 + 104} = 80\%$.

$$\frac{}{222}$$

be correctly predicted. That is to say, there are five cases in which the actor "fellow congressman" is opposed to a decision which was governed by the specified goal. Therefore, by building this loss into the overall figures, the overall performance of the model, defined as the congressman's *both* voting as the model specifies *and* avoiding colleagues who are opposed to that vote, is 90 percent. The predictive performance, in other words, remains high.

VARIATIONS

Congressmen appear to use the consensus mode of decision very regularly, regardless of the types of issues facing them, the types of congressmen they are, or the kinds of actors involved. Despite this impressive regularity, there is one possible kind of variation. Certain congressmen may find that they, more than others, must proceed through more steps in the model, that their decision-making process is somewhat more complex than that of others. In fact, Republicans are particularly prone to find more conflict in their fields than are Democrats; Northern Democrats are most likely to find their fields free of conflict. In these data, Republicans

Table 10–2. All Possible Combinations of Conflicts Among Goals, and the Resultant Outcomes

Combinations	Outcomes,[a] Expected and Actual high-salience issues[b]	low- or medium-salience issues[b]	totals
Policy and constituency vs Intra-Washington	Constituency (C2) 1/2[a]	Policy or Pres.[c] (C3) 2/2	3/4
Policy and intra-Wash. vs Constituency	Constituency (C2) 0/0	Policy (C3) 3/3	3/3
Constituency and intra-Wash. vs Policy	Constituency (C2) 0/0	Policy or Pres.[c] (C3) 0/0	0/0
Policy vs Constituency	Constituency (C2) 1/2	Policy (C3) 6/6	7/8
Constituency vs Intra-Washington	Constituency (C2) 0/0	Intra-Wash. (C4) 3/4	3/4
Policy vs Intra-Washington	President[b] (C5) 3/5	Policy[b] (C6) 3/3	6/8
Totals	5/9	17/18	22/27

[a] The goal stated in each cell is the expected outcome, the goal which the model would predict would dominate the decision. The notation in parentheses refers to the appropriate step in Figure 10–1. The actual performance is captured in the numbers in each cell. The first is the number of cases in which the outcome is as predicted by the model, the second is the total number for that cell. For instance, in the case of a conflict between the constituency and intra-Washington influence goals, on low- or medium-salience issues, the model would predict that the representative would vote according to the Intra-Washington consideration. Of the four cases in which there was such a conflict on such an issue, the congressman voted as the model expects in three.

[b] In the case of the conflict between Policy and Intra-Washington, "high salience" refers to the presidential involvement specified in Figure 10–1, Step C5, low salience to noninvolvement (Step C6). In the others, the salience of the issue refers to the general visibility of the issue in the press, in the public, and among participants. See Appendix D for the coding particulars.

[c] In these cases, since the congressman cycles through Steps C5 and C6, there is a chance that the president's request may overturn the policy consideration, and it did in fact happen in one case. Thus that case is coded as accounted for by the model, even though policy did not control, because the model predicted the outcome correctly. In the other case, the President's priority is not involved, so the congressman votes according to his policy position. See the text for further explanation.

found their fields (Step B in Figure 10–1) free of conflict only 28 percent of the time, whereas the Northern Democrats found no conflict 66 percent and Southern Democrats, 54 percent.

The first reason for this pattern emerging is concerned with administration control. Members of the party that controls the presidency are obliged at least to listen to the administration's wishes, while the administration is often not even a part of the opposition congressman's set of relevant actors. This great involvement of the administration and party leadership in the decisions of congressmen of the president's party carries with it a greater likelihood that on occasion, the administration will ask something that is not in accordance either with the congressman's own wishes or with the positions of others to whom he pays attention. Thus as we discovered in Chapter 4, Republicans found their constituencies more in conflict with the party and the administration than Democrats did. It is not clear to what extent a Democratic president would create similar problems for Democrats.

A second reason for the observed party differences lies in interest group and constituency factors. As found in Chapter 5, interest groups at least in the late 1960s, tended to be active in floor battles from a liberal, rather than a conservative, direction. This pattern brings them more often into conflict with Republicans and Southern Democrats than with Northern Democrats, who are predisposed to more liberal points of view. Furthermore, because of this interest group activity, Northern Democrats find themselves in agreement with elites in their constituencies, and thus evidence less conflict with their constituencies than either Republicans or Southern Democrats do.

Finally, since Northern Democrats have fewer problems with administration, interest groups, or constituents, they content themselves with reinforcing fellow congressmen as well, as we found in Chapter 3. When they turn to colleagues for information or guidance, they seek out those with whom they agree more often than happens with Republicans or Southern Democrats. In all these ways that have to do with a number of actors with whom they interact, Northern Democrats are simply presented with or generate less conflict in their field of forces. This is reflected in a simpler, less uncertain kind of decision-making.

This lower extent of conflict for Northern Democrats than for Republicans is consistent with party differences on a direct measure of uncertainty. During the interview, I noticed any statements made to the effect that the congressman was unsure about how he would eventually vote on the issue under discussion. If the topic of uncertainty was never mentioned in any way, I asked at the end whether he had ever been uncertain about what he would do. According to this crude index, in 69 percent of the decisions the congressmen exhibited no discernible uncertainty, at least within the several months preceding the vote. Although there are no particularly large differences in congressmen's uncertainty in terms of seniority or competitiveness of the district, there is a striking party difference. In fully 84 percent of their decisions, Northern Democrats exhibited no uncertainty about their votes, compared with 69 percent for Southern Democrats, and only 56 percent for Republicans. The most junior Republicans were particularly prone to exhibit uncertainty. Party differences persisted with seniority, district urbanness, and Americans for Democratic Action score controlled.

There might also be variations over time. As a Democrat occupies the White House, for instance, the impact of administration control might shift from Republicans to Democrats. Or as interest groups become much more vocal from the right end of an ideological spectrum, as happened through the 1970s, Democrats would be affected in much the same way that Republicans were affected by liberal groups in 1969. Beyond those changes, as politics in general become more contentious and divisive, members of Congress probably find that they must proceed through more steps in the consensus model than in a more placid time. It would be hard to argue, however, that the politics of the late 1970s were more divisive than the politics of the late 1960s. There may be more players in the game, particularly more single-issue interest groups and intra-House caucuses, but the tremendous conflict over the Vietnam war, urban and college unrest, and other issues in the late 1960s make it seem unlikely that contention in the body politic could have had a greater impact on legislative voting a decade later. Indeed, the fact that the consensus mode of decision worked as well as it did during a time that the country was in such a state of dissension as we experienced in the late 1960s argues that the fundamental logic involved in this sort of decision-making must be rather resilient. In short, although various subgroups of the Congress may find it necessary to proceed through more steps of the model than other subgroups, and although some periods of our politics may make it necessary for legislators in general to proceed further through the model than other periods, the logical structure of the model seems to apply regardless of these variations within that structure.

Finally, it is a reasonable conjecture that in votes of lower visibility than those in this core sample, congressmen find less conflict in their fields than they do with relatively information-rich, higher-visibility votes. There are no marked differences according to salience within my sample of votes. Interestingly, there are also no substantial differences according to seniority, district competitiveness, or size of state delegation.

CONCLUSIONS

Congressmen begin their decisional process on any matter before them with a great watershed distinction: Is it controversial or not? From that beginning, they use a fundamental decision rule, the consensus mode of decision. They assess their environment in terms of the degree of consensus which they can perceive in it. If they find no conflict in the total environment, they simply vote in the direction in which it impels them. If there is conflict within the total environment, the congressman then implicitly subsets the environment, and asks if there is conflict within the field of forces—his own constituency, informants, party leadership, and the like—which bears on his own decision. If there is no conflict in that field, once again the choice is simple: Vote with the field. Subsequent steps in the process are either continued uses of this consensus model on those occasions when the congressman does not find complete agreement in his perceptual field or simple decision rules that handle conflict. Republicans found more conflict in their fields than did Democrats in 1969, particularly Northern Democrats, as a consequence of more frequent administration requests, a lesser affinity with active interest groups, and a lesser tendency to select informants within the House who agreed with them. All congressmen, however, regularly use the consensus mode of decision in wide varieties of circumstances. Given their great need for simplifying decisions in the face of far too many things to do in the time available, perceiving consensus is one of the most helpful rules of thumb.

This model of the decisional process has a good fit to the data. If it accounts for votes as well as it does with this core sample, it would undoubtedly have an even better fit for legislative votes in general. In addition to this predictive power, the model is a plausible and realistic account of congressmen's behavior. It grew out of my interviewing and other observations, rather than being imposed a priori on roll call data. It is intuitively plausible, in the sense that congressmen need not engage in any extensive search for information or proceed through an impossibly complex set of decisional steps. The model is also politically sensible, because voting according to consensus in a field is entirely consistent with avoiding political trouble.

If one were interested in predictive power alone, one could get excellent results in these data by using as the sole predictors either the congressman's own attitude on the vote or the position of fellow congressmen on whom he relied. But one wants realism in a model in addition to predictive value. At various points in this book, several alternative models of decision-making are discussed, and none seems as satisfactory as the consensus mode. Interaction among fellow congressmen, for instance, is held in Chapter 3 to be highly important, but not a complete decision model. The congressman's own policy attitudes, although an important preconsensus factor, do not represent a realistic alternative model to the consensus mode for reasons detailed in Chapter 11. The same applies to an incremental model or decision-making according to past voting history. I also tried a model of constituency intensity and one of administration involvement for Republicans, neither of which proved to account for behavior very well. Further alternative formulations are detailed in Appendix F. The consensus mode of decision, on the other hand, emerged quite clearly from my research. Therefore, on the basis of my initial observations, the rereading of the interviews, and the consideration of several alternative models, I have concluded that the model not only predicts well, but that it is also an accurate representation of congressmen's decision-making process.

There may be a wider applicability of the key concepts presented here beyond the case of legislative voting, in the sense that wide varieties of decision-makers may use versions of a similar general approach to their decisions. Legislators, bureaucrats, judges, and others may all be thought to search for consensus in their environment, to subset that environment in the event that agreement is lacking and to search for consensus within the most critical subset, to identify their most important goals and ask if there is agreement among them, and to get into more complex decisions if these simpler rules fail them. The well-known use of standard operating procedures in bureaucracies, for example, may be due to consensus among the relevant actors in the bureaucrat's environment—his superiors, the agency clientele, his co-workers, his professional associates outside the agency—that given SOPs are appropriate for a given class of cases. Or judges deciding on sentencing of convicted defendants, for another example, have been found to impose the sentence recommended by police, prosecutor, and probation departments if the three agree; if they do not agree, the judge must enter a more complex set of decision rules.[9] Mass public voting behavior exhibits similar characteristics: When various important influences agree, the voting decision is made; when they do not, the voter is said to be under "cross-pressure," and the decision becomes more complicated. It is worth noting that the model presented here may represent a general decision strategy, an approach to decision-making that is widely used. Thus this work hopefully contributes not only to further understanding of legislative behavior, but also to the general building of theory about decision processes.

NOTES

1. For a discussion of similar general problems of most decision-makers and their adaptation to these problems, see James G. March and Herbert A. Simon, *Organizations* (New York: Wiley, 1958), chap. 6, entitled, "Cognitive Limits on Rationality." See also Chester I. Barnard, *The Functions of the Executive* (Cambridge, Mass.: Harvard University Press, 1966; first published, 1938), pp. 189–191; Richard Cyert and James March, *A Behavioral Theory of the Firm* (Englewood Cliffs, N.J.: Prentice-Hall, 1963), pp. 120–122; and Raymond Bauer, Ithiel Pool, and Lewis Dexter, *American Business and Public Policy* (New York: Atherton, 1964), chap. 29.

2. Richard Fenno, *Congressmen in Committees* (Boston: Little, Brown, 1973).

3. For two recent examples, see David Mayhew, *Congress: The Electoral Connection* (New Haven: Yale University Press, 1974), and Morris Fiorina, *Representatives, Roll Calls, and Constituencies* (Lexington, Mass.: D. C. Heath, 1974).

4. For a report of research on the importance of voting history, see Herbert Asher and Herbert Weisberg, "Voting Change in Congress," *American Journal of Political Science* 22(1978):391–425.

5. For a discussion of cue-taking, see Donald Matthews and James Stimson, *Yeas and Nays* (New York: Wiley-Interscience, 1975).

6. Fiorina, *op. cit.,* and Mayhew, *op. cit.*

7. The same balancing logic applies to Step C1. If constituency is not sufficiently intense to pass the critical threshold and policy position is sufficiently extreme, for example, policy dominates constituency.

8. For a recent example of the way in which congressmen use the consensus mode, see Elizabeth Drew, "A Tendency to Legislate," *The New Yorker,* June 26, 1978, pp. 80–89. Several congressmen relate their decision strategy in the case of votes on suspensions: If the bill is noncontroversial, vote for it; if there is some controversy involved, devise another way to decide, which generally is a version of cue-taking. This decision rule provides a powerful incentive for the bill's sponsors to arrange for the bill to appear noncontroversial even though it might not be, an implication to which we turn in Chapter 11.

9. Bradley Schram, "An Investigation into Disparity in Sentencing in Washtenaw County Circuit Court" (Senior Honors thesis, Department of Political Science, University of Michigan, 1972), pp. 73–74. I should mention that Schram's work done entirely independently of my own, and neither could have influenced the other.

11

Preconsensus Processes

Chapter 10 presented the consensus mode of decision, which appears to be the predominant means by which congressmen finally cast their votes. In this chapter the processes by which consensus is produced will be discussed. In this study, we cannot say with a high degree of certainty exactly how a congressman arrives at the position in which he perceives a consensus either in the total environment or in the field of forces which influences him individually. We are able, however, to point to several processes which are likely to be at work.

Generally speaking, there are two classes of such processes, environmental and personal. Either in the total legislative environment or in the field of forces which bears on his own decision, the congressman may discover an agreement or near-agreement on the direction which his vote should take. As an alternative to this environmental process of consensus-definition, the congressman himself may have some influence over the ways in which consensus is defined. His own attitude on the public policy issue facing him, for example, affects his choice of the fellow congressmen to whom he turns for advice.

ENVIRONMENTAL PROCESSES

It is possible for various actors in a congressman's environment to conspire to make consensus appear to be greater than it actually is. Such strategic manipulation, on the other hand, may not be necessary. The environment may simply exhibit no substantial conflict without it. There are thus two sets of environmental preconsensus processes: simple and contrived.

Simple Consensus

We need not be occupied long with the case of simple consensus. Often, there just is no substantial conflict in the legislative environment. If there is some, there is none in the field of forces which bears on an individual congressman's decision. Often, controversy over a given issue of public policy was settled long before a vote is taken. Very few serious political actors in the current day would argue that we should not have some kind of social security system, for instance, even though that issue was a matter of great controversy years ago. But votes on the final passage of social security bills today may either involve relatively minor changes in the basic thrust of the legislation, or may simply be opportunities for congressmen to get on the record for home consumption.

A factor contributing to simple consensus is actor involvement. As we have seen, some actors are not involved in congressmen's decisions much of the time, and others are involved only part of the time. On those votes in which a given actor is not active or is not noticed, that actor has no opportunity to contribute to conflict in a congressman's field of forces. In his field, for instance, the staff is often not involved, which leaves consensus or conflict in the field to be defined by other actors. The greater the number of actors involved in the congressman's decision, the greater is the likelihood that some conflict will result. Thus we have found, for example, that Republicans experienced a greater degree of conflict in their fields than did Northern Democrats, partly because the administration and party leadership were more often making requests of them than of the Democrats.

Contrived Consensus

Even if there is no simple consensus existing among the actors that could influence a congressman's decision, various of these actors may collaborate in order to iron out their differences and present congressmen with a version of united front, which, in turn, greatly simplifies his decisions and points out the direction which he should follow. Such prefloor collaboration both determines the consensus which emerges, and appears to be a systematic adaptation to the consensus mode of decision.

That mode clearly affects the kinds of strategies that are devised by participants in the legislative system. Knowing that the first decision rule is, "Is it controversial?" strategists inside and outside of the House deliberately attempt to structure the situation so as to minimize the controversy, at least among people who are basically like-minded. They do so partly to maximize their vote total, and partly to reduce the uncertainty about what will happen on the floor. One lobbyist stated the origins of the united education funding effort in the following, perhaps overly dramatic, way:

We concluded that if we went our separate ways, we'd be defeated. We finally made a pact that we were going to go into this thing together, that nobody was going to pull out when the chips were down and try to cut his own deal. If anybody split off, it was understood that the rest of the groups in the coalition would go against them, fight them, beat hell out of them, and never cooperate with them again.

Had these groups not coalesced in this way, the floor situation at best would have been less predictable, and at worst would have resulted in the defeat of a substantial part of the lobbying campaign.

Similar examples of this kind of strategic adaptation to the consensus mode are easy to find. The Appropriations Committee places such a high premium on coming to the floor united,[1] because they want the congressmen to answer the first question, "Is it controversial?" in the negative, and vote for the bill without amendment. In the Senate, the more united the reporting committee is, the greater is the chance that the motion will pass.[2] In another case, one Republican strategist recounted in some detail what he called "the byplay in the committee," the kinds of differences of opinion there were, even among members of the same party, and concluded after suffering a major defeat on the floor, "We had a problem there in the committee keeping the Republicans together." Another congressman referred to the problems caused for the farm-area congressmen by the internecine bickering:

I'm from a metropolitan area and I don't know much about farmers. So I talked to farm congressmen about agricultural bills. The first thing you'd find out is that they'd fight a lot among themselves. We'd get together in the bar of the Congressional Hotel, and after they were about half stiff, they'd really go at each other. It was more confusing than it was helpful. I don't talk to them about it any more.

To avoid this sort of situation, therefore, the major reference groups inside and outside of Congress who have some reasonable basis for agreement make some effort to get together, in order to approximate as closely as possible the consensus decisional mode. As we indicated in earlier chapters, furthermore, those who want to influence congressmen—interest groups, party leadership, administration—tend to avoid their opponents and to work with their friends, which further adds to the reinforcement effect. On the other hand, if one anticipates that he will lose on the floor given the current coalitions, one strategic option is to stimulate controversy in the hopes that out of the resulting chaos will come a more satisfactory result, or at least some publicity. In any event, our understanding of congressmen's decision rules helps us to understand the strategic behavior which permeates the legislative environment. This one bit of decision theory illuminates a good deal of the prefloor behavior of many legislative participants.

PERSONAL PROCESSES

In addition to the environmental processes which define consensus, a congressman himself has some control over the structure of the field of forces which influences him. He may hold a strong opinion on a given issue, for instance, and selects for informants those fellow congressmen in agreement with his view. Important interest groups in his constituency may take a strong position, for example, and he chooses to perceive the rest of the constituency as not caring about the issue a great deal. The administration may approach one of their partisans with a plea to vote with them, and he brings his own attitude into line with that position. In a number of ways, conscious and unconscious, involving cognitive dissonance reduction as well as selection of the actors to whom he turns, the congressman may personally play a part in producing consensus in his actual or perceived environment. I discuss three such influences on consensus here: the congressman's own policy attitudes, his voting history, and the weighing of individual actors.

Congressmen's Policy Attitudes

Concentrating on the influence of actors in the legislative system on congressmen's votes should not for a moment obscure the fact that congressmen themselves hold their own attitudes on questions of public policy, and that these attitudes affect their votes. When a congressman says, as several did, "I usually vote my political philosophy," it is not an idle statement. "You'll find that most guys are pretty well set most of the time," said one congressman. "People have well-formed opinions, and there's not much that can be done to shake them out of them." Examples of the importance of policy attitudes on votes abound at every hand in the interviews. On defense matters, one congressman will cite as an influence on his ABM vote his belief in a "strong national defense"; another expresses his willingness to "take some risks for peace" and adds, "it's a value judgment, not a question of fact"; yet another says, "I admit I started out predisposed to acquire just about any new weapon system that's laying around."

On education matters, one congressman told me, "I've always been for aid to education. It's the liberal position, you know"; while another explains, "I'm a conservative by inclination and I don't believe in massive federal aid to schools"; while yet another notes, "I think education is the best investment we can make." Another congressman addressed himself to the reform of the electoral college, saying: "On this issue, you're either for it or against it. You just have an immediate reaction and that's how you decide. Is this the democratic thing to do or is it not? It's as simple as that."

There is a question whether congressmen's attitudes are simply the rationalizations which they develop to justify their behavior to themselves and to others. One staffer told me that congressmen would merely tell me the rationalizations for their behavior, rather than the true reasons. This is in part a methodological point, one having to do with whether the interview data can be taken as "true" accounts of the reasons for voting. One of the virtues of the issue-by-issue interviewing technique employed here is its focus on concrete decisional contexts, and the resultant diminution of the degree to which respondents are able to engage in verbalizations which are not closely related to their actual behavior. As the quotations throughout this book should indicate, most congressmen did speak frankly.

But this methodological point masks a much more interesting substantive point. Even if congressmen do engage in a process of rationalization, this process is not "mere" in any sense. Indeed, rationalization itself is a highly important part of the decisional process. Congressmen like to believe that they are going through some sort of rational consideration which is connected to the issue of public policy they are deciding. They do not enjoy seeing themselves as being manipulated or pushed and pulled by forces beyond their control. As one congressman said, "People don't like to feel owned. They have to demonstrate their independence." Not only do they feel that they must somehow justify a vote to themselves, but they also believe that they must be prepared to explain their vote to others, particularly constituents. If the congressman cannot rationalize a vote in a given direction, it is unlikely that he will cast the vote in that direction. He must seize on some sort of argument that will justify his vote to himself and to others. For some congressmen, this is reinforcement; for others, persuasion.

All this would be rather unimportant if it were possible to get a congressman to rationalize any course of action. But it is not always possible to do so. Many Republicans, for instance, were called by their own administration to vote for an increase in the debt limit early in the Nixon administration's tenure in office, something which nearly all of them had opposed for years and years. Obtaining their votes was not easy, since they had to be persuaded, or provided with a rationalization for the vote. The rationalization that developed and one that surfaced repeatedly in interviews with Republicans went to the effect that President Nixon had inherited a deficit that was not his doing, that he would be fiscally responsible if given the time to straighten out the inherited mess, and that Republicans should thus help their president in this transitional period. This rationalization process was not mere window dressing; it was an integral part of the decision. Without it, the votes of many Republicans would not have been delivered. They had to be able to live with their decisions.

The debt limit was not the only case in which rationalization was an important part of the decision process. Many hard-liners on college unrest finally rationalized federal inaction with the argument that precipitous action would play into the hands of revolutionaries. In the cigarette advertising bill, as another example, it would be difficult to vote on the side of the tobacco interests if one were fully convinced that cigarette smoking inexorably led to lung cancer. Tobacco-area congressmen therefore took a good part of the hearing time to refute the Surgeon General's reports, to call physicians who were willing to testify that the causal link had not yet been established, and to question the statistical correlations in the absence of laboratory evidence. Whether such testimony and like information diffused to other congressmen was scientifically indisputable is quite beside the point. The result was that just enough doubt about the link between smoking and cancer was planted in the minds of congressmen so that they felt free to vote with the tobacco interests in good conscience. The fact that congressmen, in this and in many similar cases, go to considerable trouble to build a case and provide a rationalization for their colleagues, suggests that they themselves are much aware of the importance of the process.

We turn next to the form which congressmen's policy attitudes take. Several roll call studies have discovered that votes can be scaled along a rather limited number of dimensions.[3] Can we thus infer that congressmen think in a fashion that has some features of ideology? In fact, congressmen frequently did display a kind of dimensional thinking in my interviews. It is very common, for instance, to refer to a bill as being "stronger" or "weaker" because of amendments being offered. One Southern Democrat said that he voted for the Green substitute to the Elementary and Secondary Education bill "as a way of weakening the original committee bill." A Northern Democrat on the same bill stuck with the committee, because "I wanted the strongest bill possible. Then when [Chairman] Perkins offered his substitute, I of course went along, because that was the strongest thing available at that point." On coal mine safety legislation, references were often made to a general dimension of "toughness" on the mine operators: a given amendment is "too tough," or "not tough enough." Any appropriation or authorization bill, of course, is particularly amenable to this sort of dimensional thinking, since greater or lesser amounts of money are involved by definition. The general point which emerges is that congressmen are quite comfortable with thinking in terms of general evaluative dimensions and placing political objects (amendments, groups, congressmen) along those dimensions at points they perceive to be appropriate. Thus a given amendment would "weaken" the bill; or Congressman X is for a "stronger" bill, and so forth.

For many congressmen, these broad evaluative continua are an important device to structure their decisions. At least for a congressman who is at either end of a given spectrum, ideology is a means to array the amendments and the proponents on the continuum, enabling him to vote for the one nearest him. To illustrate the process, one liberal Democrat said of the Elementary and Secondary bill, "There were no decisions to make. It was a totally inadequate bill. But weak as it was, I had to vote for the strongest bill available. That was to go with Perkins." As he generalized his position later in the interview, "I usually don't have any trouble deciding. I'm probably the most progressive member of the House. It's almost always a question of not doing enough, as far as I'm concerned." Since the congressman places himself at the left in an ideological continuum on nearly everything, he simply picks the alternative closest to the left end. Other congressmen evidenced the same sort of thinking. A Northern Democrat said of the funding for water pollution abatement, "I voted for the $1 billion. We could spend $25 billion and still not have the thing licked." On the same issue, a conservative Republican had obviously decided to spend the least possible amount: "We can't spend money we haven't got to spend.

(Question: What if the committee had voted a smaller amount?) I'd have gone with that. I sure won't amend it to increase the spending."

We might speculate, however, that policy continua are much more useful for those who are near the ends of those continua than they are for those who place themselves closer to the middle. Ideologues of the left and right have an easy time using ideology as a guide; they just choose the alternative nearest to them. But ideology is somewhat less useful for the person in the middle, who cannot place proposals and proponents on evaluative dimensions as readily and cannot judge distances on those dimensions as easily. To put the same point more technically, the congressman on the end is only required to treat continua ordinally: He simply needs to see objects as closer or farther away and to choose the closest one. But the congressman in the middle must additionally treat a dimension in an interval fashion: He must judge *how far* from his middle position in either direction a given proposal is. Such a task is much more difficult, and makes ideological dimensions much less useful than they are for ideologues of the left or right.

To return to attitude as a preconsensus process, there are a number of ways in which a congressman's general policy attitudes contribute to the consensus which he perceives in the field of forces which influences his decision. Congressmen often select those portions of the environment to which they will pay attention and selectively perceive and misperceive other actors, according to the policy attitudes which they hold. The congressman's own policy attitudes are highly important guides to choosing the colleagues within the House to whom he will turn for advice in voting, for instance. A fellow congressman is a surrogate for one's own ideology, and given the wide range of choice among available colleagues, is probably a reasonably close approximation.

This highly important generalization about the importance of policy attitudes in picking informants within the House can be extended to the rest of the environment as well. Basically, the recruitment process—nominations, elections, and related events—brings people to Congress who have fairly well-formed attitudes on major directions of public policy. There can be some incremental adjustments in these attitudes, but the basic parameters of legislative decisions are set by these distributions of congressmen's attitudes. As one staffer said: "There's a lot less soul-searching and introspection than you might think. Very little midnight oil [is] burned. Most members come here with well-formed predispositions. They're very opinionated and their minds are made up beforehand. There's very little you can do to change their minds."

Once congressmen are in office, their environment is highly complex. A plethora of interest groups confronts them, and a wide spectrum of opinion exists among their colleagues. Given his initial recruitment and the constituency boundaries within which he is obliged to operate, a congressman has ample opportunity to select from the rest of the environment those sources and those bits of information which reinforce his original disposition. Once he picks out the reinforcing things as being persuasive or right, he tends to dismiss the rest as coming from the wrong crowd or as not convincing. One congressman laid out this process of original predisposition and subsequent reinforcement very nicely, in the case of the Elementary and Secondary Education Act:

First, I'm a conservative by inclination, and I don't believe in massive federal aid to schools. So I was predisposed against Perkins and the committee. Second, I'm a Republican, and I'll support the administration when I can. In this case, happily enough, the two coincided, so I didn't have any problem. And as I listened to the debate, I thought Mrs. Green was by far the most effective speaker. She knows what she's doing. So that reinforced my original feeling.

We are accustomed to thinking of influence as being closely connected to attitude or behavior change. Dahl's definition that one person influences another when he moves the other to do something that he would not otherwise have done[4] has its parallels in lay thinking, when it is alleged that a given event or person "didn't make any difference" because no change resulted. Actually, this reinforcement effect of communication and its ability to structure a consensus in a congressman's perceptual field is by no means unimportant. Given a legislative environment containing a flurry of contradictory cues and pressures, any mechanism which reinforces and, thus, promotes behavioral stability is of great importance, whether one views such an effect normatively as being a net gain or loss.

There is some fragmentary evidence in my data which indicates the importance of this selection of cues according to ideology. If one takes all the possible pairs of actors and examines only those cases in which the two actors of a given pair were in conflict, one finds in virtually every pair that liberals (as measured by a relatively high Americans for Democratic Action score) tend to vote with the liberal actor of the pair, and that conservatives tend to vote with the conservative actor, regardless of which actors are involved. While this tendency to vote with the actor with whom the congressman shares a general ideological viewpoint varies in strength from one pair to another, it is nearly always present.

In addition to this tendency to select cues according to previous general policy orientation or ideology, part of the reinforcement or consensus effect is the well-known phenomenon of selective perception. Congressmen place different constructions or interpretations on similar events, depending on their previous attitudes. A fascinating case in point were congressmen's attitudes toward the activity of Community Action Programs within the poverty program. When the Office of Economic Opportunity legislation was before the House, congressmen often referred in the interviews to the political actions of poverty workers. Those who opposed the program deplored such activity; those who favored the program tolerated it. In fact, strikingly similar incidents were given very different constructions, depending upon the congressman involved. Consider the following two reports from congressmen who are sympathetic to the poverty program:

They organized and financed a march on the Housing Board by elderly people, when all they would have had to do was place a couple of phone calls and the thing would have been taken care of. I told them this, and the guy said that it was therapy for the elderly. Okay, I guess.

We've had a few flaps, but nothing serious. You have to expect some administrative problems. They go off in strange directions sometimes. I get frantic calls at the eleventh hour that they can't meet the payroll this pay period. Or one faction is pulling out of the program over something or other. You have to expect that.

These same events reported by an opponent of the poverty program would be interpreted very differently. One such opponent referred to such incidents in his area as evidence of "agitating, political work, and promoting anarchy." In general, events are interpreted according to the attitudes and perceptions which the congressman brings to the fresh information.

In view of all the tendencies toward reinforcement, attitudinal or behavioral change is rather difficult to accomplish and infrequent in occurrence. Change does take place, but it generally comes about in one of two ways, both of them rare. One is through a sustained movement of uncontrollable events or of contrived pressure, repeated forcefully over a long period of time. The change in attitudes about Vietnam over several years both inside Congress and in the general public, and the emphasis on "reordering priorities" are both examples of this kind of long-term change. The other means of change is through a shift in the House membership. In this case, the processes of nomination and election bring new congressmen with new attitudes into the body, thus shifting the distributions. Both of these occurrences, however, are likely to reflect gross societal changes or dramatic environmental shocks. More short-run change, involving a given piece of legislation and taking place within a shorter time period, is quite unlikely.

As it happens, the decade of the 1970s produced one of those rare shifts in the membership. The combination of substantial numbers of defeats, as in 1974 with Republicans, and large numbers of retirements has resulted in quite an unusual turnover in membership. In 1979, over half of the House of Representatives had been in Congress for four or fewer years, and over half of the Senate had been in that body for six or fewer years. The results have been evident on every hand: The serious erosion of the seniority system, as evidenced by the removal of three committee chairs in 1975 and the subsequent election of relatively junior subcommittee chairs; the advent of such rules changes as recorded teller voting and open rules for Ways and Means bills; the diminution of the power of committee chairs and the strengthening of subcommittees; the beginning of the congressional budget process; and the considerable increase in staffing. Not all of these changes can be attributed solely to the change in membership, but it is clear that turnover has had an important impact. The winds of change have been blowing through Congress, related in large part to the change of membership.

But the difficulties of producing at least short-run attitude change have prominent effects on the kinds of strategies that are employed to pass or to retard legislation. By and large, attitude change is a long-term proposition. It takes time, turns of events, and constant efforts at persuasion. But lobbying strategies are generally more short-term, operating within a time frame which does not allow for attitude change. The arguments about the substance of the issue, therefore, are useful only for those who already agree with the legislative strategist, and may suffice if that core of support already exceeds the winning margin. But to attract others to the coalition, legislative strategists often avoid arguments that have to do with the substance of the issue at hand. Instead, they employ nonsubstantive arguments, such as appeals to congressional procedure, institutional loyalty, party loyalty, and like desiderata.[5]

Examples of this sort of strategic adaptation are not difficult to locate. When administration spokesmen were attempting to persuade Republicans to vote for a debt limit increase, they did not attempt to persuade them of the wisdom of a certain kind of national debt management or of a new way of economic thinking. Rather, their arguments were couched in terms that the Nixon administration was not responsible for an inherited deficit and that party loyalty pointed in the direction of administration support. Or again, farm-area congressmen and the Agriculture Department tended not to concentrate on the substance of the payment limitation, but rather on its administrative feasibility and on the argument that it should not be done in an appropriations bill. Or opponents of the House Un-American Activities Committee, in an effort to enlarge their vote, concentrated not on direct attacks against the committee, but rather on the more procedural point that its functions should be under the aegis of the Judiciary Committee. Avoidance of the "issues" is often a way to enlarge the coalition, given the dim prospects for short-term attitude change.

Finally, given the obvious importance of the congressman's own policy attitude in his voting, it would be tempting to adopt an ideological model as one's sole explanation for legislative voting behavior. For a number of reasons, however, I have chosen instead to treat general policy attitudes as one important preconsensus process which may structure a decisional context, rather than an alternative model. There should be a clear distinction made, in the first place, between general policy orientations and attitudes toward specific pieces of legislation. Congressmen may well have rather well-formed general orientations. But partly because of the sheer volume and complexity of issues upon which they are called to vote, their policy attitudes toward specific amendments and bills are likely to be much less well formed in advance of a given vote. A congressman is quite open to suggestion, particularly on questions of minor importance or low visibility, but even on rather major pieces of legislation. On some issues, he may use the consensus mode of decision without even forming a policy attitude. Everyone to whom he would pay attention is for a given course of action, and he goes along without thinking about the matter. On other issues, the information coming to the congressman or the information to which he chooses to pay attention results in the formation of a specific policy attitude toward the particular vote in question. Once this specific attitude is formed, of course, the congressman almost never votes contrary to it, as my data show. What is interesting, however, is not that this happens, but how these attitudes were arrived at.

Even if a congressman does have a fairly well-formed attitude on a particular policy issue, furthermore, he often finds some sort of communication process useful in terms of linking his attitude to votes on particular amendments or bills.[6] The fact that he is strongly for civil rights legislation, for instance, does not by itself give him sufficient guidance in voting on a given amendment to a Judiciary Committee or an Appropriations Committee bill. He needs to know what the effect of the amendment is, who favors and who opposes it, and what its substantive and political implications are. In addition, as argued previously, ideology is a much less useful guide for moderates and those in the middle of given policy continua than it is for those of either the left or right.

Consistency and Voting History

Very similar to congressmen's general policy attitudes, in terms of its operation as a preconsensus process, is a drive toward consistency. Once a congressman has established a pattern of behavior, this pattern may structure current decisions. The constituents to whom he pays the greatest attention, for instance, often let him know that they approve of his past behavior, and he often picks informants in the House who reinforce it. Thus, in much the same way that the congressman's field of forces can be structured by his ideology, so can it be structured by his previous behavior.

Congressmen most often operationalize this consistency in terms of their voting history. If they have voted one way in the past, there is a tendency for them to vote the same way again. As one said of his vote on the foreign aid bill, "I voted against it last time, the time before that, and the time before that. So I voted against it again." Another said of his vote for an education bill, "This is a matter of long-standing position." Not only does this sort of history have an impact on congressmen's individual decisions, but it structures an entire institutional context. One congressman said of the amendment to the Elementary and Secondary Education Act: "This was an old issue. Federal aid to education has been kicking around for a long time. The basic problems with it were settled several years ago. What you saw last week was a minor skirmish. This was pretty typical of a lot of legislative situations."

It is possible to obtain some quantitative indications of the degree to which a voting history was important in the decisions under study. For each decision, a classification was made as to whether a previous voting history was of major or determinative importance on the one hand, or of minor or no importance on the other.[7] In 43 percent of the cases, the voting history was of at least major importance, with the remaining 57 percent showing the history being classified as of minor or no importance. Many of the issues in this core sample were fairly new issues, ones that were either up for decision for the first time, or did not yet have a clear history established for them. Issues were selected in part because they were new issues over which the controversy and publicity were likely to be relatively intense. Considering this sampling fact, therefore, voting history would probably prove to be more important if one included a large number of relatively minor votes in the sample. This reasoning is lent some credence by the fact that in the low-salience votes within this sample, voting history seems more important than in the other votes. Of the decisions on low-salience issues, 64 percent have voting history as a major or determinative ingredient, compared with a 30 percent incidence for medium-salience and 34 percent for high-salience issues.

One might also expect that congressmen of higher seniority would vote more often according to their previous pattern. As one senior member of the House told me, "After you've been around here for several years as I have, you've plowed the ground before. You've read and studied on it, and you develop a pattern." Without the chance to establish such a pattern, the junior member would presumably find a voting history to be of less use. But contrary to this expectation, no such difference emerged among seniority levels. This lack of difference probably obtains, first, because the issues tended to be of high salience and of short history themselves, which would give a senior congressman no greater advantage in voting history than one many years his junior. Second, it is possible that one establishes a voting history very quickly indeed, and that even very junior congressmen find previous votes cast only a year or two ago as helpful in decision-making as they would histories of longer duration. One congressman with only slightly more than two years' experience in the House reflected, "I think after three or four years you develop an instinct about how to vote, and you just do it. Younger people like me agonize more, but even I am settling into a rut." If it takes such a short time to establish a voting history, then voting history would be of similar importance at all seniority levels except the very lowest. Closer inspection of the relatively junior group of congressmen, in fact, reveals exactly this quick learning of the uses of voting history. Among freshmen congressmen (those who are in their first term in the House) previous behavior is of major importance in only one vote decision.[8] But among those who have been in the House only one term before the present one, voting history is of major importance about half the time.

There are a number of reasons why a voting history, or more broadly, consistency, would be of some importance in a congressman's decisions. One is simple conditioning. Like other human beings, a congressman may simply repeat what he has done before, as a kind of conditioned reflex. If he has not been negatively reinforced for a given vote before, and to an extent has been positively reinforced, he repeats that behavior. One congressman said about seating Adam Clayton Powell, "I voted to seat Powell last time, and I expected quite a reaction. But it didn't materialize. So this time it wasn't a problem." Said another about the same vote, "It's like diving off the 10-foot board. The first time you do it, it's hard. But once you've done it, then it gets easier." As another congressman summarized the point, "I guess I voted mostly out of habit."

Second, past history is quite an important aid to rational calculation, in an incremental decision-making sense. If a congressman can take his past history as given for the most part, and use it as a guide to present and future behavior, this drastically reduces the decisional burden. As one said, "I've been over this ground before. That helps a good deal in deciding." Much of the time, nothing changes in the interim which would make the congressman change his voting behavior. Even in those instances in which they do speak of having shifted their positions, it is portrayed as a very gradual, incremental shift that was many years in the coming. Several talked of having "come around" over a period of years to favoring direct election of the president. Another referred to his gradual disenchantment with agriculture subsidies until this year when he decided to "make the break" and vote to limit them.

A final reason for consistency is more political. Congressmen find it difficult to explain inconsistency to their constituents. Rationalizations for votes, once developed, have a way of pre-judging similar issues subsequently. Said one congressman, "I came here pledged to vote against more taxes, and it's a tough thing to go back and tell radio and TV audiences that I've changed my mind." A good part of Republican discomfort over voting for a debt limit increase also had to do with the problem of explaining inconsistency with their past records. In addition to this constituency consideration, consistency is also important in terms of dealing with one's colleagues in the House. One congressman translated this general need for consistency into his particular concern with the possible disadvantages of direct election of the president for his own urban constituents: "I find opposition to direct election awfully hard for me to justify. Here I'm in favor of one man–one vote and have been fighting for it for years. There will be another fight later on over congressional election standards. Now, how can I say one man–one vote for Congress, but not for president? You just can't make a case that way."

Once again, as in the case of the congressman's ideology, it might be tempting to consider a congressman's voting history as a model of decision, sufficient in itself to explain his votes. An incremental model of decision which has been used successfully in other contexts,[9] might apply here. Instead of treating an incremental model as an alternative to the consensus decision model, however, I have opted to consider past behavior as another important preconsensus process. Voting history, first, does not seem to be sufficiently important in my data to give us the kind of confidence we would need in order to accept an incremental process as our dominant explanation for congressmen's voting decisions. Quite often on both new issues at the cutting edge of policy-making as well as on more routine but minor matters, the congressman simply may not have a strong past voting history. If he does have a voting history, furthermore, he must implicity ask himself if there is any current reason to deviate from it, which obliges him not to vote simply as he has done in the past. He wants to know if any of the parameters which had affected his original decision have changed in the interim, and whether the current situation is a meaningful reproduction of the previous one. One congressman, for instance, simply checked with the sponsor of an amendment to make sure that it was the same one that he had offered the previous year. Another respondent, in a clear allusion to both the field of forces and to voting history, said of his decision to vote for Vietnam appropriations: "I was precommitted in a way. I had fought that out with myself some time ago—a year or longer—and had decided at that time to support funding for Vietnam. I'd already been through that, and nothing in my circle of relevant factors had changed since."

Single-actor Weighting

In Chapter 2, we discussed the manner in which a congressman weighs constituency intensity. If the constituency was perceived to be particularly intense about an issue and the congressman had no strong preference, he found it convenient to vote with his constituency. This sort of intensity calculus can be extended to other actors as well, and constitutes another type of process which may be responsible for the degree of consensus which a congressman finds in the field of forces which can be thought to influence him. An intense constituency, a well-placed committee chairman with a reputation for a long memory, or the administration for congressmen of the president's party—all are capable of structuring congressmen's cues and perceptions in much the same way as his own attitude does. An intense constituency, for example, may determine what the congressman's own attitude will be toward a specific piece of legislation, which in turn influences his choice of informants within the House. Or for Republicans under the Nixon administration, a clear and vigorous presidential preference combined with party leadership activity may persuade him to go along, to formulate a new attitude toward the issue, and perhaps to perceive constituents as not being particularly interested in it.

In contrast to the effect of intensity, single actors may define consensus through default. On a low-visibility matter in which there are virtually no cues from the environment, for instance, and on which the congressman has no pronounced preference, the fellow congressman to whom he turns may simply define the direction of the field which is operative on that particular decision. Or when the congressman has no strong opinion or voting history, and few actors are concerned about the issue, a lobbyist whom he has come to trust may bend his ear. Fellow congressmen are most prone to be the single actors of great importance in such cases, for reasons discussed in Chapter 3.

CONCLUSIONS

The state of consensus in a congressman's perceptual field, which we discussed in Chapter 10, has a set of antecedents, the preconsensus processes. These processes determine the pattern of consensus which he finds in his environment on any given issue. Once that state has been established, the congressman is then free to use the consensus mode of decision as his rule of thumb for making up his mind. Preconsensus processes are not portrayed as possible alternative models to the consensus mode, but rather as factors which affect the degree of agreement to be found.

Preconsensus processes can be divided into two categories: environmental and personal. Environmental consensus can come about either because there simply is no disagreement anywhere in the set of possible influences on congressmen's decisions, or because actors in that set realize that the congressman uses the consensus mode of decision and, consequently, they contrive agreement in order to impel him in the desired direction. The congressman himself, however, is not just carried along with his environment, but rather has some personal influence in the process of consensus-definition. He structures his own environment according to his general policy attitudes, through selection of those cues to which he pays attention, and through selective perception of information which comes to him. His own past voting history plays a similar part in structuring consensus in his field. Finally, single actors, such as an aroused constituency or a determined president, are sometimes weighted by the congressman in such a fashion as to determine the degree of consensus in the field. It is not possible in this study to place an order on these various processes, in the sense either of establishing the frequency with which each occurs, singly or in combination, or of specifying which of them might control the effects of which others. What we have done is to identify the processes, describe their workings and effects, and connect them logically to the consensus mode of decision as antecedents.

It is worth noting, finally, that an understanding of congressmen's decision-making tells us some interesting things about the wider political system. A tremendous amount of prefloor activity, for instance, can be seen essentially as consensus-building, an adaptation to the congressmen's use of the consensus mode on the part of those who would want to influence legislative outcomes. Other strategies in the legislative process can be understood in the same terms, as adaptations to congressmen's decision rules, such as the avoidance of attempts at attitude change and the importance of providing rationalizations for votes. A decision-making approach, in short, has broader implications than simply a description of the decisions themselves.

NOTES

1. Richard F. Fenno, Jr., *Power of the Purse* (Boston: Little, Brown, 1966), pp. 163–166.
2. Donald R. Matthews, *U.S. Senators and their World* (Chapel Hill: University of North Carolina Press, 1960; Vintage Books), pp. 168–169. Other examples in the literature include Manley's discussion of executive branch attention to the problem, in John F. Manley, *The Politics of Finance* (Boston: Little, Brown, 1970), pp. 357 and 374; and Mayhew's portrayal of the breakdown of the agriculture consensus, in David R. Mayhew, *Party Loyalty among Congressmen* (Cambridge, Mass.: Harvard University Press, 1966), p. 37.
3. Duncan MacRae, Jr., *Dimensions of Congressional Voting* (Berkeley: University of California Press, 1958); Aage R. Clausen, "Measurement Identity in the Longitudinal Analysis of Legislative Voting," *American Political Science Review* 61(1967):1020–1035; Clausen, *How Congressmen Decide* (New York: St. Martin's, 1973); Herbert Weisberg, "Scaling Models for Legislative Roll Call Analysis," *American Political Science Review* 66(1972):1306–1315; Weisberg, "Dimensional Analysis of Legislative Roll Calls." Ph.D. dissertation, University of Michigan, 1968; Jerrold Schneider, *Ideological Coalitions in Congress* (Westport, Conn.: Greenwood Press, 1979). A fascinating argument for the importance of politicians' policy attitudes is Anthony King, "Ideologies as Predictors of Public Patterns," paper prepared for the 1971 Annual Meeting of the *American Political Science Association;* see also King, "Ideas, Institutions, and the Policies of Governments," *British Journal of Political Science* 3(1973):291–314, 409–424; and David Cameron, "The Expansion of the Public Economy," *American Political Science Review* 72(1978):1243–1261.
4. Robert A. Dahl, "The Concept of Power," *Behavioral Science* 2 (1957):202–203.
5. As majority leader of the Senate, Lyndon Johnson often appealed to senators' party loyalty and institutional patriotism. See Ralph K. Huitt, "Democratic Party Leadership in the Senate," *American Political Science Review* 55 (1961):333–344.
6. See Donald R. Matthews and James A. Stimson, "Decision-Making by U.S. Representatives," in *Political Decision-Making*, ed. S. Sidney Ulmer (New York:

Van Nostrand, 1970), pp. 20–21, on the question of an ideological model of legislative voting.

7. The original coding was fourfold as indicated—no, minor, major, determinative—but was collapsed into a dichotomy in order to diminish problems with intercoder reliability. See Appendix C for a complete discussion.

8. In that one, the freshman congressman had taken a strong position on the same issue in the state legislature, and referred to that previous position in such a way as to indicate that it had markedly affected his current decision.

9. Charles E. Lindblom, "Decision-making in Taxation and Expenditures," in *Public Finances: Needs, Sources, and Utilization* (Princeton, N.J.: National Bureau of Economic Research, 1961); Lindblom, "The Science of 'Muddling Through,'" *Public Administration Review* 19(1959):79–88; and Aaron Wildavsky, *The Politics of the Budgetary Process* (Boston: Little, Brown, 1964), pp. 13–16.

12

Structural Decision Features

The bulk of this book is about political choice: With a given set of alternatives facing them, how do congressmen choose among them? This concentration on choice should not be allowed to obscure the fact that there are other features of the decision process which are highly important and which deserve some discussion. From time to time throughout the book, we have made passing references to agenda-setting and decision boundaries. The data on voting decisions reported in this book do allow some informed speculation on these structural decision features

THE AGENDA AND ALTERNATIVES

Throughout most of this book, we have concentrated on the final step in the decision process: choice. Actually, one can conceive of two previous steps which are also highly important in terms of understanding the outcomes of the legislative process. The first step is the setting of the agenda for decision, that is, the collection of topics which become subjects for governmental policy. Then within these topics or policy concerns, the second step is the specifying of the alternatives among which a choice is to be made. In the third and final step, a choice is made among the alternatives. The processes by which the agenda and alternatives are determined, and which actors in the political system have a primary role in these processes, are as crucial to an understanding of governmental policy-making as the choice processes themselves.

It is important to keep in mind that in the process of setting the agenda and specifying the alternatives, a good many policy options are eliminated from consideration. There is a myriad of subjects that could conceivably be decided by Congress or by any other authoritative decision body. Governmental decision-makers, particularly congressmen, cannot attend to them all or even to a very large fraction of them. The subjects that do become part of the decisional agenda, therefore, represent only a part of the population of subjects that are potential agenda items. This selection of which subjects to address and which ones to overlook is a kind of structural "decision" of major consequence.[1] In the process, a goodly number of potential agenda items are left untouched. Similarly, once a matter does reach the decisional agenda, the process by which alternatives are evoked and seriously considered is also crucial. At this stage, many alternatives will be eliminated from serious consideration, and only a few are left for the final choice stage. Many of the decisional possibilities, both in terms of subjects to be considered and alternatives to be weighed, are screened out before the final choice stage is reached.

Attention-getting

The first agenda process in the legislative case is what I choose to label "attention-getting." There are so many people, events, and pieces of information that compete for a congressman's attention, that his conscious or unconscious choice about which matters will receive his attention is a decision of great moment. Apart from the congressman's choices about attention, furthermore, the communication net which brings certain things to his attention and screens out other things is also of crucial importance in determining which matters will be left untouched, which problems will be left unsolved.

Congressmen themselves continually refer to the mechanisms by which information penetrates their consciousness and thus has some potential for an impact on their decisions. They themselves use the phrase, "bringing it to our attention." One said of a doctor's testimony about the terrible shortages of supplies and personnel at D.C. General Hospital, "If people don't bring these problems to our attention, we never hear about them." Another said about his relationship with a member of the Ways and Means Committee, "Every now and then someone would write me with some problem they were having, and if I thought it was something that should be brought to his attention, I'd send him a copy." Another referred to the tax reform bill: "Bolling caught this thing on the rate structure, or whoever brought it to his attention." An unusually reflective congressman, after having described his considerable efforts to study the antiballistic missile issue, mused, "One interesting question: Why am I studying *this?* What made me pick it? Usually, this would just zip through

—another piece of hardware for the military—what else is new? I don't know the answer."

It is difficult to exaggerate the importance of attention-getting. If a matter is not brought to congressmen's attention, it will not become a subject of legislative action, in statute or otherwise. In an effort to conserve time and handle an impossible job, congressmen often start by assuming implicitly that if a problem is not brought to their attention, then the problem does not exist. The intensity with which people hold their attitudes is often measured by contact with the congressman. If constituents do not contact him, for instance, he assumes they have little interest. Or if the administration is not actively lobbying for its position, he assumes the administration regards the matter as being of low priority. In other words, unless something is forcibly brought to his attention and kept there, it tends to be shunted aside in the terrific press of other business.

There appear to be several agents of attention-getting, that is, several sources of agenda items. First, as argued in Chapter 8, the mass media appear to be important in setting the agenda. Printed and broadcast media are capable of the kind of continuous and prominent coverage of a story which makes it virtually impossible for a congressman to ignore. Since congressmen follow the media, they themselves notice such coverage. But indirectly as well, there is no other actor in the system which is in quite the same position to arouse the attention of constituents or to stimulate the avalanche of "spontaneous" mail as is the media. Conversely, the media also play a prominent part in selecting out the subjects which fail to appear on the agenda. There are surely many congressmen and other political actors who have abandoned attempts to get subjects considered for want of media attention.

A second actor in the system which appears to have a negligible independent effect on the final choice, but which has a rather more important effect on the agenda, is the collection of Washington-based policy elites. Many authors have discussed their importance.[2] The boundaries of such an elite are not particularly well defined, but they include lobbyists, academics, think-tank members, and governmental officials. A good bit of lobbying may not have much effect except to keep a subject on the agenda, as discussed in Chapter 5, but in view of the competition for a place on the agenda, this is no mean accomplishment.

Another attention-getting force is the congressman's own colleagues. A few particularly innovative or ambitious congressmen are acutely aware of the importance of the agenda, and participate actively in its definition. They take on causes, and by repeated and insistent talking in various forums, through which they communicate directly with their colleagues and indirectly through the media, they manage to force other congressmen to pay attention to what they are saying. One Northern Democrat reflected: "This notion of national priorities is catching on, I think. (Kingdon: It's almost a cliché) Well, sometimes you have to repeat things and repeat and repeat until you almost gag on the words before people will finally grasp it. You may be up to your nose in the water, but it's barely washed over their boots. This is one of those cases." Media coverage patterns enhance the importance of these congressmen in affecting the public agenda, since they capture headlines by virtue of the journalists' tendency to display congressional activities prominently.

Finally, it should not be forgotten that inescapable turns of events that are not particularly under the control of any identifiable set of system actors often structure the agenda, perhaps more than anything else. A mine disaster at Farmington, West Virginia, placed the subject of coal mine safety on the agenda in a forceful way, and resulted finally in new safety legislation. The 1968 presidential candidacy of George Wallace threw a scare into leaders of the two major parties both in and out of Congress, resulting in active interest in electoral college reform. As one congressman wryly observed, "I've always favored reform, whenever it would come up. Now that it was forcibly brought to our attention, it is up." Congressmen and others may seize upon such events to dramatize the need for governmental attention to a problem. A group of congressmen waged a fight early in 1969 to refuse the counting of a North Carolina Republican elector's vote for Wallace, not so much to affect that vote as to dramatize the need for electoral reform. But crisis events are often important in and of themselves, and not particularly controllable.

One kind of event which is worth notice is what I call a "focusing event." Once a matter is in the congressman's attention field, events may take place which have a powerful focusing effect. A former Treasury Secretary's comment that there was a "taxpayer revolt" in progress, for instance, obviously summarized the experience of many congressmen in talks with their constituents, and was repeatedly cited in interviews on tax matters. Or Senator Eastland's substantial agricultural payment came up over and over again in my interviews about the farm payment limitation. Or the Ford Foundation grants to aides of the late Senator Robert Kennedy symbolized to many congressmen everything that they had found wrong with foundations. It is not clear that this sort of event has an effect on legislative outcomes independent of other factors at work. But such a focusing event often does serve as an important catalytic agent. It strikes a responsive chord in congressmen because it symbolizes something in their own experience. They pick it up, and from then on the focusing event proves to have a dynamic of its own.[3]

The Legislative Agenda
Once a subject is on the public agenda, the focus of attention in a rather wide circle of attentive people, it must still be placed on the legislative agenda. In this substep of agenda-setting, the standing committees and the party leadership, particularly of the majority party, are of major importance. Some of this influence on the legislative agenda has to do with the scheduling function, through which the timing of votes can be manipulated to maximize the chances that the view of the leadership will prevail. The committees also serve as legislative agenda-setters, particularly through their power to block legislation and prevent it from ever reaching the floor. Many subjects never reach the whole House because of the influence of the standing committees, party leaders, and the Rules Committee on the legislative agenda, and those that do are affected by the timing of their consideration.

Decision-making changes in several respects as a congressional session progresses, due in part to committee and leadership timing. It is possible to divide the issues which form the core sample of this study according to the time of the session in which they were considered: the first five as being at the early part of the session, the middle five votes at midsession, and the last five at the end of the session. As the session moves along, two features of congressmen's decisions change markedly.[4] First, decisions become less routine. At the beginning of the session, there is more voting by previous history, less search for information, and less uncertainty about the decision than there is later in the session. Second, more information and more varieties of information are brought to bear on later decisions than on those made earlier in the session. Congressmen go outside their state delegation more, receive more conflicting cues and fewer strictly procedural cues, receive more information from their constituency and more mail, and increase their supply of information from staffs and reading. As the session proceeds, then, decisions become less routine and more information-laden.

Reasons for these changes are rooted in the behavior of House agenda agents. The committees and the leadership tend to get routine and minor pieces of legislation out of the way early in the session and take longer to consider the more major bills in committee. This tendency was exacerbated in the session under study because it was the first term of a new administration, though it probably is true of most sessions to some extent. To this natural rhythm of committee consideration of legislation, which may have no necessary conscious design, should be added an explicitly strategic possibility: Committee and party leaders may delay some of the legislation for which they anticipate trouble on the floor until later in the session, in the hope that the committee bill and the conference report encounter fewer serious attempts at amendment at the end of the session. This would presumably occur since in the rush for adjournment, the legislative process often becomes terribly confused; congressmen's attention is much more diffused and less focused on particular features of given bills, and the chances are better than they would have been earlier for a committee bill or conference report to come through floor consideration unscathed.

Alternative Specification

After the agenda has been set, the alternatives among which the final choice will be made are specified. In this step, members of the standing committee that consider the bill assume a primary importance, at least in terms of setting the alternatives for floor choices. As we pointed out in Chapter 4, congressmen largely leave to committee members these choices about which alternatives to pose. If they are not presented with the alternatives they would ideally prefer, they feel nearly powerless to change them. They can, of course, choose fairly freely among the alternatives presented by majority and minority members of the committee. But they find it very difficult to change those alternatives or to generate new ones. One congressman said, "You just take what you're presented with."

In this process of structuring the alternatives which will be presented to their colleagues for ultimate decision, the com-

mittee members engage in a number of crucial behavior patterns in addition to simply deciding which alternatives will and
will not be presented. They may paper over their differences in
the committee, for instance, and never present alternatives to the
whole House at all. They are also instrumental in translating the
concern which placed a subject on the agenda into concrete
proposals. This translation process does not always accurately
mirror the original concerns. In the tax reform case, for instance,
it was public outcry at the level of taxes which played a large
part in placing the item on the agenda, but this outcry was
translated, not only into simple tax cuts, but also into a degree of
tax reform. In other words, the committee members evoke the
alternatives to be seriously considered.[5] Finally, in the alternatives which they do present, committee majorities and dissenters who offer amendments often package their amendments
in such a way as to prevent congressmen from picking and choosing among provisions as they see fit. The Joelson amendment to
the Health, Education, and Welfare appropriations bill was a
classic case in point: The popular impacted aid was joined to
the unpopular education programs, many of which if considered
separately would go down to defeat. Or on occasion, if a package
approach appears unlikely to succeed, the proposers of amendments may break up a package in order to salvage what they can
from it.

DECISION BOUNDARIES

In the entire discussion of the importance of agenda-setting and
alternative-specifying agents in the political system, it is well
to keep in mind that rank-and-file congressmen deciding how to
vote on the floor of the House are not without their own influence
on the prechoice processes. As I argued at some length in Chapter 4, alternatives are not simply presented to congressmen. Instead, committee members' and others' calculations about "what
will go," based on congressmen's preferences, play a vital part
in structuring the alternatives in the first place. Agenda- and
alternative-setters find that they are obliged to operate within
the boundaries set for them by the whole House. Thus, the Ways
and Means Committee members calculated the effects of various
tax reform provisions on floor votes, Appropriations Committee
members were continually concerned about "getting rolled" on
the floor, amendment-writers would ask themselves whether or

not they could "sell" a given amendment on the floor, and so forth.

As I also discussed in Chapter 4, the consequences of failing to anticipate floor reactions adequately are painfully evident. The Appropriations Committee's failure to build sufficient impacted aid funds into the education appropriation, for example, resulted in getting rolled to the spectacular tune of about one billion dollars. The move of the Education and Labor Committee majority to extend the Elementary and Secondary Education Act for five years went down to decisive defeat. By contrast, Wilbur Mills's reputation for care in anticipating floor reaction was repeatedly confirmed through the session under study.

The notion that committees must operate within the boundaries set for them by the whole House, of course, has been discussed in several other legislative studies. A major theme of Fenno's work on the Appropriations Committee, for instance, is that even as powerful a committee as Appropriations finds that it must make decisions within the constraints set by the parent body.[6] And as Manley has convincingly argued, one key to Wilbur Mills's reputation for power in Congress is his ability to anticipate the reactions of his colleagues and take account of their preferences.[7] It has in fact long been argued in the legislative literature that the whole House sets boundaries which the committees transgress at their peril, and within which they must exercise the discretion left to them by the whole House.

Furthermore, as I argued in Chapter 2, a congressman's constituency sets boundaries within which he is obliged to stay without risking serious political trouble. The boundaries set by the mass public in the district, of course, are quite vague and allow the congressman a good deal of discretion. Those set by elites in the district, however, particularly the elites that form his supporting coalition, are better defined and allow him less discretion as compared to the mass public's constraints.[8] Once again, this notion that a constituency sets boundaries for a legislator is not new to the literature of political science.[9]

This entire line of argument leads us to a general model of the political system which I call the model of "successively narrowing boundaries." According to this notion, one could conceive of a full range of possible alternatives in given arenas of public policy. A congressman, however, is not entirely free to select any of these alternatives. The distribution of attitudes within the mass public in his constituency sets (admittedly broad) boundaries within which he is able to choose among the alternatives remaining after the mass public has effectively eliminated several alternatives from serious consideration. Similarly, within the range of alternatives still permitted by the mass public, elites in the district further constrain the congressman by not tolerating some alternatives that were tolerated by the mass. Basically, these elite and mass attitude distributions make up the congressman's decision parameters. He still has a range of choice available, but it is considerably narrower than the full range of conceivable policy options.

Within these boundaries, there is a distribution of congressmen's attitudes in the whole House.[10] The committees are obliged to make their choices from among the range of alternatives which would be permitted in the whole House. Just as in the case of constituency constraints on individual congressmen, committees do have discretion, but it is limited by the whole House. The Appropriations Committee may be able to report out a bill containing anywhere from $600 million to $1 billion in funds for water pollution abatement, for instance, but they would not be permitted to report only $200 million and expect that figure to stand. Of the original full range of conceivable options, furthermore, the committees seriously consider only a rather narrow set, since decisional boundaries have been successively narrowed through a number of steps.

This notion of successively narrowing boundaries is similar to a notion of sets and subsets.[11] Out of the total range of all conceivable policy options (i.e., the full set), the mass public makes some of these options politically improbable, and allows only a subset to be seriously considered. From that mass public subset, constituency elites constrain congressmen further to an elite subset of policy alternatives. From that elite subset, congressmen themselves choose the alternatives which they will allow to be seriously considered, leaving a comparatively narrow whole-House subset of alternatives from which the committees are free to choose. This model of successively narrowing subsets is presented schematically in Figure 12-1.

This conceptual framework is a model which emphasizes constraints on decision, rather than causes. Instead of saying that constituents influence or cause some configuration of congressmen's behavior, for instance, we say that constraints set by constituents make certain congressional behaviors highly *un*likely. Similarly, instead of saying that the distribution of attitudes in

Figure 12–1 Successively Narrowing Boundaries

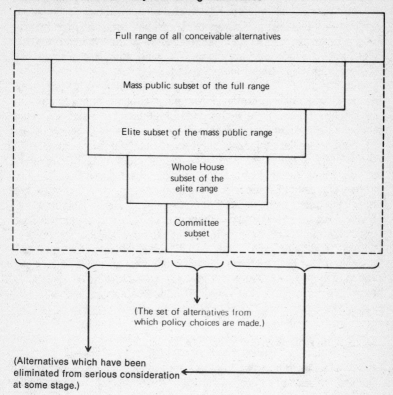

Full range of all conceivable alternatives

Mass public subset of the full range

Elite subset of the mass public range

Whole House subset of the elite range

Committee subset

(The set of alternatives from which policy choices are made.)

(Alternatives which have been eliminated from serious consideration at some stage.)

the whole House determines committee behavior, we would say that the distribution of attitudes in the whole House makes certain committee behaviors highly *im*probable. Note too that this is a kind of *negative* model. It would be difficult according to this notion of successively narrowing boundaries to determine precisely which behaviors will occur. But we can say something about which behaviors are *un*likely or *im*probable. This notion, therefore, essentially narrows the range of the behaviors that are likely to occur.

This whole discussion, of course, is only suggested by this study and must remain highly speculative. Some interesting further possibilities for research, however, do come to mind. How much of the range of conceivable alternatives is rendered unlikely at each stage, for instance? I would conjecture that the mass public rules out rather few possible alternatives, but that elites rule out rather more. To cite another interesting question, are alternatives from the left of an ideological spectrum made improbable as additions to public policy more than alternatives from the right, or vice versa, and at what step in the process? More possibilities could be suggested.

Finally, the interpretations which one attaches to these speculations constitute another interesting aspect. The concept of successively narrowing boundaries emphasizes the limits placed on elites. At each stage, I would hypothesize, the narrower set of people is limited by the broader set. But one interpretive question is whether the limits are important. Are they true limits on behavior, or are they so vague as to be meaningless? And conversely, are the more narrow questions mere details, or are they the guts of the issue? If leaders really do lead their followers, furthermore, what influence do they themselves have on the attitudes that would presumably define their constraints? It would be difficult to resolve such questions here. But one can still postulate that the boundaries at each stage do exist and are definable, and that behaviors outside these boundaries are improbable.

BEYOND FLOOR VOTING

Our concentration in this book on congressmen's decisions about how to vote on the floor of the legislature helps to contribute to an understanding of a larger set of political phenomena. It is unlikely, first of all, that congressmen's voting decisions are totally dissimilar from decisions which they make in other contexts. I would expect, for instance, that the consensus mode of decision is employed in committee work as well as in floor voting, albeit with probably a somewhat different set of actors. Or the importance of constituency carries over to a degree into committee work as well, since congressmen are assigned to committees partly on the basis of which assignments will help them politically back home.[12] While committee or other decisions are different from floor voting, to be sure, many of the decision rules discussed in this book may still apply.

Knowing about the decisions of congressmen, furthermore, contributes to an understanding of the behavior of other actors in the political system. To the extent that they wish to influence legislative outcomes, their behavior can often be seen as a strategic adaptation to congressmen's decision rules. Thus the consensus mode of decision, for instance, provides a powerful incentive for coalition formation among like-minded groups and people, which simplifies congressmen's decisions and makes outcomes more predictable. Similarly, interest groups adapt their strategies to congressmen's decision rules, by working through constituencies and through fellow congressmen, for instance. Or again, congressmen's decision-making helps us to understand the constraints on prefloor activity, such as the problem of correct timing of lobbying efforts. It is also possible that decision-makers other than congressmen use decision rules and take measures to cope with their problems that are similar to those described in this study; the logic of the consensus mode of decision, for instance, may have a rather wide applicability.

We have also been led in this chapter to speculate about such prechoice processes as the setting of the public and legislative agendas and the specification of the alternatives from which choice is made. We have argued that the mass media, Washington-based policy elites, certain innovative congressmen, and uncontrollable turns of events all play a part in getting the attention of congressmen and thus setting the agenda. Members of the House standing committees appear to prescribe the alternatives from which congressmen choose on the floor. These committees and the party leadership have a good deal to do with the timing of consideration, which is partly responsible for the changes in congressmen's decision-making that take place as the session progresses. Throughout, a model of successively narrowing boundaries prevails, in which congressmen are restricted by their constituents and committees are restricted by the whole House.

This study and the book which reports its results hopefully make a number of contributions. We know more about congressmen's voting decisions themselves, about the rules they employ, the explanations for and consequences of these rules. We also learn something about congressmen's sources of information, their search for and uses of information, and the effects which information has on them. The importance of various actors in the political system is somewhat better illuminated. We consider the conditions under which various patterns of decision, information flow, and actor importance obtain. But beyond these questions of some moment, it is hoped we have contributed to a better understanding of the larger political system and the place of congressmen in it.

NOTES

1. Many scholars have recently turned their attention to the agenda stage. See for example Peter Bachrach and Morton S. Baratz, "Two Faces of Power," *American Political Science Review* 56(1962):947–952; Bachrach and Baratz, "Decisions and Nondecisions: An Analytical Framework," *American Political Science Review* 57(1963):632–642; Thomas J. Anton, "Power, Pluralism, and Local Politics," *Administrative Science Quarterly* 7(1963):425–457; Jack L. Walker, "A Critique of the Elitist Theory of Democracy," *American Political Science Review* 60(1966):285–295; Walker, "Setting the Agenda in the U.S. Senate," *British Journal of Political Science* 7(1977):423–445. James L. Sundquist, *Politics and Policy* (Washington, D.C.: Brookings, 1968); and Matthew A. Crenson, *The Un-Politics of Air Pollution* (Baltimore: Johns Hopkins Press, 1971). An early statement of the problem is Chester I. Barnard, *The Functions of the Executive* (Cambridge, Mass.: Harvard University Press, 1966; first published, 1938), pp. 193–194. See also Roger W. Cobb and Charles D. Elder, *Participation in American Politics: The Dynamics of Agenda-Building* (Boston: Allyn and Bacon, 1972); and Cobb, Jennie Keith-Ross, and Marc Ross, "Agenda Building as a Comparative Political Process," *American Political Science Review* 70(1976):126–138.

2. See Sundquist, *ibid.;* Edward Schneier, "The Intelligence of Congress: Information and Public Policy Patterns," The *Annals* of the American Academy of Political and Social Science, 388(1970):16–18; and Theodore J. Lowi, *The End of Liberalism* (New York: Norton, 1969), chaps. 3–4. Cater's notion of "subgovernments" includes these policy elites; see Douglas Cater, *Power in Washington* (New York: Vintage, 1964).

3. For an analysis of symbols and politics, see Murray Edelman, *The Symbolic Uses of Politics* (Urbana: University of Illinois Press, 1964).

4. The following account is based on examination of eleven cross-tabulations. They are simply summarized verbally here, rather than presented in their entirety.

5. For a discussion of the importance of the process by which alternatives are evoked, see James G. March and Herbert A. Simon, *Organizations* (New York: Wiley, 1958), pp. 53–64.

6. Richard F. Fenno, Jr., *The Power of the Purse* (Boston: Little, Brown, 1966), chaps. 1–2.

7. John F. Manley, *The Politics of Finance* (Boston: Little, Brown, 1970), chap. 4. Manley also emphasizes the importance of election results at p. 381.

8. See John W. Kingdon, *Candidates for Office* (New York: Random House, 1968), chap. 3.

9. See Robert A. Dahl, *A Preface to Democratic Theory* (Chicago: University of Chicago Press, 1956), p. 132; and V. O. Key, Jr., *Public Opinion and American Democracy* (New York: Knopf, 1961), p. 552. The boundaries are sometimes set through the mechanism of potential sanctions; see Warren E. Miller and Donald E. Stokes, "Constituency Influence in Congress," *American Political Science Review* 57(1963):55. See also Roger H. Davidson, *The Role of the Congressman* (New York: Pegasus, 1969), p. 121, and John W. Kingdon, *Candidates for Office* (New York: Random House, 1968), pp. 81 and 154.

10. Legislative outcomes seem fundamentally determined by that distribution. See Gary Orfield, *Congressional Power: Congress and Social Change* (New York: Harcourt Brace Jovanovich, 1975), chaps. 1, 12, 13, and pp. 319–325.

11. For a particularly inventive discussion of related problems, see Andrew S. McFarland, *Power and Leadership in Pluralist Systems* (Stanford, Calif.: Stanford University Press, 1969), chap. 7 and p. 174.

12. Nicholas A. Masters, "Committee Assignments in the House of Representatives," *American Political Science Review* 55(1961):345–357.

PART IV

Appendixes

Appendix A

Sampling

Chapter 1 has set forth the background of this study, the shortcomings of roll call data, and the problems of studying the topic of voting decisions by means of a standard survey instrument. These appendixes are designed to fill in the details of this study's method, and in the process to discuss in more general terms some methodological considerations. The design, interviewing, coding, and analysis were done by the author.

Appendix A is devoted to some questions of sampling, which actually divide quite naturally into two problems: The first is sampling the congressmen, a relatively standard, precise kind of exercise; the second is sampling the votes, a more complex and less precise enterprise.

SAMPLING THE CONGRESSMEN

The central sample in this study is a probability sample of the House, selected such that each member has an equal statistical chance of falling into the sample. To this basic randomness was added a stratification of the sample. In a population as small as the size of the House ($n = 435$), stratification by a number of variables which are relevant to the subject matter of the study is highly desirable. It allows for more precision in the sample, and greatly reduces the likelihood that the sample will turn out by chance to be unrepresentative of the House in some major way.

Table A-1 presents the stratification. First, 10 party leaders and 5 non-randomly selected congressmen were excluded from the sampling universe.[1] The remaining 420 were divided into nine strata arranged by party, length of service in the House, and one regional category, that of Southern Democrats. As is customary in such a procedure, a few arbitrary assignments to strata were made on the margins in order to preserve the feature of equal chance of selection. Names were randomly drawn within the strata in proportion to the number in the strata. Fifteen such names for each vote decision were drawn.

Once four draws of 15 congressmen each ($n = 60$) had been made, I started to return to the first 15-member sample, and went through the sample in this fashion for the rest of the session, 15 per vote, returning to a given congressman every fourth vote. In practice, this meant that I

Table A–1. Stratification

length of service	Southern Democrats	Northern Democrats	Republicans	Total
Short	28 (1)[a]	56 (2)	84 (3)	168 (6)
Medium	28 (1)	56 (2)	56 (2)	140 (5)
Long	28 (1)	28 (1)	56 (2)	112 (4)
Total	84 (3)	140 (5)	196 (7)	420 (15)

[a] The first number in each cell is the number of congressmen in the cell. The number of names drawn from that stratum is in parentheses.

was seeing each respondent for a short interview once per month at the most, and sometimes the time lapse between interviews was longer. Under such conditions, very little respondent fatigue—annoyance, contamination, interviewer effects—was in evidence.

There were several reasons for adopting this repeating feature, rather than continuing to draw a fresh 15-member sample each time. Seeing the same respondents repeatedly would result in an increasing rapport and frankness as the session went along. Making appointments was also easier. And as the session progresses, congressmen become more hurried and harassed, and the issues they are deciding become less routine and more controversial. It was better to have seen them early in the session in order to overcome these hazards. In short, this procedure allowed me to reap the benefits of increased rapport and frankness, while at the same time it avoided the potential cost of annoying the respondents and affecting their responses with too much interviewing.

The response rate on the first round of four draws was 83 percent. If a sampled respondent was not interviewed, he was replaced by someone randomly drawn from his stratum. Thus, the full complement of 60 was maintained throughout. Once respondents did consent to be interviewed, they dropped out of the sample subsequently only very rarely; in those three or four cases, they were also replaced from within their strata.

It should be emphasized that the *decision,* not the congressman, is the unit of analysis throughout most of this study. Since each congressman was interviewed about several voting decisions, the resultant number of cases for analysis is approximately the number of congressmen interviewed times the number of decisions each was asked about, or precisely, 222 decisions.

The sample just described forms the quantitative data base for the study. But a good deal of additional information was gathered through other kinds of interviewing and observation. Congressmen were asked about minor votes as well as the major focus of the interview. I supplemented my interviews of the probability sample of congressmen with other interviews of congressmen who various contacts told me were particularly uncertain or under pressure, who were particularly helpful and informative, or who were in a pivotal position on a given vote. I also talked to staff people, journalists, and lobbyists who were acquainted with the politics that had surrounded given issues. Throughout the session, finally, I immersed myself in the process, by witnessing committee sessions and floor debates and by having many conversations with contacts on the Hill. Information gathered in these ways, though not quantified, was highly instructive.

SAMPLING THE VOTES

At the heart of this study is an issue-by-issue approach, in which congressmen are asked about specific voting decisions which they made. Once one has decided on such an approach, the question of how one will select the decisions to be studied inevitably arises. This sampling of voting decisions was not nearly as easy to design as was the sample of congressmen. One reason for this difficulty is the simple physical absence of a sampling frame or population list. Generally speaking, one samples a population by first enumerating that population. But given the week-by-week interviewing procedure in this study, which concentrated on votes cast within the week, a list of the population of votes for the whole session of Congress cannot be used, since it would be available only after the session had ended. That simple feature of the design alone dictated an unorthodox sampling procedure.

But beyond this design feature, on more conceptual grounds I would not have elected to study either a total population of votes cast over a given time span or a random sample of those votes. The simple fact is that most votes cast in Congress are politically uninteresting. The final passage of a bill, for instance, is often entirely mundane by comparison with a vote on a key amendment or the motion to recommit. Or the renewal of a small agency's statutory authorization pales in significance next to matters such as the antiballistic missile or tax reform. Despite these obvious differences among bills and votes, many studies have made only passing attempts, if any, to distinguish among them.[2] Except for the standard practices of excluding private bills and unanimous and near-unanimous votes, the literature on legislative voting behavior has generally bypassed this problem. For my purposes, therefore, I wanted to select bills that were politically important in some sense. I believe that the costs I paid in a degree of imprecision were far outweighed by the benefit which followed from having made the attempt.

In my selection of the votes, I first excluded the vast number that appeared to be noncontroversial and routine, for several reasons. First, these votes would present the congressman with no decisional or psychological problem. In order to illuminate congressmen's decisional processes with any degree of subtlety, one would need to deal with decisions of at least some minimal degree of complexity. This conceptual problem has its practical counterpart: If an academic interviewer walked into a congressman's office and asked him about a thoroughly mundane, routine vote that was hardly noticed by anybody at all, he would appear to be far more naïve than he would wish to appear. Even as it was, I had the impression some of the time that congressmen could not fathom why I was interested in a given vote, which they themselves regarded as entirely uninteresting.

A second reason for excluding routine or minor votes is that much of floor action is mere ratification of committee action. Presumably, if one is interested in studying legislative voting on the floor, then one is at least partially interested in its independent effects. If a vote is simple ratification of the committee, then the policy decisions were presumably made in committee and a committee study would be more appropriate than a study of floor action.

Third, if one wishes in part to determine the relative importance of various actors in the legislative system, as I did, then one should select those votes for study which at least allow for their possible involvement in congressmen's decisions. But the fact is that most political actors are not concerned with most bills most of the time. For example, I could obtain a better test of the proposition that the House party leadership is more important than a congressman's constituents if both of these actors had at least some potential for being either interested in the decision or for being considered by the congressman.

In choosing the votes on which I did interview, I used a number of rough guidelines. One was the amount of attention which the issue seemed to be getting. If congressmen seemed to be interested in the issue (as measured, for example, by attendance on the floor), if other actors such as the administration or interest groups appeared to notice it and become involved, if it was reported in the press at all extensively, then it stood a better chance of falling into my sample of votes than if it had received little attention. Second, I attempted to judge how many political actors were involved. The vote for which constituency, administration, interest groups, and party leadership were all relevant was more desirable for this sample than one which was handled by only a few members of the reporting committee in the absence of other actors' involvement. Third, I made some judgment about the extent and intensity of the conflict over the legislation. I preferred controversial votes on which people appeared to be expending considerable amounts of energy and political resources. I made the judgments about whether a given vote seemed to have conformed to these guidelines by consulting with various informants (congressmen, staff people, lobbyists, journalists, other observers), attending both floor and committee sessions, and reading the press, *Congressional Quarterly,* and the *Congressional Record.*

The result is primarily a sample of the "big" votes of the session, which include some of the major issues of the decade. Some touched on general issues of war and peace. Others raised the broad issue of national priorities. Still others were concerned with the health of the economy. In short, these were issues that mattered to many people. Figure A–1 contains a chronological listing of the votes which constitute the core sample of this study, together with the number of cases (total $n = 222$) on each of the votes and a short paragraph on each vote which summarizes the general dimensions of each issue. For some of the interviewing and coding, one vote concerning the bill in question stood out as being more important than the others. There were a number of amendments offered to the Health, Education, and Welfare appropriation bill, for example, but in the eyes of virtually every participant, the important question was the Joelson amendment to add nearly $1 billion to the bill, which a coalition of education groups was supporting vigorously. Thus Figure A-1 also defines a "key vote" for each bill, on which the interviewing and coding concentrated when it was appropriate to differentiate among several votes on the bill.

There are a number of features of this selection process which should be emphasized. First, the votes in the core sample were not necessarily won or lost by close margins. Roll call analysis has often excluded unanimous and near-unanimous votes from consideration,[3] and one index proposed to weight votes partly according to how close the vote turned out to be.[4] But even lopsided votes may be of great political interest, and several are included here. Considerable leadership efforts may be undertaken, for example, to insure that a vote will be won by a large margin. Or consider the following quotation from a defeated Republican leader on a crucial vote: "The final margin was much wider than it had to be, just because a lot of Republicans saw the ship was going down and decided to take care of themselves." Or another legislative strategist, seeing that he will be defeated, lowers his sights and accepts an amendment, resulting in another lopsided vote. The politically interesting vote,

1. - Seating of Adam Clayton Powell. (13 cases, January 3) Powell had been excluded from the House two years earlier, and had been reelected twice since then. The compromise which finally prevailed, 254-158, seated him with a $25,000 fine. The key votes found liberals willing to seat him even without a fine, moderates and conservatives against such a proposal.

2. House Un-American Activities Committee. (15 cases, February 18) Committee Chairman Richard Ichord (D.-Mo.) requested that the committee's name be changed to the Internal Security Committee. Opponents of the committee staged a fight against the previous question, which if successful, would have opened up the resolution to amendments such as transferring the committee's functions to the Judiciary Committee or abolishing the committee. Key vote: the previous question, which was adopted 262-123.

3. Debt limit increase. (15 cases, March 19) A perfectly routine extension request was made interesting by the fact that Republicans had overwhelmingly voted against it in the past, but that now their own administration was asking for their support. Many Democrats had threatened to withhold their support unless Republican votes were forthcoming. Key vote: final passage, 313-93.

4. Elementary and Secondary Education Act. (15 cases, April 23) The Education and Labor Committee reported a bill extending the act for 5 years. Representatives Edith Green (D.-Ore.), William Ayers (R.-Ohio), and Albert Quie (R.-Minn.) introduced a package amendment that finally prevailed, which provided the 2-year extension requested by the Nixon administration and consolidated several previously separated programs. This was the first time in the session that there was any extensive lobbying activity, in this case several education groups. Key vote: the Green-Ayers-Quie amendment, which passed 235-184.

5. Supplemental appropriation bill. (15 cases, May 21) There were a number of provisions here, and each respondent specified his own key vote. Of major interest was the first imposition of a spending ceiling on federal expenditures. Other controversial provisions included funds for Southeast Asia military operations and funds for federal and congressional pay increases. An amendment was passed restricting federal funds to colleges and universities which had not cut off aid to student disrupters.

6. Agriculture payment limitation. (14 cases, May 26-27) Key vote was an amendment to the agriculture appropriation bill, sponsored by Silvio Conte (R.-Mass.) and Paul Findley (R.-Ill.), which would limit federal subsidy payments to individual farmers to $20,000 per year. That limitation passed on a teller vote, 112-100, and then on a roll call vote, 225-142.

7. Cigarette advertising bill. (14 cases, June 14) The committee bill, supported by the tobacco interests, strengthened the health warning on packages but prohibited the Federal Communications Commission from restricting advertising. Key vote: the motion to recommit, which was offered by anticigarette congressmen who wanted to kill the bill, and which failed 137-252.

8. Surtax extension package. (16 cases, June 30) The committee bill extended the 10 percent surtax, and included a repeal of the investment credit and a low income allowance. Liberals argued against the bill, saying that it should be combined with tax reform. Key vote: final passage, 210-205.

9. Health, Education, and Welfare appropriation. (15 cases, July 29-31) The key vote here is an amendment by Charles Joelson (D.-N.J.), vigorously supported by education groups, to increase spending for various education programs by more than $1 billion over the administration request and about $900 million over the committee bill. The amendment passed 242-106 on tellers, and 293-120 on roll call.

10. Tax reform bill. (15 cases, August 6-7) This was a wide-ranging reform bill which gave some tax relief to low- and middle-income taxpayers and tightened up some loopholes. When a key vote was needed in the coding, it was on the previous question, which if defeated would have opened up the bill for amendment. It passed, 265-145; final passage, 394-30.

11. Electoral college reform. (15 cases, September 15-18) The committee bill provided for direct election of the president. The key vote was an amendment (and subsequently the motion to recommit) which would have provided for a district plan rather than direct election; rejected on tellers, 159-192, and in the motion to recommit, 162-245.

12. Military procurement. (15 cases, October 1-3) There were a number of controversial measures in this bill, including the C-5A transport, extra funds for shipbuilding, and several others. But the key vote was the teller vote on an amendment to cut ABM procurement, defeated 105-219.

13. Public works appropriation. (15 cases, October 8) The key vote here was an amendment to raise the committee figure for water pollution abatement through federal grants for sewage treatment facilities from the committee figure of $600 million to the authorized figure of $1 billion, which failed to pass by two votes on tellers, 146-148.

14. Foreign aid authorization. (15 cases, November 19) The key vote was a surprise amendment offered by Robert Sikes (D.-Fla.), adding $54 million in military aid to Nationalist China. The amendment was hotly contested, and its passage (175-169) nearly brought the entire bill to defeat. Final passage 176-163.

15. Poverty program. (15 cases, December 12) The key vote was on a substitute amendment offered by Edith Green (D.-Ore.), William Ayers (R.-Ohio), and Albert Quie (R.-Minn.), which would have provided for greater state control over the poverty program, had it passed. Defeated on tellers 167-183 and in roll call motion to recommit, 163-231.

Figure A–1 Sampled Votes

in short, is not necessarily the close vote; nor is the close vote necessarily politically interesting.

A second caveat is that even within this sample of the big votes of the session, there is a considerable variance in the degree of public visibility and the degree to which congressmen routinize the decision. A good bit of analysis according to differences in salience is in fact possible. So they are all votes that are worthy of note in some respect, but they are not all the same by any means. The supplemental bill, for instance, was hardly noticed, in contrast to ABM deployment or the surtax.

Third, I also did some interviewing on more minor votes, just to ascertain how congressmen went about making decisions on such matters. I usually worked such a vote into an interview on a more substantial matter, rather than devoting an entire session to it. But I did want to provide a contrast to the more major matters, in order to fill in a more complete picture of the decision-making process.

Finally, and quite important, these procedures were adapted to explore some "nondecisions,"[5] matters which could very well have come up for a vote but did not. I also investigated not only congressmen's choices among the available alternatives, but also the manner in which the alternatives were posed in the first place, and the setting of the agenda for decision. While these matters, like the minor votes, are not a part of the core quantitative sample of this study, they still form an important part of this book.

NOTES

1. At the beginning of the study, I had conceived of a set of five nonrandomly selected congressmen representing different types, who were to be interviewed quite intensively and who were to serve as sources of information to supplement the probability sample. When I discarded this idea of the parallel informants' sample, I kept three of these nonrandomly selected respondents in the final core sample, because they represented strata that might be expected to be resistant to academic interviewers. So three of the eventual 60 respondents, while taking their places in the appropriate strata, have not been selected randomly.

2. For one exception, an interesting attempt to distinguish among issues, see McFarland's discussion of critical and routine decisions. Andrew S. McFarland, *Power and Leadership in Pluralist Systems* (Stanford, Calif.: Stanford University Press, 1969), Chap. 5.

3. This is particularly true of most index constructions and of cluster-bloc analysis. See Lee F. Anderson, Meredith W. Watts, Jr., and Allen R. Wilcox, *Legislative Roll-Call Analysis* (Evanston, Ill.: Northwestern University Press, 1966), Chaps. 2–4.

4. William H. Riker, "A Method for Determining the Significance of Roll Calls in Voting Bodies," in *Legislative Behavior: A Reader in Theory and Research,* ed. John C. Wahlke and Heinz Eulau (Glencoe, Ill.: Free Press, 1959), pp. 377–384.

5. On the concept of nondecisions, see two articles by Peter Bachrach and Morton S. Baratz, "Two Faces of Power," *American Political Science Review* 56(1962):947–952; and "Decisions and Non-Decisions: An Analytical Framework," *American Political Science Review* 57(1963):632–642.

Appendix B

Interviewing Procedure

There are certain difficulties posed by academic interviewing on Capitol Hill. Congressmen are preoccupied with many concerns and have little time to devote to interviews. Professors do not lighten the burden when they send their unprepared undergraduates to Washington in droves for term paper research. In addition to these general problems, this study posed some peculiar to this design. Asking a congressman to divulge how he went about casting a vote in a specific instance is a potentially touchy subject. In addition, I wanted a complete record of his decision-making process on a given vote, and waiting for any period of time after the vote might result in problems of inadequate recall.

Several features of the interviewing procedure were developed in response to these various problems.[1] First, the interview was kept short. It often took only ten or fifteen minutes to obtain all the information needed about one single vote, though some interviews were longer. The project was intentionally designed to keep the interview short and to conserve the congressman's valuable time. Second, to minimize recall deficiencies I took the interview very soon after the vote was cast. Many were conducted within two or three days of the vote, and rarely did a week pass before I had talked to the member. Most interviews were conducted in respondents' offices, but many also took place off the floor, in hallways, and the like.

Some interviews were taken before the votes were cast, in order to catch congressmen in mid-decision, so to speak. But such timing had to be limited, for two reasons: First, the whole story sometimes is not complete right up until the hour of the vote. On the revision of the debt limit, for instance, many Republicans were unconvinced that they should vote with the administration right up to the day of the vote. Or the Sikes amendment to the foreign aid bill was unanticipated even by committee leaders. Second, some congressmen are reticent to talk about their votes before they cast them, but the reluctance evaporates once the vote is over. One runs the risk, of course, that one will obtain only after-the-vote rationalizations from the respondents. Thus, the interview schedule was specifically designed to probe beyond rationalizations, and comparisons between those interviews conducted before and after the fact were re-assuring in this respect.

I made every effort to conduct these interviews in an entirely conversational, relaxed manner. The fact that respondents saw me more than once was helpful in developing rapport. I also assured them of their anonymity. In the interview itself, the questions and probes were worded conversationally, and I took no notes during the interview. The write-up which I did immediately after each interview was successful in capturing quite a complete record of the responses.

As the quotations throughout this book testify, most respondents appeared to be very frank in their responses. A number of factors help to account for this frankness. One is the conversational, no-notes type of interview. Another was the fact that this was an issue-by-issue interview, which placed questions in a context which was both familiar to the congressman and less susceptible than most academic interviews to general, nonspecific, nonbehavioral responses. Third, since I saw them several times, congressmen came to know me a bit. There were several dramatic improvements in frankness between the first and second interviews. One congressman, for instance, told me during the first interview: "There are three things I take into account. Is it constitutional? Is it right? Can we afford it? That's what I always tell my constituents, and that's what I'd tell you. That pretty well sums up what I do. My constituency never affects me." In subsequent interviews, however, this same congressman was describing in great detail how the education lobby had "boxed him in" on the Joelson amendment because of the low amount of impacted aid in the committee bill, how he "had" to vote for limiting farm payments because of potential political reaction back home, and so forth.

Finally, so far as the degree of structure is concerned, I believe that I have combined good features of both structured and unstructured interviewing.[2] I did have an interview schedule and did ask the questions as they are worded in Figure B–1, though the order was sometimes varied. The record of the interview is quite complete. So these data are capable of quantification. But to capture desirable features of unstructured interviewing, I liberally inserted probes, comments, and other inquiries after the general questions when they were appropriate either to the issue under discussion or to the respondent. I specifically asked them on the Elementary and Secondary Education Act extension, for example—after the general question on interest groups—whether the school people in their districts had contacted them, since I had known that such a lobbying effort was underway. So there was this measure of adaptation to the individual respondent and the specific issue, and this combined with the conversational style of the interview without note-taking, lends some of the

Figure B–1   Interview Schedule

---

1. (Cite the vote picked.) How did you go about making up your mind? What steps did you go through?

2. Were there any fellow congressmen that you paid attention to? If no: I don't mean just following them; I mean looking to them for information and guidance. If yes: Who? Why them?

3. What did the party leadership do? How about informal groups within the party? (e.g., Democratic Study Group)

4. Did you talk to staff people about this?

5. What do you think your constituents wanted you to do on this? How was your mail?

6. Did anyone in the administration or executive branch contact you?

7. Did you hear anything from any organizations?

8. Was there anything that you read that affected how you saw it?

9. At any point along the way, were you ever uncertain about how to vote?

---

desirable features of less structure. The result is obtaining the quantifiable data that one desires from a structured interview, while at the same time preserving rapport and responses that are relevant to the particular respondent.

NOTES

1. A pretest of the interviewing procedures and interview schedule was run on three members of the Michigan state legislature, two congressmen during the second session of the Ninetieth Congress, and five congressmen at the beginning of the first session of the Ninety-first.
2. For a discussion of structured and unstructured interviewing in studies of Congress, see Robert L. Peabody's essay in Ralph K. Huitt and Peabody, *Congress: Two Decades of Analysis* (New York: Harper & Row, 1969), pp. 28–34.

Appendix C

Coding

I coded these data myself. The major advantage of doing it myself was that I was close to the field process and could correctly interpret the responses in the interview protocols. The major disadvantage, aside from my personal loss of time, was that by virtue of my very involvement, a good bit of unreliability might creep into the coding.

To check on the degree of unreliability, I instituted a check-coding procedure. At the point at which I had coded one-third of the interviews, I took the variables on which there were likely to be the greatest errors of judgment. For these 22 variables, I had someone else independently code 25 randomly selected respondents. The check-coder and I then totaled the variables on which we had agreed and disagreed; in those cases in which we had disagreed, we discussed each one individually and made a common judgment about whose coding had been correct.

The results of this process were encouraging. In these most judgmental columns, in which the intercoder reliability would be expected to be the lowest, the check-coder and I deemed necessary a change in my original coding only 7 percent of the time. Inasmuch as these errors were corrected in the relevant variables, there would be about a 6 percent coding error in the final data set, assuming that I did not revise my coding procedures at all in the light of the check-coding. But since I presumably did learn something from the check-coding, the final error is probably lower than 6 percent. It should be stressed that this is the result in the variables *most* susceptible to coding error.

In terms of the variables that are most often used throughout this study, the results are slightly better. The proportion of the spontaneous mentions of actors that was changed, for instance, was 5 percent. Only 4 percent of the cases involving the subjective importance of the actors were changed. The objective positions of the actors used in the correlation analysis are virtually free of error.

In those cases in which there is an abnormally high rate of error, I have in some instances elected not to use the variable at all, believing that it would be better to lose this information rather than to base some sort of interpretation on misleading data. In other cases with high rates, I have collapsed categories to reduce the problems. In the importance of voting history, for instance, several of the disagreements between the check-coder and myself involved differing judgments about whether history was of "major" or "determinative" importance, or whether it was of "minor" or "no" importance. By collapsing "major" and "determinative" into one category and "minor" and "no" into another, I paid the cost of losing information, but obtained a more reliable code for use in the analysis.

Appendix D

Variables and Indexes

The purpose of this appendix is to present the mechanics involved in some of the variables and indexes used throughout this book. We start with discussion of several standard independent variables that were used throughout the analysis, and then proceed to a few indexes used at various points.

STANDARD INDEPENDENT VARIABLES

There were a number of independent variables which were used repeatedly in the analysis of these data and referred to repeatedly in this book. They were first defined in the way described below, and then run in cross-tabulations against many of the other variables in the data, to produce substantial numbers of tables for analysis. Though the raw numbers and finer divisions were sometimes used when it seemed desirable, for the most part these independent variables were trichotomized for the purposes of the cross-tabulations, such that they would produce three categories of roughly equal numbers of cases. Two costs of this procedure are recognized and deliberately paid. One is that the analysis thus loses some information which regression, for example, could use. But I see little payoff for most purposes in relating a virtually continuous variable (e.g., size of largest city in the district) to variables which have only a few categories as most of my dependent variables do, without somehow collapsing that independent variable. Second, in some cases, the cutting points seem arbitrary and also tend to lump divergent cases into the same category. This is necessitated, however, by the small sample size, which dictates as even a spread on the independent variable as possible to avoid prohibitively small cell sizes. I have also tried to draw the cutting points in such a way as to avoid doing violence to the concepts being measured.

Party

It makes a good deal of sense to treat the U.S. Congress as a three-party system. Southern Democrats are such a different grouping from Northern Democrats, that I have predominantly treated them separately throughout this book. Thus the party variable is divided into Northern Democrats, Southern Democrats, and Republicans. Naturally, this is not a trichotomy which produces equal numbers in the categories. The numbers of decisions are: Northern Democrats = 74; Southern Democrats = 52; and Republicans = 96, which is almost identical to the proportions in the House. (Numbers cited throughout refer to decisions in my sample, not to numbers of congressmen.)

Size of State Party Delegation
For many purposes, we want to know whether a congressman comes from a large or small state delegation. But communication within delegation or region is almost entirely within party, rather than between parties. Thus, in this measure, we use the number of congressmen from the respondent's state and party. In this sample, these state party delegations ranged in size from 2 to 26. The categories are: small ($n = 75$), 2 to 5 congressmen in the state party delegation; medium ($n = 79$), 6 to 12 congressmen; large ($n = 68$), 13 to 26 congressmen.

Length of Service in the House
Seniority is defined by the number of years the respondent has served in the House. Freshmen were defined as having served 1 year, and the number of years ranged upward in this sample to 27. The categories are: junior ($n = 75$), 1 to 5 years; medium ($n = 85$), 6 to 11 years; senior ($n = 62$), 12 to 27 years.

District Competitiveness
I took as my measure of the party competitiveness of the district the percentage of the two-party vote which the congressman received in the previous election, that of 1968. I did so on the theory that the congressman's most recent election experience would probably both generally reflect the pattern in the district in recent years, and would also be the experience that was freshest in his mind and thus be one that would have the greatest impact on him. In addition, I used an "Index of Comparative Margins," described below, to combine the results of the previous two elections for another measure. The categories by the percentage of the two-party vote in 1968 are: competitive ($n = 64$), 50 to 57 percent; medium ($n = 76$), 58 to 66 percent; safe ($n = 82$), 67 to 100 percent.

Urbanness of District
It is difficult to devise a measure of urbanness which would please everyone. Surely the census definition creates far too many urban areas. For my purposes, I took as my measure the size of the largest city in the con-

gressman's district, on the reasoning that in a political sense, the congressman would respond to population concentrations in any event. It happened that there were very few congressional districts with truly small towns as their largest city, and there were several within huge metropolises (e.g., New York or Chicago). The categories by size of largest city are: small ($n = 86$), 0–74,999; medium ($n = 79$), 75,000–494,999; large ($n = 57$), 495,000+.

Liberalism–Conservatism

A convincing argument can be made that one should allow self-professed liberals and conservatives to define for themselves what they mean by liberalism and conservatism.[1] Using such reasoning, I defined this variable by use of the voting record scores of the Americans for Democratic Action and the Americans for Constitutional Action for the session under study. It turns out that when one trichotomizes each of these and crosstabulates them, the ADA and ACA scores are nearly true reciprocals (*tau-b* $= -.75$; *gamma* $= -.94$). Throughout the analysis, therefore, I simply used the trichotomized ADA score as the measure of liberalism-conservatism. The categories are: conservative ($n = 70$), ADA score of 0–9; moderate ($n = 86$), ADA score of 10–60; liberal ($n = 66$), ADA score of 61–100.

Time in the Session

The last two standard independent variables are categorizations of the 15 issues discussed in Appendix A. First, I simply wanted to know whether the vote took place relatively early or relatively late in the session. Thus the first five votes in chronological order are classified as early, the next five as middle, and the last five as occurring late in the session. That procedure results in the cutting points being about the end of May and the end of August.

Salience of Issue

It proved quite useful to have at least a rough indication of the salience of the issue. Some of these issues were far more visible than others, with demonstrable consequences. There is no ready way in which a classification could easily be accomplished. So as a rough coding, I made a judgment about how much attention the issue appeared to have received in the press, among congressmen, and among other participants in the legislative system. The categories are: low-salience—Powell seating,[2] House Un-American Activities Committee name change, debt limit, suplemental appropriation, and foreign aid; medium-salience—Elementary and Secondary Education, farm payment limitation, cigarette bill, electoral college reform, and water pollution abatement in public works; high-salience—surtax extension, Joelson amendment for education funding, tax reform bill, ABM in military procurement, and Quie-Green-Ayres amendment to the poverty program.

OTHER INDEXES

Index of Comparative Margins

Simple margins of victory may not be an entirely satisfactory index of the degree of electoral competition in a given congressional district. Even cumulations of such margins over time may still lack a certain validity. The reason is that congressmen may not think in terms of simple election margins. They may instead make trend comparisons from one election to another. The congressman who won by 60 percent in 1966 and then by 54 percent in 1968, for instance, would view his margin as having slipped from one election to another, which would be cause for some concern. But another congressman who also won by the same margin in 1968, 54 percent, would be much encouraged if his margin in 1966 had been only 51 percent. Thus, in terms of the interpretation which congressmen place on margins of victory, and hence in terms of the effects that electoral margins are likely to have on their behavior, a kind of comparison of margins over time would seem to yield a better measure of electoral competition.

Taking the previous two election margins, the congressman's last two experiences with electoral competition in his district, I constructed an Index of Comparative Margins. This index starts with the difference between half of the two-party vote and the vote which the congressman (or in the case of freshmen, the congressman's party) won in the 1966 election. I take this figure as the base from which the congressman works, the amount of margin which he can afford to lose. If he won by 60 percent in 1966, for example, he would have to drop to 49 percent in order to be defeated in 1968. Hence his base, the margin of free electoral slack in 1966, is 60 minus 49, or 11 percent. The sign is always positive.

I next compare this base to the change which the congressman experienced between 1966 and 1968. This is the simple arithmetic difference between the 1968 and 1966 margins. If he won by 65 percent in 1968 and 60 percent in 1966, for instance, the electoral gain was 5 percent. The sign in this case is positive if he gained over the two-year period, negative if he lost. This gain or loss must be compared to his base since, for example, a loss of 5 percent means something entirely different to two congressmen, one of whom started with 70 percent and the other with 56 percent.

The Index of Comparative Margins is a ratio of this gain or loss to the 1966 base. Its formula reads:

$$I_{cm} = \frac{\% \text{ in } 1968 - \% \text{ in } 1966}{\% \text{ in } 1966 - 49\%}$$

Thus to use the example above, if the member won by 60 percent in 1966 and 65 percent in 1968, the Index of Comparative Margins would be:

$$\frac{65 - 60}{60 - 49} = \frac{5}{11} = +.45$$

In my sample, the values thus obtained ranged from −.78 through +8.00, the latter value being true of a congressman who had been redistricted from a very marginal district into a safe one. Trichotomizing this variable produces the following categories: insecure ($n = 73$), −.78 through −.24; medium ($n = 63$), −.23 through +.29; and secure ($n = 75$), +.30 through +8.00.

Conflict Codes

One set of variables in the data is composed of conflict codes. If one conceives of all the possible actors in the legislative system which could influence the congressman's vote, the list in these data would be as follows: the congressman's own attitude, his constituency, interest groups, fellow congressmen, his staff, the administration, and his party leadership. One can pose a conflict between any given pair among these actors, for example, constituency versus party leadership, and state with which actor the congressman voted. In the current example, one could code the pair as showing no conflict for a number of reasons, or as showing conflict between constituency and party leadership. In the case of conflict, one can then code which actor's position was the same as the congressman's vote. The full conflict code for this pair is as follows:

1. No conflict, because neither is involved in his decision.
2. No conflict, because constituency is involved and party leadership is not.
3. No conflict, because party leadership is involved and constituency is not.
4. No conflict, because both are involved, but they agree.
5. Constituency is more liberal than party leadership, and constituency "wins" (i.e., congressman votes with the constituency position).

6. Constituency is more conservative than party leadership, and constituency wins.
7. Constituency is more liberal than party leadership, and party leadership wins.
8. Constituency is more conservative than party leadership, and party leadership wins.

In these cases, "not involved" means either that the congressman took no account of the actor's position, or that the actor took no position at all.

This sort of coding was done for all possible pairs among the seven actors cited above which could influence the congressman's vote. There are 21 such possible pairs, including for example, attitude versus constituency, administration versus party leadership, and so forth. In addition, it would be possible that a respondent would be particularly prone to say that the administration or party leadership was not involved in his decision, even though each may have taken some sort of position on the issue. Thus the objective administration and party leadership positions were also added, whether or not the respondent felt them relevant to his own decision. In this case of objective positions, "not involved" would mean that the administration or party leadership took no discernible position at all. There are 11 possible pairs which involve the objective administration and the objective party leadership positions.

Procedural versus Substantive Cues

In Chapter 3, we made a distinction between procedural and substantive cues. A procedural cue is given to a congressman who already has made up his mind, and simply needs to straighten out the parliamentary situation so that he knows that his vote will express his intention properly. He thus checks with an informant in the House, for example, to find out the content of the motion to recommit, or to discover whether the vote on the previous question is strictly routine or a mask for a substantive vote, and so forth. Substantive cues contain more content information. They may simply provide the congressman with more information about the bill or amendment than he possessed previously, or they may influence him to vote one way or another, either through a change in his attitude, or through providing direction to a vote on which he had not previously formulated an opinion.

When I say in Chapter 3 that 31 percent of the cues received from fellow congressmen were coded as "primarily procedural," I mean that they were either purely procedural, or that they were procedural combined with some reality checking, in which the congressman simply checks around to be sure that his first reaction to the bill or amendment was right. The cues that are more substantive and not primarily procedural are those either with more information to them, or with a greater degree of influence on the congressman's vote from the fellow congressman. The coding was more complex at first than this simple dichotomy between procedural and substantive cues. But the check-coding procedure revealed that the intercoder reliability was not very good. Hence, the categories were collapsed in order to provide for a code which was more reliable.

NOTES

1. For such an argument, see Robert A. Schoenberger, "Conservatism, Personality, and Political Extremism," *American Political Science Review* 62(1968):868–877.
2. The vote on the seating of Adam Clayton Powell in 1967 was entirely different, a high-salience vote accompanied by extensive press coverage of Powell's activities, newspaper editorials, and floods of mail. In 1969, the year of this study, the Powell seating vote was of much lower visibility.

Appendix E

Actor–Vote Agreement Analysis

A major part of this study was to assess the importance of various actors in the legislative system in terms of accounting for congressmen's voting decisions. One way in which this was done was to canvass the interviews and code the responses in two ways: according to whether the congressman spontaneously mentioned the actor in question, and according to how he appeared to talk about the actor, whether the actor could be seen as of determinative, major, minor, or no importance in the decision. These two codes have been called the "subjective" importance modes of assessing actor importance.

The other way in which actor importance has been assessed in this study is through determining objective agreement between the actor position and the congressman's vote. In this case, we arrive at our best estimate of a given actor's position, and determine how closely it agrees with the congressman's vote. This appendix is devoted to a discussion of these "objective" agreement techniques.

THE GROUNDWORK

On the basis of review of previous legislative behavior literature, conversations and pretest interviews with those knowledgeable about legislatures and particularly Congress, and thinking through my own experiences and knowledge, I arrived at a list of six actors in the legislative system who could conceivably have an influence on congressmen's votes. These actors are the following: the congressman's constituency, fellow congressmen, interest groups, the administration and executive branch, his party leadership, and his staff. For the purposes of considering predictors of the vote, I eliminated at this stage the congressman's own specific attitude on the legislation at hand, both because I was more interested in antecedents to his attitude and because as a practical matter, given that these interviews were conducted on an issue-by-issue basis, the congressman nearly always voted according to his specific attitude toward that provision. The more interesting question would be how he arrived at his attitude in the first place. (See Chapter 11 for a discussion of the place of congressmen's general policy attitudes.)

For each of these six actors, I tried to get a best estimate of their position on the issue at hand. This task was more easily accomplished with some actors than with others. For the party leadership, there was no problem, since the party leadership always voted on the issue and hence always took a clear position which could be objectively defined. There was also an objective administration position measured, not only by what appeared in the press and other public statements, but also by what "the word" was about the administration's desires, particularly on the Republican side of the aisle. In the case of fellow congressmen, the respondent would name those colleagues, if any, to whom he had paid attention, and ascertaining their objective position was not overly difficult. A congressman could fairly accurately report his own staff's position, if the staff were involved in his decision at all. For interest groups, I would first ascertain independently which interest groups were active on the issue, and then ask a respondent about whether that group had been to see him or had otherwise been important at all in his decision, in addition to recording any other interest group positions which he reported.

In these last two cases—interest groups and staff—there is an element of reliance on congressmen's perceptions of the actor position in determining our best estimate of that position. Probably a congressman's misperceptions would not be too serious in these cases, since he presumably sees his staff daily, and would not find it difficult to ascertain a lobby's position on a given vote, for example, educators on school funding. But in the case of the final actor, the constituency, there is more possibility that the congressman might misperceive. I am obliged to rely on the congressman's perception of the constituency position as my measure. There are two considerations, however, which somewhat mitigate the effects of this indicator. First, congressmen were often judging the positions of elites in their districts, unlike some other treatments of perceptions of constituency. It is much less likely that the congressman will seriously misperceive the elites than the masses. It is also likely that on issues of high salience, the congressman's perceptions even of the attitudes of the masses in his district are at least roughly accurate. While the issues in this sample do vary considerably according to public visibility, they still are disproportionately those of relatively high salience.

On each issue, the congressman's position, that which is to be predicted, is defined as being in either the liberal or the conservative direction. Then for each of the six actors, their position on balance is defined as tending to urge the congressman in a liberal direction, or in the conservative direction, or in no direction at all. This neutral case occurs never with the party leadership, with the administration only when the administration takes no discernible position at all, with fellow congressmen only when the respondent names nobody to whom he paid attention, and with interest groups, staff, and constituency only when these actors are of no importance at all in the decision, either because they took no position or because they are not involved in the decision. Since we are simply assessing the direction of the position, these data are highly reliable. The terms "liberal" and "conservative" are put to no particular ideological use, but are simply convenient ways of identifying that direction.

For the relationship of each actor's position to the congressman's vote, therefore, one can generate the basic cross-tabulation presented in Table E–1. These cross-tabulations were in fact generated, not only for the whole sample, but also controlling for various of the standard independent variables in the study. They were examined partly for their own sake, and partly as the functional analogue to a scatterplot in a regression analysis, where there are only six locations in the two-dimensional space and the actor position is taken as a predictor of a congressman's vote.[1]

MANIPULATIONS OF THE BASIC RELATIONSHIP

There are two ways of looking at the basic relationship between actor position and congressman's vote which summarize that relationship. One is to ask oneself how much the congressman's vote agrees with the actor's position on those occasions in which the actor takes a position, for which conditional probability is appropriate. The other is to consider the general relationship between actor position and vote, using rather than excluding the "neutral" category, for which correlation is appropriate.

Conditional Probability
The conditional probability in this study is defined as the probability that the congressman will vote in accordance with the actor's position, given that the actor has a position. Referring to Table E–1, where the

Table E–1.   The Basic Cross-Tabulation

Congressman's Vote	actor position		
	Liberal	Neutral	Conservative
Liberal	Cell A	Cell C	Cell E
Conservative	Cell B	Cell D	Cell F

letters in the following formula are the raw numbers in each of the cells noted, this probability for each actor is computed thus:

$$\frac{A + F}{A + B + E + F}$$

In other words, excluding all the cases in which the actor is neutral, it computes the proportion of the remaining cases in which the congressman votes with the actor in question.

Interpretation of this statistic depends upon some statement of a null value. One can state what the figure would be by chance alone in two different ways, which fortunately yield almost no practical difference. If the congressman were flipping coins between a liberal and conservative vote, and an involved actor were also flipping coins between a liberal and conservative position, the conditional probability figure would be .50. On the other hand, if one computes the expected values in each cell from the marginal frequencies, the values differ from one actor to another. Those expected values range from a low of .47 to a high of .52, with three of the six being .50 exactly. For all practical purposes, therefore, one can say that on the basis of chance alone, the congressman could be expected to vote with any involved actor about half the time, or that by chance the conditional probability figure would be about .50. This gives a usable benchmark against which to compare the observed values, which range from very slight improvement on chance performance with some actors to a very strong showing with others.

The conditional probability figure has a number of advantages. For one thing, it is fairly straightforward and open to rather few ambiguities of interpretation, a not inconsiderable accomplishment. For another, it is substantively appealing in this study. For some purposes, one might want to consider an actor as an influence on the vote only on those occasions in which the actor was involved. Given that staffs rarely are involved in congressmen's floor voting decisions, for instance, how does the congressman's vote square with his staff's position when the staff *is* involved? So this measure adds another way of looking at the importance of the actors in addition to the correlation model and the subjective importance.

Correlation

Product-moment correlations are computed in a two-variable space with six possible locations equivalent to Table E–1, with the actor's position (liberal, neutral, or conservative) interpreted as being a predictor of the congressman's vote (liberal or conservative). The correlations were computed for the whole sample and for subsets of the sample (e.g., within party or seniority groupings). This mode provided another measure of actor–vote agreement, and was used partly to take account of the total spectrum of actors' positions including a possible neutral position, and partly to sort out the separate effects of various actors through partial correlation.

I have elected not to report regression coefficients in this study, by and large, following the reasoning of Blalock that the first concern in this exploratory sort of study should be with the strength of the relationships rather than their form.[2] As a practical matter, furthermore, it would be somewhat unproductive to consider the form of a relationship in a space with so few possible locations as six. Some may also ask whether product-moment correlation is appropriate, since I do not have interval-level data as we usually define the term.[3] The distinction between ordinal- and interval-level measurement may possibly be overdrawn.[4] Aside from this argument, it is possible to conceptualize these data as having interval characteristics. A dichotomy (e.g., the congressman's vote) is often treated as an interval variable. So far as the actor positions are concerned, if one conceives of the neutral position as a zero point, then the distance in the liberal direction can be thought to be equal to the distance in the conservative direction. For a more empirical test, furthermore, it turns out that the values for the product-moment correlation coefficients computed from the data such as Table E–1 correspond very closely to those for tau-b, an ordinal statistic. Thus as a practical matter, there is not a very great empirical leap from ordinal to interval measurement in this case.

Generally, the model just described has a good fit to the data. If one uses the six actor positions as variables predicting a congressman's vote, the multiple correlation between the six and the vote is .83 for the entire sample, and does not vary much from that value within party groupings. The residuals for this equation were also plotted against the dependent variable, and they showed no pattern which would lead one to suspect the adequacy of the equation. Because fellow congressmen and staff share their capacity of being freely selected by the congressman, for some purposes we may want to eliminate them from the model and leave only four independent variables. The multiple correlation for these four and the vote is .53.

Controlling

Some of the results reported in this book rely on simple bivariate correlations between the actor position and the congressman's vote. But others depend on an attempt to control such a bivariate relationship for the effects of other independent variables. I have thus presented partial correlations in the six-variable model, that is, the relationship between a given actor's position and the vote, controlling for the effects of the other five. Again, to screen out the effect of the freely selected variables of fellow congressmen and staff, I have also presented partial correlations in a four-variable model that uses only the remaining four as predictors.

If two independent variables are themselves highly correlated, it is difficult to assess their independent effects on the dependent variable.[5] In my data, there are several pairs of independent variables that show some relationship. In terms of the substance of the analysis, the two pairs that are potentially the most troublesome are the administration and the party leadership ($r = .44$) and constituency and interest groups ($r = .40$). According to various rules of thumb for deciding whether or not the correlations between pairs of independent variables are high enough to create substantial multicollinearity problems, these values probably are not very troublesome in any event. To the extent that the independent effects of these related variables can be sorted out, I have done so largely by re-sorting to considerations other than the correlation analysis itself, such as the theoretical or intuitive importance of the actors and the subjective and other codes.

Partial correlations have added some evidence at various points in this book. In Chapter 5, for instance, the correlation between interest group position and the vote disappeared when controlling for constituency position, but controlling constituency for interest group positions (in Chapter 1, four-variable model) did not affect the rather strong relationship between constituency and the vote. This meant that interest group position had no unique contribution to an explanation of the vote, independent of constituency, but that constituency retained its contribution faced with the same test. The partial correlations are not definitive by themselves, but the fact that they corroborate the other evidence in this and other cases lends support to the generalizations which have emerged.

I have also used a stepwise regression procedure, with results that fit those of other analyses. Stepwise regression essentially inserts the variable with the highest predictive value (in this case, fellow congressmen) into a regression model first, and then asks what additional increment of predictive value a second variable can add, and so forth, through subsequent variables.

It turned out that in the six-variable model, fellow congressmen were introduced into the model first, and constituency added a significant ($p = .05$) increment of predictive value in all party subgroups, as well as in the sample as a whole. In addition, staff added a significant value for Republicans (and hence for the whole sample) but not for Democrats, and administration was nearly significant at the .05 level for Republicans as well. In the four-variable model, constituency was introduced first in all party subgroups, and it was the only significant variable for Northern Democrats. The administration position added a statistically significant increment for Republicans and Southern Democrats, and thus for the sample as a whole. An examination of the regression coefficients themselves, furthermore, confirmed the results of the partial correlation analysis reported throughout the book.

This procedure, although again not definitive by itself, produces results which are consistent with the other types of analysis employed. As I have argued in the substantive chapters of the book, the interest groups appear to have little if any effect on congressmen's votes aside from their effect through the constituencies, an argument which squares with the results of this stepwise regression. Furthermore, in the case of Republicans and Southern Democrats it has appeared that the administration is more important than the party leadership, a conclusion which again is borne out here.

Another problem which may arise with the pairs of correlated independent variables is that the two in combination with one another might have an effect on the vote different from the two taken separately. To test for this possibility, two new variables were introduced into the regression model that were designed to represent an interaction effect in the case of each pair—administration-party leadership and constituency-interest groups. In each case, the term was the product of the values of the two variables in the pair taken separately. When these interaction terms were added to the model, this addition produced no significant increment in the model's multiple correlation, and in a stepwise regression procedure, these two variables came in a decided last in terms of adding to the predictive capabilities of the other variables.

NOTES

1. On the importance of analyzing scatterplots, see Hubert M. Blalock, *Social Statistics* (New York: McGraw-Hill, 1960), pp. 279–280.
2. *Ibid.,* p. 285.
3. For a discussion of different levels of data—nominal, ordinal, and interval—see Blalock, *ibid.,* pp. 11–16.
4. Tufte argues that the distinction is often taken too seriously. See Edward R. Tufte, *The Quantitative Analysis of Social Problems* (Reading, Mass.: Addison-Wesley, 1970), pp. 440–441.
5. On the problem of multicollinearity, see Tufte, *ibid.,* pp. 446–447.

Appendix F

The Consensus Decision Model

This appendix explains the procedures involved in developing the consensus decision model which is discussed in Chapter 10 and portrayed in Figure 10–1. That development begins with a definition of the "field of forces" which could conceivably affect the congressman's decision. For the purposes of this model, there are seven such forces: the congressman's own specific attitude on the issue at hand, his constituency, fellow congressmen to whom he paid attention, interest groups, his staff, his party leadership, and the administration. In the latter two cases, the party leadership and the administration, the "objective" position is not used as it was in the case of the regression model. For these purposes, we want a measure of the congressman's own subjective field. Hence, for example, the administration is not involved in the decisions of many Northern Democrats, even though they may have taken a position. Except for the use of these two subjective positions and the addition of the congressman's own attitude, the actor positions are defined as they are in the correlation model in Appendix E. For each of these forces, the actor can be conceived as tending toward a liberal or conservative direction, or as being neutral or not involved in the decision.

The next step is to count the number of actors in each decisional case who are liberal and the number who are conservative. If four of the seven are liberal, none are conservative, and three are neutral, for example, that configuration is defined as evidencing no conflict in the field. If three are liberal, one conservative, and three neutral, however, there is conflict, with a three-to-one liberal split. The basic table for the resultant calculations appears here as Table F–1. Cases of no conflict in the field appear in either the zero column or the zero row; that is, there were either no conservative actors and some liberal ones, or there were no liberal actors and some conservative ones. In these cases, regardless of the number of neutral actors on that particular decision, there is no liberal-conservative split, and these cases are hence defined as being free of conflict in the field. In these 104 cases, the congressman always votes with the field.

In Table F–1, the cases on the upper left to lower right diagonal ex-

Table F–1.   Raw Data for Calculations on the Consensus Mode[a]

		\0	1	2	3	4	5	6	7	Total
				Count of Liberal Actors						
	0	0	5	6	16	17	11	2	0	57
	1	2	2	8	7	9	8	1		37
Count	2	7	9	10	8	4	4			42
of	3	11	12	11	2	0				36
Conser-	4	8	9	5	0					22
vative	5	10	5	4						19
Actors	6	8	0							8
	7	1								1
	Total	47	42	44	33	30	23	3	0	222

[a] The entry in each cell is the number of cases displaying that configuration. For example, 16 cases show 3 liberal actors, no conservative, and 4 neutral; 12 cases show 1 liberal actor, 3 conservative, and 3 neutral. There are always 7 actors; thus the number of neutral actors is 7 minus the combined number of liberal and conservative actors.

emplify an evenly split field; that is, there are either one liberal and one conservative actor (with five neutral), two liberal and two conservative, or three and three. Cases in which there is one actor out of line from the rest of the field appear in either Row 1 or Column 1, excluding the cases in which there was either no conflict or a split field. Thus such configurations may range from a one-to-two liberal-conservative split to one-to-six. Finally, cases in which there are two actors out of line appear in either Row 2 or Column 2, again exclusive of even splits, no conflict cases, or one-actor cases. These range from a two-to-three liberal-conservative split to two-to-five.

The model which begins with these counts has a good predictive power, as presented in Chapter 10. Aside from the reasons for this performance discussed there, and aside from the likelihood that the model is simply an accurate description of congressmen's decision processes, a number of features of the study design and analysis should be remembered. First, this study has good measurement of the impact of the relevant actors. Instead of a set of agreement scores for colleagues in the House, for example, we have an accounting of specifically to which fellow congressmen on each issue the deciding congressman paid attention; instead of a publicly stated administration position, we have a notion of whether that position was involved in the congressman's decision. Second, the measurements are vote-specific. Instead of comparing congressmen's ideologies to a roll call scale position, for instance, we compare a congressman's attitude on that particular issue to his vote on that issue; instead of a constituency's demographic makeup or general attitudinal distribution, we have a measure of the congressman's perception of constituency opinion on the issue at hand. Finally, intra-actor conflict has been eliminated in the coding. For example, a respondent may name several congressmen to whom he paid attention, not all of them of the same persuasion. But to determine a position for the "fellow congressmen" actor, I code the direction in which the whole set tends. Conflict is then defined as conflict among actors, not within actors. The key question is whether a given *consideration* (constituency, party, etc.) points in one or another direction, and what is the state of conflict among these considerations.

On the other hand, there are two methodological points which would lead one to conclude that there is a surprising amount of consensus in these fields. First, some of the actors that are counted into the field are often not truly among those that a congressman would seriously consider. The education lobby, for instance, is defined as being in the field of conservative Republicans if educators talked to them, in spite of the fact that many probably did not take them very seriously. The same point may apply, for example, to ultraconservatives in a liberal Northern Democrat's constituency. Second, I have not built any intensity factor into the first two steps of the model, although I do take account of intensity in later steps and as a preconsensus process in Chapter 11. It could be that much of the time, conflicts which are counted are not of sufficient intensity to make a real difference to the congressman. He may note, for example, that his constituents may disapprove of his vote for foreign aid, but that they certainly do not feel strongly enough about it to give him any pause whatever. This sort of conflict is duly noted, even though it makes no practical difference.

THE ORIGINAL MODEL

The original version of the consensus model appeared in the first edition of this book. It differed in some respects from the version presented in Chaper 10 of this edition. Some readers might find it useful to see the original version here, partly for reference purposes and partly because the comparisons between the two versions are instructive in several ways that are discussed below.

The first two steps of the two models are the same and are discussed in Chapter 10. Starting with the third step, the models diverge. Figure F–1 shows the original formulation, which showed subsequent steps in the model as logical extensions of the drive to vote with a consensus in the field. If the deciding congressman found conflict within his usual field of forces, he was portrayed in that formulation as proceeding to the third step in Figure F–1. It could be that even within his own immediate field of forces, there is only one isolated actor who is out of line with the rest of the actors and is thus causing some conflict. A Republican congressman, for instance, may find an interest group pressing him for something that every other actor in the field, including his own attitude, opposes. In an instance in which one actor in the field is out of line with the rest, the congressman is very likely to vote against that one actor. If there are two actors that are out of line with the rest of the field, the congressman is likely to vote against that pair. In large part, this is because the two are actually defined as one in his own cognitive makeup, and that one pair is thus effectively the same as one actor out of line. Republicans, for instance, may find their party leadership and the administration out of line with the rest of their field of forces, but because the party leadership is the administration's spokesman on the Hill, this pair is conceived by the congressman as one actor for all practical purposes. Similarly, interest groups and constituency are two separable actors in this model, although an interest group is often nothing more nor less than a constituency elite.

The sequence just discussed was not necessarily thought to be a conscious process in the mind of the congressman. It may be in some instances, but on other occasions it may be more implicit in the way he decides. Conscious or not, the deciding congressman, of course, was not conceived as mechanically totaling up the actors and voting with the plurality. He instead perceived his entire field as having a predominant consensus in it, and behaved accordingly. The final steps in the model simply represented a recognition that the congressman need not find complete agreement in his perceptual field in order to use the convenient consensus mode.

In addition to the 104 cases in which the congressman finds no conflict in his field at all, there are 68 cases in which one actor is out of line with the rest. Of those, the congressman votes against that one actor 93 percent of the time. Once again, this encouraging result obtains in a sample of relatively high-conflict votes which should be much harder to explain than most legislative votes. It is interesting to note, furthermore, that of the five decisions left unexplained, the "actor" out of line in four of them is the congressman's own attitude, and in all but one of them, the field is a two-to-one split with four other actors neutral; thus these deviations from the predicted result are entirely understandable. Table F–2 shows how often each actor is out of line.

The next step is a logical extension of the previous one. There is a pair of actors out of line with the rest of the field in an additional 36 cases, and the congressman votes against that pair in 30 of them. A number of examples will clarify why Step 4 is as successful as it is in predicting

Figure F–1.   The Original Consensus Model

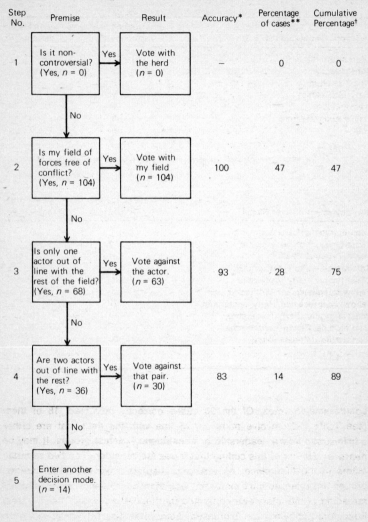

Step No.	Premise	Result	Accuracy*	Percentage of cases**	Cumulative Percentage†
1	Is it non-controversial? (Yes, *n* = 0) → Yes → Vote with the herd (*n* = 0)		–	0	0
2	Is my field of forces free of conflict? (Yes, *n* = 104) → Yes → Vote with my field (*n* = 104)		100	47	47
3	Is only one actor out of line with the rest of the field? (Yes, *n* = 68) → Yes → Vote against the actor. (*n* = 63)		93	28	75
4	Are two actors out of line with the rest? (Yes, *n* = 36) → Yes → Vote against that pair. (*n* = 30)		83	14	89
5	Enter another decision mode. (*n* = 14)				

*Accuracy equals the percentage of the cases in which the congressman votes as the result specifies, given a "yes" answer to the premise question. For example, in Step 3, Accuracy = 63 ÷ 68 = 93%. The number of cases left unexplained in that step can also be ascertained; in Step 3, it is 68 − 63 = 5.

**Percentage of cases equals percentage of the total *n* (222) accounted for by that decision step. For example, in Step 3, it is 63 ÷ 222 = 28 percent.

† The cumulative percentage equals percentage of 222 accounted for by that decision step plus all the previous steps. For example, in Step 3, it is

$$\frac{63 + 104}{222} = 75 \text{ percent.}$$

Table F–2.   Actors Out of Line with the Field

One actor out of line (Step 3)	voted against the one (n)	voted with the one (n)
Interest groups	22	0
Constituency	19	1
Administration	11	0
Party leadership	5	0
Own attitude	4	4
Fellow congressmen	1	0
Staff	1	0
Total n	63	5

Two actors out of line (Step 4)	voted against the pair (n)	voted with the pair (n)
Administration/Party leadership	10	0
Constituency/Interest groups	8	0
Interest groups/Staff	4	0
Administration/Interest groups	3	0
Constituency/Party leadership	2	0
Fellow congressmen/Administration	1	0
Fellow congressmen/Party leadership	1	0
Interest groups/Party leadership	1	0
Own attitude/Fellow congressmen	0	5
Own attitude/Constituency	0	1
Total n	30	6

congressmen's votes. Of the 30 cases correctly predicted, 18 of them (see Table F–2) involve pairs out of line with the field that are either administration-party leadership or constituency-interest groups. It may be nearly an artifact of this coding that those are considered as two separate actors in the first place. As previous chapters have indicated, interest groups are often nothing more nor less than constituency elites, and my rereading of the interviews confirmed that model in many of these cases. Educators lobbying for increased appropriations, for instance, were classified as both interest groups and constituency elites, when all were part of one coordinated effort. Similarly the Republican party leadership, and even the leadership on the Democratic side, often worked very closely with the administration. When the congressman looks at one of these two "pairs," then, he may see only one actor out of line with the rest of the field. If he does conceive of them as one, then the field exhibits at least a three-to-one split, and it may be four- or five-to-one. These are fields in which a dominant consensus is not difficult to discern. Further-more, the next most numerous category in Table F–2—the pairing of in-terest groups and staff—included a number of cases in which peace groups and liberal staff members were out of line with hawkish Republi-cans and Southern Democrats and the rest of their fields on the ABM question. Once again, the resultant vote against the pair of actors is entirely understandable in terms of the model.

As in the case of Step 3, the deviant cases are rather to be expected. Of the six cases incorrectly predicted, the "pair" out of line with which the congressman votes is his own attitude reinforced by another actor—fellow congressmen in five instances. All but one of the six is also a three-to-two split in the field, where it should, of course, be more difficult to discern consensus than in a field exhibiting a wider margin.

Another way to view the cases in which a pair of actors is out of line with the rest of the field is to conceive of the congressman as voting ac-cording to his own policy attitude on the matter before him, an attitude which is buttressed by the confirming pressure of other actors. The unexplained cases in Table F–2, in fact, tend to be cases in which the congressman votes according to his own attitude. It must be remembered, however, that the attitudes at this decisional stage are specific to the legislative provision under consideration, and measured at the time of decision or shortly thereafter. By that time, of course, the congressman has formed some articulated policy attitude, expresses it, and votes in a fashion consistent with it. But earlier in the process of decision, he may not have formed that attitude, and even if he does have some policy atti-tude to guide him, he still needs some communication with other actors to link it with the piece of legislation at hand. Among the actors with which his attitude is aligned in this step in the model, indeed, the con-gressman nearly always speaks of constituents, fellow congressmen, or administration as being of major or determinative importance in his de-cision. Of greater interest than these specific attitudes toward given bills or amendments, however, is the place of the congressman's general policy predispositions in his decision-making. These general attitudes are treated in some detail in Chapter 11 as forces which constitute an important preconsensus process.

SOME CODING PARTICULARS

Most of the codes are described in Appendixes C and D. Two other coding matters are confined to the consensus model and should therefore be discussed here: (1) the use of the criterion of major or determinative importance in setting the thresholds in Steps C and D and (2) the actual operations of the ADA–ACA index discussed in Chapter 10.

First, it might be possible that coding the constituency as being of "major" or "determinative" importance would be closely associated with the congressman's vote in accordance with the constituency position. If such were the case, the test of the model would not be as good as could be hoped, since passing the critical threshold would by itself imply a constituency-oriented vote, lending an artificial predictive power to the model. It turns out, however, that these apprehensions can be alleviated somewhat. Of the cases in which there is some conflict in the congressman's field, constituency is coded as being of major or determinative importance in 42 cases. Of these 42 cases, the congressman votes with the constituency position 62 percent of the time, a performance somewhat better than chance (which is ½), but not dramatically better. By contrast, the model correctly predicts 93 percent of those cases. Thus, although there is naturally some association between the importance coding and the vote, it is not so strong as to negate the value of defining the critical threshold in the fashion described. The coding does not by itself produce the predictive performance.

To turn to the second coding matter, in Chapter 10 I described the use of ADA and ACA scores to determine the extremity of members' policy positions. Either a coding of voting history as major or determinative importance or an "extreme" ADA–ACA score evokes the policy goal at Step C. Operationally, the ADA and ACA scores are used to form an index in which a congressman is considered to be sufficiently extreme if either the ADA and ACA score is 90 to 100 or 0 to 10, and if the opposite score is in the opposite three deciles among my respondents. If the ADA score is zero, for instance, and the ACA score is in the upper three deciles, the congressman is considered to be a conservative; if the ADA score is 100 and the ACA score is in the bottom three deciles, for another example, the congressman is defined as liberal. Congressmen who do not meet these criteria are considered to have a sufficiently "moderate" record that ADA–ACA position is not a guide to votes, and thus does not evoke the policy goal.

An impressionistic scanning of the members so classified confirms that those labeled the most liberal and conservative by the ADA–ACA criterion would be clearly regarded by most observers of the House as being correctly labeled. The index fails to identify some members for whom certain policy goals are clearly relevant, as, for instance, some very public doves on ABM deployment. In that sense, it may underestimate the importance of policy goals, since it discards some members for whom policy goals may be highly important. That underestimation also lowers the overall predictive performance of the model a bit. But the index does not make the other error: Those who are identified as liberal or conservative are not mislabeled.[1] As far as triggering the policy goal is concerned, the ADA-ACA index and the coding for the importance of voting history make a roughly equal contribution. Of the cases which exhibit some conflict in the field of forces in which the policy goal is evoked, the ADA-ACA index alone is responsible for that triggering in 30 cases, voting history alone in 27, and the two together in 25.

ALTERNATIVE FORMULATIONS

There are a number of alternative formulations of the consensus model presented in Figure 10-1. This portion of Appendix F tests some of these alernative formulations, to see if the version in Figure 10–1 works best in the sense of correctly accounting for outcomes. Such an analysis would help to evaluate some plausible alternative hypotheses about the structure of the model and the place of several of the variables in it. I present here two types of alternative formulations: (1) changes in the basic structure of the model and (2) changes in certain parts of the model.

The Basic Stucture

There are three changes in the basic structure which have been tried on the data: bypassing the first consensus steps in the model, bypassing the nonconsensus part of the model, and substituting one simple decision rule for the nonconsensus part.

First, to bypass the first steps, we postulate that the 104 cases correctly accounted for by the consensus step (Step B) can be predicted by subsequent steps in the model (Steps C and D). In other words, we start the model running at Step C. One logical feature of the model becomes immediately clear, namely, that the only way for the goals step (Step C) to fail to predict decisions correctly is for none of the three goals to exceed their critical thresholds. If any do exceed their thresholds, then it is logically impossible in the 104 censusus cases for the goal agreement step (Step C1) not to account correctly for the outcome. If goals pass their thresholds, in other words, there is agreement among them by definition, since the original Step B filtered the cases according to the consensus criterion. Of the 104 cases at issue, then, Step C would correctly account for 82. Of the remaining cases, which then reach Step D, following fellow congressmen of major importance picks up an additional nine cases. Thus Steps C and D account for 91 of the 104 cases, for an 88 percent accuracy rate; the original Step B accounted for all 104, a 100 percent accuracy rate.

Second, to bypass the nonconsensus parts of the model, we drop out Steps C2 through C6, and observe what difference it makes. In other words, if there is conflict among the evoked goals (at Step C1), the model proceeds immediately to considering the position of fellow congressmen (Step D), rather than going through the decision rules designed to sort out the goal conflict. The issue then is how many of the 27 cases originally classified as Steps C2 through C6 cases are accounted for by Step D, which turns out to be 12 of the 27, or 44 percent. This compares to 22 of the 27 (81 percent) in the original formulation. As with the first reformulation, this one does not improve on the original; in fact, it performs worse.

The third basic structural reformulation, instead of bypassing the nonconsensus steps (C2 through C6), substitutes a simple but plausible decision rule for them, namely, that in the event of serious conflict among his goals, the legislator votes in accord with his policy position. Of the 27 cases at issue, the policy goal is evoked in 23, and of those 23, the legislator does vote with his policy position in 17. Thus the hypothesized decision rule accounts for 63 percent (17/27) of the cases compared to 81 percent (22/27) in the original model's Steps C2 through C6.

Changes in Certain Parts

The last structural reformulation leads directly to some possible reformulations of parts of the model, particularly concentrating on various parts of the goals steps (Step C and substeps thereof). These changes fall into three categories: one concerned with the constituency goal, those concerned with the intra-Washington influence goal, and one which eliminates the threshold requirement at the beginning of Step C.

First, in the steps of the original model which show a conflict between constituency and other goals (C2 through C4), one could state an hypothesis that if constituency is of major importance, given the primacy of reelection to a seasoned politician, the congressman should be expected to vote with the constituency every time. That model, however, would account for only 3 of the 19 cases, whereas the model presented in Figure 10–1 accounts for 16. Thus this reformulation would represent a distinct loss of ability to account for the outcomes quantitatively.

Second, taking up reformulations having to do with the goal of intra-Washington influence, one plausible hypothesis would be that congressmen of the president's party would follow his lead. In the session under study, the hypothesis would state that when Republicans were aware of an administration position and when it played some part in their thinking, they would vote with the administration position. It turns out that when the administration was involved in Republican decisions, they voted with the administration position 68 percent of the time. By contrast, the model presented in this book accounts for 85 percent of the same 59 cases.

Another reformulation involving intra-Washington influence would allow more than simply a president of the legislator's own party to be involved at Steps C5 and C6. Suppose, at that step in the model, that either the president of one's own party, or one's own party leadership, or colleagues within the House engaged in a logrolling exchange could overturn one's own policy position; in other words, the entire set of evoked intra-Washington considerations could be swung into play, rather than simply a president of one's own party. It turns out that only two cases are affected by that change, and the reformulation fails to predict them correctly, whereas the original model had correctly predicted them.

The final reformulation eliminates the requirement that a goal must pass a critical threshold in order to be evoked (beginning at Step C), and then asks how the 79 cases originally disposed of at the goal consensus stage (C1) fare without that threshold requirement. Operationally, then, the goals are evoked as follows: (1) if either constituency or interest groups are of *any* importance in the congressman's decision (rather than of major or determinative importance), then the constituency goal is evoked; (2) if either administration, party leadership, or fellow congressmen are of any importance, the goal of intra-Washington influence is evoked; (3) the policy goal threshold remains unchanged, since the ADA–ACA index must provide some sort of direction. Then because some conflict among the goals is now introduced into the 79 cases that would previously have been filtered out due to the threshold requirement, we run the 79 cases through the nonconsensus steps (C2 through C6) under the new conditions. The result is that Steps C2 through C6 correctly predict 62 of the 79 cases (78 percent), predict a result which does not in fact occur in 13 cases, and fail to provide a decision rule in four cases. If we allow those four cases to proceed to fellow congressmen for resolution (Step D), three of the four are correctly predicted there. Thus, by the combination of the nonconsensus and fellow congressmen steps, we have correctly accounted for 65 of the 79 cases (82 percent), whereas the original model at Step C1 accounted for 74 of the 79 (94 percent).

In conclusion, after testing of several alternative formulations, it appears that the original model presented in Figure 10–1 emerges largely intact. None of the reformulations perform better in a quantitative sense, and many of them perform substantially worse. The good quantitative performance, however, does not address all of the questions which one might have about a model's usefulness. We now turn to some further questions.

A CAUTION ABOUT QUANTITATIVE PERFORMANCE

It is appropriate to close with a caution that models of legislative voting should not be accepted solely because of their good ability to account for cases in quantitative terms.[2] In some situations in the social sciences, a good fit to the data is regarded as a sufficient condition to accept a model, since it is difficult to predict outcomes. In other situations, such as the case of legislative voting models, a good quantitative performance is a necessary, but not sufficient condition to accept a model, since outcomes are quite easy to predict. The null hypothesis in the legislative case predicts 50 percent of the cases by itself, since if a congressman were flipping coins between "yes" and "no" in order to decide, and a random model were also flipping coins, the random model and the congressman's behavior would agree half the time. Beyond this "impressive" chance performance, quite a simple model constructed from commonplaces in the literature—for example, some combination of party, region, constituency, and president position—would probably do quite nicely in a statistical sense. Indeed, a model which simply postulated that all congressmen vote "yea," although not theoretically interesting, would yield a fairly good prediction.[3] As a matter of fact, most of the previous models discussed in this book do quite nicely on their data sets, and we have become accustomed to models which predict about 85 percent of the cases. This is not to say that all possible models do well in terms of a criterion of ability to predict, as we have seen. Some models can be falsified, but that still leaves a number of models which do well.

In evaluating those remaining models of legislative voting, then, one should add to conventional criteria of statistical fit and quantitative performance, and use more conceptual and theoretical considerations. In Chapter 10, I outlined some of these considerations, including plausibility, simplicity, political realism, and comprehensiveness. The advantages of the model presented in Chapter 10 have to do with those considerations. The model is quite comprehensive, and yet does not achieve this comprehensiveness at the expense of simplicity, plausibility, or realism. There is also a compelling logic to the progression portrayed, for congressmen are seen as moving from the simple to the complex, from a simple judgment about the whole environment, to a subsetting of that environment, to a further subsetting which concentrates explicitly on goals. These sorts of considerations, rather than simply an impressive ability to account for cases quantitatively, commend the model.

An instructive illustration may be the juxtaposition of the model in Figure 10–1 with the analysis found elsewhere in this book. I will discuss two of those analyses: the correlation analysis, which attempts to determine the influence of each of a set of actors on voting decisions, and the original consensus model presented earlier in this appendix. Taking the correlation analysis first, I identify six actors in the legislative system who could conceivably have an influence on a congressman's votes: the congressman's constituency, fellow congressmen, interest groups, the administration and executive branch, his party leadership, and his staff. The position of each on the issue at hand (for, against, neutral) is treated as an independent variable affecting the vote; and agreement scores, bivariate correlations, partial correlations, and stepwise regression are generated from the basic correlation model. The results are presented in great detail in Chapters 1 through 8 and Appendix E, and need not be repeated here. What is relevant to this discussion is that the multiple correlation between the six variables and the vote is .83, and that the residuals exhibit no pattern that would lead one to suspect the adequacy of the equation. Thus the quantitative performance is good, and for some purposes, such as the ability to sort out the influence of various actors on legislative voting decisions, the analysis is quite useful.

As a model of decisional processes, however, the correlation approach does not appear to be entirely satisfying. A major point of a model such as the one discussed in Chapter 10 is that most of the time legislators do not "weight influences" as regression, correlation, or some computer simulations portray them as doing. If legislators were to make decisions in a fashion analogous to regression, they would be required to weight each potential influence and to consider simultaneously the entire set of weighted influences. Given the severe time constraints on decision, and perhaps a general tendency for human beings to avoid thinking in such a simultaneous weighting fashion, this mode would not seem to be a plausible model of decisional processes. Furthermore, such a mode of decision is simply unnecessary on most votes. If the various possible influences agree, or the critical subsets of them agree, as they often do, then there is no need to engage in the weighting procedure that many other types of analysis require. A more minor consideration is that one would come away from the correlation analysis with the impression that fellow congressmen drive the decisions, which for a series of technical and conceptual reasons is probably not a complete model of decision, as I argue in Chapter 3. At any rate, it is important to distinguish the objectives of a regression mode of thought from those of a process modeling approach.

The other juxtaposition is between the model presented in Chapter 10 and the earlier consensus mode of decision, which is found in this appendix. The final steps of the earlier model, unlike the current one, portray a deciding congressman as identifying the actors who were out of line with the dominant consensus in the field, and voting against them. The gain in predictive power of the new model over that earlier version is trivial. What this new model does provide are important theoretical additions to the earlier work.

To elaborate, the original consensus model in its last steps was not simply a matter of "majority rule" or mechanical counting. Somehow, there are processes at work, conceptualized in Chapter 11 as "preconsensus" processes, which lead the congressman to the conclusion that these actors against which he votes are isolated, of little consequence, and capable of being safely slighted. The model presented in Chapter 10 provides a way to interpret the pattern portrayed in the earlier model. For example, there are 19 cases in my data in which the constituency is the one actor out of line with the rest of the field and in which the congressman votes against the constituency position. In 15 of those 19 cases, constituency is coded as being of minor importance, meaning, in terms of the new model, that the goal of satisfying constituents has not been evoked. The remaining four were all low-salience issues, in which the constituency interest could be overruled. Thus the operation of the model presented in Chapter 10 helps us to understand why the deciding congressmen could vote against constituency wishes in these instances. Or to take the other most numerous example, respondents voted against interest groups in 22 cases, of which 18 found constituency to be of minor importance and the remaining four found constituency opposed to the interest group position. Because interest groups are vulnerable without a constituency connection, it seems quite understandable that congressmen should find it possible to vote against an interest group when the constituency consideration is either not evoked or is opposed to the lobby position. Other examples could be discussed.

The point is that deciding congressmen are indeed voting against these actors, as the original model portrays them as doing. This new model adds some further thinking about *why* they are doing so.

NOTES

1. It is also true that ADA and ACA scores relate strongly to other such indexes, lending an additional validity to the measure. See Carol Goss, "House Committee Characteristics and Distributive Politics" (paper prepared for delivery at the 1975 American Political Science Association meeting), p. 7.
2. For a general discussion, see Herbert Simon, "On Judging the Plausibility of

Theories," in *Logic, Methodology, and Philosophy of Sciences,* III, ed. van Rootselaar and Staal (Amsterdam: North-Holland, 1968), pp. 439–459.

3. For a discussion which makes the same point, see Donald Matthews and James Stimson, *Yeas and Nays,* (New York: Wiley, 1975) p. 115. Weisberg has calculated various null models in addition to the 50 percent model, and has concluded that some of them can account for well into the 80 percent range. That fact places all the more importance on such considerations as plausibility, simplicity, and comprehensiveness. See Herbert Weisberg, "Evaluating Theories of Congressional Roll Call Voting," *American Journal of Political Science* 22(1978):554–577.

Index

81 82 83 9 8 7 6 5 4 3 2